PHP Programming: Versatile, Server-Side, Multi-Purpose Programming Language

By Theophilus Edet

Theophilus Edet

 theo.edet@comprequestseries.com

 facebook.com/theoedet

twitter.com/TheophilusEdet

Instagram.com/edettheophilus

Table of Contents

iv

Preface

PHP has been a cornerstone of web development for over two decades, evolving from a simple scripting language into a powerful, versatile tool for building modern applications. As a server-side programming language, PHP powers millions of websites, from personal blogs to large-scale enterprise applications. Its flexibility, ease of use, and extensive ecosystem of frameworks and libraries make it an essential skill for developers at all levels. This book, *PHP Programming: Versatile, Server-Side, Multi-Purpose Programming Language*, is designed to provide a structured and comprehensive exploration of PHP, equipping readers with the knowledge to build robust, scalable, and secure applications.

Why This Book?

PHP has often been underestimated in comparison to newer programming languages, but its adaptability and continuous evolution have kept it at the forefront of web development. Unlike many resources that focus solely on basic syntax or framework-specific knowledge, this book delves deep into PHP's core strengths, covering its programming models, frameworks, design patterns, and specialized applications. Whether you are a beginner aiming to grasp PHP's fundamentals or an experienced developer looking to refine your expertise, this book provides a structured learning path that emphasizes both theoretical knowledge and practical application.

Structure and Approach

This book is designed to follow a logical progression, ensuring that readers build a strong foundation before moving on to more advanced topics. It begins with the fundamentals of PHP, covering syntax, data structures, and essential programming paradigms. From there, it explores PHP's diverse programming models, including object-oriented, functional, asynchronous, and metaprogramming concepts. Readers will then delve into PHP frameworks, learning how to leverage Laravel, Symfony, CodeIgniter, and other popular tools to build scalable applications. Advanced topics such as API development, security, cryptography, and PHP's role in IoT and game development are also covered, ensuring a well-rounded understanding of the language's capabilities.

One of the distinguishing features of this book is its emphasis on **design patterns** and **architectural best practices**. Many PHP applications suffer from poor structure, making them difficult to maintain and scale. By integrating software design principles and patterns throughout the book, readers will learn how to write clean, maintainable code that adheres to industry standards. Case studies and real-world projects further reinforce these concepts, bridging the gap between theory and practical implementation.

Who Should Read This Book?

This book is suitable for a broad audience, from beginners to experienced developers. If you are new to PHP, the structured approach will help you gain a solid grasp of the language, while intermediate developers will benefit from the in-depth exploration of frameworks and advanced programming concepts. Even experienced PHP developers will find valuable insights in the sections on design patterns, performance optimization, and modern application architectures. Whether you are a freelancer, web developer, software engineer, or system architect, this book will serve as a valuable resource in your PHP journey.

Final Thoughts

PHP continues to evolve, adapting to the changing landscape of web development. Mastering PHP is not just about learning its syntax but understanding how to use it effectively to build scalable and maintainable applications. This book aims to empower developers with the knowledge and best practices needed to harness PHP's full potential.

Theophilus Edet

PHP Programming: Versatile, Server-Side, Multi-Purpose Programming Language

PHP remains one of the most influential programming languages in web development, powering over 75% of websites worldwide. From personal blogs to enterprise-grade applications, PHP's versatility has made it a preferred choice for developers seeking a balance of flexibility, scalability, and ease of use. This book, *PHP Programming: Versatile, Server-Side, Multi-Purpose Programming Language*, is designed to provide a comprehensive and structured approach to mastering PHP, covering its fundamental constructs, programming paradigms, frameworks, design patterns, and specialized applications. Whether you are a beginner or an experienced developer, this book will serve as a roadmap to understanding PHP's vast capabilities and leveraging them effectively.

Book Structure and Approach

The book is divided into four major parts, each focusing on a distinct aspect of PHP development. The first part establishes a strong foundation by covering PHP's fundamental constructs, including variables, data types, control structures, functions, loops, and object-oriented programming. These building blocks are essential for any PHP developer, ensuring a deep understanding of how the language works before moving on to more advanced topics.

The second part introduces PHP's diverse programming models, exploring the various paradigms that PHP supports. While many programming languages adhere strictly to a single paradigm, PHP's strength lies in its ability to support multiple approaches, including procedural, object-oriented, functional, event-driven, and asynchronous programming. This part of the book covers best practices for structuring PHP applications using different paradigms and provides case studies to illustrate real-world applications.

The third part focuses on API development, web development, command-line scripting, content management systems, e-commerce platforms, and PHP's use in specialized areas such as game development and the Internet of Things (IoT). PHP is more than just a web development tool—it is a multi-purpose language that can be used for automating tasks, handling large-scale data processing, and even interfacing with hardware devices. This part provides in-depth insights into building scalable and secure applications with PHP while incorporating authentication, encryption, and performance optimization techniques.

The final part delves into PHP frameworks and design patterns, equipping developers with the knowledge to build enterprise-level applications efficiently. Popular frameworks such as Laravel, Symfony, CodeIgniter, and Yii are explored in detail, along with their design patterns and architectural principles. Understanding software design patterns is crucial for writing maintainable and scalable code, and this final part ensures that developers can apply these patterns effectively in their PHP projects.

A Deep Dive into PHP Programming Constructs

Before mastering advanced PHP applications, developers must first understand the core constructs of the language. Part 1 of the book introduces PHP variables, data types, and the dynamic nature of PHP's type system. This is followed by a detailed discussion of functions, scope, control structures, and array manipulation techniques. Readers will also explore PHP's object-oriented programming model, covering access modifiers, namespaces, and the latest enhancements introduced in PHP 8.1, such as enumerations (enums).

One of the key aspects of this part is ensuring that developers write clean and maintainable code by adhering to best practices and documentation standards. PHPDoc and annotation-based documentation techniques are introduced to help developers create well-documented codebases that facilitate collaboration and long-term maintenance.

Exploring PHP's Programming Models

PHP supports multiple programming paradigms, making it one of the most adaptable languages for modern application development. Part 2 of the book explores these paradigms in depth, beginning with array programming and data-driven development. The ability to work efficiently with data structures is critical in PHP, especially when dealing with databases, APIs, and large data sets.

Asynchronous and event-driven programming are also covered, focusing on libraries such as ReactPHP and Swoole that enable PHP applications to handle real-time events and background tasks. Readers will also learn about component-based and service-oriented programming, which are essential for building modular, maintainable applications. Object-oriented and procedural programming models are compared, with real-world case studies demonstrating how to refactor procedural code into well-structured OOP implementations.

Other key topics include functional programming, metaprogramming, structured programming, and API development techniques. By the end of this part, developers will have a clear understanding of how to choose the right programming model for their PHP projects based on scalability, maintainability, and performance considerations.

Practical PHP Applications and Use Cases

While PHP is primarily known for web development, its applications extend far beyond dynamic web pages. Part 3 of the book highlights PHP's versatility by exploring various domains in which it excels. API development is covered extensively, teaching readers how to build secure and scalable RESTful and GraphQL APIs using frameworks such as Laravel and Symfony.

Web development is explored in detail, covering frontend-backend interactions, user authentication, form handling, and content management systems such as WordPress, Joomla, and Drupal. PHP's capabilities in e-commerce platforms are also discussed, with practical guidance on integrating payment gateways, managing user sessions, and handling product inventory.

Beyond web applications, this section delves into PHP's use in command-line scripting, automation, game development, IoT, and cybersecurity. PHP's ability to process large-scale data, interact with hardware devices, and secure applications using cryptographic techniques makes it an invaluable tool for developers working in diverse fields.

Mastering PHP Frameworks and Design Patterns

The final part of the book is dedicated to PHP frameworks and design patterns, ensuring that developers can build efficient, scalable, and maintainable applications. This part begins with an overview of popular PHP frameworks, including Laravel, Symfony, CodeIgniter, Yii, and Phalcon. Each framework is examined in terms of its strengths, use cases, and underlying design patterns.

PHP's implementation of software design patterns is explored in detail, covering creational, structural, and behavioral patterns. These patterns play a crucial role in building reusable, scalable, and testable code. Developers will learn how to apply the Singleton, Factory, Adapter, Observer, and Composite patterns, among others, to solve common programming challenges.

The book concludes with real-world case studies that illustrate how PHP frameworks and design patterns are used to build high-performance applications. Readers will gain insights into best practices for architecting PHP applications, optimizing performance, and adhering to coding standards that ensure long-term maintainability.

PHP remains one of the most versatile and powerful programming languages available today. This book provides a structured and in-depth guide to mastering PHP, from its core constructs to advanced frameworks and design principles. By following this learning path, developers will gain the skills to build secure, scalable, and high-performance applications, ensuring their success in the ever-evolving world of PHP development.

Part 1:

PHP Programming Constructs - Building Blocks of PHP Development

PHP's fundamental programming constructs form the backbone of dynamic web development. This part introduces essential elements such as variables, data types, functions, control structures, collections, loops, and object-oriented programming (OOP). Mastering these core concepts ensures developers can write efficient, maintainable, and scalable PHP applications. This section also covers documentation standards, enumeration (introduced in PHP 8.1+), and best practices for structuring code. By understanding these foundational principles, developers gain the skills needed to build robust applications, optimize performance, and transition seamlessly into more advanced topics such as frameworks, security, and design patterns.

PHP Variables & Data Types

PHP's dynamic typing system allows variables to store different types of data without explicit declaration. Primitive types include integers, floats, strings, and booleans, while complex types such as arrays, objects, and resources enable structured data management. Type juggling in PHP automatically converts values between types, which simplifies operations but can also lead to unintended behaviors. Type casting provides an explicit way to convert values, ensuring greater control over data representation. Understanding how PHP manages variables and data types is crucial for preventing type-related errors, improving performance, and ensuring compatibility when handling user input or interacting with databases.

Functions and Scope in PHP

Functions in PHP promote modularity and code reusability by encapsulating logic into callable blocks. Defining functions with parameters and return types ensures better data integrity, while type hints enforce strict input validation. PHP's variable scope defines how variables are accessed within functions—local variables exist only inside functions, while global variables can be accessed throughout the script. Static variables retain their values across function calls. Anonymous functions and closures allow flexible callback mechanisms, particularly useful in functional programming and event-driven scenarios. Understanding function behavior and scope enhances PHP code organization and maintainability.

Conditional Statements and Control Flow

Control flow statements determine how a PHP program executes logic based on conditions. The if-else and switch-case structures help developers define branching logic, while PHP's truthy and falsy evaluation rules impact conditional checks. The ternary operator and null coalescing operator provide concise alternatives to standard conditionals. Writing readable and maintainable conditional logic involves avoiding deep nesting and redundant checks. Effective use of conditional statements ensures code executes efficiently, improves readability, and helps prevent logical errors in applications, making them more reliable and easier to debug.

Collections and Array Manipulation

Arrays are fundamental data structures in PHP, allowing storage and manipulation of indexed, associative, and multidimensional data. PHP's array functions facilitate operations like mapping, filtering, and reducing, enabling functional programming approaches. Sorting arrays, merging datasets, and splitting values into smaller chunks help manage large collections effectively. Iterators and generators improve performance when handling extensive datasets by processing data lazily rather than loading entire collections into memory. Understanding these concepts allows developers to efficiently manage and manipulate structured data in PHP applications.

Loops and Iteration Constructs

Loops allow repetitive execution of code, enabling efficient data processing. PHP provides four primary loop structures: while, do-while, for, and foreach, each suited for different use cases. The break and continue statements control loop execution, helping manage flow efficiently. Iterating over arrays—both indexed and associative—requires choosing the optimal loop for performance. Handling large datasets necessitates minimizing unnecessary iterations and using optimized loop constructs. Understanding iteration mechanisms in PHP is essential for writing performant applications that can process large amounts of data without unnecessary overhead.

Comments and Documentation Standards

Code documentation is crucial for maintainability and collaboration. PHP supports single-line and multi-line comments for explaining logic within scripts. PHPDoc, a standardized documentation format, enhances code readability by providing structured annotations for functions, parameters, return types, and exceptions. Proper documentation improves team collaboration and ensures future developers can understand and extend codebases easily. Annotations further automate code generation and validation in frameworks. Writing well-documented code is a best practice that leads to more maintainable and scalable PHP applications.

Enumerations (Enums in PHP 8.1+)

Enums provide a structured way to define a fixed set of values, improving type safety and code clarity. PHP 8.1 introduced pure enums, which define named constants, and backed enums, which map names to scalar values like integers or strings. Using enums enhances readability and prevents invalid values from being used. Enums are particularly useful in defining application states, handling user roles, or managing configuration options. Implementing enums in PHP leads to cleaner, more maintainable code by reducing reliance on arbitrary constants and hardcoded values.

Object-Oriented Programming (OOP) Basics

OOP principles in PHP provide a structured approach to software development. Classes and objects define reusable blueprints for organizing code. Constructors and destructors handle initialization and cleanup processes. Inheritance promotes code reuse, polymorphism allows flexible function overriding, and abstract classes enforce structure. Traits and interfaces extend functionality across classes, enabling multiple inheritance-like behaviors. Mastering OOP principles enables developers to create scalable, modular applications by organizing code into reusable, maintainable components that align with real-world business logic.

Accessors, Modifiers, and Namespaces

Encapsulation is a key OOP principle that controls data access using visibility modifiers—public, private, and protected. Getters and setters regulate how class properties are retrieved and modified, ensuring controlled data access. Namespaces prevent class name conflicts in large projects, allowing structured code organization. PHP's PSR-4 autoloading standard simplifies class management, eliminating the need for manual includes. Understanding these concepts leads to better-structured applications, reducing conflicts and improving maintainability, particularly in large-scale PHP projects.

This part establishes the essential programming constructs for PHP development, equipping developers with the knowledge needed to write efficient, structured, and maintainable code. Mastering these fundamentals ensures a solid foundation for more advanced PHP topics, including frameworks, security, and database integration.

Module 1:
PHP Variables & Data Types

PHP is a dynamically typed, server-side scripting language widely used for web development. Understanding PHP variables and data types is fundamental for writing efficient and maintainable code. This module explores PHP's dynamic typing system, primitive and complex data types, and how type juggling and type casting affect data handling in PHP.

Understanding PHP Variables and Dynamic Typing

PHP variables store and manipulate data dynamically. Unlike statically typed languages, PHP does not require explicit type declarations, making it highly flexible. Variables in PHP are prefixed with a dollar sign ($) and can store different types of data. PHP's **dynamic typing** system determines a variable's type based on its assigned value. This flexibility speeds up development but requires careful handling to prevent unexpected behavior. PHP variables have different scopes: **local**, **global**, **static**, and **superglobal**, each suited for specific situations. Local variables exist within functions, while global variables are accessible throughout the script. Understanding dynamic typing and scope is essential for effective PHP programming.

Primitive Data Types and Their Usage in PHP

PHP supports several **primitive data types**, including integers, floats, strings, and booleans. **Integers** are whole numbers, used for arithmetic and loop counters. **Floats**, also called doubles, store decimal numbers and are useful for precise calculations. **Strings** are sequences of characters enclosed in single (') or double (") quotes and play a key role in text processing and data storage. **Booleans** represent true/false values and control logical operations and conditionals. Each data type behaves differently, affecting operations like concatenation, mathematical calculations, and comparisons. Proper use of primitive data types enhances performance, readability, and maintainability of PHP applications.

Complex Data Types: Arrays, Objects, and Resources

Beyond primitive types, PHP provides complex data types for advanced programming. **Arrays** store multiple values in indexed or associative formats, making them essential for data handling. Indexed arrays use numeric keys, while associative arrays use named keys. **Objects** represent instances of classes and facilitate object-oriented programming (OOP), promoting reusable and modular code. **Resources** manage external references, such as database connections and file handles. Since PHP is widely used for web applications, efficient handling of complex data types is crucial for managing large datasets, structuring applications, and interacting with external services.

Type Casting and Type Juggling in PHP

PHP's **type juggling** automatically converts data types when needed. This feature simplifies coding but can lead to unexpected results. For example, PHP may convert a string to a number in arithmetic operations, which could cause errors if not properly managed. **Type casting**, on the other hand, allows explicit conversion between types, providing better control over data handling. It is useful when processing user input, performing strict comparisons, or ensuring compatibility with APIs. Understanding type juggling and type casting is critical for preventing type-related bugs and ensuring predictable behavior in PHP applications.

Mastering PHP variables and data types is fundamental for writing efficient and scalable applications. PHP's dynamic nature offers flexibility but requires an understanding of how different data types interact. By leveraging primitive and complex data structures effectively and controlling type conversion, developers can build robust and maintainable PHP applications.

Understanding PHP Variables and Dynamic Typing

Variables are one of the core building blocks of PHP programming, allowing developers to store and manipulate data dynamically. Unlike statically typed languages, PHP follows a **loosely typed** approach, meaning variables do not need explicit type declarations. Instead, PHP determines a variable's type based on the value assigned to it, making it highly flexible. This dynamic typing simplifies development but can introduce unexpected behavior if not handled correctly.

Declaring and Using Variables

A PHP variable is declared using the dollar sign ($) followed by an identifier. The variable's type is automatically assigned based on the data it holds. For example:

```
$name = "John Doe";   // String
$age = 30;            // Integer
$height = 5.9;        // Float
$isAdmin = true;      // Boolean
```

Here, $name holds a string, $age is an integer, $height is a floating-point number, and $isAdmin is a boolean. PHP does not require explicit type definitions, allowing developers to change the type of a variable by assigning a new value of a different type.

Variable Scope in PHP

PHP provides different **variable scopes**, determining where a variable can be accessed within a script. The four main types are:

1. **Local Scope** – Variables declared inside a function are only accessible within that function.

2. **Global Scope** – Variables declared outside functions have a global scope but are not accessible within functions unless explicitly stated.

3. **Static Variables** – Static variables retain their value between function calls.

4. **Superglobals** – Predefined global arrays (e.g., $_POST, $_GET, $_SESSION) that provide access to external data.

Example of **local and global scope**:

```php
$globalVar = "I am global";  // Global variable

function testScope() {
    $localVar = "I am local";  // Local variable
    global $globalVar;  // Accessing global variable inside function
    echo $globalVar;
}

testScope();
echo $localVar; // This will cause an error since $localVar is not accessible
            outside the function
```

Dynamic Typing and Type Changes

Since PHP variables are dynamically typed, their data type can change at runtime.

```php
$var = "10";    // String
$var = $var + 5;  // Now treated as an integer (15)
```

Here, $var starts as a string ("10") but is automatically converted to an integer when used in an arithmetic operation. This is an example of **type juggling**, where PHP determines the best data type based on the operation being performed.

Understanding PHP's variable system and dynamic typing is crucial for writing efficient and maintainable code. While PHP's flexible approach simplifies development, developers must be cautious of unexpected type conversions. By mastering variable scope and data handling, PHP programmers can ensure clarity and avoid unintended errors in their scripts.

Primitive Data Types and Their Usage in PHP

PHP provides several **primitive data types** that form the foundation of all variable assignments and data manipulations. These include **integers, floats, strings, and booleans**. Understanding how these data types work is essential for performing calculations, handling user input, and structuring application logic efficiently.

1. Integers

An **integer** is a whole number without a decimal point. It can be positive, negative, or zero. PHP supports decimal (base 10), hexadecimal (base 16, prefixed with 0x), octal (base 8, prefixed with 0), and binary (base 2, prefixed with 0b) integer representations.

Example:

```
$positive = 100;    // Decimal integer
$negative = -50;    // Negative integer
$hex = 0x1A;        // Hexadecimal (26 in decimal)
$octal = 0123;      // Octal (83 in decimal)
$binary = 0b1101;   // Binary (13 in decimal)
```

PHP integers have platform-dependent size limits, typically **32-bit or 64-bit**, and exceeding this limit converts the number into a **float**.

2. Floating-Point Numbers (Floats)

A **float** (or **double**) represents numbers with decimal points or in scientific notation. Floats are used for calculations requiring precision, such as measurements or currency operations.

Example:

```
$price = 19.99;       // Regular float
$scientific = 5.2e3;  // Scientific notation (5.2 × 10³ = 5200)
```

Since floats have precision limitations, comparing them directly can cause issues:

```
$a = 0.1 + 0.2;
$b = 0.3;
var_dump($a == $b); // false due to floating-point precision errors
```

To compare floats correctly, use round() or bcmath functions.

3. Strings

A **string** is a sequence of characters enclosed in single (') or double (") quotes. Double-quoted strings support variable interpolation and escape sequences (\n, \t, etc.), while single-quoted strings do not.

Example:

```
$name = "John";
echo "Hello, $name"; // Outputs: Hello, John
echo 'Hello, $name'; // Outputs: Hello, $name (no variable expansion)
```

Strings can be manipulated using functions like strlen(), strtoupper(), strtolower(), and substr().

```
$text = "PHP is powerful!";
echo strlen($text); // 17
echo strtoupper($text); // "PHP IS POWERFUL!"
```

4. Booleans

A **boolean** represents true or false, commonly used in conditionals and loops. PHP treats **empty strings, 0, null, and empty arrays** as false.

18

Example:

```php
$isUserLoggedIn = true;
if ($isUserLoggedIn) {
    echo "Welcome back!";
} else {
    echo "Please log in.";
}
```

PHP's primitive data types—integers, floats, strings, and booleans—are the foundation of all variable handling and computations. Understanding how to declare, manipulate, and compare these data types ensures efficient PHP programming and minimizes errors in applications.

Complex Data Types: Arrays, Objects, and Resources

Beyond primitive data types, PHP provides **complex data types** that allow developers to work with structured data, objects, and external resources. These include **arrays, objects, and resources**, each serving a unique role in managing application data efficiently.

1. Arrays

An **array** is a data structure that holds multiple values in a single variable. PHP supports two types of arrays:

- **Indexed Arrays** – Use numeric keys (starting from 0).

- **Associative Arrays** – Use named keys instead of numeric indices.

Example of an **indexed array**:

```php
$fruits = ["Apple", "Banana", "Cherry"];
echo $fruits[1]; // Outputs: Banana
```

Example of an **associative array**:

```php
$user = [
    "name" => "John Doe",
    "email" => "john@example.com",
    "age" => 30
];
echo $user["email"]; // Outputs: john@example.com
```

PHP also supports **multidimensional arrays**, useful for storing complex datasets like tables.

Example:

```php
$students = [
    ["John", 20, "A"],
    ["Alice", 22, "B"]
];

echo $students[1][0]; // Outputs: Alice
```

19

Array functions like count(), array_push(), array_pop(), and foreach loops help manipulate arrays effectively.

2. Objects

PHP supports **object-oriented programming (OOP)**, allowing developers to define **classes** and create **objects**. Objects are instances of classes that encapsulate properties (variables) and methods (functions).

Example of an object in PHP:

```php
class Car {
    public $brand;
    public $color;

    public function setBrand($brand) {
        $this->brand = $brand;
    }

    public function getBrand() {
        return $this->brand;
    }
}

$myCar = new Car();
$myCar->setBrand("Toyota");
echo $myCar->getBrand(); // Outputs: Toyota
```

Using objects makes PHP applications more **structured, reusable, and scalable**.

3. Resources

A **resource** is a special type in PHP used to reference external entities like **database connections, file handles, and streams**. Unlike other types, resources do not hold actual data but instead act as handles to these external connections.

Example of a database connection resource (using MySQLi):

```php
$conn = mysqli_connect("localhost", "root", "", "test_db");

if ($conn) {
    echo "Connected successfully!";
} else {
    echo "Connection failed!";
}
```

Resources are commonly used for **file handling (fopen()), database access, and API requests**. They must be properly **closed (fclose(), mysqli_close())** to free system resources.

PHP's complex data types—arrays, objects, and resources—enhance the ability to handle structured data, implement OOP principles, and interact with external systems. Mastering these types enables developers to build more efficient and scalable PHP applications.

Type Casting and Type Juggling in PHP

PHP is a loosely typed language, meaning variables do not have a fixed type and can change based on the assigned value or operation performed. This dynamic behavior is known as **type juggling**, where PHP automatically converts variables between types as needed. Developers can also enforce specific data types through **type casting**, which explicitly converts a variable to another type. Understanding both mechanisms is crucial for writing reliable PHP code and avoiding unexpected results.

1. Type Juggling in PHP

Type juggling occurs when PHP **automatically converts a variable's data type** based on the context in which it is used.

Example:

```php
$var = "5" + 10; // PHP converts "5" (string) to an integer and performs
            addition
echo $var; // Outputs: 15
```

PHP converted "5" (a string) into an integer before performing the addition. This automatic conversion can sometimes lead to **unexpected behavior**, especially when comparing values of different types.

Example of a **loose comparison (==)**:

```php
var_dump("123" == 123); // true, because PHP converts the string to an integer
var_dump("123abc" == 123); // true, because PHP extracts the numeric part before
            comparison
```

To avoid unintended type juggling, use **strict comparison (===)**, which checks both the value and the data type:

```php
var_dump("123" === 123); // false, because one is a string and the other is an
            integer
```

2. Type Casting in PHP

Unlike type juggling, **type casting** is an explicit way to convert variables to a specific data type. PHP provides several type casting options:

- (int) or (integer) – Converts to integer

- (float) or (double) – Converts to floating-point number

- (string) – Converts to string

- (bool) or (boolean) – Converts to boolean

- (array) – Converts to an array

- (object) – Converts to an object

Example:

```
$var = "42";
$intVar = (int) $var; // Explicitly converts string "42" to an integer
echo $intVar; // Outputs: 42
```

Example of **boolean casting**:

```
var_dump((bool) 0); // false
var_dump((bool) 1); // true
var_dump((bool) ""); // false
var_dump((bool) "hello"); // true
```

3. Common Pitfalls of Type Conversion

- **Unexpected results with arithmetic operations**:

```
echo "10" + "20hello"; // Outputs: 30 (PHP ignores non-numeric part)
```

- **Boolean conversion quirks**:

```
var_dump((bool) "0"); // false (empty string "0" is treated as false)
var_dump((bool) 0.0001); // true (any nonzero value is true)
```

- **Unintended comparisons**:

```
var_dump(0 == "hello"); // true (PHP converts "hello" to 0)
```

PHP's type juggling allows flexibility but can lead to unexpected behavior if not properly managed. Using **explicit type casting** helps ensure accuracy in data handling. Developers should be cautious when working with automatic conversions, always considering strict comparisons and controlled type conversions for better code reliability.

Module 2:
Functions and Scope in PHP

Functions play a fundamental role in PHP by allowing developers to encapsulate reusable blocks of code, improving maintainability and efficiency. PHP supports various function types, from named functions to anonymous functions and closures. Understanding function parameters, return types, and variable scope ensures structured and predictable code execution. This module explores function definitions, scope management, and advanced function types such as closures and callbacks.

Defining and Calling Functions in PHP

In PHP, functions serve as reusable code units that perform specific tasks. A function is defined once and can be called multiple times within a script, eliminating redundancy. Properly designed functions enhance readability and reduce development effort. Functions can accept inputs, process data, and return results, making them powerful building blocks in PHP applications. PHP functions can be either **user-defined** or **built-in**. Built-in functions provide essential functionalities, while user-defined functions enable customization based on application needs. A well-structured function includes a meaningful name, optional parameters, and a return value when necessary. Understanding function creation and invocation is crucial for efficient programming.

Function Parameters, Return Types, and Type Hints

Functions in PHP can accept parameters to process data dynamically. Parameters allow functions to handle variable inputs rather than relying on fixed values. PHP also supports **default parameter values**, enabling functions to be called without explicitly passing all arguments. Additionally, **return types** specify the type of value a function returns, enforcing consistency in function output. **Type hints** further improve function reliability by enforcing expected data types for parameters and return values. With PHP's flexible type system, developers can use **strict typing** to prevent unintended type conversions, ensuring robust and predictable function behavior across different application scenarios.

Understanding Scope: Global, Local, and Static Variables

Variable scope defines where a variable can be accessed within a PHP script. PHP has three primary variable scopes: **local, global, and static**. **Local variables** exist only within the function where they are declared, ensuring data encapsulation. **Global variables** are accessible throughout the script but require special handling when used inside functions. The global keyword or $GLOBALS array provides access to global variables within functions. **Static variables**, on the other hand, retain their values across multiple function calls, making them useful for maintaining stateful data without using global variables. Understanding scope is essential for preventing conflicts and improving code maintainability.

Anonymous Functions, Closures, and Callback Functions

PHP supports **anonymous functions**, which are functions without a name, often assigned to variables or passed as arguments. These are useful for short, one-time-use functionalities. **Closures** extend anonymous functions by capturing variables from their surrounding scope, enabling more dynamic behavior. **Callback functions** are functions passed as arguments to other functions, commonly used in event-driven programming, array operations, and asynchronous tasks. These advanced function types enhance PHP's flexibility, allowing developers to create modular, reusable, and event-driven code structures. Mastering these concepts enables efficient handling of functional programming patterns within PHP applications.

Understanding functions and scope in PHP is crucial for writing clean, modular, and maintainable code. This module covers defining functions, handling parameters and return types, managing variable scope, and leveraging advanced function types like closures and callbacks. By mastering these concepts, PHP developers can build efficient, scalable, and well-structured applications.

Defining and Calling Functions in PHP

Functions are fundamental building blocks in PHP programming, allowing developers to create reusable, modular, and efficient code. Instead of repeating the same logic multiple times, functions enable encapsulating logic into a single unit that can be called whenever needed. PHP supports both **built-in functions** and **user-defined functions**, providing a robust approach to code organization. This section explores how to define and call functions in PHP, outlining key principles such as function names, parameters, return values, and best practices for function implementation.

Defining a Function

A function in PHP is defined using the function keyword followed by a unique function name and parentheses (). The function body, enclosed within curly braces {}, contains the executable code.

```php
function greet() {
    echo "Hello, World!";
}
```

This function does not take any parameters and simply outputs a message when called.

Calling a Function

A function must be **called** for its code to execute. A function call is made by writing the function name followed by parentheses:

24

```
greet(); // Outputs: Hello, World!
```

Since PHP does not require functions to be declared before they are used (except for functions inside conditional blocks), they can be defined anywhere in the script.

Functions with Parameters

Functions can accept **parameters** that allow them to process dynamic values. Parameters are declared inside the parentheses and can be used within the function body.

```
function greetUser($name) {
    echo "Hello, $name!";
}

greetUser("Alice"); // Outputs: Hello, Alice!
```

Multiple parameters can be passed by separating them with commas:

```
function add($a, $b) {
    return $a + $b;
}

echo add(5, 3); // Outputs: 8
```

Returning Values from Functions

The return statement allows a function to send back a value to the caller instead of just printing it.

```
function square($num) {
    return $num * $num;
}

$result = square(4);
echo $result; // Outputs: 16
```

A function stops executing once it encounters a return statement. Any code after return within the function will not be executed.

Best Practices for Defining Functions

- **Use meaningful function names** that describe their purpose.

- **Keep functions small and focused** on a single task.

- **Avoid using global variables** inside functions to prevent unintended side effects.

- **Use default parameter values** for flexibility.

- **Document functions** with comments for better readability.

Functions in PHP improve code organization, reusability, and maintainability. By defining functions properly, handling parameters effectively, and using return values efficiently, developers can write cleaner and more structured PHP code. Mastering function usage is essential for building scalable and well-optimized PHP applications.

Function Parameters, Return Types, and Type Hints

Functions in PHP become more powerful when they accept parameters and return values. Parameters allow functions to process dynamic input, while return values enable functions to send results back to the caller. Additionally, **type hints** enforce data types for function arguments and return values, making code more predictable and reducing potential errors. This section explores the different ways to define function parameters, use return values effectively, and implement type hints for stricter data control.

Function Parameters

A function can accept parameters inside parentheses. Parameters act as placeholders for values passed during the function call.

```php
function greet($name) {
    echo "Hello, $name!";
}

greet("Alice"); // Outputs: Hello, Alice!
```

Multiple parameters are separated by commas:

```php
function add($a, $b) {
    return $a + $b;
}

echo add(5, 3); // Outputs: 8
```

Default Parameter Values

PHP allows setting default values for parameters, making them optional during function calls.

```php
function greet($name = "Guest") {
    echo "Hello, $name!";
}

greet();        // Outputs: Hello, Guest!
greet("John"); // Outputs: Hello, John!
```

Default values ensure that a function works even when no arguments are provided.

Return Values

Functions can return values using the return statement. The returned value can be stored in a variable or used directly in expressions.

```
function multiply($a, $b) {
    return $a * $b;
}

$result = multiply(4, 5);
echo $result; // Outputs: 20
```

Functions stop execution when they encounter return, ignoring any code after it.

Type Hints in Function Parameters

Type hints enforce strict data types for function arguments, reducing errors caused by unexpected input. PHP supports type hints such as int, float, string, bool, array, object, and custom class names.

```
function addNumbers(int $a, int $b): int {
    return $a + $b;
}

echo addNumbers(5, 10); // Outputs: 15
```

Passing an incorrect type (e.g., a string instead of an integer) results in a TypeError when strict typing is enabled.

Return Type Declarations

Return type declarations specify the expected return type of a function.

```
function getGreeting(string $name): string {
    return "Hello, $name!";
}

echo getGreeting("Alice"); // Outputs: Hello, Alice!
```

This ensures that the function always returns a string. If it tries to return a different type, an error will occur.

Using function parameters, return types, and type hints improves function clarity, reliability, and maintainability. Type hints prevent invalid data types, while return types enforce predictable outputs. These techniques help developers write robust PHP applications with fewer runtime errors and better data handling.

Understanding Scope: Global, Local, and Static Variables

Variable scope in PHP determines where a variable can be accessed within a script. PHP has three primary types of variable scope: **local, global, and static**. Understanding these scopes is essential for managing data effectively and preventing unintended conflicts between variables. This section explores how variable scope works in PHP, along with best practices for using global and static variables responsibly.

Local Variables

A **local variable** is declared inside a function and is only accessible within that function. It **cannot** be accessed from outside the function, ensuring encapsulation and preventing accidental modifications.

```
function example() {
    $message = "Hello, World!";
    echo $message;
}

example(); // Outputs: Hello, World!
// echo $message; // Error: Undefined variable $message
```

Local variables exist **only while the function is executing** and are destroyed when the function completes. This prevents unnecessary memory usage and conflicts between variables in different functions.

Global Variables

A **global variable** is declared outside of a function and can be accessed anywhere in the script. However, by default, global variables **are not accessible within functions** unless explicitly specified using the global keyword.

```
$siteName = "PHP Programming";

function showSiteName() {
    global $siteName; // Accessing the global variable
    echo $siteName;
}

showSiteName(); // Outputs: PHP Programming
```

Alternatively, the $GLOBALS array can be used to access global variables inside functions:

```
function display() {
    echo $GLOBALS['siteName'];
}

display(); // Outputs: PHP Programming
```

Using too many global variables can make code harder to maintain and debug, as changes in one part of the script may affect other unrelated parts.

Static Variables

A **static variable** retains its value between function calls. Unlike local variables, which are reinitialized every time a function runs, static variables **persist** their values across multiple calls but remain function-scoped.

```
function counter() {
    static $count = 0; // Retains value between function calls
    $count++;
    echo $count;
}
```

```
counter(); // Outputs: 1
counter(); // Outputs: 2
counter(); // Outputs: 3
```

Static variables are useful for tracking values across multiple function calls without using global variables.

Best Practices for Managing Variable Scope

- **Prefer local variables** when possible to avoid unintended side effects.

- **Limit global variables** and use them only when necessary.

- **Use static variables** for maintaining function-specific state without polluting the global scope.

- **Encapsulate variables within functions** to improve modularity and reusability.

Understanding variable scope is crucial for writing clean and efficient PHP code. Local variables provide function-level isolation, global variables allow script-wide access, and static variables enable persistent values within functions. Managing scope properly enhances code maintainability, reduces conflicts, and prevents unexpected behavior in PHP applications.

Anonymous Functions, Closures, and Callback Functions

PHP provides advanced function capabilities such as **anonymous functions**, **closures**, and **callback functions**, which enhance flexibility and modularity in programming. These function types allow developers to write cleaner, more concise, and more dynamic code. This section explores how each of these function types works, their use cases, and best practices for implementation.

Anonymous Functions

An **anonymous function** (also called a **lambda function**) is a function **without a name**. It is often assigned to a variable or used as an argument in other functions. Anonymous functions are useful for short, one-time operations where defining a named function would be unnecessary.

```
$greet = function($name) {
    return "Hello, $name!";
};

echo $greet("Alice"); // Outputs: Hello, Alice!
```

Anonymous functions are commonly used for event handlers, short computations, or passing functions as arguments.

Closures

A **closure** is an anonymous function that can **access variables from its surrounding scope**, even after the original scope has ended. Closures allow for more **dynamic and encapsulated** functionality.

To use an external variable inside an anonymous function, the use keyword is required:

```php
$message = "Welcome";

$greet = function($name) use ($message) {
    return "$message, $name!";
};

echo $greet("Alice"); // Outputs: Welcome, Alice!
```

Without use, the function would not have access to $message from the outside scope. Closures are useful in scenarios where a function needs to retain access to specific data while being executed in a different context.

Callback Functions

A **callback function** is a function passed as an argument to another function. Callbacks allow flexible and reusable function behavior, making them essential for **event-driven programming, array operations, and custom processing functions**.

PHP functions like array_map() and array_filter() commonly use callbacks:

```php
$numbers = [1, 2, 3, 4, 5];

$squaredNumbers = array_map(function($num) {
    return $num * $num;
}, $numbers);

print_r($squaredNumbers);
// Outputs: [1, 4, 9, 16, 25]
```

Alternatively, a named function can be used as a callback:

```php
function double($num) {
    return $num * 2;
}

$results = array_map("double", $numbers);
print_r($results); // Outputs: [2, 4, 6, 8, 10]
```

Best Practices for Using Anonymous Functions, Closures, and Callbacks

- **Use anonymous functions** for short, temporary logic.

- **Utilize closures** when a function needs access to external variables.

- **Leverage callback functions** for dynamic behavior in array operations and event handling.

- **Keep functions small and focused** to improve readability and maintainability.

Anonymous functions, closures, and callback functions add flexibility to PHP programming, enabling cleaner and more modular code. By mastering these function types, developers can write more efficient and maintainable PHP applications, making full use of functional programming techniques..

Module 3:

Conditional Statements and Control Flow

Conditional statements and control flow mechanisms are fundamental in PHP programming, allowing scripts to make decisions based on conditions. They help execute specific blocks of code depending on variable states or user input. This module explores PHP's key conditional constructs, including **if-else statements, switch-case logic, truthy and falsy evaluations, ternary and null coalescing operators,** and **best practices for writing maintainable conditional logic**. Mastering these control flow techniques enables developers to build dynamic, efficient, and readable PHP applications.

Implementing If-Else and Switch-Case Logic

Conditional execution is primarily handled using if, else, and elseif statements. The if statement checks a condition and executes a block of code if it evaluates to true. If the condition is false, an else block may provide an alternative execution path. The elseif statement allows multiple conditions to be checked in sequence.

For scenarios requiring multiple condition checks against a single variable, the switch statement provides a more structured approach. It evaluates an expression and executes the corresponding case block. This prevents excessive if-elseif chains, improving readability and performance. Proper use of break statements ensures that execution does not unintentionally continue into subsequent cases.

Evaluating Truthy and Falsy Values in PHP

In PHP, values are evaluated as **truthy** or **falsy** when used in conditional expressions. A value is **truthy** if it evaluates to true in a boolean context, while a **falsy** value evaluates to false. PHP considers 0, "" (empty string), null, false, [] (empty array), and 0.0 as falsy, while non-zero numbers, non-empty strings, and arrays are truthy.

Understanding truthy and falsy values helps prevent unexpected behavior in conditionals. Developers must be cautious when comparing values using == (loose comparison) versus === (strict comparison), as PHP may perform type juggling, leading to unintended results. Explicit type checks (is_null(), empty(), isset()) improve reliability in condition evaluations.

Using the Ternary and Null Coalescing Operators

PHP provides shorthand operators to simplify conditional expressions. The **ternary operator (? :)** is a compact alternative to an if-else statement, making code more concise. It returns one value if a condition is true and another if false. However, excessive nesting can harm readability.

The **null coalescing operator (??)** simplifies checks for null values. It returns the first operand if it exists and is not null; otherwise, it returns the second operand. This is particularly useful for handling user input or database results where variables may be undefined. Using these operators effectively can make code cleaner and reduce verbosity.

Writing Readable and Maintainable Conditional Logic

Well-structured conditional logic improves code maintainability and reduces errors. Best practices include **keeping conditions simple, using descriptive variable names, avoiding deeply nested conditions, and leveraging functions for reusable logic**. The early return pattern (guard clauses) prevents unnecessary nesting by handling exceptions or invalid states at the beginning of a function.

Consistent indentation and spacing also contribute to readability. When using multiple conditions, **logical operators (&&, ||)** should be used judiciously to enhance clarity. By following these principles, developers can write efficient, scalable, and maintainable PHP applications.

Mastering conditional statements and control flow is essential for writing dynamic and responsive PHP applications. Using if-else, switch-case, truthy and falsy evaluations, ternary and null coalescing operators, and structured logic ensures efficient decision-making in scripts. Writing clear, maintainable conditional logic enhances both code quality and developer productivity.

Implementing If-Else and Switch-Case Logic

Conditional statements allow PHP scripts to make decisions based on specific conditions. The two primary structures for implementing conditional logic in PHP are **if-else statements** and **switch-case statements**. These control structures enable developers to create dynamic applications by executing different blocks of code depending on variable values. This section covers the syntax, use cases, and best practices for both if-else and switch-case logic.

Using If-Else Statements

The if statement is the most common conditional structure. It evaluates a condition and executes a block of code if the condition is true.

```
$age = 18;

if ($age >= 18) {
    echo "You are eligible to vote.";
}
```

An else block provides an alternative execution path when the if condition evaluates to false.

```
$age = 16;
```

```php
if ($age >= 18) {
    echo "You are eligible to vote.";
} else {
    echo "You are not old enough to vote.";
}
```

For multiple conditions, elseif statements allow checking additional conditions in sequence.

```php
$score = 85;

if ($score >= 90) {
    echo "Grade: A";
} elseif ($score >= 80) {
    echo "Grade: B";
} elseif ($score >= 70) {
    echo "Grade: C";
} else {
    echo "Grade: F";
}
```

Using elseif prevents redundant condition evaluations and enhances efficiency.

Using Switch-Case Statements

The switch statement is an alternative to multiple if-elseif statements, particularly when comparing a single variable against multiple fixed values. It improves readability and performance in cases where multiple conditions depend on the same variable.

```php
$day = "Monday";

switch ($day) {
    case "Monday":
        echo "Start of the workweek.";
        break;
    case "Friday":
        echo "Weekend is near.";
        break;
    case "Sunday":
        echo "It's a rest day!";
        break;
    default:
        echo "A regular day.";
}
```

Each case represents a possible value of $day, and the break statement ensures that execution stops after a match is found. The default case provides a fallback when none of the specified cases match the variable.

Best Practices for Conditional Logic

1. **Use if-else for range-based conditions** (e.g., numerical comparisons).

2. **Use switch-case when checking multiple fixed values** of a single variable.

3. **Avoid deeply nested conditionals**, as they reduce readability.

4. **Use strict comparisons (=== instead of ==)** to prevent unintended type coercion.

5. **Keep conditions simple and readable** for maintainability.

The if-else and switch-case statements provide essential control flow mechanisms in PHP. While if-else is more flexible for handling conditions with ranges or different variables, switch is more efficient when evaluating a single variable against multiple possible values. Following best practices ensures clear, maintainable, and efficient conditional logic in PHP applications.

Evaluating Truthy and Falsy Values in PHP

In PHP, conditions often depend on whether a value is considered **truthy** or **falsy**. Truthy values evaluate to true when used in a conditional statement, while falsy values evaluate to false. Understanding how PHP determines truthiness and falsiness is crucial for avoiding logical errors and writing reliable code. This section explores truthy and falsy values, their impact on conditional logic, and best practices for handling them effectively.

Truthy and Falsy Values in PHP

PHP considers certain values **falsy**, meaning they evaluate to false in a boolean context. These include:

- false (Boolean false)

- 0 (Integer zero)

- 0.0 (Float zero)

- "" (Empty string)

- "0" (String containing zero)

- [] (Empty array)

- null (Null value)

Any value not in this list is **truthy**, meaning it evaluates to true when used in a condition. Examples of truthy values include:

- Non-zero numbers (1, -1, 3.14)

- Non-empty strings ("hello", "false")

35

- Non-empty arrays ([1, 2, 3])

- Objects

- Resource handles

Truthy and Falsy Behavior in Conditional Statements

Since PHP automatically converts values to boolean when used in conditionals, improper handling can lead to unexpected behavior.

```
if ("0") {
    echo "This is truthy!";
} else {
    echo "This is falsy!";
}
// Outputs: "This is falsy!"
```

In this case, the string "0" is falsy, which can be surprising to developers unfamiliar with PHP's type juggling.

Strict Comparisons for Reliable Evaluations

To avoid unintended truthy or falsy evaluations, use **strict comparisons (=== and !==)** rather than loose comparisons (==).

```
$value = "0";

if ($value === true) {
    echo "True";
} else {
    echo "False";
}
// Outputs: "False"
```

This prevents PHP from converting "0" to false, ensuring an explicit boolean check.

Using empty(), isset(), and is_null() for Safer Checks

- empty($var): Returns true if $var is falsy (e.g., "", 0, null, false, []).

- isset($var): Returns true if $var is defined and not null.

- is_null($var): Returns true if $var is null.

```
$value = "";

if (empty($value)) {
    echo "Value is empty!";
}
// Outputs: "Value is empty!"
```

Using these functions helps avoid unintended behavior caused by PHP's automatic type conversions.

Understanding truthy and falsy values is critical for writing reliable PHP conditionals. While PHP's flexible type system can simplify coding, it can also lead to unexpected results. Using strict comparisons and functions like empty(), isset(), and is_null() ensures predictable and maintainable conditional logic in PHP applications.

Using the Ternary and Null Coalescing Operators

PHP provides shorthand operators to simplify conditional expressions: **the ternary operator (? :)** and **the null coalescing operator (??)**. These operators enhance code readability and reduce verbosity, making conditional checks more concise. This section explores their syntax, use cases, and best practices for efficient conditional logic.

The Ternary Operator (? :)

The **ternary operator** is a compact alternative to an if-else statement. It evaluates a condition and returns one of two values depending on whether the condition is true or false.

Syntax:

```
condition ? value_if_true : value_if_false;
```

Example:

```
$age = 20;
$message = ($age >= 18) ? "Eligible to vote" : "Not eligible to vote";
echo $message; // Outputs: Eligible to vote
```

Instead of writing a full if-else statement, the ternary operator provides a one-liner alternative, improving readability for simple conditional assignments.

Chaining Ternary Operators

Multiple ternary expressions can be chained, but excessive nesting can reduce readability.

```
$score = 75;
$grade = ($score >= 90) ? "A" : (($score >= 80) ? "B" : "C");
echo $grade; // Outputs: C
```

Using parentheses improves clarity in chained ternary expressions, but if conditions become complex, a traditional if-else structure is preferable.

The Null Coalescing Operator (??)

The **null coalescing operator (??)** provides a clean way to check if a variable is set and not null. It returns the first operand if it exists and is not null; otherwise, it returns the second operand. This is useful for handling optional values, default settings, and user inputs.

Syntax:

```
$variable = value_if_set ?? alternative_value;
```

Example:

```
$username = $_GET['user'] ?? "Guest";
echo $username; // Outputs: "Guest" if 'user' is not set
```

This eliminates the need for isset() checks, making the code cleaner and more efficient.

Differences Between ?? and ?:

- The **ternary operator (? :)** evaluates a condition and returns one of two values based on truthiness.

- The **null coalescing operator (??)** strictly checks for null and does not evaluate truthiness.

Example Comparison:

```
$value = 0;
echo $value ?: "Default"; // Outputs: "Default" (because 0 is falsy)
echo $value ?? "Default"; // Outputs: 0 (because $value exists and is not null)
```

Best Practices for Using These Operators

1. **Use the ternary operator for simple conditional assignments**, but avoid excessive nesting.

2. **Prefer ?? for handling default values**, especially in user input or configuration settings.

3. **Avoid using ?: when strict null checks are needed**, as it evaluates truthiness rather than null status.

4. **Prioritize readability**—if a condition is complex, use if-else instead of multiple ternary operations.

The ternary and null coalescing operators provide a concise way to handle conditional logic in PHP. While the ternary operator is useful for simple if-else replacements, the null coalescing operator is ideal for handling default values. Using them correctly improves code efficiency and readability, reducing unnecessary boilerplate code.

Writing Readable and Maintainable Conditional Logic

Writing clean and maintainable conditional logic is essential for ensuring that PHP applications remain easy to understand, debug, and extend. Poorly structured conditions can lead to spaghetti code, making it difficult to track logic errors or modify functionality. This section explores best practices for writing conditional statements that are readable, efficient, and maintainable.

1. Keeping Conditions Simple and Clear

Complex conditions reduce readability and increase the likelihood of errors. Instead of writing long, nested conditions, break them down into meaningful boolean variables or functions.

Example (Hard to Read):

```php
if (($userRole == "admin" && $status == "active") || ($userRole == "editor" &&
        $status != "banned")) {
    grantAccess();
}
```

Refactored for Readability:

```php
$isAdmin = ($userRole == "admin" && $status == "active");
$isEditor = ($userRole == "editor" && $status != "banned");

if ($isAdmin || $isEditor) {
    grantAccess();
}
```

By using well-named variables, the condition becomes self-explanatory and easier to modify later.

2. Avoiding Deep Nesting

Nested if statements can make the code difficult to follow. Instead, use **early returns** or **guard clauses** to simplify logic.

Example (Deep Nesting):

```php
function processOrder($order) {
    if ($order) {
        if ($order->status == "pending") {
            if ($order->paymentConfirmed) {
                approveOrder($order);
            }
        }
    }
}
```

Refactored with Early Return:

```php
function processOrder($order) {
    if (!$order || $order->status != "pending" || !$order->paymentConfirmed) {
        return;
    }
```

```
        approveOrder($order);
}
```

By handling invalid cases first, the function remains clean and avoids excessive indentation.

3. Using Switch-Case for Multiple Conditions

When a single variable is being compared against multiple values, a switch statement can enhance readability over multiple if-elseif conditions.

Example (Multiple if-elseif):

```
if ($status == "pending") {
    $message = "Order is pending.";
} elseif ($status == "shipped") {
    $message = "Order has been shipped.";
} elseif ($status == "delivered") {
    $message = "Order delivered successfully.";
} else {
    $message = "Unknown status.";
}
```

Refactored with switch:

```
switch ($status) {
    case "pending":
        $message = "Order is pending.";
        break;
    case "shipped":
        $message = "Order has been shipped.";
        break;
    case "delivered":
        $message = "Order delivered successfully.";
        break;
    default:
        $message = "Unknown status.";
}
```

Using switch improves clarity and ensures efficient branching.

4. Using the Null Coalescing and Ternary Operators Wisely

Short-hand operators like ?? and ?: help streamline conditions, but overuse can hurt readability.

Example (Readable Usage of ??):

```
$username = $_GET['user'] ?? "Guest";
```

Example (Unclear Overuse of Ternary Operators):

```
$message = ($status == "active") ? "Welcome" : (($status == "pending") ? "Please
            wait" : "Access denied");
```

This ternary chain can be refactored into a switch or if-elseif structure for clarity.

40

Maintaining clean, readable, and efficient conditional logic improves code maintainability and reduces errors. Using strategies like simplifying conditions, avoiding deep nesting, leveraging switch-case, and applying shorthand operators appropriately ensures that PHP applications remain scalable and easy to understand. Prioritizing readability leads to better collaboration and long-term maintainability.

Module 4:
Collections and Array Manipulation

Arrays are a fundamental data structure in PHP, allowing developers to store, manipulate, and process collections of data efficiently. PHP offers powerful built-in functions for working with arrays, making it easy to perform operations such as sorting, filtering, and transformation. This module explores different types of arrays, functional array operations, sorting techniques, and advanced data handling using iterators and generators. Mastering these concepts is crucial for writing efficient and scalable PHP applications that handle large datasets effectively.

Working with Indexed, Associative, and Multidimensional Arrays

PHP supports three primary types of arrays: **indexed**, **associative**, and **multidimensional** arrays. Indexed arrays use numeric keys to store ordered values, making them ideal for sequential data like lists or numerical datasets. Associative arrays, on the other hand, use named keys, allowing developers to store key-value pairs, which is useful for configuration settings or mapping relationships. Multidimensional arrays enable hierarchical data storage by nesting arrays within arrays, making them useful for representing complex structures such as matrices or JSON-like datasets. Understanding how to create, access, and manipulate these different types of arrays is essential for effective PHP programming.

Functional Array Operations: Mapping, Filtering, and Reducing

PHP provides powerful functional programming capabilities for working with arrays through functions like array_map(), array_filter(), and array_reduce(). These functions allow developers to **transform** array elements, **extract specific values** based on conditions, and **aggregate** values efficiently. Mapping applies a function to each element in an array, filtering removes elements that do not meet a condition, and reducing collapses an array into a single computed value. By leveraging these operations, developers can write more expressive and concise code, reducing the need for complex loops and improving code maintainability.

Sorting, Merging, and Splitting Arrays in PHP

Sorting is a critical operation when dealing with collections of data. PHP provides various sorting functions, such as sort(), asort(), and ksort(), which allow sorting by values or keys, while maintaining or discarding key associations. In addition to sorting, PHP allows for **merging** arrays using functions like array_merge() and array_combine(), enabling the combination of multiple datasets into a single array. Splitting arrays into smaller chunks using array_chunk() or extracting specific portions with array_slice() is useful for pagination and batch processing. Mastering these array manipulation techniques allows developers to efficiently manage data structures in PHP.

42

Implementing Iterators and Generators for Efficient Data Handling

When dealing with large datasets, iterators and generators provide **memory-efficient solutions** for traversing data without loading the entire dataset into memory. PHP offers built-in iterators, such as ArrayIterator and IteratorAggregate, which provide enhanced control over array traversal. Generators, implemented using the yield keyword, allow on-the-fly data generation, reducing memory consumption when processing large files, database records, or API responses. These techniques are especially useful in performance-critical applications, where memory optimization is essential for scalability and responsiveness.

Mastering array manipulation in PHP is key to efficient data processing and application performance. This module covers different array types, functional transformations, sorting and merging techniques, and advanced iteration strategies. By leveraging PHP's built-in array functions, developers can write more optimized, readable, and maintainable code, improving both functionality and performance in PHP applications.

Working with Indexed, Associative, and Multidimensional Arrays

Arrays are a core data structure in PHP, used for storing multiple values in a single variable. PHP provides three main types of arrays: **indexed arrays**, **associative arrays**, and **multidimensional arrays**. Each type serves a different purpose, making it essential to understand their differences, how to manipulate them, and when to use them effectively.

Indexed Arrays

An **indexed array** is a collection of values assigned numerical keys automatically starting from 0. They are best suited for storing ordered lists, such as product names, numbers, or user IDs.

Creating an Indexed Array:

```php
$fruits = ["Apple", "Banana", "Cherry"];
```

Accessing Elements:

```php
echo $fruits[1]; // Outputs: Banana
```

Indexed arrays can be iterated using loops like foreach or for:

```php
foreach ($fruits as $fruit) {
    echo $fruit . "<br>";
}
```

Associative Arrays

An **associative array** uses named keys instead of numerical indexes, making it ideal for storing key-value pairs such as user information, configurations, or mappings.

Creating an Associative Array:

```
$user = [
    "name" => "John Doe",
    "email" => "john@example.com",
    "age" => 30
];
```

Accessing Values:

```
echo $user["email"]; // Outputs: john@example.com
```

Associative arrays provide flexibility when dealing with structured data, allowing meaningful key names instead of numerical indices.

Multidimensional Arrays

A **multidimensional array** is an array that contains other arrays, enabling hierarchical data storage. It is useful for representing complex structures like tables, JSON data, or nested configurations.

Creating a Multidimensional Array:

```
$users = [
    ["name" => "Alice", "email" => "alice@example.com"],
    ["name" => "Bob", "email" => "bob@example.com"]
];
```

Accessing Nested Elements:

```
echo $users[1]["name"]; // Outputs: Bob
```

Looping Through Multidimensional Arrays:

```
foreach ($users as $user) {
    echo $user["name"] . " - " . $user["email"] . "<br>";
}
```

Best Practices for Using Arrays

1. **Choose the right type**: Use indexed arrays for lists, associative arrays for key-value pairs, and multidimensional arrays for structured data.

2. **Ensure proper indexing**: Avoid missing or duplicate keys to maintain consistency.

3. **Use loops effectively**: Utilize foreach for associative and multidimensional arrays to improve readability.

Understanding indexed, associative, and multidimensional arrays is fundamental in PHP development. By selecting the appropriate array type and employing efficient iteration techniques, developers can store and manipulate data effectively, leading to cleaner, more maintainable code.

Functional Array Operations: Mapping, Filtering, and Reducing

PHP provides a rich set of functional programming tools for working with arrays efficiently. Among these are **array mapping**, **filtering**, and **reducing**, which enable developers to process and transform array data concisely. These functions eliminate the need for explicit loops, making code more readable and expressive. Understanding these techniques is essential for writing efficient and maintainable PHP applications.

Mapping Arrays with array_map()

The array_map() function applies a callback function to each element in an array and returns a new array with the modified values. This is useful for transforming data without modifying the original array.

Example: Converting a List of Names to Uppercase

```
$names = ["alice", "bob", "charlie"];
$uppercaseNames = array_map("strtoupper", $names);

print_r($uppercaseNames);
// Output: ["ALICE", "BOB", "CHARLIE"]
```

Alternatively, an anonymous function (closure) can be used for custom transformations:

```
$prices = [100, 200, 300];
$discountedPrices = array_map(function ($price) {
    return $price * 0.9;
}, $prices);

print_r($discountedPrices);
// Output: [90, 180, 270]
```

Filtering Arrays with array_filter()

The array_filter() function removes elements that do not satisfy a given condition, keeping only values that return true when passed to the callback.

Example: Filtering Even Numbers from an Array

```
$numbers = [1, 2, 3, 4, 5, 6];
$evenNumbers = array_filter($numbers, function ($num) {
    return $num % 2 == 0;
});

print_r($evenNumbers);
// Output: [2, 4, 6]
```

Unlike array_map(), array_filter() preserves array keys, which might need reindexing using array_values().

Reducing Arrays with array_reduce()

The array_reduce() function collapses an array into a single value by applying a function iteratively. This is useful for operations such as summing values or concatenating strings.

Example: Calculating the Sum of an Array

```
$numbers = [10, 20, 30, 40];
$total = array_reduce($numbers, function ($carry, $num) {
    return $carry + $num;
}, 0);

echo $total; // Output: 100
```

Another common use case is string concatenation:

```
$words = ["Hello", "world", "!"];
$sentence = array_reduce($words, function ($carry, $word) {
    return $carry . " " . $word;
});

echo trim($sentence); // Output: "Hello world!"
```

Best Practices for Functional Array Operations

- Use array_map() when transforming all elements of an array.

- Use array_filter() to extract specific elements based on conditions.

- Use array_reduce() when aggregating values into a single result.

PHP's functional array operations provide a powerful way to manipulate and process data efficiently. By leveraging array_map(), array_filter(), and array_reduce(), developers can replace verbose loops with concise, readable code, improving maintainability and performance.

Sorting, Merging, and Splitting Arrays in PHP

Manipulating arrays effectively is crucial in PHP development, especially when dealing with large datasets. Sorting, merging, and splitting arrays allow developers to structure and process data efficiently. PHP provides built-in functions for these operations, making it easy to organize and manage arrays. This section explores various sorting techniques, merging strategies, and splitting methods to optimize array handling.

Sorting Arrays in PHP

PHP offers multiple sorting functions depending on whether sorting is based on keys, values, or custom comparison logic.

Sorting by Values (sort() and rsort())

- sort() arranges an array in ascending order.

- rsort() sorts in descending order.

```
$numbers = [3, 1, 4, 1, 5, 9];
sort($numbers);
print_r($numbers); // Output: [1, 1, 3, 4, 5, 9]
```

Sorting Associative Arrays (asort(), arsort(), ksort(), krsort())

- asort() sorts associative arrays by values, preserving keys.

- ksort() sorts by keys.

- arsort() and krsort() perform reverse sorting for values and keys, respectively.

```
$ages = ["Alice" => 25, "Bob" => 22, "Charlie" => 30];
asort($ages);
print_r($ages); // Output: ["Bob" => 22, "Alice" => 25, "Charlie" => 30]
```

Custom Sorting (usort())

For complex sorting, usort() allows a user-defined function to determine order.

```
$people = [
    ["name" => "Alice", "age" => 25],
    ["name" => "Bob", "age" => 22]
];

usort($people, function ($a, $b) {
    return $a["age"] - $b["age"];
});

print_r($people); // Output: Bob first, then Alice
```

Merging Arrays in PHP

PHP provides several ways to combine arrays.

Using array_merge()

array_merge() merges multiple arrays into one. If keys conflict, numeric keys are reindexed, and string keys are overridden.

```
$array1 = ["a" => "apple", "b" => "banana"];
$array2 = ["b" => "blueberry", "c" => "cherry"];
$result = array_merge($array1, $array2);

print_r($result);
// Output: ["a" => "apple", "b" => "blueberry", "c" => "cherry"]
```

Using array_combine()

array_combine() creates an associative array by using one array as keys and another as values.

```
$keys = ["name", "email"];
$values = ["Alice", "alice@example.com"];
$combined = array_combine($keys, $values);

print_r($combined);
// Output: ["name" => "Alice", "email" => "alice@example.com"]
```

Splitting Arrays in PHP

PHP allows arrays to be divided into smaller parts.

Using array_chunk()

array_chunk() splits an array into equally sized chunks.

```
$numbers = [1, 2, 3, 4, 5, 6];
$chunks = array_chunk($numbers, 2);

print_r($chunks);
// Output: [[1, 2], [3, 4], [5, 6]]
```

Using array_slice()

array_slice() extracts a portion of an array without modifying the original.

```
$fruits = ["apple", "banana", "cherry", "date"];
$sliced = array_slice($fruits, 1, 2);

print_r($sliced);
// Output: ["banana", "cherry"]
```

Sorting, merging, and splitting arrays are fundamental operations in PHP that help manage and structure data effectively. By using built-in functions like sort(), array_merge(), and array_chunk(), developers can optimize data handling, improve performance, and write cleaner, more efficient code.

Implementing Iterators and Generators for Efficient Data Handling

When working with large datasets in PHP, processing every item at once can lead to memory inefficiencies. Iterators and generators provide a solution by allowing elements to be processed one at a time, reducing memory consumption and improving performance. This section explores PHP's **Iterator** interface and **generators**, demonstrating how they enhance efficiency in handling data streams.

Using Iterators in PHP

An **iterator** is an object that allows traversal over a dataset without loading it all into memory. PHP provides built-in iterators through the **Iterator interface**, which requires implementing five methods:

- current(): Returns the current element.

- key(): Returns the current index or key.

- next(): Moves to the next element.

- rewind(): Resets the iterator to the first element.

- valid(): Checks if the current position is valid.

Example: Creating a Custom Iterator

```php
class NumberIterator implements Iterator {
    private $numbers;
    private $index = 0;

    public function __construct($numbers) {
        $this->numbers = $numbers;
    }

    public function current() {
        return $this->numbers[$this->index];
    }

    public function key() {
        return $this->index;
    }

    public function next() {
        $this->index++;
    }

    public function rewind() {
        $this->index = 0;
    }

    public function valid() {
        return isset($this->numbers[$this->index]);
    }
}

$numbers = new NumberIterator([10, 20, 30, 40]);

foreach ($numbers as $key => $value) {
    echo "$key => $value\n";
}
```

Iterators are particularly useful for database results, file handling, and paginated APIs, where processing data sequentially is more efficient than loading everything at once.

Using Generators in PHP

A **generator** simplifies iteration by using the yield keyword instead of storing all values in memory. This allows PHP to produce values on demand, significantly improving performance.

Example: Creating a Generator for a Large Dataset

49

```
function numberGenerator($limit) {
    for ($i = 1; $i <= $limit; $i++) {
        yield $i;
    }
}

foreach (numberGenerator(5) as $num) {
    echo $num . "\n";
}
```

Unlike arrays, a generator does not hold all elements in memory, making it ideal for handling large datasets efficiently.

Combining Generators with File Handling

Generators are useful for processing large files line by line without loading the entire file into memory.

Example: Reading a Large File Line by Line

```
function readLargeFile($filename) {
    $file = fopen($filename, "r");
    while (!feof($file)) {
        yield fgets($file);
    }
    fclose($file);
}

foreach (readLargeFile("large.txt") as $line) {
    echo $line;
}
```

This approach ensures that only one line is loaded into memory at a time, preventing excessive memory usage when processing large files.

When to Use Iterators vs. Generators

- **Use iterators** when you need advanced control over dataset traversal, such as rewinding, seeking, or counting elements.

- **Use generators** when working with large data streams that should be processed lazily to minimize memory usage.

Iterators and generators enhance PHP's efficiency when handling large datasets by reducing memory consumption and improving performance. By implementing custom iterators or leveraging generators, developers can build scalable applications that process data efficiently, making them essential tools for handling files, databases, and large data collections.

Module 5:
Loops and Iteration Constructs

Loops and iteration constructs are fundamental in PHP for automating repetitive tasks, processing data structures, and managing large datasets efficiently. PHP provides several looping structures, including while, do-while, for, and foreach, each suited to different scenarios. This module explores these constructs, execution flow control mechanisms, and performance considerations for handling large datasets optimally.

Implementing While, Do-While, For, and Foreach Loops

Loops allow PHP to execute a block of code multiple times based on specified conditions. The while loop executes code as long as a condition remains true, making it useful for indefinite iterations. The do-while loop is similar but guarantees at least one execution before checking the condition. The for loop is ideal for iterating a known number of times, using an initialization, condition, and increment. The foreach loop simplifies iterating over arrays and objects by handling index tracking automatically. Understanding when to use each loop type improves code efficiency and readability.

Controlling Execution Flow with Break and Continue

PHP provides break and continue statements to control loop execution dynamically. The break statement immediately terminates a loop, useful when a certain condition is met, preventing unnecessary iterations. The continue statement skips the current iteration and proceeds to the next one, enabling selective execution within a loop. These constructs are particularly useful when processing large datasets, filtering results, or managing nested loops efficiently. Properly applying break and continue enhances performance and ensures that only necessary iterations execute, reducing computational overhead and improving response times in data-intensive applications.

Iterating Over Associative and Multidimensional Arrays

PHP arrays store complex data structures, including key-value pairs (associative arrays) and nested arrays (multidimensional arrays). The foreach loop is the most efficient method for iterating over associative arrays, as it automatically assigns keys and values for each iteration. When handling multidimensional arrays, nested loops become necessary to access elements within nested structures. Using proper iteration techniques prevents unnecessary computations and optimizes data traversal. Understanding how to iterate over complex arrays effectively is crucial for working with configuration files, database results, and structured datasets in PHP applications.

Performance Considerations When Handling Large Data Sets

When dealing with large datasets, choosing the right loop and optimization strategy is critical. Iterating over extensive data collections can lead to memory exhaustion and slow execution. Using iterators and generators instead of traditional loops reduces memory usage, as they process data lazily rather than loading everything at once. Batch processing techniques, such as breaking large data into smaller chunks, prevent excessive resource consumption. Efficiently structured loops, early termination with break, and selective iteration with continue further enhance performance. Profiling and benchmarking code ensures that loops are optimized for minimal resource consumption and maximum speed.

Loops and iteration constructs are essential for automating tasks, processing arrays, and managing large datasets in PHP. Understanding when to use while, do-while, for, and foreach loops, along with execution control mechanisms like break and continue, helps write efficient and scalable code. Optimizing loop structures improves performance, making PHP applications more responsive and resource-efficient.

Implementing While, Do-While, For, and Foreach Loops

Loops in PHP allow developers to execute a block of code multiple times based on conditions or iterations. PHP provides four primary loop structures: while, do-while, for, and foreach, each designed for different scenarios. Understanding when to use each loop helps in writing efficient, maintainable, and optimized code.

The while Loop

The while loop executes as long as a specified condition remains true. It is ideal for cases where the number of iterations is unknown beforehand, such as reading from a database or processing user input dynamically.

```
$counter = 1;
while ($counter <= 5) {
    echo "Iteration: $counter\n";
    $counter++;
}
```

Here, the loop runs as long as $counter is less than or equal to 5. If the condition never becomes false, an infinite loop occurs, so it is important to ensure proper termination.

The do-while Loop

The do-while loop functions similarly to while, but it guarantees at least one execution before checking the condition. This is useful when an operation should execute at least once regardless of the condition.

```
$counter = 1;
do {
    echo "Executed at least once: $counter\n";
    $counter++;
```

52

```
} while ($counter <= 5);
```

This loop is particularly useful for scenarios like user authentication prompts, where at least one attempt must be made before validating conditions.

The for Loop

The for loop is ideal when the number of iterations is known beforehand. It consists of three parts: initialization, condition, and iteration step.

```
for ($i = 1; $i <= 5; $i++) {
    echo "For Loop Iteration: $i\n";
}
```

This loop is commonly used for processing arrays with a fixed number of elements, iterating over form fields, or performing calculations.

The foreach Loop

The foreach loop is designed specifically for iterating over arrays. It automatically assigns the current element to a variable without requiring manual index handling.

```
$fruits = ["Apple", "Banana", "Cherry"];
foreach ($fruits as $fruit) {
    echo "Fruit: $fruit\n";
}
```

For associative arrays, foreach can extract both keys and values:

```
$ages = ["Alice" => 25, "Bob" => 30];
foreach ($ages as $name => $age) {
    echo "$name is $age years old.\n";
}
```

Choosing the Right Loop

- **Use while** when the number of iterations is unknown and depends on a condition.

- **Use do-while** when the block must execute at least once before condition checking.

- **Use for** when iterating a specific number of times.

- **Use foreach** when working with arrays and objects.

PHP loops enable efficient repetition of code blocks, making them essential for handling dynamic data, automating tasks, and optimizing performance. Choosing the right loop structure ensures readable, efficient, and maintainable code.

Controlling Execution Flow with Break and Continue

PHP provides two essential statements for controlling loop execution flow: break and continue. These statements help optimize performance by terminating loops early (break) or skipping iterations (continue). Using them effectively ensures efficient execution, especially when handling large datasets or processing user input dynamically.

Using the break Statement

The break statement is used to exit a loop immediately, regardless of the loop's condition. This is particularly useful when searching for a specific value, processing large data sets, or handling early termination conditions.

```
$numbers = [10, 20, 30, 40, 50];

foreach ($numbers as $num) {
    if ($num == 30) {
        echo "Number found: $num\n";
        break; // Exit loop when 30 is found
    }
    echo "Checking: $num\n";
}
```

Here, the loop stops when it finds 30, preventing unnecessary iterations. This technique is beneficial in database searches or pagination logic where stopping early improves performance.

break is also useful for exiting nested loops when working with multidimensional arrays. By specifying a numeric argument, it can break out of multiple levels at once.

```
for ($i = 1; $i <= 3; $i++) {
    for ($j = 1; $j <= 3; $j++) {
        echo "$i, $j\n";
        if ($i == 2 && $j == 2) {
            break 2; // Exit both loops
        }
    }
}
```

This approach helps prevent excessive looping, particularly in computationally expensive operations.

Using the continue Statement

The continue statement skips the current iteration and moves to the next cycle without terminating the loop entirely. It is useful when filtering unwanted values or optimizing logic within iterations.

```
for ($i = 1; $i <= 5; $i++) {
    if ($i == 3) {
        continue; // Skip iteration when $i is 3
    }
    echo "Iteration: $i\n";
}
```

In this example, the output excludes Iteration: 3 since the loop skips that iteration. This technique is useful when handling invalid inputs, skipping empty data, or implementing selective processing.

Using break and continue Together

Combining break and continue allows for precise control over execution flow. For example, in a search function, continue can skip invalid values while break stops execution upon finding a match.

```php
$values = [5, 10, 15, 0, 20];

foreach ($values as $val) {
    if ($val == 0) {
        continue; // Skip invalid value
    }
    echo "Processing: $val\n";
    if ($val == 15) {
        break; // Stop after finding 15
    }
}
```

The break and continue statements enhance loop efficiency by reducing unnecessary iterations. break ensures early termination when conditions are met, while continue allows selective execution. Proper usage of these statements improves script performance, particularly when processing large data sets or implementing dynamic conditions.

Iterating Over Associative and Multidimensional Arrays

PHP provides robust methods for iterating over different types of arrays. Associative arrays store key-value pairs, while multidimensional arrays contain nested arrays. Understanding how to traverse these structures efficiently ensures optimal data handling, particularly when working with configuration files, database results, or API responses.

Iterating Over Associative Arrays

Associative arrays allow indexing by custom keys instead of numeric indices. The foreach loop is the best way to iterate over them since it automatically assigns keys and values during iteration.

```php
$userAges = ["Alice" => 25, "Bob" => 30, "Charlie" => 35];

foreach ($userAges as $name => $age) {
    echo "$name is $age years old.\n";
}
```

This method is ideal for handling key-value data, such as user details, settings, or form submissions.

Using array_keys() and array_values() for Iteration

Sometimes, iterating over only keys or values is necessary. PHP provides array_keys() to extract all keys and array_values() to retrieve all values.

```php
$prices = ["Apple" => 1.2, "Banana" => 0.8, "Cherry" => 2.5];

foreach (array_keys($prices) as $fruit) {
    echo "Fruit: $fruit\n";
}

foreach (array_values($prices) as $price) {
    echo "Price: $price\n";
}
```

This is useful when dealing with indexed and associative arrays selectively.

Iterating Over Multidimensional Arrays

Multidimensional arrays store nested arrays, requiring nested loops to access their elements.

```php
$students = [
    ["name" => "Alice", "age" => 25, "grade" => "A"],
    ["name" => "Bob", "age" => 30, "grade" => "B"],
    ["name" => "Charlie", "age" => 35, "grade" => "A"]
];

foreach ($students as $student) {
    echo "Name: {$student['name']}, Age: {$student['age']}, Grade:
        {$student['grade']}\n";
}
```

Here, each inner array represents a student's details, and the foreach loop iterates through them efficiently.

Using Recursive Functions for Deeply Nested Arrays

For deeply nested arrays, recursion can be an effective way to iterate over elements.

```php
function printArray($array, $level = 0) {
    foreach ($array as $key => $value) {
        if (is_array($value)) {
            printArray($value, $level + 1);
        } else {
            echo str_repeat(" ", $level * 4) . "$key: $value\n";
        }
    }
}
```

This method is particularly useful for working with JSON data, hierarchical structures, or nested configurations.

Iterating over associative and multidimensional arrays is a core PHP skill for handling structured data. Using foreach, array_keys(), and recursive functions ensures efficient traversal. Mastering these techniques allows developers to work with large datasets, complex configurations, and API responses effectively.

Performance Considerations When Handling Large Data Sets

Handling large data sets efficiently in PHP is crucial for optimizing memory usage and execution time. Poorly managed loops and data structures can lead to performance bottlenecks, high memory consumption, and slow script execution. By implementing techniques like optimized loops, lazy loading, and memory-efficient data handling, developers can improve PHP application performance when working with extensive data.

Using Generators Instead of Large Arrays

PHP arrays consume significant memory, especially when handling large datasets. Instead of loading all data into memory at once, generators provide a memory-efficient alternative by yielding values one at a time.

```php
function generateNumbers($limit) {
    for ($i = 1; $i <= $limit; $i++) {
        yield $i;
    }
}

foreach (generateNumbers(1000000) as $number) {
    // Process each number without storing all in memory
}
```

Generators prevent excessive memory usage by processing data incrementally instead of storing everything at once.

Using array_chunk() for Batch Processing

When dealing with large arrays, processing them in smaller chunks reduces memory usage. The array_chunk() function splits arrays into smaller segments, enabling batch processing.

```php
$largeArray = range(1, 1000000);
$chunks = array_chunk($largeArray, 10000);

foreach ($chunks as $chunk) {
    // Process 10,000 elements at a time
}
```

This technique is particularly useful when working with database queries or large CSV files.

Optimizing Loops with foreach Instead of for

Using foreach is generally more efficient than for loops when iterating over arrays, as it avoids manual index manipulation.

```php
$data = range(1, 1000);

foreach ($data as $value) {
    // Process each value
}
```

Unlike for, foreach does not require calling count() on every iteration, making it faster for large datasets.

Using Indexed Arrays Instead of Associative Arrays

Indexed arrays consume less memory compared to associative arrays since they do not require additional key storage.

```php
// More memory-efficient
$indexedArray = [10, 20, 30];

// Less memory-efficient
$associativeArray = ["a" => 10, "b" => 20, "c" => 30];
```

For large datasets, choosing indexed arrays whenever possible improves performance.

Reading Large Files Line-by-Line Instead of Loading into Memory

Using fgets() instead of file_get_contents() prevents memory exhaustion when reading large files.

```php
$file = fopen("largefile.txt", "r");

while (($line = fgets($file)) !== false) {
    // Process each line without loading the entire file
}

fclose($file);
```

This method ensures scalability when handling gigabyte-sized logs or CSV files.

Efficiently handling large data sets in PHP requires memory optimization, batch processing, and lazy loading techniques. Using generators, array chunking, and optimized loops significantly improve script performance. By implementing these best practices, developers can ensure that PHP applications remain scalable, responsive, and efficient when processing extensive data.

Module 6:
Comments and Documentation Standards

Effective documentation is essential for writing maintainable and readable PHP code. Comments and documentation help developers understand the purpose of different parts of a script, making it easier to debug, modify, and collaborate on projects. This module explores the different types of comments in PHP, introduces PHPDoc for structured documentation, and highlights best practices for improving code clarity and maintainability. Additionally, it covers the use of annotations for automating tasks such as validation, routing, and dependency injection in modern PHP frameworks.

Writing Single-Line and Multi-Line Comments in PHP

Comments allow developers to add explanatory notes to their code without affecting execution. PHP supports single-line comments using // or #, and multi-line comments using /* */. Single-line comments are useful for brief explanations, while multi-line comments help document larger sections of code. Proper use of comments enhances code readability, reduces confusion, and assists future maintenance efforts. However, excessive or redundant commenting should be avoided, as it can clutter the codebase. Instead, comments should clarify the logic behind complex operations, highlight potential issues, and document assumptions that may not be immediately apparent from the code structure.

Utilizing PHPDoc for Code Documentation

PHPDoc is a widely used standard for documenting PHP code. It enables developers to generate structured documentation using special comment blocks that describe classes, functions, and variables. A PHPDoc block typically includes tags such as @param for function parameters, @return for return types, and @author for contributor details. This approach improves code organization and helps developers understand the intended usage of different components. Many IDEs and tools can parse PHPDoc comments, providing auto-generated documentation and code insights. Following PHPDoc standards ensures consistency in large projects and facilitates seamless collaboration among development teams.

Improving Code Readability and Maintainability

Readable and maintainable code is crucial for long-term project sustainability. Well-documented code with clear naming conventions, logical structure, and properly placed comments ensures that new developers can quickly grasp the logic. Instead of writing unnecessary comments, developers should strive to write self-explanatory code with meaningful variable names and structured formatting. Additionally, breaking complex functions into smaller, well-defined methods improves maintainability. Proper indentation, spacing, and consistent coding styles also enhance readability. Adhering to best practices in commenting and documentation prevents technical debt, reduces debugging time, and improves overall software quality.

Leveraging Annotations for Automated Code Generation

Annotations are metadata tags used in many modern PHP frameworks to simplify common programming tasks. They provide additional context for classes and functions, enabling automated features such as routing, validation, and dependency injection. Frameworks like Symfony and Doctrine use annotations extensively to define database entities, API routes, and security rules. Unlike traditional comments, annotations influence application behavior by serving as directives for code execution. Using annotations effectively can streamline development, reduce boilerplate code, and improve maintainability. However, they should be used judiciously to prevent excessive dependency on framework-specific implementations.

Proper documentation and commenting practices are essential for writing professional PHP code. Single-line and multi-line comments improve clarity, while PHPDoc ensures structured documentation. Readable and maintainable code benefits from clear logic, meaningful naming conventions, and proper formatting. Additionally, annotations facilitate automation in modern PHP frameworks. By following these best practices, developers can enhance collaboration, debugging efficiency, and overall code quality.

Writing Single-Line and Multi-Line Comments in PHP

Comments in PHP help developers document code, making it easier to understand and maintain. PHP supports both single-line and multi-line comments, allowing programmers to add explanations and notes without affecting the execution of the script. Using comments effectively enhances code readability and simplifies debugging, particularly in large projects.

Single-Line Comments

Single-line comments in PHP begin with either // or #. These are typically used to describe a single statement or provide a brief explanation.

```
// This is a single-line comment
$price = 100; // Assigning value to $price

# Another way to write a single-line comment
echo "Total: " . $price;
```

Using single-line comments is ideal for short notes about code functionality or marking sections of a script for easy reference. However, excessive commenting should be avoided in favor of self-explanatory code.

Multi-Line Comments

Multi-line comments begin with /* and end with */. They are useful for providing detailed explanations, documenting functions, or temporarily disabling blocks of code during debugging.

```
/*
This function calculates the total price after discount.
It accepts the original price and a discount percentage as parameters.
*/
function calculateDiscount($price, $discount) {
    return $price - ($price * $discount / 100);
}
```

Multi-line comments are beneficial when describing complex algorithms, defining project-specific coding standards, or explaining modifications in collaborative projects.

Best Practices for Writing Comments

- **Comment only when necessary**: Avoid redundant comments that merely restate the code. Instead, explain *why* a particular approach was taken.

- **Use meaningful variable and function names**: Well-named variables reduce the need for excessive comments.

- **Place comments close to the code they describe**: This prevents confusion and ensures clarity.

- **Update comments as the code evolves**: Outdated comments can mislead developers and cause misunderstandings.

```
// Bad practice
$y = 200; // Assigning 200 to variable y

// Good practice
$productPrice = 200; // Initial price of the product before tax
```

Proper use of single-line and multi-line comments improves code clarity and maintainability. Single-line comments (//, #) are suitable for short notes, while multi-line comments (/* */) provide detailed explanations. By following best practices, developers can write well-documented PHP code that is easy to understand and maintain over time.

Utilizing PHPDoc for Code Documentation

PHPDoc is a standardized documentation format used to describe PHP code in a structured way. It provides essential metadata about classes, functions, variables, and return types. By following PHPDoc conventions, developers can generate automated documentation, improve code maintainability, and enhance collaboration in team projects. Many modern IDEs support PHPDoc, offering autocomplete suggestions and inline documentation for better development efficiency.

Basic PHPDoc Syntax

PHPDoc comments start with /** and end with */. Inside, tags like @param, @return, and @var describe function parameters, return types, and variables, respectively.

```php
/**
 * Adds two numbers and returns the sum.
 *
 * @param int $a The first number
 * @param int $b The second number
 * @return int The sum of $a and $b
 */
function addNumbers(int $a, int $b): int {
    return $a + $b;
}
```

This format helps both human readers and documentation tools understand the function's purpose, expected inputs, and output type.

Common PHPDoc Tags

- @param – Describes function parameters.

- @return – Specifies the function's return type.

- @var – Documents class properties and variables.

- @throws – Indicates exceptions that a function may throw.

- @deprecated – Marks outdated functions or methods.

- @author – Specifies the author of the code.

Example usage in a class:

```php
class Product {
    /**
     * @var string The product name
     */
    private string $name;

    /**
     * @var float The product price
     */
    private float $price;

    /**
     * Sets the product details.
     *
     * @param string $name
     * @param float $price
     */
    public function __construct(string $name, float $price) {
        $this->name = $name;
        $this->price = $price;
    }
}
```

Generating Documentation from PHPDoc

PHPDoc comments are not just for readability—they can be used to generate documentation using tools like **phpDocumentor**. Running phpDocumentor on a well-commented codebase produces structured documentation that can be shared with a development team.

```
phpDocumentor -d /path/to/project -t /path/to/output
```

PHPDoc is an essential tool for maintaining well-documented PHP projects. It improves readability, aids in automated documentation generation, and enhances developer productivity. By incorporating PHPDoc in functions, classes, and properties, PHP developers can ensure that their code remains clear, scalable, and easy to manage.

Improving Code Readability and Maintainability

Readable and maintainable code is essential for long-term software development. Code that is easy to understand reduces debugging time, improves collaboration, and enhances overall efficiency. PHP developers should follow best practices such as consistent formatting, meaningful variable names, structured commenting, and modular programming to ensure clarity and maintainability.

Using Meaningful Naming Conventions

Clear and descriptive names for variables, functions, and classes make code self-explanatory. Instead of using generic names like $x or $data, meaningful names should describe the purpose of the variable or function.

```php
// Poor naming
$n = 100;
function calc($a, $b) { return $a * $b; }

// Improved naming
$productPrice = 100;
function calculateTotalPrice(float $price, float $taxRate): float {
    return $price + ($price * $taxRate / 100);
}
```

Well-named variables and functions reduce the need for excessive commenting and make code intuitive.

Structuring Code with Proper Indentation and Spacing

Consistent indentation and spacing improve readability. PHP follows a flexible syntax, but following PSR-12 (PHP Standards Recommendation) ensures consistency.

```php
// Poor formatting
if($userRole=='admin'){echo "Access granted";}else{echo "Access denied";}

// Improved formatting
if ($userRole == 'admin') {
    echo "Access granted";
```

63

```
    } else {
        echo "Access denied";
    }
```

Adopting a consistent coding style across a project helps developers quickly understand and modify the codebase.

Writing Modular and Reusable Code

Breaking code into smaller, reusable functions or classes enhances maintainability. Large blocks of code should be avoided in favor of modular programming.

```
// Without modularization
$discountedPrice = $price - ($price * 0.1);

// Using a function
function applyDiscount(float $price, float $discountRate): float {
    return $price - ($price * $discountRate / 100);
}
```

This approach simplifies debugging, testing, and extending functionality.

Keeping Comments Relevant and Up-to-Date

Comments should clarify complex logic, but redundant or outdated comments should be removed.

```
// Outdated comment
// This function applies a fixed 10% discount
function applyDiscount(float $price, float $discountRate): float {
    return $price - ($price * $discountRate / 100);
}
```

Comments should align with actual code behavior to avoid confusion.

Readable and maintainable PHP code follows best practices such as meaningful naming conventions, proper formatting, modular design, and relevant comments. By prioritizing clarity and structure, developers can create codebases that are easier to understand, modify, and scale over time.

Leveraging Annotations for Automated Code Generation

Annotations in PHP provide metadata that can be used for automation, configuration, and enhanced code organization. While PHP does not have built-in annotation support like Java, it leverages **docblocks**, attributes, and third-party libraries like Doctrine Annotations to define structured metadata. Annotations improve code maintainability by enabling automated dependency injection, validation, and routing in frameworks.

Understanding Annotations in PHP

Annotations are special comments within PHPDoc blocks that provide metadata for classes, methods, and properties. They are commonly used in frameworks like Laravel and Symfony for configuration purposes.

```php
/**
 * @Route("/users", methods={"GET"})
 */
function getUsers() {
    return ["John", "Jane"];
}
```

Here, the @Route annotation is used by a framework to define an HTTP route without manually configuring it.

Using Attributes as Native PHP Annotations

Starting from PHP 8, **attributes** provide a native way to implement annotations. Unlike traditional PHPDoc annotations, attributes are processed at runtime, making them more powerful.

```php
use Attribute;

#[Attribute]
class Route {
    public function __construct(public string $path, public string $method) {}
}

class UserController {
    #[Route("/users", "GET")]
    public function getUsers() {
        return ["Alice", "Bob"];
    }
}
```

Attributes allow PHP to move away from comment-based annotations, improving performance and reliability.

Leveraging Annotations for ORM and Validation

Annotations are widely used in **Object-Relational Mappers (ORMs)** like Doctrine to map PHP objects to database tables.

```php
use Doctrine\ORM\Mapping as ORM;

/**
 * @ORM\Entity
 * @ORM\Table(name="users")
 */
class User {
    /** @ORM\Id @ORM\Column(type="integer") @ORM\GeneratedValue */
    private int $id;

    /** @ORM\Column(type="string", length=100) */
    private string $name;
}
```

This eliminates the need for separate configuration files, making database interaction more intuitive.

Automating Code Behavior with Annotations

Annotations can automate processes such as:

- **Routing** (e.g., defining API endpoints)

- **Validation** (e.g., enforcing data constraints)

- **Dependency Injection** (e.g., auto-wiring services in frameworks)

For instance, Symfony uses annotations for **form validation**:

```
use Symfony\Component\Validator\Constraints as Assert;

class Product {
    /**
     * @Assert\NotBlank
     * @Assert\Length(min=3, max=50)
     */
    private string $name;
}
```

This ensures name cannot be empty and must be between 3-50 characters.

Annotations streamline PHP development by automating routing, validation, ORM mapping, and dependency injection. While PHP 8 attributes provide a native approach, traditional PHPDoc-based annotations remain widely used in frameworks. Leveraging annotations enhances code clarity, reduces configuration overhead, and promotes maintainability in modern PHP applications.

Module 7:
Enumerations (Enums in PHP 8.1+)

Enumerations (Enums) were introduced in PHP 8.1 as a way to define a fixed set of possible values for a given type. They enhance code clarity, prevent invalid values, and improve maintainability. This module explores the role of Enums in PHP, how to define and use them, their application in clean code design, and a practical case study demonstrating Enums for managing application states. By the end of this module, readers will understand how Enums can replace traditional constants and string-based values to create more structured and reliable applications.

Introduction to Enums and Their Role in PHP Development

Enums provide a structured way to handle predefined values, reducing the risk of invalid inputs in PHP applications. Before PHP 8.1, developers relied on constants or string values to define fixed sets of options, which often led to inconsistencies and errors. Enums solve this problem by enforcing type safety, making it impossible to assign an invalid value. They are especially useful in scenarios like defining user roles, order statuses, or HTTP response codes. This section introduces the concept of Enums, their syntax, and how they contribute to better code structure, validation, and readability in PHP projects.

Defining and Using Pure and Backed Enums

PHP supports two types of Enums: **pure Enums** and **backed Enums**. Pure Enums consist of a set of named values without associated data, while backed Enums allow each value to be mapped to a scalar type (integer or string). This section explains how to define both types of Enums and their practical use cases. Readers will learn when to use pure Enums for strict value constraints and backed Enums for seamless integration with databases, APIs, and other data-driven applications. By structuring code with Enums, developers can replace error-prone string-based values with a more robust and type-safe alternative.

Implementing Enum-Based Logic for Clean Code Design

Enums not only define values but also support methods, properties, and logic, making them powerful tools for writing cleaner, more maintainable code. This section demonstrates how to integrate Enums into application logic, reducing the reliance on long switch-case statements or conditionals. By encapsulating logic within Enums, developers can centralize behaviors and ensure consistency throughout the codebase. Examples include handling user permissions, configuring feature flags, and managing workflow states. Readers will see how Enum-based logic simplifies debugging, improves maintainability, and enhances overall application design by promoting a more structured approach.

Case Study: Using Enums for Managing Application States

To showcase the practical benefits of Enums, this section presents a case study on managing application states using Enums. Real-world applications often involve multiple states, such as pending, active, suspended, or completed. Using Enums for state management eliminates invalid state transitions, ensures consistency across the application, and enhances readability. The case study walks through defining Enums for application states, integrating them with database storage, and utilizing them in business logic. By the end of this section, readers will have a solid understanding of how to leverage Enums to build more robust and scalable PHP applications.

Enums in PHP 8.1+ provide a structured, type-safe alternative to traditional constants and string-based values. They enhance code clarity, prevent errors, and improve maintainability by enforcing strict value constraints. This module has covered the fundamentals of Enums, their practical use in clean code design, and a case study demonstrating their effectiveness in real-world applications.

Introduction to Enums and Their Role in PHP Development

Enums, introduced in PHP 8.1, offer a structured way to define a fixed set of related values. Before Enums, PHP developers typically relied on constants or string-based values to represent predefined options, which often led to inconsistencies and type-related issues. Enums solve these problems by ensuring type safety and restricting values to a defined set, improving both code reliability and readability.

Why Use Enums in PHP?

Enums provide several advantages over traditional constants and string values:

- **Type Safety**: Ensures only valid values are assigned to variables.

- **Readability**: Improves code clarity by grouping related values under a common type.

- **Maintainability**: Makes it easier to update allowed values without modifying multiple files.

- **Error Reduction**: Prevents the use of incorrect or unintended values in the codebase.

Defining a Basic Enum in PHP

In PHP, Enums are defined using the enum keyword, followed by a set of possible values.

```php
enum UserRole {
    case Admin;
    case Editor;
    case Subscriber;
}
```

Here, UserRole defines three valid roles: Admin, Editor, and Subscriber. Unlike string-based representations, an invalid role cannot be mistakenly assigned, ensuring greater consistency in the application.

Using Enums in Code

Once defined, Enums can be used as type hints in function arguments and return types:

```
function getUserPermissions(UserRole $role): string {
    return match ($role) {
        UserRole::Admin => "Full Access",
        UserRole::Editor => "Edit Access",
        UserRole::Subscriber => "Read Access",
    };
}
```

This function ensures only valid UserRole values are accepted, reducing potential bugs and improving maintainability.

Comparison with Constants and Strings

Traditionally, PHP developers used class constants or string values to represent predefined options:

```
class UserRole {
    const ADMIN = "admin";
    const EDITOR = "editor";
    const SUBSCRIBER = "subscriber";
}
```

However, this approach lacks type safety, as any string value—including invalid ones—can be assigned to a variable. Enums enforce stricter value constraints, making them a better alternative.

Enums in PHP 8.1+ improve code structure, enforce strict value constraints, and enhance readability. They replace error-prone string-based values and constants, making PHP applications more maintainable and robust. By understanding Enums and their role in PHP development, developers can write cleaner, more reliable code that reduces bugs and simplifies logic management.

Defining and Using Pure and Backed Enums

PHP supports two types of Enums: **pure Enums** and **backed Enums**. Pure Enums consist of a fixed set of named cases without associated values, while backed Enums associate each case with a string or integer value. Understanding when to use each type allows developers to write more robust and maintainable code.

Pure Enums

A **pure Enum** is a simple enumeration that defines a list of possible values. These Enums enforce strict type safety and prevent unexpected values from being assigned.

Defining a Pure Enum

```
enum OrderStatus {
    case Pending;
    case Processing;
    case Shipped;
    case Delivered;
}
```

This OrderStatus Enum defines four possible order states: Pending, Processing, Shipped, and Delivered. These values cannot be altered or assigned arbitrary values, ensuring consistency in the application.

Using a Pure Enum in Code

A pure Enum can be used for type checking, ensuring that only valid values are passed to a function:

```
function updateOrderStatus(OrderStatus $status): void {
    echo "The order status is now: " . $status->name;
}
```

Calling this function with OrderStatus::Shipped guarantees type safety while improving readability.

Backed Enums

A **backed Enum** is an Enum where each case has an associated scalar value, either a string or an integer. This is useful when working with databases, APIs, or when serialization is required.

Defining a Backed Enum (String Values)

```
enum UserRole: string {
    case Admin = 'admin';
    case Editor = 'editor';
    case Subscriber = 'subscriber';
}
```

Each case has a specific string value, making it easy to store and retrieve from a database.

Defining a Backed Enum (Integer Values)

```
enum HttpStatus: int {
    case OK = 200;
    case NotFound = 404;
    case InternalServerError = 500;
}
```

This Enum maps common HTTP status codes to their respective integer values.

Using Backed Enums

Backed Enums allow retrieval of their scalar values:

```php
echo UserRole::Admin->value; // Outputs: admin
```

They can also be used for lookups:

```php
function getHttpMessage(HttpStatus $status): string {
    return match ($status) {
        HttpStatus::OK => "Success",
        HttpStatus::NotFound => "Not Found",
        HttpStatus::InternalServerError => "Server Error",
    };
}
```

Choosing Between Pure and Backed Enums

- **Use pure Enums** when you only need a fixed set of values without associated data.

- **Use backed Enums** when you need to store, retrieve, or compare Enum values with external data sources like databases or APIs.

Enums in PHP provide a structured way to manage fixed values while enforcing type safety. Pure Enums are useful for strict categorization, while backed Enums help when working with databases or external systems. Understanding both types ensures more robust and maintainable PHP applications.

Implementing Enum-Based Logic for Clean Code Design

Enums in PHP are not just about defining a fixed set of values—they also help enforce structured, maintainable, and error-free logic. By integrating Enums into application workflows, developers can write cleaner, more predictable code. This section explores how to implement Enum-based logic effectively.

Using Enums in Conditional Statements

Enums can replace error-prone string-based comparisons in conditional logic. Instead of checking raw strings, Enum cases make conditions clearer and safer:

```php
enum PaymentStatus {
    case Pending;
    case Completed;
    case Failed;
}

function handlePayment(PaymentStatus $status): string {
    return match ($status) {
        PaymentStatus::Pending => "Payment is pending.",
        PaymentStatus::Completed => "Payment successful!",
        PaymentStatus::Failed => "Payment failed, try again.",
    };
}
```

This ensures only valid statuses are passed, reducing potential runtime errors.

Leveraging Methods in Enums

PHP Enums support methods, allowing logic to be encapsulated within the Enum itself. This improves modularity by keeping related logic close to the Enum definition.

```php
enum UserRole {
    case Admin;
    case Editor;
    case Subscriber;

    public function getPermissions(): array {
        return match ($this) {
            self::Admin => ['read', 'write', 'delete'],
            self::Editor => ['read', 'write'],
            self::Subscriber => ['read'],
        };
    }
}
```

Now, permissions can be retrieved directly from the Enum:

```php
$userRole = UserRole::Editor;
$permissions = $userRole->getPermissions();
```

This approach eliminates the need for separate permission-checking functions.

Using Backed Enums for Database Operations

Backed Enums are particularly useful when working with databases, as they allow for easy storage and retrieval of values.

Saving Enum Values in a Database

```php
enum OrderStatus: string {
    case Pending = 'pending';
    case Shipped = 'shipped';
    case Delivered = 'delivered';
}

// Storing in a database
$orderStatus = OrderStatus::Shipped;
$query = "INSERT INTO orders (status) VALUES ('{$orderStatus->value}')";
```

Retrieving and Converting Enum Values

When retrieving an Enum from a database, it can be converted back into an Enum instance:

```php
$statusFromDB = 'delivered';
$orderStatus = OrderStatus::tryFrom($statusFromDB); // Returns
          OrderStatus::Delivered
```

This prevents invalid values from being assigned and ensures strict type enforcement.

Enums as Keys in Associative Arrays

Since Enums are objects, they can serve as associative array keys for structured data storage:

```
$taxRates = [
    UserRole::Admin => 0.15,
    UserRole::Editor => 0.10,
    UserRole::Subscriber => 0.05,
];

echo $taxRates[UserRole::Editor]; // Outputs: 0.10
```

This enhances code readability and maintainability.

Enum-based logic simplifies code structure, enhances maintainability, and prevents invalid value assignments. By using Enums in conditional statements, encapsulating logic within Enum methods, and integrating them with databases, PHP developers can build cleaner and more robust applications.

Case Study: Using Enums for Managing Application States

Enums in PHP provide a structured approach to managing application states. By defining predefined values, Enums enhance code reliability, maintainability, and readability. This case study explores how Enums can be used effectively to handle various application states, improving consistency in workflows like order processing, user authentication, and API responses.

Scenario: Managing Order States in an E-commerce Application

In an e-commerce system, an order can transition through several states: Pending, Processing, Shipped, and Delivered. Using Enums ensures that only valid states are used, preventing inconsistent or incorrect values from being assigned.

Defining the OrderStatus Enum

```
enum OrderStatus: string {
    case Pending = 'pending';
    case Processing = 'processing';
    case Shipped = 'shipped';
    case Delivered = 'delivered';

    public function next(): ?self {
        return match ($this) {
            self::Pending => self::Processing,
            self::Processing => self::Shipped,
            self::Shipped => self::Delivered,
            self::Delivered => null, // No next state
        };
    }
}
```

This Enum not only defines order states but also includes a next() method that determines the next valid state.

Using the Enum in Order Processing

```php
function processOrder(OrderStatus $status): void {
    echo "Current order status: " . $status->value . PHP_EOL;

    $nextStatus = $status->next();
    if ($nextStatus) {
        echo "Updating status to: " . $nextStatus->value . PHP_EOL;
    } else {
        echo "Order has been delivered. No further updates." . PHP_EOL;
    }
}

processOrder(OrderStatus::Pending);
```

This ensures that orders transition only through predefined states, preventing incorrect status assignments.

Using Enums for User Roles in Authentication

In a role-based authentication system, Enums can represent user roles such as Admin, Editor, and Subscriber.

Defining the UserRole Enum

```php
enum UserRole {
    case Admin;
    case Editor;
    case Subscriber;

    public function hasAccess(string $permission): bool {
        return match ($this) {
            self::Admin => true, // Full access
            self::Editor => in_array($permission, ['edit', 'view']),
            self::Subscriber => $permission === 'view',
        };
    }
}
```

This ensures that user roles dictate access permissions logically.

Checking User Permissions

```php
$userRole = UserRole::Editor;
if ($userRole->hasAccess('delete')) {
    echo "Access granted.";
} else {
    echo "Access denied.";
}
```

By using Enums, permission handling becomes more structured and avoids hardcoded string comparisons.

Handling API Response States with Enums

Enums can also standardize API response statuses, improving consistency across applications.

```php
enum ApiResponseStatus: int {
    case Success = 200;
    case BadRequest = 400;
    case Unauthorized = 401;
    case NotFound = 404;
}
```

When handling API responses:

```php
function sendResponse(ApiResponseStatus $status, string $message): void {
    http_response_code($status->value);
    echo json_encode(["status" => $status->name, "message" => $message]);
}

sendResponse(ApiResponseStatus::Success, "Request successful.");
```

This approach ensures that API responses always adhere to predefined status codes.

Enums provide a structured way to manage application states, ensuring consistency in workflows. By applying Enums to order processing, authentication, and API responses, PHP developers can enforce strict rules, reduce bugs, and create maintainable codebases.

Module 8:
Object-Oriented Programming (OOP) Basics

Object-Oriented Programming (OOP) is a fundamental paradigm in PHP that enhances code organization, reusability, and maintainability. This module explores the essential concepts of OOP, including classes, objects, inheritance, polymorphism, traits, and interfaces. By understanding these principles, developers can build scalable, efficient, and modular PHP applications while adhering to best coding practices.

Understanding Classes and Objects in PHP

Classes and objects form the backbone of OOP in PHP. A class acts as a blueprint for creating objects, which represent real-world entities. Each object instantiated from a class has its own attributes (properties) and behaviors (methods). Using classes and objects allows developers to encapsulate functionality within reusable components. For example, a User class can define properties such as name and email, and methods like register() or login(). The ability to instantiate multiple objects from a class promotes modularity and avoids repetitive code. Understanding how to declare and use classes and objects is the first step toward mastering PHP's OOP capabilities.

Implementing Constructors, Destructors, and Class Methods

Constructors and destructors play a crucial role in object lifecycle management. A constructor is a special method that initializes an object's properties when it is created. This ensures that essential values are set immediately upon object instantiation. Conversely, a destructor is executed when an object is no longer needed, making it useful for resource cleanup, such as closing database connections. In addition to these lifecycle methods, class methods define the behavior of an object. Methods can be public, private, or protected, depending on their intended accessibility. By leveraging constructors, destructors, and methods, developers can structure their classes efficiently.

Applying Inheritance, Polymorphism, and Abstract Classes

Inheritance allows one class to derive properties and methods from another, promoting code reusability. A subclass inherits from a parent class, enabling it to extend or override functionalities. Polymorphism further enhances code flexibility by allowing different classes to define their own implementations of the same method. This concept enables a more dynamic approach to handling objects. Abstract classes serve as blueprints for other classes and cannot be instantiated on their own. Instead, they define required methods that must be implemented by subclasses. By applying these principles, PHP developers can create robust, hierarchical structures that simplify application development.

Using Traits and Interfaces to Extend Functionality

Traits and interfaces provide additional ways to extend class functionality in PHP. While PHP does not support multiple inheritance, traits allow classes to include methods from multiple sources. Traits are particularly useful for code reuse across unrelated classes. Interfaces, on the other hand, define method signatures that implementing classes must adhere to. This ensures a consistent contract across multiple classes, making them useful in designing scalable applications. By combining traits and interfaces, developers can create flexible, maintainable code structures that adhere to industry standards. These tools are essential for enhancing PHP's OOP capabilities.

OOP in PHP provides a structured approach to application development by encapsulating data, promoting code reuse, and enforcing modularity. By mastering classes, objects, inheritance, polymorphism, traits, and interfaces, developers can write cleaner, more scalable applications. This module lays the groundwork for building robust PHP systems using fundamental OOP principles.

Understanding Classes and Objects in PHP

Object-Oriented Programming (OOP) in PHP revolves around **classes** and **objects**, which structure code into reusable, modular components. A **class** is a blueprint that defines properties (variables) and methods (functions), while an **object** is an instance of a class. By leveraging OOP principles, PHP developers can build scalable applications with better organization and maintainability.

Defining and Instantiating Classes

A PHP class is defined using the class keyword, followed by a class name and a pair of curly braces {} that encapsulate its properties and methods.

```php
class Car {
    public $brand;
    public $color;

    public function setBrand($brand) {
        $this->brand = $brand;
    }

    public function getBrand() {
        return $this->brand;
    }
}
```

In this example, Car is a class with two **properties** ($brand and $color) and two **methods** (setBrand() and getBrand()).

To create an **object** from this class, use the new keyword:

```
$myCar = new Car();
$myCar->setBrand("Toyota");

echo $myCar->getBrand(); // Output: Toyota
```

Here, $myCar is an **instance** of the Car class, and the methods modify and retrieve object data.

Understanding Class Properties and Methods

Properties store object data and are defined using access modifiers:

- **public** – Accessible from anywhere in the program

- **private** – Accessible only within the class

- **protected** – Accessible within the class and its subclasses

```
class Person {
    private $name;

    public function setName($name) {
        $this->name = $name;
    }

    public function getName() {
        return $this->name;
    }
}
```

Here, $name is private, meaning it can't be accessed directly outside the class:

```
$person = new Person();
// $person->name = "John"; // This would cause an error
$person->setName("John");
echo $person->getName(); // Output: John
```

Methods are class functions that operate on properties and define object behavior. They use $this to reference the current object instance.

Creating Multiple Instances

Each object instantiated from a class has its own copy of the properties, making OOP ideal for managing multiple entities with different attributes.

```
$car1 = new Car();
$car1->setBrand("Honda");

$car2 = new Car();
$car2->setBrand("Ford");

echo $car1->getBrand(); // Output: Honda
echo $car2->getBrand(); // Output: Ford
```

Each object ($car1 and $car2) holds independent values while sharing the same class structure.

Classes and objects are fundamental to PHP's OOP paradigm, providing a structured way to organize and manipulate data. By defining properties and methods within classes, developers can create reusable, maintainable, and scalable applications. The ability to instantiate multiple objects ensures flexibility and efficiency in software development.

Implementing Constructors, Destructors, and Class Methods

In Object-Oriented Programming (OOP), constructors and destructors play a crucial role in managing object lifecycle, while class methods define the behavior of objects. Constructors initialize objects with predefined values, destructors handle cleanup, and methods encapsulate functionality. These features make PHP applications more structured, efficient, and easier to maintain.

Using Constructors for Automatic Initialization

A **constructor** is a special method executed when an object is created. It initializes object properties and ensures essential values are set immediately. In PHP, constructors are defined using the __construct() method.

```php
class User {
    public $name;
    public $email;

    public function __construct($name, $email) {
        $this->name = $name;
        $this->email = $email;
    }

    public function getUserInfo() {
        return "Name: {$this->name}, Email: {$this->email}";
    }
}

$user1 = new User("John Doe", "john@example.com");
echo $user1->getUserInfo();
// Output: Name: John Doe, Email: john@example.com
```

When $user1 is instantiated, the constructor automatically assigns values to $name and $email. This eliminates the need to call a separate method for initialization.

Using Destructors for Cleanup

A **destructor** is called when an object is destroyed or goes out of scope. It is useful for cleanup tasks like closing database connections or freeing resources. PHP defines destructors using the __destruct() method.

```php
class Connection {
    public function __construct() {
        echo "Connection established.\n";
    }
}
```

```
        public function __destruct() {
            echo "Connection closed.\n";
        }
    }

    $conn = new Connection();
    unset($conn);
    // Output: Connection established.
    //         Connection closed.
```

In this example, the destructor runs when the object is explicitly unset, ensuring proper cleanup. If not manually unset, PHP will invoke the destructor when the script ends.

Defining Class Methods for Object Behavior

Class methods define what an object can do. They are functions inside a class and use the $this keyword to access properties. Methods can be **public**, **private**, or **protected**, controlling their accessibility.

```
    class Calculator {
        private $result = 0;

        public function add($num) {
            $this->result += $num;
        }

        public function getResult() {
            return $this->result;
        }
    }

    $calc = new Calculator();
    $calc->add(10);
    $calc->add(5);
    echo $calc->getResult(); // Output: 15
```

Here, the add() method modifies the internal $result property, while getResult() returns the final value.

Constructors automate initialization, destructors handle cleanup, and class methods define object behavior. By leveraging these features, developers can create structured, reusable, and maintainable PHP applications. Understanding these concepts is essential for building robust OOP-based solutions.

Applying Inheritance, Polymorphism, and Abstract Classes

Object-Oriented Programming (OOP) in PHP provides powerful mechanisms for code reuse and flexibility. **Inheritance** allows one class to derive properties and behaviors from another. **Polymorphism** enables objects to be treated interchangeably based on shared interfaces. **Abstract classes** define a blueprint for subclasses while enforcing specific methods. These principles enhance maintainability and scalability.

Implementing Inheritance in PHP

Inheritance enables a class to inherit properties and methods from another class using the extends keyword. The parent class provides common functionality, while the child class can extend or override it.

```php
class Animal {
    public $name;

    public function __construct($name) {
        $this->name = $name;
    }

    public function makeSound() {
        return "Some generic sound";
    }
}

class Dog extends Animal {
    public function makeSound() {
        return "Bark";
    }
}

$dog = new Dog("Buddy");
echo $dog->name;          // Output: Buddy
echo $dog->makeSound();   // Output: Bark
```

The Dog class inherits the name property and makeSound() method but overrides it to provide specific behavior.

Understanding Polymorphism

Polymorphism allows different classes to be used interchangeably if they share the same method signatures. This is achieved through **method overriding** and **interfaces**.

```php
class Cat extends Animal {
    public function makeSound() {
        return "Meow";
    }
}

$animals = [new Dog("Rex"), new Cat("Whiskers")];

foreach ($animals as $animal) {
    echo $animal->name . " says " . $animal->makeSound() . "\n";
}

// Output:
// Rex says Bark
// Whiskers says Meow
```

Since both Dog and Cat inherit from Animal, they can be treated as Animal objects, demonstrating polymorphism.

Using Abstract Classes

An **abstract class** defines methods that must be implemented by any subclass. It cannot be instantiated directly and ensures a structured approach to class design.

```php
abstract class Shape {
    abstract public function getArea();
}

class Rectangle extends Shape {
    private $width, $height;

    public function __construct($width, $height) {
        $this->width = $width;
        $this->height = $height;
    }

    public function getArea() {
        return $this->width * $this->height;
    }
}

$rect = new Rectangle(5, 10);
echo $rect->getArea(); // Output: 50
```

Here, Shape enforces the getArea() method, ensuring that all subclasses implement it.

Inheritance enables code reuse, polymorphism allows flexibility, and abstract classes enforce structured design. These concepts form the backbone of PHP OOP, making applications modular, scalable, and maintainable. Understanding and applying these principles is key to writing efficient and reusable code.

Using Traits and Interfaces to Extend Functionality

PHP provides **traits** and **interfaces** to enhance flexibility and modularity in Object-Oriented Programming. **Traits** allow code reuse across unrelated classes, overcoming single inheritance limitations. **Interfaces** define method contracts that multiple classes can implement, ensuring consistency without enforcing inheritance. These features promote clean, maintainable, and scalable code structures in PHP applications.

Using Traits for Code Reusability

PHP does not support multiple inheritance, meaning a class can only inherit from one parent. **Traits** solve this by allowing code to be shared across multiple classes without direct inheritance. Traits are defined using the trait keyword and included in classes using use.

```php
trait Logger {
    public function log($message) {
        echo "[LOG]: $message\n";
    }
}

class User {
    use Logger;

    public function createUser($name) {
        $this->log("User '$name' created.");
    }
}

$user = new User();
```

82

```php
$user->createUser("Alice");
// Output: [LOG]: User 'Alice' created.
```

Here, Logger provides a reusable log() method. Any class using Logger gains access to this functionality without inheritance.

Handling Conflicts in Traits

When multiple traits define the same method, **method precedence** can be controlled using insteadof and as.

```php
trait A {
    public function hello() {
        echo "Hello from A";
    }
}

trait B {
    public function hello() {
        echo "Hello from B";
    }
}

class MyClass {
    use A, B {
        B::hello insteadof A;
        A::hello as helloA;
    }
}

$obj = new MyClass();
$obj->hello();   // Output: Hello from B
$obj->helloA(); // Output: Hello from A
```

This ensures controlled method resolution when using multiple traits.

Implementing Interfaces for Consistency

An **interface** defines a contract that a class must implement. Unlike abstract classes, interfaces cannot have properties or method implementations.

```php
interface PaymentGateway {
    public function processPayment($amount);
}

class PayPal implements PaymentGateway {
    public function processPayment($amount) {
        echo "Processing $$amount via PayPal.";
    }
}

class Stripe implements PaymentGateway {
    public function processPayment($amount) {
        echo "Processing $$amount via Stripe.";
    }
}

$payment = new Stripe();
$payment->processPayment(100);
// Output: Processing $100 via Stripe.
```

Both PayPal and Stripe implement PaymentGateway, ensuring consistency while allowing different implementations.

Combining Traits and Interfaces

Traits and interfaces can be used together for maximum flexibility.

```php
interface LoggerInterface {
    public function log($message);
}

trait LoggerTrait {
    public function log($message) {
        echo "[LOG]: $message\n";
    }
}

class App implements LoggerInterface {
    use LoggerTrait;
}

$app = new App();
$app->log("Application started.");
// Output: [LOG]: Application started.
```

This approach ensures method standardization while enabling code reuse.

Traits allow code reuse across classes, while interfaces enforce method consistency. Using both effectively leads to modular, maintainable PHP applications. These features overcome inheritance limitations and improve code organization, making them essential tools for PHP developers.

Module 9:
Accessors, Modifiers, and Namespaces

PHP provides essential mechanisms to control data access, encapsulation, and organization within codebases. This module covers visibility modifiers, which define access levels for class properties and methods, the role of getters and setters in controlled data access, the importance of namespaces in preventing naming conflicts, and PSR-4 autoloading for maintaining scalable, well-structured applications.

Implementing Visibility Modifiers: Public, Private, and Protected

Visibility modifiers in PHP determine how properties and methods can be accessed within and outside a class. **Public** members are accessible from anywhere, including outside the class. **Private** members are only accessible within the class itself, ensuring data encapsulation. **Protected** members allow access within the class and its child classes, promoting inheritance-based control. Using visibility modifiers ensures that sensitive data remains secure while providing necessary access control. These modifiers enforce best practices in object-oriented programming by restricting direct manipulation of properties and requiring controlled interactions through defined methods. Proper use of visibility enhances security, maintainability, and code clarity.

Using Getters and Setters to Manage Data Access

Getters and setters act as intermediaries for accessing and modifying class properties, providing controlled interaction with object data. Direct property access can lead to unintended modifications, but encapsulating properties using getters (for retrieval) and setters (for modification) ensures validation and security. Setters can enforce rules like input sanitization or validation before assigning values, preventing inconsistencies and security risks. Getters allow read-only access to certain properties, maintaining data integrity. This approach is particularly useful in large applications where strict data handling is required. Implementing getters and setters improves code maintainability, making it easier to introduce changes without breaking functionality.

Understanding Namespaces to Avoid Class Name Conflicts

Namespaces in PHP help organize code and prevent naming conflicts, especially in large applications or when integrating third-party libraries. Without namespaces, multiple classes with the same name can cause collisions, leading to runtime errors. By defining a namespace, developers can group related classes logically and reference them explicitly when needed. Namespaces allow developers to structure code better by avoiding ambiguous class names, enabling modular development. They are particularly important in modern PHP applications that use frameworks, libraries, or APIs. Understanding namespaces ensures clean code organization, making it easier to scale applications while avoiding conflicts between different components.

Autoloading and Following PSR-4 Standards for Clean Code

Autoloading simplifies the inclusion of class files, reducing the need for manual require or include statements. The **PSR-4 standard**, defined by the PHP-FIG (Framework Interoperability Group), provides a structured way to autoload classes based on their namespaces and directory structure. PSR-4 encourages a standardized approach where each class is mapped to a file path, improving maintainability and reducing dependency issues. By adhering to PSR-4, developers can seamlessly integrate third-party libraries and frameworks, ensuring compatibility. Autoloading improves application performance by loading only the required classes when needed, making PHP applications more efficient and scalable.

This module emphasizes essential PHP features for structured and maintainable code. Visibility modifiers ensure controlled data access, getters and setters provide validation mechanisms, namespaces prevent naming conflicts, and autoloading with PSR-4 enhances project organization. Mastering these concepts enables developers to write secure, modular, and efficient PHP applications that follow modern coding standards.

Implementing Visibility Modifiers: Public, Private, and Protected

Visibility modifiers in PHP determine how class properties and methods are accessed, ensuring proper encapsulation and security. PHP provides three visibility levels: **public**, **private**, and **protected**, each serving a specific purpose in object-oriented programming.

Public Modifier

A **public** property or method is accessible from anywhere, both inside and outside the class. This provides flexibility but can expose class internals, leading to unintended modifications.

```php
class User {
    public $name = "John";

    public function getName() {
        return $this->name;
    }
}

$user = new User();
echo $user->getName(); // Output: John
```

Private Modifier

A **private** property or method is only accessible within the class itself. This ensures strict data protection, preventing external modifications.

```php
class User {
    private $password = "secret";
```

```php
    private function getPassword() {
        return $this->password;
    }
}

$user = new User();
// echo $user->password; // Error: Cannot access private property
// echo $user->getPassword(); // Error: Cannot access private method
```

Protected Modifier

A **protected** property or method is similar to private but allows access within the class and its subclasses. This is useful when designing an inheritance structure.

```php
class User {
    protected $role = "subscriber";

    protected function getRole() {
        return $this->role;
    }
}

class Admin extends User {
    public function showRole() {
        return $this->getRole();
    }
}

$admin = new Admin();
echo $admin->showRole(); // Output: subscriber
```

Best Practices

- Use **private** properties to enforce encapsulation.

- Use **protected** properties when designing inheritance-based access control.

- Use **public** properties sparingly to avoid accidental modifications.

Mastering visibility modifiers is crucial for writing secure and maintainable PHP applications.

Using Getters and Setters to Manage Data Access

Encapsulation is a core principle of object-oriented programming (OOP), and getters and setters provide controlled access to class properties. Instead of allowing direct property modifications, these methods enable validation, transformation, and data protection, ensuring consistency in an application.

Why Use Getters and Setters?

PHP allows direct property access when declared as public, but this can lead to unintended modifications. Getters and setters provide:

- **Encapsulation**: Protects properties from unintended external modifications.

- **Validation**: Ensures that only valid data is assigned to properties.

- **Flexibility**: Allows modification of how data is retrieved or stored without breaking existing code.

Implementing Getters and Setters

Basic Getter and Setter

A **getter** retrieves a property's value, while a **setter** assigns a value after validation.

```php
class User {
    private $email;

    public function getEmail() {
        return $this->email;
    }

    public function setEmail($email) {
        if (filter_var($email, FILTER_VALIDATE_EMAIL)) {
            $this->email = $email;
        } else {
            throw new Exception("Invalid email format");
        }
    }
}

$user = new User();
$user->setEmail("test@example.com");
echo $user->getEmail(); // Output: test@example.com
```

Read-Only and Write-Only Properties

- **Read-only**: No setter is provided, meaning the property can only be retrieved.

- **Write-only**: No getter is provided, restricting access to the property's value.

```php
class Product {
    private $price;

    public function setPrice($price) {
        if ($price > 0) {
            $this->price = $price;
        } else {
            throw new Exception("Price must be positive");
        }
    }

    public function getPrice() {
        return $this->price;
    }
}

$product = new Product();
$product->setPrice(100);
echo $product->getPrice(); // Output: 100
```

Magic Methods: __get() and __set()

PHP provides magic methods __get() and __set() for dynamic property access without explicitly defining getters and setters.

```
class Person {
    private $data = [];

    public function __get($name) {
        return isset($this->data[$name]) ? $this->data[$name] : null;
    }

    public function __set($name, $value) {
        $this->data[$name] = $value;
    }
}

$person = new Person();
$person->age = 30; // Calls __set()
echo $person->age; // Calls __get(), Output: 30
```

Best Practices

- Use **explicit getters and setters** for strict control.

- Validate inputs inside setters to prevent incorrect data storage.

- Avoid overusing __get() and __set() as they reduce explicit property declaration.

By implementing getters and setters, developers enforce data integrity and security, making their PHP applications more maintainable and reliable.

Understanding Namespaces to Avoid Class Name Conflicts

As PHP applications grow, the risk of class name conflicts increases, especially when integrating third-party libraries or organizing large codebases. **Namespaces** help mitigate these issues by allowing developers to group related classes, functions, and constants under unique identifiers, ensuring a well-structured and conflict-free codebase.

Why Use Namespaces?

- **Prevents Name Collisions**: Different libraries may define the same class names.

- **Improves Code Organization**: Groups related components logically.

- **Enhances Readability**: Helps distinguish between similarly named classes in large projects.

- **Supports Autoloading**: Works seamlessly with autoloading mechanisms like Composer.

Defining and Using Namespaces

To define a namespace, use the namespace keyword at the beginning of a PHP file.

```
namespace App\Models;

class User {
    public function getName() {
        return "John Doe";
    }
}
```

To use the class, either refer to it with its **fully qualified name** or import it with the use keyword.

```
require 'User.php';

$user = new \App\Models\User();
echo $user->getName(); // Output: John Doe
```

Alternatively, importing with use simplifies access:

```
use App\Models\User;

$user = new User();
echo $user->getName();
```

Nested and Sub-Namespaces

Namespaces can be nested to create a hierarchical structure.

```
namespace App\Controllers\Admin;

class Dashboard {
    public function show() {
        return "Admin Dashboard";
    }
}
```

To use this class:

```
use App\Controllers\Admin\Dashboard;

$dashboard = new Dashboard();
echo $dashboard->show(); // Output: Admin Dashboard
```

Global Namespace and Aliases

By default, PHP operates in the **global namespace**. If a namespaced class conflicts with a global function, explicitly prefix it with \.

```
namespace App\Utils;

class File {
    public function read() {
        return "Reading file...";
    }
}
```

To differentiate from a PHP built-in function:

```php
$file = new \App\Utils\File(); // Custom class
echo $file->read(); // Output: Reading file...
```

Aliases simplify class names when importing multiple namespaces:

```php
use App\Models\User as AppUser;
use Vendor\Package\User as VendorUser;

$user1 = new AppUser();
$user2 = new VendorUser();
```

Best Practices

- Use **meaningful namespaces** based on project structure (e.g., App\Models, App\Controllers).

- Follow **PSR-4 autoloading standards** for consistency.

- Avoid **deeply nested namespaces**, as they complicate class resolution.

By leveraging namespaces, PHP developers can build scalable, modular, and conflict-free applications.

Autoloading and Following PSR-4 Standards for Clean Code

As PHP projects expand, manually including files with require or include becomes cumbersome and error-prone. **Autoloading** simplifies dependency management by dynamically loading classes when they are needed. The **PSR-4 autoloading standard**, established by the PHP-FIG (Framework Interoperability Group), ensures a structured and efficient way to organize and load PHP classes automatically.

Why Use Autoloading?

- **Eliminates Manual Includes**: No need to use require or include for each class file.

- **Improves Maintainability**: Automatically loads the correct class file based on namespace structure.

- **Encourages Standardized Code**: Following PSR-4 ensures consistency across projects and frameworks.

- **Enhances Performance**: Loads only the required classes, reducing memory usage.

Understanding PSR-4 Autoloading

PSR-4 maps namespaces directly to directory structures, making class loading intuitive. The structure follows:

```
project-root/
|— src/
|    |— Models/
|    |    |— User.php
|    |    |— Post.php
|    |— Controllers/
|    |    |— UserController.php
|— vendor/
|— composer.json
|— index.php
```

Each class resides in a directory that mirrors its namespace. For example, a User class in the App\Models namespace should be stored in src/Models/User.php.

```
namespace App\Models;

class User {
    public function getName() {
        return "John Doe";
    }
}
```

Implementing Autoloading with Composer

PHP's built-in spl_autoload_register() function can be used for custom autoloading, but **Composer** provides a more robust solution.

1. **Initialize Composer**
   Navigate to the project root and run:

   ```
   composer init
   ```

2. **Define PSR-4 Autoloading in composer.json**

   ```
   {
       "autoload": {
           "psr-4": {
               "App\\": "src/"
           }
       }
   }
   ```

3. **Run Composer Dump-Autoload**
   After defining the autoload configuration, generate the autoload files:

   ```
   composer dump-autoload
   ```

4. **Use Autoloading in PHP Scripts**
   Include Composer's autoloader in your application:

   ```
   require 'vendor/autoload.php';

   use App\Models\User;
   ```

```
$user = new User();
echo $user->getName(); // Output: John Doe
```

Best Practices for PSR-4 Autoloading

- **Follow a logical namespace structure** that mirrors the folder hierarchy.

- **Use singular names for class directories** (Model instead of Models).

- **Avoid unnecessary nesting** to keep file paths manageable.

- **Leverage Composer's autoload optimizations** (composer dump-autoload -o) for better performance.

By implementing PSR-4 autoloading, PHP developers ensure cleaner, maintainable, and scalable applications.

Part 2:

PHP Programming Models - Strong Core Support for 14 Programming Paradigms

PHP's flexibility allows it to support multiple programming paradigms, enabling developers to choose the best approach for different problem domains. This part explores how PHP accommodates array programming, event-driven execution, service-oriented development, object-oriented and procedural paradigms, functional and imperative methodologies, metaprogramming, structured programming, and API-driven development. Understanding these models empowers developers to build robust applications with optimized performance, modular design, and improved security. By exploring these diverse paradigms, developers can refine their programming style and effectively address the needs of modern web applications across different industries and use cases.

Array Programming and Data-Driven Development

Array programming is central to PHP, providing built-in support for handling structured data efficiently. PHP's extensive array functions allow developers to manipulate large datasets using operations such as mapping, filtering, and reducing. These functions enable developers to adopt a more functional approach, making code more concise and expressive. Array-based data structures are particularly useful in data-driven applications, where PHP interacts with relational databases like MySQL and PostgreSQL, as well as NoSQL solutions like MongoDB. Mastering PHP's array capabilities allows developers to process and analyze data efficiently, as demonstrated in the case study of a data processing and reporting system.

Asynchronous and Event-Driven Programming

PHP is traditionally synchronous, executing tasks sequentially. However, modern applications demand real-time responsiveness, which PHP achieves through asynchronous programming with tools like Swoole and ReactPHP. These libraries enable non-blocking execution, allowing PHP to handle concurrent tasks efficiently. Event-driven programming in PHP is facilitated by frameworks like Laravel and Symfony, which provide event dispatchers for handling user interactions, system notifications, and background tasks. Implementing these concepts allows developers to build real-time applications, such as the case study demonstrating a fully functional real-time chat system powered by PHP's event-driven capabilities.

Component-Based and Service-Oriented Programming

Component-based programming allows PHP applications to be modular and reusable. Frameworks such as Symfony and Laravel encourage component reuse through service providers and dependency injection, enhancing maintainability and scalability. Service-oriented programming extends this principle by structuring applications as independent services communicating via APIs. PHP is well-suited for building RESTful and microservices architectures, ensuring interoperability between different systems. Implementing a microservices architecture in PHP optimizes performance and scalability, as illustrated in the case study of a PHP-based scalable microservices application.

Object-Oriented and Procedural Programming

Object-oriented programming (OOP) in PHP introduces encapsulation, inheritance, and polymorphism, making code more reusable and maintainable. While procedural programming follows a linear execution flow, OOP structures applications into reusable components. Design patterns such as Factory, Singleton, and Observer help optimize OOP implementations in PHP. Refactoring procedural code into an object-oriented structure improves maintainability, as demonstrated in the case study of migrating a legacy codebase from procedural to object-oriented PHP.

Functional and Imperative Programming

PHP supports functional programming features such as closures, higher-order functions, and array transformations, allowing developers to write concise, expressive code. Functional programming minimizes side effects and enhances code reusability, making it well-suited for data manipulation and algorithmic processing. Conversely, imperative programming focuses on explicit step-by-step execution, maintaining strict control over program flow. Developers must decide between functional and imperative styles based on application needs, as illustrated in the case study comparing these approaches for different scenarios.

Metaprogramming and Reflective Programming

Metaprogramming in PHP enables dynamic code execution and class manipulation at runtime. Magic methods such as __call and __get provide flexible, dynamic interactions. PHP's Reflection API allows developers to inspect and modify class structures programmatically, enabling runtime behavior modifications. These techniques are particularly useful in extensible applications, where plugins and modules require dynamic behavior. The case study on developing a dynamic plugin system showcases the power of metaprogramming in creating extensible PHP applications.

Structured and Security-Oriented Programming

Structured programming ensures code follows a logical and organized flow, reducing complexity and improving readability. Security-oriented programming in PHP involves writing secure code by preventing common vulnerabilities such as SQL injection, cross-site scripting (XSS), and cross-site request forgery (CSRF). PHP provides robust authentication and encryption tools for securing applications. Implementing security best practices is crucial for protecting user data, as highlighted in the case study on developing a secure user authentication system.

Imperative and Procedural Programming Best Practices

Imperative and procedural programming remain relevant in PHP, especially for scripts and command-line applications. Writing clear control flow statements enhances code readability, while modular function design improves maintainability. Organizing procedural code effectively ensures that even non-OOP applications remain structured. Creating reusable functions and libraries helps scale procedural applications efficiently. These principles are demonstrated in the case study on developing a command-line PHP tool using procedural best practices.

Service-Oriented and Reflective API Development

Service-oriented API development in PHP enables applications to expose and consume services efficiently. PHP supports both RESTful and SOAP APIs, allowing flexible integration between different systems. Microservices architecture enhances scalability, while PHP's Reflection API enables dynamic API routing and metadata handling. Designing APIs with extensibility and maintainability in mind is crucial for long-term viability. The case study on building a flexible API gateway system illustrates how PHP can power service-oriented applications effectively.

This part equips developers with a deep understanding of PHP's diverse programming models, enabling them to build flexible, scalable, and efficient applications. Mastering these paradigms ensures adaptability across different project requirements and software architectures.

Module 10:
Array Programming and Data-Driven Development

PHP's powerful array handling capabilities and seamless database integration make it a preferred language for data-driven development. This module explores PHP's extensive array functions, functional programming paradigms using arrays, and database integration with MySQL, PostgreSQL, and MongoDB. It culminates in a case study demonstrating how to build a data processing and reporting system using PHP. Mastering these concepts allows developers to efficiently manipulate data, optimize performance, and build scalable applications that rely on structured and unstructured datasets.

Working with PHP's Extensive Array Functions

Arrays are fundamental to PHP development, enabling efficient data storage, manipulation, and retrieval. PHP provides a rich set of built-in array functions that simplify tasks such as searching, sorting, filtering, and transformation. Functions like array_map(), array_filter(), and array_reduce() allow developers to apply functional programming principles. Associative arrays help store key-value pairs, making data retrieval straightforward, while multidimensional arrays support complex data structures. This section explores these array functions in detail, covering common use cases and best practices for optimizing array operations in PHP applications. Understanding these functions enhances data processing efficiency and improves code readability.

Implementing Array-Based Functional Programming Concepts

Functional programming techniques can significantly improve code modularity and maintainability. PHP supports higher-order functions that operate on arrays without explicit loops. array_map() applies transformations to array elements, array_filter() removes unwanted data, and array_reduce() condenses an array into a single value. Combining these functions eliminates the need for manual iteration, making code more concise and expressive. This section delves into how functional programming concepts can be leveraged in PHP, focusing on immutability, composition, and functional purity. Developers will learn to write clean, efficient, and reusable code while minimizing side effects and enhancing application performance.

Database Integration with MySQL, PostgreSQL, and MongoDB

PHP's database connectivity extends to relational databases like MySQL and PostgreSQL, as well as NoSQL databases like MongoDB. The choice between these databases depends on application needs, with MySQL and PostgreSQL excelling in structured data storage and

MongoDB offering flexibility for document-based storage. PHP's PDO extension provides a secure and consistent way to interact with SQL databases, preventing SQL injection. For MongoDB, the PHP MongoDB driver facilitates seamless integration. This section covers connection handling, querying, prepared statements, and performance optimizations to help developers build robust, data-driven applications.

Case Study: Building a Data Processing and Reporting System

Applying theoretical knowledge to practical scenarios is essential for mastering PHP. This case study guides readers through building a data processing and reporting system using PHP's array functions and database integration. The system aggregates, filters, and visualizes data, demonstrating efficient handling of large datasets. Topics include importing data, structuring reports, optimizing queries, and generating dynamic reports. This real-world example highlights best practices for writing maintainable and scalable PHP applications, reinforcing concepts from previous sections.

Mastering PHP's array functions and database integration capabilities equips developers to build powerful data-driven applications. This module lays the foundation for efficient data processing, functional programming techniques, and best practices in database connectivity. By implementing these concepts, PHP developers can create scalable and performance-driven systems that handle complex data operations with ease.

Working with PHP's Extensive Array Functions

Arrays are a fundamental data structure in PHP, providing powerful ways to store and manipulate collections of data. PHP offers a rich set of built-in functions to work with arrays efficiently, reducing the need for manual loops and complex logic. This section explores essential array functions, demonstrating their applications through practical examples.

Creating and Manipulating Arrays

PHP supports three types of arrays: **indexed arrays** (numerically indexed), **associative arrays** (key-value pairs), and **multidimensional arrays** (arrays within arrays). Below is how they are created and manipulated:

```php
// Indexed Array
$fruits = ["Apple", "Banana", "Cherry"];
array_push($fruits, "Mango"); // Adds an element
array_pop($fruits); // Removes the last element

// Associative Array
$user = ["name" => "John", "age" => 30];
$user["email"] = "john@example.com"; // Adding a key-value pair

// Multidimensional Array
$students = [
    ["name" => "Alice", "score" => 90],
    ["name" => "Bob", "score" => 85]
];
```

```php
echo $students[0]["name"]; // Outputs: Alice
```

Searching and Filtering Arrays

PHP provides functions to **search and filter** array values efficiently.

```php
$numbers = [10, 20, 30, 40, 50];

if (in_array(30, $numbers)) {
    echo "30 is in the array.";
}

$key = array_search(40, $numbers);
echo "40 is at index: $key"; // Outputs: 40 is at index: 3

// Filtering even numbers
$filtered = array_filter($numbers, fn($n) => $n % 20 == 0);
print_r($filtered); // Outputs: [20, 40]
```

These functions improve data retrieval and enhance performance when dealing with large datasets.

Sorting Arrays in PHP

Sorting arrays helps organize data efficiently.

```php
$fruits = ["Banana", "Apple", "Mango"];
sort($fruits); // Alphabetical sorting
print_r($fruits); // Outputs: ["Apple", "Banana", "Mango"]

$ages = ["John" => 30, "Alice" => 25, "Bob" => 35];
asort($ages); // Sorts associative array by values
print_r($ages); // Outputs: ["Alice" => 25, "John" => 30, "Bob" => 35]

$names = ["John", "Alice", "Bob"];
usort($names, fn($a, $b) => strlen($a) - strlen($b)); // Sort by string length
print_r($names); // Outputs: ["Bob", "John", "Alice"]
```

Sorting improves data presentation and efficiency in applications.

Applying Functional Programming Techniques

PHP supports **functional programming** with array functions like array_map(), array_reduce(), and array_walk().

```php
$numbers = [1, 2, 3, 4, 5];

// Square each number
$squared = array_map(fn($n) => $n * $n, $numbers);
print_r($squared); // Outputs: [1, 4, 9, 16, 25]

// Sum of all numbers
$total = array_reduce($numbers, fn($carry, $n) => $carry + $n, 0);
echo $total; // Outputs: 15

// Modifying array values
array_walk($numbers, fn(&$n) => $n *= 2);
print_r($numbers); // Outputs: [2, 4, 6, 8, 10]
```

These functions enhance code efficiency, making transformations seamless.

PHP's array functions provide a powerful toolkit for managing data structures efficiently. By leveraging built-in methods for searching, sorting, and functional programming, developers can create clean, maintainable, and high-performing applications. Mastering these functions is essential for writing scalable PHP code that handles data effectively.

Implementing Array-Based Functional Programming Concepts

Functional programming in PHP allows for concise and expressive data transformations, particularly when dealing with arrays. Functions like array_map(), array_filter(), array_reduce(), and array_walk() enable developers to apply transformations, filter data, and aggregate values without relying on traditional loops. This section explores these functions and how they simplify array operations.

Using array_map() for Element-Wise Transformation

The array_map() function applies a given callback to each element of an array, returning a new transformed array.

```
$numbers = [1, 2, 3, 4, 5];

// Square each number
$squared = array_map(fn($n) => $n * $n, $numbers);

print_r($squared); // Outputs: [1, 4, 9, 16, 25]
```

This function is particularly useful for modifying data structures without mutating the original array.

Filtering Data with array_filter()

The array_filter() function removes elements that do not meet a specified condition, returning a refined subset of the array.

```
$ages = [12, 25, 17, 30, 15];

// Keep only adults (18+)
$adults = array_filter($ages, fn($age) => $age >= 18);

print_r($adults); // Outputs: [25, 30]
```

This method is commonly used for data validation and refining datasets.

Aggregating Data with array_reduce()

The array_reduce() function processes an array to produce a single aggregated value, such as a sum or concatenated string.

```
$prices = [100, 200, 150, 50];
```

```
// Calculate total cost
$total = array_reduce($prices, fn($sum, $price) => $sum + $price, 0);

echo $total; // Outputs: 500
```

This approach is efficient for reducing an array to a meaningful summary.

Applying array_walk() for In-Place Modifications

While array_map() creates a new array, array_walk() modifies the existing array.

```
$words = ["hello", "world", "php"];

array_walk($words, fn(&$word) => $word = strtoupper($word));

print_r($words); // Outputs: ["HELLO", "WORLD", "PHP"]
```

This method is useful when applying transformations without generating a new array.

PHP's functional programming capabilities offer elegant ways to process arrays efficiently. By leveraging functions like array_map(), array_filter(), and array_reduce(), developers can write cleaner and more maintainable code, reducing the reliance on traditional loops and enhancing performance in data-driven applications.

Database Integration with MySQL, PostgreSQL, and MongoDB

PHP provides robust database connectivity through extensions like MySQLi, PDO (PHP Data Objects), and MongoDB drivers. This section explores how to integrate PHP with relational databases (MySQL, PostgreSQL) and NoSQL databases (MongoDB), enabling efficient data management in modern web applications.

Connecting to a MySQL Database with PDO

PDO (PHP Data Objects) is a database abstraction layer that supports multiple database systems, including MySQL and PostgreSQL.

```
$dsn = "mysql:host=localhost;dbname=testdb;charset=utf8mb4";
$username = "root";
$password = "password";

try {
    $pdo = new PDO($dsn, $username, $password, [
        PDO::ATTR_ERRMODE => PDO::ERRMODE_EXCEPTION
    ]);
    echo "Connected to MySQL successfully!";
} catch (PDOException $e) {
    die("Connection failed: " . $e->getMessage());
}
```

Using PDO ensures secure, flexible, and portable database interactions.

Executing Queries in MySQL

To fetch and insert data securely, use prepared statements to prevent SQL injection.

100

```php
// Insert data
$stmt = $pdo->prepare("INSERT INTO users (name, email) VALUES (:name, :email)");
$stmt->execute(["name" => "John Doe", "email" => "john@example.com"]);

// Retrieve data
$stmt = $pdo->query("SELECT * FROM users");
$users = $stmt->fetchAll(PDO::FETCH_ASSOC);

print_r($users);
```

Prepared statements enhance security by ensuring safe handling of user inputs.

Integrating with PostgreSQL

PostgreSQL, a powerful relational database, is also supported via PDO.

```php
$dsn = "pgsql:host=localhost;dbname=testdb";
$pdo = new PDO($dsn, "postgres", "password", [PDO::ATTR_ERRMODE =>
        PDO::ERRMODE_EXCEPTION]);
```

The syntax for executing queries remains similar to MySQL, making it easy to switch between database engines.

Working with MongoDB in PHP

MongoDB, a NoSQL database, stores data in flexible JSON-like documents. The mongodb PHP extension provides an efficient interface for working with MongoDB.

```php
require 'vendor/autoload.php'; // Load MongoDB driver via Composer

$client = new MongoDB\Client("mongodb://localhost:27017");
$collection = $client->testdb->users;

// Insert a document
$collection->insertOne(["name" => "Jane Doe", "email" => "jane@example.com"]);

// Fetch all documents
$users = $collection->find()->toArray();
print_r($users);
```

MongoDB allows for high-performance, schema-free data storage, making it ideal for applications requiring flexibility.

PHP supports seamless database integration with both relational (MySQL, PostgreSQL) and NoSQL (MongoDB) databases. Using PDO for relational databases ensures security and flexibility, while MongoDB provides scalable and document-based storage. Choosing the right database depends on the project's requirements, ensuring efficient data handling and application performance.

Case Study: Building a Data Processing and Reporting System

In this section, we develop a simple yet powerful data processing and reporting system using PHP. The system reads data from a MySQL database, processes it, and generates a report in JSON and HTML formats. This case study highlights best practices for efficient data retrieval, manipulation, and presentation.

Step 1: Database Setup and Sample Data

We begin with a MySQL database containing a sales table that stores transaction data.

```
CREATE TABLE sales (
    id INT AUTO_INCREMENT PRIMARY KEY,
    product_name VARCHAR(255),
    quantity INT,
    price DECIMAL(10,2),
    sale_date DATE
);

INSERT INTO sales (product_name, quantity, price, sale_date)
VALUES
('Laptop', 2, 1000.00, '2024-03-01'),
('Keyboard', 5, 50.00, '2024-03-02'),
('Monitor', 3, 300.00, '2024-03-03');
```

This table records product sales, including the quantity sold and price per unit.

Step 2: Fetching and Processing Data with PHP

Using PDO, we retrieve and process data to calculate total sales revenue per product.

```
$pdo = new PDO("mysql:host=localhost;dbname=testdb", "root", "", [
    PDO::ATTR_ERRMODE => PDO::ERRMODE_EXCEPTION
]);

$query = "SELECT product_name, SUM(quantity) AS total_quantity, SUM(quantity *
          price) AS total_revenue
          FROM sales GROUP BY product_name";
$stmt = $pdo->query($query);
$salesData = $stmt->fetchAll(PDO::FETCH_ASSOC);

echo json_encode($salesData, JSON_PRETTY_PRINT);
```

This script aggregates sales data, providing insights into total units sold and revenue per product.

Step 3: Generating an HTML Report

To make the report visually accessible, we generate an HTML table.

```
echo "<table border='1'>
<tr><th>Product</th><th>Total Quantity</th><th>Total Revenue ($)</th></tr>";

foreach ($salesData as $row) {
    echo "<tr>
        <td>{$row['product_name']}</td>
        <td>{$row['total_quantity']}</td>
        <td>{$row['total_revenue']}</td>
    </tr>";
}

echo "</table>";
```

This table neatly presents sales data, making it easy for users to analyze.

Step 4: Exporting Data as a CSV File

For further analysis, we enable CSV export.

```
$filename = "sales_report.csv";
$fp = fopen($filename, "w");
fputcsv($fp, ["Product", "Total Quantity", "Total Revenue"]);

foreach ($salesData as $row) {
    fputcsv($fp, [$row['product_name'], $row['total_quantity'],
            $row['total_revenue']]);
}

fclose($fp);
echo "CSV report generated: <a href='$filename'>Download</a>";
```

This script creates a CSV file, allowing users to download and analyze sales data in spreadsheet applications.

This case study demonstrates how PHP can handle data retrieval, aggregation, and reporting efficiently. By integrating MySQL, generating HTML reports, and exporting data in multiple formats, we create a dynamic and useful reporting system. These techniques form the foundation for building scalable data-driven applications in PHP.

Module 11:
Asynchronous and Event-Driven Programming

Asynchronous and event-driven programming in PHP has gained traction with advancements in frameworks and libraries that support non-blocking execution. Traditional PHP is synchronous, executing tasks sequentially. However, modern applications require real-time responses and high concurrency, which asynchronous programming enables. This module explores PHP's synchronous nature, introduces asynchronous execution with Swoole and ReactPHP, explains event-driven systems in Laravel and Symfony, and culminates with a real-time chat application case study.

Understanding PHP's Synchronous Nature and Challenges

PHP, by default, follows a synchronous execution model where each instruction executes sequentially. This means that a script handling multiple tasks—such as processing requests, querying a database, and sending emails—must complete each step before moving to the next. While this approach simplifies development, it introduces performance bottlenecks, particularly in applications requiring real-time interactions, such as chat systems, live notifications, or high-traffic APIs.

Blocking operations like file handling, network requests, and database queries further exacerbate PHP's synchronous limitations. These processes halt execution until a response is received, making PHP inefficient for concurrent tasks. To overcome these challenges, asynchronous execution and event-driven architectures provide solutions that enhance performance, scalability, and responsiveness.

Implementing Asynchronous Execution with Swoole and ReactPHP

Swoole and ReactPHP are two powerful tools that enable asynchronous programming in PHP. Swoole is a high-performance coroutine-based framework that allows PHP to handle thousands of concurrent connections efficiently. It provides built-in features for asynchronous I/O operations, WebSockets, and task scheduling. With Swoole, PHP can function similarly to Node.js, reducing the overhead of handling concurrent requests.

ReactPHP, on the other hand, offers event-driven programming with a non-blocking architecture. It provides event loops, promises, and streams that allow developers to execute multiple tasks simultaneously without waiting for each to complete. ReactPHP is particularly useful for real-time applications and microservices that require continuous data streaming or asynchronous HTTP requests.

104

Both tools drastically improve PHP's concurrency, making it feasible to build real-time applications with superior performance.

Using Laravel Events and Symfony Event Dispatcher for Event-Driven Systems

Event-driven programming is a paradigm that decouples event producers from consumers, allowing applications to respond dynamically to events without tightly coupling components. Laravel simplifies this approach through its event system, where events are dispatched and listeners execute associated tasks. For example, a user registration event can trigger welcome emails, profile creation, and logging without explicitly calling each function.

Symfony's Event Dispatcher component provides similar capabilities, allowing developers to define events, register listeners, and dispatch them efficiently. This approach improves modularity and maintainability, as new functionalities can be added without modifying core logic.

By leveraging event-driven programming, PHP applications can become more scalable and responsive, particularly in scenarios like messaging systems, job queues, and background task execution.

Case Study: Building a Real-Time Chat Application

To demonstrate the power of asynchronous and event-driven programming in PHP, this module concludes with a real-time chat application. By combining WebSockets with Swoole or ReactPHP, the application enables instant message exchange between users without polling the server repeatedly. Laravel's event broadcasting or Symfony's event dispatcher can be used to handle message events, ensuring efficient data flow.

The chat application exemplifies PHP's ability to handle real-time communications efficiently. Asynchronous execution enables high concurrency, while event-driven programming ensures modularity and maintainability. These concepts are essential for building modern PHP applications that demand responsiveness, scalability, and real-time processing capabilities.

Understanding PHP's Synchronous Nature and Challenges

PHP is traditionally a synchronous programming language, meaning each line of code executes sequentially. When a script runs, it processes each instruction before moving to the next, making it simple to develop but inefficient for handling multiple concurrent tasks. This synchronous nature can cause delays in applications requiring real-time responses, such as chat systems, live notifications, or high-traffic APIs.

For example, if a PHP script fetches data from an external API and then queries a database, it must wait for the API response before executing the database query. This blocking behavior reduces performance when handling multiple users simultaneously.

Synchronous Execution Example

```php
function fetchData() {
    $data = file_get_contents("https://api.example.com/data");
    return json_decode($data, true);
}

$result = fetchData();
echo "Data received: " . $result['message'];
```

In this example, the script waits for file_get_contents() to complete before moving forward. If the API is slow, the entire script execution is delayed.

Challenges of PHP's Synchronous Model

1. **Blocking Operations:** File handling, database queries, and API calls halt execution until they complete. This limits PHP's ability to scale efficiently under heavy loads.

2. **Scalability Issues:** Traditional PHP applications handle concurrent requests using multiple threads or processes, which increases resource consumption.

3. **Real-Time Limitations:** Features like live updates, WebSockets, and push notifications require event-driven programming, which is difficult to achieve with PHP's default synchronous model.

4. **Inefficient Resource Usage:** PHP's synchronous execution means a single slow operation can degrade the performance of the entire application.

Workarounds Before Asynchronous PHP

Before asynchronous solutions like Swoole and ReactPHP, developers used workarounds such as:

- **AJAX Polling:** Continuously sending requests to the server to check for new data.

- **Message Queues (RabbitMQ, Redis):** Delaying processing by queuing tasks.

- **Multithreading via Forking:** Using pcntl_fork() to create multiple processes, which is complex and resource-heavy.

Why Asynchronous PHP Matters

Modern web applications demand real-time interactions, efficient resource management, and high concurrency. Asynchronous execution solves these problems by allowing non-blocking operations, enabling PHP to handle multiple tasks in parallel. This is crucial for applications like:

- **Real-time messaging (chat apps, notifications)**

- **High-frequency API calls and data streaming**

- **Concurrent database access without blocking**

With tools like Swoole and ReactPHP, PHP can now execute tasks concurrently, improving efficiency and scalability. The following sections will explore these solutions in detail.

Implementing Asynchronous Execution with Swoole and ReactPHP

Traditional PHP applications execute code synchronously, causing performance bottlenecks in high-concurrency environments. Asynchronous execution allows PHP to handle multiple tasks simultaneously without blocking the execution flow. Two popular solutions for achieving this are **Swoole** and **ReactPHP**, both of which enhance PHP's concurrency model by enabling non-blocking operations, event loops, and coroutines.

Swoole: High-Performance Asynchronous Framework

Swoole is a powerful extension for PHP that brings coroutine-based programming, asynchronous networking, and multi-threading capabilities. It enables PHP applications to run efficiently, similar to Node.js, handling thousands of concurrent requests without blocking.

Installing Swoole

```
pecl install swoole
```

Asynchronous HTTP Server with Swoole

```php
<?php
use Swoole\Http\Server;

$server = new Server("0.0.0.0", 9501);

$server->on("request", function ($request, $response) {
    $response->end("Hello, Swoole!");
});

$server->start();
?>
```

This script creates a non-blocking HTTP server that listens on port **9501** and responds to incoming requests asynchronously. Unlike traditional PHP servers, Swoole allows concurrent processing of requests without waiting for previous requests to complete.

ReactPHP: Event-Driven Asynchronous Framework

ReactPHP is a lightweight, event-driven PHP library for asynchronous programming. It provides an event loop, non-blocking I/O operations, and real-time networking capabilities.

Unlike Swoole, ReactPHP does not require a PHP extension and can be installed via Composer.

Installing ReactPHP

```
composer require react/event-loop
```

Creating an Asynchronous TCP Server with ReactPHP

```php
<?php
require 'vendor/autoload.php';

use React\EventLoop\Factory;
use React\Socket\Server;

$loop = Factory::create();
$server = new Server('127.0.0.1:8080', $loop);

$server->on('connection', function ($conn) {
    $conn->write("Hello from ReactPHP!\n");
    $conn->end();
});

$loop->run();
?>
```

This example creates a TCP server that listens for incoming connections, responds with a message, and then closes the connection—handling multiple requests simultaneously without blocking execution.

Comparing Swoole and ReactPHP

Feature	Swoole	ReactPHP
Requires PHP Extension	Yes	No
Event Loop	Built-in	External (LibEvent, LibUV)
Performance	High	Moderate
WebSocket Support	Yes	Yes
Multi-threading	Yes	No

Swoole is best suited for high-performance applications requiring coroutine support and multi-threading, while ReactPHP is ideal for event-driven programming without additional PHP extensions.

When to Use Asynchronous PHP?

- **High-concurrency applications** (e.g., chat apps, WebSockets)

- **Non-blocking database queries**

108

- **Microservices and real-time APIs**

- **Streaming large amounts of data**

By leveraging **Swoole** and **ReactPHP**, PHP developers can overcome traditional blocking constraints, significantly improving application performance and responsiveness.

Using Laravel Events and Symfony Event Dispatcher for Event-Driven Systems

Event-driven programming enables PHP applications to respond dynamically to actions and changes in the system without tightly coupling components. This approach enhances maintainability, scalability, and modularity. Two widely used frameworks for event-driven development in PHP are **Laravel's Events** and **Symfony's Event Dispatcher**.

Laravel Events: Decoupled Event Handling

Laravel provides a built-in event system that allows applications to listen for and respond to specific occurrences. This is useful for logging, notifications, and real-time updates.

Defining an Event in Laravel

```
php artisan make:event UserRegistered
```

This command generates an app/Events/UserRegistered.php file.

Creating an Event Class

```php
<?php

namespace App\Events;

use App\Models\User;
use Illuminate\Queue\SerializesModels;

class UserRegistered
{
    use SerializesModels;

    public $user;

    public function __construct(User $user)
    {
        $this->user = $user;
    }
}
```

The UserRegistered event stores user data, making it available to listeners.

Defining an Event Listener

```
php artisan make:listener SendWelcomeEmail --event=UserRegistered
```

This generates app/Listeners/SendWelcomeEmail.php, which processes the event.

```php
<?php

namespace App\Listeners;

use App\Events\UserRegistered;
use Illuminate\Contracts\Queue\ShouldQueue;
use Mail;

class SendWelcomeEmail implements ShouldQueue
{
    public function handle(UserRegistered $event)
    {
        Mail::to($event->user->email)->send(new \App\Mail\WelcomeMail($event-
            >user));
    }
}
```

This listener sends a welcome email asynchronously when a user registers.

Registering Events and Listeners

In app/Providers/EventServiceProvider.php, register the event and listener:

```php
protected $listen = [
    UserRegistered::class => [
        SendWelcomeEmail::class,
    ],
];
```

Now, Laravel will automatically trigger the event when dispatched:

```php
event(new UserRegistered($user));
```

Symfony Event Dispatcher: Flexible Event Management

Symfony's Event Dispatcher is a standalone component that allows applications to dispatch and listen for events, making it ideal for modular applications.

Installing Symfony Event Dispatcher

```
composer require symfony/event-dispatcher
```

Creating an Event Class

```php
<?php

use Symfony\Contracts\EventDispatcher\Event;

class UserRegisteredEvent extends Event
{
    public const NAME = 'user.registered';

    private $user;

    public function __construct($user)
    {
```

```php
        $this->user = $user;
    }

    public function getUser()
    {
        return $this->user;
    }
}
```

This defines an event with a NAME constant for identification.

Creating an Event Listener

```php
<?php

use Symfony\Component\EventDispatcher\EventSubscriberInterface;

class UserEventListener implements EventSubscriberInterface
{
    public static function getSubscribedEvents()
    {
        return [
            UserRegisteredEvent::NAME => 'onUserRegistered',
        ];
    }

    public function onUserRegistered(UserRegisteredEvent $event)
    {
        echo "User registered: " . $event->getUser();
    }
}
```

This listener reacts when the UserRegisteredEvent is triggered.

Dispatching an Event

```php
<?php

use Symfony\Component\EventDispatcher\EventDispatcher;

$dispatcher = new EventDispatcher();
$dispatcher->addSubscriber(new UserEventListener());

$userEvent = new UserRegisteredEvent('JohnDoe');
$dispatcher->dispatch($userEvent, UserRegisteredEvent::NAME);
```

Choosing Between Laravel Events and Symfony Event Dispatcher

Feature	Laravel Events	Symfony Event Dispatcher
Framework Dependency	Laravel-specific	Standalone Component
Ease of Use	Simplified event handling	Requires explicit setup
Async Support	Yes (queues)	Requires manual handling

Laravel's event system is more developer-friendly for Laravel projects, while Symfony's Event Dispatcher is suitable for standalone applications needing decoupled event management.

Event-driven programming allows PHP applications to react to changes efficiently, making them more modular and maintainable. Laravel provides a streamlined way to handle events within its ecosystem, while Symfony's Event Dispatcher offers a flexible, framework-agnostic approach. By leveraging these tools, PHP developers can build highly scalable and event-driven applications.

Case Study: Building a Real-Time Chat Application

Building a real-time chat application in PHP requires handling asynchronous communication efficiently. With traditional PHP being synchronous, we need tools like **Swoole** or **ReactPHP** to achieve real-time updates. This case study explores how to implement a simple real-time chat application using WebSockets with **Swoole**, combined with Laravel for backend processing.

1. Setting Up the Environment

To begin, install **Swoole**, a high-performance networking framework that enables WebSockets in PHP:

```
composer require open-swoole/swoole
```

Ensure that the Swoole extension is enabled in php.ini.

Next, create a Laravel project:

```
composer create-project --prefer-dist laravel/laravel chat-app
```

Install Laravel WebSockets package:

```
composer require beyondcode/laravel-websockets
```

Run migrations:

```
php artisan migrate
```

2. Creating the WebSocket Server

Swoole acts as a WebSocket server, handling bidirectional real-time communication between users.

Create websocket.php in the app directory:

```
<?php
```

112

```php
use Swoole\WebSocket\Server;

$server = new Server("0.0.0.0", 8080);

$server->on("open", function ($server, $request) {
    echo "Connection opened: {$request->fd}\n";
});

$server->on("message", function ($server, $frame) {
    foreach ($server->connections as $fd) {
        $server->push($fd, $frame->data);
    }
});

$server->on("close", function ($server, $fd) {
    echo "Connection closed: {$fd}\n";
});

$server->start();
```

Run the WebSocket server:

```
php app/websocket.php
```

3. Creating a Laravel API for Message Storage

Defining a Migration for Messages

```
php artisan make:migration create_messages_table
```

Modify the migration file:

```php
public function up()
{
    Schema::create('messages', function (Blueprint $table) {
        $table->id();
        $table->string('sender');
        $table->text('message');
        $table->timestamps();
    });
}
```

Run the migration:

```
php artisan migrate
```

Creating a Model for Messages

```
php artisan make:model Message
```

Modify app/Models/Message.php:

```php
<?php

namespace App\Models;

use Illuminate\Database\Eloquent\Model;

class Message extends Model
{
```

113

```
    protected $fillable = ['sender', 'message'];
}
```

Creating a Controller for Messages

```
php artisan make:controller ChatController
```

Modify app/Http/Controllers/ChatController.php:

```php
<?php

namespace App\Http\Controllers;

use Illuminate\Http\Request;
use App\Models\Message;

class ChatController extends Controller
{
    public function store(Request $request)
    {
        $message = Message::create([
            'sender' => $request->sender,
            'message' => $request->message,
        ]);

        return response()->json($message);
    }

    public function index()
    {
        return response()->json(Message::all());
    }
}
```

Define API routes in routes/api.php:

```php
use App\Http\Controllers\ChatController;

Route::get('/messages', [ChatController::class, 'index']);
Route::post('/messages', [ChatController::class, 'store']);
```

4. Creating a Frontend with JavaScript WebSockets

Modify resources/views/chat.blade.php:

```html
<!DOCTYPE html>
<html lang="en">
<head>
    <meta charset="UTF-8">
    <meta name="viewport" content="width=device-width, initial-scale=1.0">
    <title>Chat</title>
</head>
<body>
    <h2>Real-Time Chat</h2>
    <div id="chat"></div>
    <input type="text" id="message" placeholder="Type a message">
    <button onclick="sendMessage()">Send</button>

    <script>
        let socket = new WebSocket("ws://localhost:8080");

        socket.onmessage = function(event) {
```

```
        let chat = document.getElementById("chat");
        chat.innerHTML += "<p>" + event.data + "</p>";
    };

    function sendMessage() {
        let message = document.getElementById("message").value;
        socket.send(message);
    }
    </script>
</body>
</html>
```

5. Running the Real-Time Chat Application

1. **Start Laravel server**:

    ```
    php artisan serve
    ```

2. **Start the WebSocket server**:

    ```
    php app/websocket.php
    ```

3. **Open the chat application** in the browser:

    ```
    http://127.0.0.1:8000/chat
    ```

This case study demonstrated how to build a real-time chat application using **Swoole WebSockets** for live messaging and Laravel for message storage. The combination of **event-driven programming**, **WebSockets**, and **database persistence** provides a scalable, real-time PHP solution suitable for various applications like customer support, gaming, and collaboration tools.

Module 12:
Component-Based and Service-Oriented Programming

Component-based and service-oriented programming (SOP) in PHP allows for modular, reusable, and scalable application design. By breaking software into independent components and services, PHP applications can be developed efficiently and maintained with ease. This module explores component-based architecture, dependency injection, RESTful API development, and microservices. A case study on scalable microservices implementation rounds off the discussion.

Developing Modular Applications Using PHP Components

Modular application development in PHP involves structuring software into independent, reusable components. This approach enhances maintainability, testing, and scalability. PHP supports component-based programming through package managers like **Composer**, which allows developers to integrate external libraries and custom-built modules. A well-structured modular application separates concerns into different layers, such as **controllers, models, views, and services**. Frameworks like **Symfony** and **Laravel** promote modularity by providing reusable components that can be independently maintained. Developers can also build custom **PHP components** to encapsulate specific functionalities and share them across multiple projects, ensuring **code reusability and consistency**.

Using Service Providers and Dependency Injection in PHP Frameworks

Service Providers and **Dependency Injection (DI)** are essential for writing clean and maintainable PHP applications. Service providers register application services, enabling the dynamic loading of dependencies only when needed. Laravel, for instance, allows the registration of services in the AppServiceProvider class. DI facilitates **loose coupling**, making it easier to swap dependencies without altering core application logic. This approach enhances testability by allowing **mocking of dependencies** during unit testing. PHP frameworks like Symfony and Laravel implement dependency injection containers to manage class dependencies automatically, reducing **boilerplate code** and improving **code readability**.

Building RESTful APIs and Microservices in PHP

RESTful APIs and microservices provide a way to develop **scalable and distributed** PHP applications. A **REST API** follows standard HTTP methods (GET, POST, PUT, DELETE) and returns **JSON responses**. PHP frameworks such as **Laravel, Slim, and Lumen** simplify API development by providing built-in routing, authentication, and middleware support.

Microservices, on the other hand, decompose an application into small, independent services that communicate via HTTP or message queues. PHP-based microservices rely on frameworks like **Lumen (a lightweight Laravel variant)** or **RoadRunner (a Golang-powered PHP application server)** for optimized performance and asynchronous processing.

Case Study: Implementing a Scalable Microservices Architecture

A **scalable microservices architecture** in PHP involves breaking down an application into loosely coupled services that interact via REST APIs or event-driven messaging. In this case study, we explore designing an **e-commerce platform** where separate microservices handle **user authentication, orders, payments, and inventory management**. Each microservice runs independently and communicates through **API gateways** or message brokers like **RabbitMQ**. The use of **Docker and Kubernetes** allows microservices to scale horizontally based on demand. By adopting **service-oriented architecture (SOA)**, PHP applications can achieve **high availability, fault tolerance, and easy deployment**, making them suitable for cloud-based environments.

Component-based and service-oriented programming enhances the **scalability, reusability, and maintainability** of PHP applications. This module has covered modular development with PHP components, dependency injection, and building RESTful APIs and microservices. The case study demonstrated how microservices enable a scalable architecture for complex PHP applications. These concepts empower developers to build **efficient, enterprise-grade PHP systems**.

Developing Modular Applications Using PHP Components

Modular programming in PHP is an approach that structures an application into independent, reusable, and interchangeable components. This methodology enhances maintainability, promotes reusability, and reduces complexity by dividing software into distinct modules that can function independently. PHP facilitates modular development through **Composer**, the PHP package manager, which allows developers to integrate third-party libraries and create their own modular components. By designing applications with components, developers ensure **better scalability, testability, and maintainability**.

A modular application typically consists of multiple components, each responsible for specific functionality. For instance, an application can have separate modules for **user authentication, database interaction, API handling, and payment processing**. These modules can be packaged as **PHP libraries** and reused across different projects. A well-structured modular application uses the **Model-View-Controller (MVC)** architecture or **Service-Oriented Architecture (SOA)** to keep concerns separate.

Creating a Modular Component in PHP

To create a modular PHP component, developers define a self-contained class with a clear responsibility. Consider a simple **Logger** component that can be reused in multiple projects:

```php
namespace App\Components;

class Logger {
    public function log($message) {
        $timestamp = date('Y-m-d H:i:s');
        file_put_contents('app.log', "[$timestamp] $message\n", FILE_APPEND);
    }
}
```

This Logger class encapsulates logging functionality and can be reused across applications by including it as a module.

Managing PHP Components with Composer

Composer simplifies dependency management by enabling developers to install and manage third-party and custom components. To create a modular package, follow these steps:

1. Initialize a new package using Composer:

   ```
   composer init
   ```

2. Define the package structure and dependencies.

3. Publish the package on **Packagist** or use it locally in projects.

4. Install the package via Composer in another project:

   ```
   composer require vendor/package-name
   ```

By using Composer, PHP developers **avoid code duplication** and benefit from a vast ecosystem of reusable libraries.

Encapsulating Functionality with PHP Namespaces

Namespaces prevent naming conflicts when using multiple components in an application. By defining modules inside namespaces, different libraries can have **classes with the same names** without interference. For example, if two different logging modules define a Logger class, namespaces help distinguish them:

```php
use App\Components\Logger;

$logger = new Logger();
$logger->log("Application started.");
```

With proper namespace management, modular applications remain **organized and scalable**.

Developing modular PHP applications using components improves **code organization, maintainability, and reusability**. PHP provides tools like Composer for managing modular packages efficiently. By structuring software into independent modules, developers ensure **better code separation** and **scalability**, making it easier to extend applications over time. The next section will explore **service providers and dependency injection** to enhance modular development further.

Using Service Providers and Dependency Injection in PHP Frameworks

Service providers and dependency injection are core principles of modern PHP frameworks such as Laravel, Symfony, and Zend. These mechanisms enable **loose coupling** between components, making applications **more maintainable, testable, and modular**. Service providers manage class dependencies within an application, while dependency injection ensures that objects receive their required dependencies without hardcoded instantiation.

A **service provider** in PHP frameworks is responsible for registering and bootstrapping services, ensuring they are available throughout the application. Dependency injection, on the other hand, allows objects to receive dependencies externally rather than creating them within the class. This practice adheres to the **Inversion of Control (IoC)** principle, reducing direct dependencies and improving flexibility.

Understanding Dependency Injection

Dependency injection (DI) is a design pattern where **a class receives its dependencies from an external source rather than creating them internally**. This makes the class independent of specific implementations, allowing for greater flexibility.

For example, consider a simple Mailer class that sends emails:

```
class Mailer {
    public function send($to, $message) {
        echo "Sending email to $to: $message";
    }
}
```

If another class depends on Mailer, it should not instantiate it directly. Instead, the dependency should be **injected**:

```
class Notification {
    protected $mailer;

    public function __construct(Mailer $mailer) {
        $this->mailer = $mailer;
    }

    public function notify($user, $message) {
        $this->mailer->send($user, $message);
    }
}
```

119

Here, the Mailer dependency is injected via the constructor, making Notification **loosely coupled** and allowing different mail implementations to be used without modifying the Notification class.

Implementing Dependency Injection with Laravel's Service Container

Laravel provides a **service container** for managing dependencies. Instead of manually injecting dependencies, Laravel automatically resolves them using **service binding**.

1. **Binding a Service in a Laravel Service Provider**

Service providers register dependencies in Laravel's AppServiceProvider:

```
use App\Services\Mailer;
use Illuminate\Support\ServiceProvider;

class AppServiceProvider extends ServiceProvider {
    public function register() {
        $this->app->singleton(Mailer::class, function ($app) {
            return new Mailer();
        });
    }
}
```

This binds the Mailer class as a singleton, ensuring that the same instance is used throughout the application.

2. **Using Dependency Injection in a Controller**

Laravel's service container automatically injects dependencies into classes:

```
use App\Services\Mailer;

class NotificationController {
    protected $mailer;

    public function __construct(Mailer $mailer) {
        $this->mailer = $mailer;
    }

    public function sendNotification($user, $message) {
        $this->mailer->send($user, $message);
    }
}
```

By using Laravel's service container, developers avoid manual dependency resolution, improving **scalability and testability**.

Service providers and dependency injection **enhance modularity, flexibility, and maintainability** in PHP frameworks. By leveraging these patterns, developers create **loosely coupled** components that are **easier to test and extend**. The next section will focus on **building RESTful APIs and microservices in PHP** to support service-oriented architecture.

Building RESTful APIs and Microservices in PHP

RESTful APIs and microservices have become fundamental for modern web applications, enabling efficient communication between systems. PHP, with frameworks like Laravel, Symfony, and Slim, provides powerful tools to build scalable APIs. RESTful APIs follow standard HTTP methods (GET, POST, PUT, DELETE) to interact with resources, ensuring interoperability across platforms.

Microservices architecture further **decomposes applications into smaller, independent services**, each handling a specific functionality. These services communicate via RESTful APIs or message queues, enhancing **scalability, maintainability, and deployment flexibility**. In this section, we explore how to build RESTful APIs in PHP and design microservices that integrate efficiently.

Setting Up a Basic RESTful API in PHP

A RESTful API in PHP requires **routing, request handling, and response formatting**. The following example demonstrates a simple API using **Laravel**:

1. **Defining API Routes (routes/api.php in Laravel)**

```php
use App\Http\Controllers\UserController;
use Illuminate\Support\Facades\Route;

Route::get('/users', [UserController::class, 'index']);
Route::get('/users/{id}', [UserController::class, 'show']);
Route::post('/users', [UserController::class, 'store']);
Route::put('/users/{id}', [UserController::class, 'update']);
Route::delete('/users/{id}', [UserController::class, 'destroy']);
```

Each route corresponds to an API endpoint that performs CRUD operations on user data.

2. **Creating the Controller to Handle API Requests**

```php
namespace App\Http\Controllers;

use App\Models\User;
use Illuminate\Http\Request;
use Illuminate\Http\Response;
class UserController extends Controller {
    public function index() {
        return response()->json(User::all(), Response::HTTP_OK);
    }

    public function show($id) {
        $user = User::find($id);
        return $user ? response()->json($user, Response::HTTP_OK)
                    : response()->json(['error' => 'User not found'],
            Response::HTTP_NOT_FOUND);
    }

    public function store(Request $request) {
        $user = User::create($request->all());
        return response()->json($user, Response::HTTP_CREATED);
    }
```

```php
    public function update(Request $request, $id) {
        $user = User::find($id);
        if (!$user) {
            return response()->json(['error' => 'User not found'],
        Response::HTTP_NOT_FOUND);
        }
        $user->update($request->all());
        return response()->json($user, Response::HTTP_OK);
    }

    public function destroy($id) {
        $user = User::find($id);
        if (!$user) {
            return response()->json(['error' => 'User not found'],
        Response::HTTP_NOT_FOUND);
        }
        $user->delete();
        return response()->json(['message' => 'User deleted'],
        Response::HTTP_OK);
    }
}
```

This controller **handles user CRUD operations** and returns JSON responses with appropriate HTTP status codes.

Building a PHP Microservice

A microservices architecture **splits functionalities into independent services**, each managing a specific domain. A user service, for example, may expose RESTful APIs for user management.

1. **Designing a Microservice Structure**

    o   **User Service**: Manages user authentication and profiles.

    o   **Order Service**: Handles product purchases.

    o   **Notification Service**: Sends emails or push notifications.

Each microservice communicates via API endpoints or message brokers like **RabbitMQ** or **Redis Pub/Sub**.

2. **Consuming a Microservice API in PHP**

A PHP application can interact with a microservice using **cURL or Guzzle**:

```php
use GuzzleHttp\Client;

$client = new Client();
$response = $client->get('http://user-service.local/api/users');
$users = json_decode($response->getBody(), true);

print_r($users);
```

Guzzle simplifies **HTTP requests** between services, ensuring efficient API consumption.

RESTful APIs and microservices **enable scalable, decoupled, and high-performance architectures**. PHP frameworks like Laravel and Symfony provide robust tools for API development, while services like **Guzzle, RabbitMQ, and Redis** facilitate microservices communication. In the next section, we will explore a **real-world case study** on implementing a scalable microservices architecture.

Case Study: Implementing a Scalable Microservices Architecture

In modern web development, **microservices architecture** enables applications to be broken into small, independent services, each handling a specific business functionality. This approach **improves scalability, maintainability, and fault isolation**, ensuring that services can evolve independently. This case study demonstrates how to implement a **scalable microservices architecture using PHP** with Laravel for API services and RabbitMQ for communication.

Overview of the Microservices Architecture

In this case study, we build a **user management and order processing system** using three core microservices:

1. **User Service**: Manages authentication, user registration, and profiles.

2. **Order Service**: Handles orders, payments, and transactions.

3. **Notification Service**: Sends emails or push notifications for order confirmations.

These services communicate via **RESTful APIs** and **message queues (RabbitMQ)** for event-driven interactions.

Designing the User Service

The **User Service** handles user authentication and registration, exposing endpoints for CRUD operations. It stores user data in **MySQL** and provides JWT-based authentication.

User Service API Routes (routes/api.php)

```
use App\Http\Controllers\UserController;
use Illuminate\Support\Facades\Route;

Route::post('/register', [UserController::class, 'register']);
Route::post('/login', [UserController::class, 'login']);
Route::get('/users/{id}', [UserController::class, 'show']);
```

User Registration Controller Method

```
namespace App\Http\Controllers;
```

```
use App\Models\User;
use Illuminate\Http\Request;
use Illuminate\Support\Facades\Hash;
use Illuminate\Support\Facades\Validator;

class UserController extends Controller {
    public function register(Request $request) {
        $validator = Validator::make($request->all(), [
            'name' => 'required',
            'email' => 'required|email|unique:users',
            'password' => 'required|min:6'
        ]);

        if ($validator->fails()) {
            return response()->json($validator->errors(), 400);
        }

        $user = User::create([
            'name' => $request->name,
            'email' => $request->email,
            'password' => Hash::make($request->password)
        ]);

        return response()->json($user, 201);
    }
}
```

Order Service: Processing Orders and Payments

The **Order Service** is responsible for managing orders. It communicates with the **User Service** to validate users before processing orders.

Creating an Order (routes/api.php)

```
use App\Http\Controllers\OrderController;
use Illuminate\Support\Facades\Route;

Route::post('/orders', [OrderController::class, 'store']);
```

Order Controller: Storing Orders and Sending Events

```
namespace App\Http\Controllers;

use App\Models\Order;
use Illuminate\Http\Request;
use Illuminate\Support\Facades\Http;

class OrderController extends Controller {
    public function store(Request $request) {
        $userResponse = Http::get("http://user-
            service.local/api/users/{$request->user_id}");

        if ($userResponse->failed()) {
            return response()->json(['error' => 'User not found'], 404);
        }

        $order = Order::create([
            'user_id' => $request->user_id,
            'product' => $request->product,
            'amount' => $request->amount
        ]);

        // Send event to RabbitMQ for notification processing
```

```
            event(new \App\Events\OrderPlaced($order));

            return response()->json($order, 201);
        }
    }
```

This service **validates users by making API requests** to the User Service and triggers an **event for notifications** upon order creation.

Notification Service: Handling Asynchronous Events

To avoid performance bottlenecks, notifications are processed **asynchronously** using RabbitMQ. The Notification Service **listens for new orders** and sends an email to users.

Setting Up RabbitMQ Listener for Order Events

```
namespace App\Listeners;

use App\Events\OrderPlaced;
use Illuminate\Contracts\Queue\ShouldQueue;
use Illuminate\Support\Facades\Mail;
use App\Mail\OrderConfirmationMail;

class SendOrderNotification implements ShouldQueue {
    public function handle(OrderPlaced $event) {
        Mail::to($event->order->user->email)
            ->send(new OrderConfirmationMail($event->order));
    }
}
```

This service ensures that email notifications are processed in the background, **reducing API response time** for order placements.

Microservices Communication: RESTful APIs vs. Message Queues

- **RESTful APIs**: Used for synchronous operations like fetching user data.

- **Message Queues (RabbitMQ)**: Used for asynchronous tasks like sending notifications.

This hybrid approach **optimizes system performance and responsiveness**.

This case study demonstrates how to **build a scalable PHP microservices architecture** using Laravel, RESTful APIs, and RabbitMQ. By **separating services into independent components**, this design ensures better **scalability, maintainability, and fault tolerance**, making it ideal for **large-scale applications**.

Module 13:
Object-Oriented and Procedural Programming

PHP supports both **object-oriented programming (OOP)** and **procedural programming**, allowing developers to choose the best approach based on project requirements. While procedural programming follows a step-by-step execution flow using functions and global variables, object-oriented programming organizes code into reusable objects and classes. This module explores the differences between these approaches, their use cases, and best practices for writing maintainable PHP code. It also covers design patterns, refactoring procedural code into OOP, and a case study on migrating a legacy PHP codebase to an object-oriented structure for better scalability and maintainability.

Comparing Object-Oriented and Procedural Programming Approaches

Procedural programming structures code as a **sequence of function calls and conditional statements**, making it simple and easy to follow. This approach is best suited for **small projects and scripts** where complexity is minimal. However, as projects grow, maintaining procedural code becomes challenging due to **tight coupling and lack of modularity**.

Object-oriented programming (OOP), on the other hand, organizes code into **classes and objects**, encapsulating logic within reusable structures. OOP promotes **code reusability, maintainability, and scalability** by following principles like **encapsulation, inheritance, and polymorphism**. While OOP adds an abstraction layer that may introduce a slight performance overhead, its benefits in large-scale applications outweigh this trade-off. The choice between OOP and procedural programming depends on the project's size, complexity, and long-term maintainability goals.

Implementing Design Patterns in Object-Oriented PHP

Design patterns provide **reusable solutions to common programming problems** in software development. In PHP, implementing **creational, structural, and behavioral patterns** improves code organization, efficiency, and maintainability.

Singleton Pattern ensures that only one instance of a class exists, commonly used for database connections. **Factory Pattern** simplifies object creation by encapsulating logic within a dedicated class. **Observer Pattern** enables event-driven programming by allowing objects to subscribe to state changes in another object. By leveraging these design patterns, developers **enhance code organization, reduce redundancy, and facilitate easier debugging**. Applying

126

the right pattern improves software scalability and maintains **separation of concerns**, making applications easier to extend and modify.

Refactoring Procedural Code into Object-Oriented Structures

Refactoring procedural code into OOP improves code maintainability and scalability. The process involves **identifying related functions**, grouping them into **classes**, and encapsulating **shared data** as class properties. Procedural scripts often contain **global variables and tightly coupled logic**, which can be structured into **modular, self-contained objects** with clear responsibilities.

The refactoring process involves:

1. **Encapsulating related functions into classes**

2. **Replacing global variables with class properties**

3. **Implementing constructors to initialize dependencies**

4. **Utilizing inheritance and interfaces for extensibility**

By converting procedural code to OOP, developers **improve code clarity, reduce redundancy, and enhance modularity**, making future modifications and expansions more manageable.

Case Study: Migrating a Legacy Codebase to OOP

Migrating a legacy PHP application from procedural code to OOP requires **strategic planning and incremental refactoring**. The migration process starts by **analyzing the existing codebase**, identifying **modular components**, and **gradually introducing classes and objects** while maintaining functionality.

A practical approach includes:

1. **Identifying repeated code blocks** and refactoring them into reusable classes.

2. **Introducing MVC architecture** to separate logic, presentation, and data.

3. **Replacing hardcoded dependencies** with dependency injection.

This transformation results in **a more scalable, maintainable, and testable application**. By adopting OOP principles, developers can future-proof their PHP projects, making them easier to extend and integrate with modern frameworks.

Understanding the differences between **procedural and object-oriented programming** helps developers choose the right approach for their projects. While procedural programming is simpler, **OOP provides modularity, reusability, and maintainability**, making it ideal for **large-scale applications**. Implementing **design patterns**, refactoring procedural code, and **migrating legacy systems to OOP** enhances PHP development efficiency, ensuring robust and scalable software solutions.

Comparing Object-Oriented and Procedural Programming Approaches

PHP supports both **procedural programming (PP)** and **object-oriented programming (OOP)**, each with distinct methodologies. Procedural programming follows a **linear execution flow**, using functions and global variables to process data step-by-step. OOP, on the other hand, structures code into **classes and objects**, encapsulating functionality for better reusability and maintainability.

Procedural Programming in PHP

Procedural programming is straightforward and suitable for small applications. Here's an example of a procedural approach:

```
function calculateTotal($price, $quantity) {
    return $price * $quantity;
}

$price = 20;
$quantity = 5;
$total = calculateTotal($price, $quantity);
echo "Total: $total";
```

This approach is **functional but lacks modularity**. If the application scales, maintaining and extending this code becomes difficult due to **tight coupling** between functions.

Object-Oriented Programming in PHP

OOP organizes code into reusable objects. The same functionality using OOP would be:

```
class Order {
    private $price;
    private $quantity;

    public function __construct($price, $quantity) {
        $this->price = $price;
        $this->quantity = $quantity;
    }

    public function calculateTotal() {
        return $this->price * $this->quantity;
    }
}

$order = new Order(20, 5);
echo "Total: " . $order->calculateTotal();
```

Here, **data and behavior are encapsulated in the class**. This makes the code more maintainable and **extensible**.

Key Differences Between Procedural and OOP

Feature	Procedural Programming	Object-Oriented Programming
Structure	Linear, function-based	Modular, object-based
Reusability	Limited	High (via inheritance, encapsulation)
Scalability	Hard to maintain as complexity grows	Easier to extend
Encapsulation	Uses global variables	Uses private/protected properties

When to Use Procedural vs. OOP

- **Use procedural programming** for **simple scripts**, small utilities, or quick processing tasks.

- **Use OOP** for **large applications**, where modularity, scalability, and reusability are required.

PHP's **modern frameworks (Laravel, Symfony)** rely heavily on OOP. Thus, adopting OOP ensures better **long-term project maintainability**.

Implementing Design Patterns in Object-Oriented PHP

Design patterns are **proven solutions** to common software design problems. In PHP, applying **object-oriented design patterns** enhances **code reusability, scalability, and maintainability**. This section explores some essential design patterns widely used in PHP development.

1. Singleton Pattern

The **Singleton Pattern** ensures that a class has **only one instance** throughout the application lifecycle. It is useful for managing **database connections, configuration settings, or logging mechanisms**.

```
class Database {
    private static $instance = null;
    private $connection;

    private function __construct() {
        $this->connection = new PDO("mysql:host=localhost;dbname=test", "root",
            "");
    }

    public static function getInstance() {
        if (self::$instance === null) {
```

129

```
            self::$instance = new self();
        }
        return self::$instance;
    }

    public function getConnection() {
        return $this->connection;
    }
}

// Usage
$db1 = Database::getInstance();
$db2 = Database::getInstance();

var_dump($db1 === $db2); // true (same instance)
```

This pattern **prevents multiple database connections** and optimizes resource usage.

2. Factory Pattern

The **Factory Pattern** is used to **create objects without specifying the exact class**. This enhances flexibility and **decouples object creation** from implementation.

```
interface Product {
    public function getType();
}

class Book implements Product {
    public function getType() {
        return "This is a Book";
    }
}

class Electronic implements Product {
    public function getType() {
        return "This is an Electronic item";
    }
}

class ProductFactory {
    public static function createProduct($type) {
        switch ($type) {
            case 'book': return new Book();
            case 'electronic': return new Electronic();
            default: throw new Exception("Invalid product type");
        }
    }
}

// Usage
$product = ProductFactory::createProduct('book');
echo $product->getType(); // Output: This is a Book
```

The **Factory Pattern** helps manage **object creation dynamically** without modifying existing code.

3. Strategy Pattern

The **Strategy Pattern** allows selecting different **algorithms or behaviors at runtime**. It is useful for **payment processing, authentication methods, or sorting algorithms**.

```
interface PaymentStrategy {
    public function pay($amount);
}

class PayPal implements PaymentStrategy {
    public function pay($amount) {
        return "Paid $amount via PayPal";
    }
}

class CreditCard implements PaymentStrategy {
    public function pay($amount) {
        return "Paid $amount via Credit Card";
    }
}

class PaymentProcessor {
    private $strategy;

    public function __construct(PaymentStrategy $strategy) {
        $this->strategy = $strategy;
    }

    public function executePayment($amount) {
        return $this->strategy->pay($amount);
    }
}
// Usage
$payment = new PaymentProcessor(new PayPal());
echo $payment->executePayment(100); // Output: Paid 100 via PayPal
```

This pattern **improves flexibility** by allowing different payment methods without modifying existing classes.

Design patterns enhance **code maintainability and scalability** in OOP PHP. The **Singleton Pattern** ensures a single instance, the **Factory Pattern** abstracts object creation, and the **Strategy Pattern** enables dynamic behavior switching. Understanding these patterns **helps build robust, reusable PHP applications**.

Refactoring Procedural Code into Object-Oriented Structures

Refactoring procedural PHP code into an object-oriented (OOP) structure **improves maintainability, reusability, and scalability**. Procedural programming relies on functions and global variables, whereas OOP organizes code into **classes and objects**, encapsulating logic within reusable components. This section demonstrates the **step-by-step conversion** of procedural code into an object-oriented design.

1. Identifying Procedural Code

A typical procedural script may consist of **functions that operate on global data**. Consider the following **procedural user authentication system**:

```
// Procedural Code
function connectDatabase() {
```

```php
        return new PDO("mysql:host=localhost;dbname=test", "root", "");
}

function authenticateUser($username, $password) {
    $db = connectDatabase();
    $stmt = $db->prepare("SELECT * FROM users WHERE username = ? AND password =
        ?");
    $stmt->execute([$username, md5($password)]);
    return $stmt->fetch(PDO::FETCH_ASSOC);
}

// Usage
$user = authenticateUser("john_doe", "securepass");
if ($user) {
    echo "Login successful!";
} else {
    echo "Invalid credentials.";
}
```

2. Creating a User Class

Instead of handling everything in **global functions**, we **encapsulate** database interactions inside a User class.

```php
class User {
    private $db;

    public function __construct(PDO $db) {
        $this->db = $db;
    }

    public function authenticate($username, $password) {
        $stmt = $this->db->prepare("SELECT * FROM users WHERE username = ? AND
            password = ?");
        $stmt->execute([$username, md5($password)]);
        return $stmt->fetch(PDO::FETCH_ASSOC);
    }
}
```

Now, authentication logic is encapsulated within a **self-contained class**, promoting **reusability**.

3. Creating a Database Class

To **separate concerns**, a dedicated Database class is introduced for managing database connections.

```php
class Database {
    private static $instance = null;
    private $connection;

    private function __construct() {
        $this->connection = new PDO("mysql:host=localhost;dbname=test", "root",
            "");
    }

    public static function getInstance() {
        if (self::$instance === null) {
            self::$instance = new self();
        }
        return self::$instance->connection;
```

```
    }
}
```

This follows the **Singleton Pattern**, ensuring only **one database connection** is created.

4. Implementing OOP Authentication

With the User and Database classes, we **refactor the procedural script**:

```
$db = Database::getInstance();
$user = new User($db);

$authenticatedUser = $user->authenticate("john_doe", "securepass");
if ($authenticatedUser) {
    echo "Login successful!";
} else {
    echo "Invalid credentials.";
}
```

By refactoring procedural code into **OOP structures**, we achieve **better organization, reusability, and scalability**. The **User class** handles authentication, and the **Database class** manages connections. This approach **reduces redundancy, improves maintainability, and makes the codebase more extensible** for future enhancements.

Case Study: Migrating a Legacy Codebase to OOP

Migrating a **legacy procedural PHP codebase** to an **object-oriented (OOP) structure** enhances maintainability, reusability, and scalability. This case study demonstrates how an **existing procedural e-commerce system** can be transformed into a **modular OOP-based architecture**, ensuring **cleaner, well-structured, and extensible** code.

1. Understanding the Legacy Codebase

A procedural approach typically involves **global variables, functions, and repetitive logic**. Consider the following **legacy shopping cart system**:

```
// Procedural Approach
$cart = [];

function addToCart($product, $quantity) {
    global $cart;
    $cart[$product] = $quantity;
}

function getCartTotal() {
    global $cart;
    $total = 0;
    foreach ($cart as $product => $quantity) {
        $total += getProductPrice($product) * $quantity;
    }
    return $total;
}

function getProductPrice($product) {
    $prices = ["laptop" => 1000, "phone" => 500];
    return $prices[$product] ?? 0;
}
```

```
// Usage
addToCart("laptop", 1);
addToCart("phone", 2);
echo "Total: $" . getCartTotal();
```

2. Designing an Object-Oriented Structure

To **improve code maintainability**, we identify key **entities**:

- **Cart**: Manages shopping cart items.

- **Product**: Represents individual products.

- **CartService**: Handles business logic, such as calculating totals.

3. Implementing the OOP Version

Creating the Product Class

Encapsulating product details in a dedicated class:

```
class Product {
    private $name;
    private $price;

    public function __construct($name, $price) {
        $this->name = $name;
        $this->price = $price;
    }

    public function getName() {
        return $this->name;
    }

    public function getPrice() {
        return $this->price;
    }
}
```

Creating the Cart Class

The Cart class **manages items and quantities**:

```
class Cart {
    private $items = [];

    public function addProduct(Product $product, $quantity) {
        $this->items[$product->getName()] = [
            "product" => $product,
            "quantity" => $quantity
        ];
    }

    public function getItems() {
        return $this->items;
    }
}
```

Creating the CartService Class

This class **handles cart-related logic**, such as computing totals:

```
class CartService {
    public static function calculateTotal(Cart $cart) {
        $total = 0;
        foreach ($cart->getItems() as $item) {
            $total += $item["product"]->getPrice() * $item["quantity"];
        }
        return $total;
    }
}
```

4. Using the OOP Approach

Now, we instantiate **objects** and call methods instead of using global functions:

```
$laptop = new Product("laptop", 1000);
$phone = new Product("phone", 500);

$cart = new Cart();
$cart->addProduct($laptop, 1);
$cart->addProduct($phone, 2);

echo "Total: $" . CartService::calculateTotal($cart);
```

Refactoring procedural code into **OOP enhances maintainability, scalability, and reusability**. By introducing **Product, Cart, and CartService** classes, we eliminate **global state dependencies** and **improve code organization**. This structured approach ensures **modularity and easier future enhancements**, such as integrating databases or payment gateways.

Module 14:
Functional and Imperative Programming

PHP supports both **functional and imperative programming paradigms**, allowing developers to choose an approach that best suits their application requirements. **Functional programming** focuses on immutability and function composition, leveraging **closures, higher-order functions, and functional array methods**. Meanwhile, **imperative programming** emphasizes step-by-step execution using loops and conditionals. This module explores the differences between these paradigms, their use cases, and how they impact code readability and maintainability. It concludes with a case study demonstrating when to use functional or imperative approaches in a PHP project.

Understanding Functional Constructs: Closures and Higher-Order Functions

Functional programming in PHP relies on **first-class functions**, meaning functions can be assigned to variables, passed as arguments, and returned from other functions. **Closures (anonymous functions)** allow encapsulating functionality within a variable without requiring a named function, while **higher-order functions** accept functions as arguments, enabling efficient and reusable logic. This approach minimizes side effects by emphasizing **pure functions**, which return the same output given the same input and do not modify external states. Functional programming helps **simplify complex logic**, enhances modularity, and reduces redundancy by enabling function composition and concise expressions.

Applying Functional Array Methods Instead of Traditional Loops

PHP provides built-in **functional array methods** such as array_map(), array_filter(), and array_reduce(), which offer cleaner alternatives to traditional loops like foreach and for. Instead of **explicitly iterating over arrays**, functional array methods operate on data declaratively, improving readability and reducing boilerplate code. These methods facilitate transformations, filtering, and aggregations in a concise manner, particularly when working with collections of data. By replacing loops with functional methods, developers can write **less error-prone and more expressive** code, avoiding unnecessary temporary variables and repetitive logic while improving overall performance in many scenarios.

Writing Clean, Imperative Code for Step-by-Step Execution

While functional programming emphasizes **declarative programming**, imperative programming follows a **step-by-step execution model**, making the code execution flow more explicit. PHP's imperative features include **sequential statements, loops, and conditional structures** such as if, switch, and for loops. This approach is often preferred when direct state manipulation is required, such as managing application state or executing sequential operations with dependencies. Imperative code provides **greater control over execution flow**, making it easier to follow and debug in scenarios that demand **procedural clarity**. However, excessive imperative programming can lead to **verbose and less modular** code, requiring careful structuring for maintainability.

Case Study: Choosing Between Functional and Imperative Styles

This section explores a **real-world PHP scenario** where both functional and imperative programming approaches are applicable. By comparing two implementations of the same task—one using functional constructs and the other using imperative structures—developers can evaluate **readability, maintainability, and performance trade-offs**. The case study highlights the **advantages and disadvantages** of each style and provides guidelines on when to apply functional programming for **concise, reusable logic** versus imperative programming for **clear, step-by-step execution**. By understanding these paradigms, PHP developers can write **more efficient and adaptable** code, leveraging both approaches where appropriate.

Functional and imperative programming each offer distinct advantages in PHP development. **Functional constructs** provide a concise, declarative approach that reduces redundancy, while **imperative programming** offers explicit control over execution. This module equips developers with the **knowledge to choose the right paradigm** for their specific use cases, improving code clarity, maintainability, and efficiency.

Understanding Functional Constructs: Closures and Higher-Order Functions

PHP supports **functional programming constructs**, allowing developers to write modular and reusable code. Two key features of functional programming in PHP are **closures (anonymous functions)** and **higher-order functions**. These features enable **function composition, encapsulation of logic, and immutability**, reducing side effects in application design.

Closures (Anonymous Functions)

A **closure** in PHP is an **anonymous function** that can be assigned to a variable, passed as an argument, or returned from another function. Closures allow for **encapsulation of logic** within a function, making it reusable and modular.

```php
$greet = function($name) {
    return "Hello, $name!";
};

echo $greet("Alice"); // Output: Hello, Alice!
```

Closures can also **capture variables** from their surrounding scope using the use keyword:

```php
$message = "Welcome";
$welcomeUser = function($name) use ($message) {
    return "$message, $name!";
```

137

```
};
echo $welcomeUser("Bob"); // Output: Welcome, Bob!
```

Higher-Order Functions

A **higher-order function** is a function that takes another function as a **parameter** or **returns a function**. This enables **dynamic and reusable** logic, reducing the need for repetitive code.

Example of a **higher-order function** accepting a function as an argument:

```
function applyFunction($callback, $value) {
    return $callback($value);
}

$square = function($num) {
    return $num * $num;
};

echo applyFunction($square, 5); // Output: 25
```

A function returning another function:

```
function multiplier($factor) {
    return function($num) use ($factor) {
        return $num * $factor;
    };
}

$double = multiplier(2);
echo $double(10); // Output: 20
```

Benefits of Functional Constructs in PHP

• **Encapsulation:** Closures keep logic self-contained and modular.

• **Code Reusability:** Higher-order functions reduce redundancy.

• **Immutability:** Functional programming reduces unintended side effects.

• **Readability:** More concise and expressive code.

Using **closures and higher-order functions** allows PHP developers to write more **efficient, scalable, and maintainable** applications by leveraging **functional programming paradigms** within a traditionally imperative language.

Applying Functional Array Methods Instead of Traditional Loops

PHP provides **functional array methods** that allow developers to process arrays in a **concise and declarative** manner, eliminating the need for explicit loops. These methods— such as array_map(), array_filter(), and array_reduce()—enable more readable and maintainable code while promoting **functional programming principles** like immutability and function composition.

Replacing Loops with array_map()

The array_map() function applies a **callback function** to each element in an array, returning a new transformed array. This eliminates the need for a foreach loop.

Using a traditional loop:

```
$numbers = [1, 2, 3, 4, 5];
$squared = [];

foreach ($numbers as $num) {
    $squared[] = $num * $num;
}

print_r($squared);
```

Using array_map() instead:

```
$numbers = [1, 2, 3, 4, 5];
$squared = array_map(fn($num) => $num * $num, $numbers);

print_r($squared);
```

This approach eliminates the need for manually defining and updating an output array.

Filtering Arrays with array_filter()

Instead of iterating over an array with a loop and conditionally adding elements to a new array, array_filter() allows elements that satisfy a condition to be retained.

Using a loop:

```
$numbers = [1, 2, 3, 4, 5, 6];
$evens = [];

foreach ($numbers as $num) {
    if ($num % 2 === 0) {
        $evens[] = $num;
    }
}

print_r($evens);
```

Using array_filter() instead:

```
$numbers = [1, 2, 3, 4, 5, 6];
$evens = array_filter($numbers, fn($num) => $num % 2 === 0);

print_r($evens);
```

This approach **removes the need for explicit iteration** and makes the condition clearer.

Reducing Arrays with array_reduce()

The array_reduce() function processes an array into a **single accumulated value**, which is useful for computing sums, products, or concatenations.

Using a loop to sum an array:

```php
$numbers = [1, 2, 3, 4, 5];
$sum = 0;

foreach ($numbers as $num) {
    $sum += $num;
}

echo $sum;
```

Using array_reduce() instead:

```php
$numbers = [1, 2, 3, 4, 5];
$sum = array_reduce($numbers, fn($carry, $num) => $carry + $num, 0);

echo $sum;
```

Functional array methods make code **more expressive, readable, and modular**, reducing the reliance on explicit loops. By using array_map(), array_filter(), and array_reduce(), developers can **write more declarative PHP code**, improving maintainability and performance.

Writing Clean, Imperative Code for Step-by-Step Execution

Imperative programming in PHP follows a **step-by-step approach**, where the logic is executed in a **sequential manner** using loops, conditionals, and variables to manipulate state. Unlike functional programming, which focuses on expressions and immutability, imperative programming provides more **control over program flow** and is often more intuitive for developers accustomed to procedural coding.

Understanding Imperative Programming in PHP

Imperative code **directly modifies state** by defining a sequence of instructions that must be executed in order. Consider a simple example where we find the sum of numbers in an array.

Imperative approach:

```php
$numbers = [1, 2, 3, 4, 5];
$sum = 0;

for ($i = 0; $i < count($numbers); $i++) {
    $sum += $numbers[$i];
}

echo "Sum: $sum";
```

This code explicitly **iterates** over the array, modifying the $sum variable at each step.

Using Conditionals and Loops

Imperative programming relies heavily on **loops** and **conditional statements** to control execution flow. Here's an example that finds even numbers in an array using an imperative approach:

```
$numbers = [1, 2, 3, 4, 5, 6];
$evens = [];

foreach ($numbers as $num) {
    if ($num % 2 === 0) {
        $evens[] = $num;
    }
}

print_r($evens);
```

This step-by-step execution modifies the $evens array as the loop progresses.

Mutable State in Imperative Programming

Unlike functional programming, which favors **immutable data**, imperative programming often modifies existing variables. Consider reversing an array **in place** using an imperative approach:

```
$numbers = [1, 2, 3, 4, 5];
$length = count($numbers);

for ($i = 0; $i < $length / 2; $i++) {
    $temp = $numbers[$i];
    $numbers[$i] = $numbers[$length - $i - 1];
    $numbers[$length - $i - 1] = $temp;
}

print_r($numbers);
```

This algorithm **swaps** elements in the array, modifying its structure **without creating a new array**, which is a key characteristic of imperative programming.

Comparing Imperative vs. Functional Approaches

To contrast imperative and functional programming, let's look at squaring numbers in an array.

Imperative approach:

```
$numbers = [1, 2, 3, 4, 5];
$squared = [];

foreach ($numbers as $num) {
    $squared[] = $num * $num;
}
```

```
print_r($squared);
```

Functional approach using array_map():

```
$numbers = [1, 2, 3, 4, 5];
$squared = array_map(fn($num) => $num * $num, $numbers);

print_r($squared);
```

The imperative approach **modifies** an array using loops, while the functional approach **transforms** it using expressions.

Imperative programming in PHP is useful for **explicit control over execution**, making it ideal for algorithms requiring **state mutation and step-by-step instructions**. While it can be more verbose than functional programming, it remains a **core paradigm** in PHP development, especially in procedural and object-oriented codebases.

Case Study: Choosing Between Functional and Imperative Styles

When developing in PHP, choosing between **functional and imperative programming** depends on factors such as code readability, maintainability, and efficiency. While **functional programming** emphasizes immutability and declarative expressions, **imperative programming** focuses on step-by-step execution and modifying state. This case study explores when to use each paradigm and provides practical examples.

Scenario: Processing User Data in a Web Application

Assume we have a list of users and need to filter active users, extract their emails, and format them for display. We can solve this problem using both **imperative** and **functional** styles.

Imperative Approach

The imperative solution uses loops and conditionals to **manually iterate** over data and modify variables.

```
$users = [
    ['name' => 'Alice', 'email' => 'alice@example.com', 'active' => true],
    ['name' => 'Bob', 'email' => 'bob@example.com', 'active' => false],
    ['name' => 'Charlie', 'email' => 'charlie@example.com', 'active' => true],
];

$activeEmails = [];

foreach ($users as $user) {
    if ($user['active']) {
        $activeEmails[] = strtoupper($user['email']);
    }
}

print_r($activeEmails);
```

This approach:

- Uses a **foreach loop** to iterate over the array.

- **Modifies** the $activeEmails array inside the loop.

- Uses **conditional statements** to check the user's status.

Functional Approach

The same problem can be solved using **array functions** like array_filter(), array_map(), and array_column(), making the solution **more concise and declarative**.

```
$activeUsers = array_filter($users, fn($user) => $user['active']);
$emails = array_map(fn($user) => strtoupper($user['email']), $activeUsers);

print_r($emails);
```

This approach:

- Uses array_filter() to select **only active users**.

- Applies array_map() to **transform** the emails into uppercase.

- Avoids **explicit loops and mutable state**, making the code more readable.

Comparing Performance and Maintainability

1. **Readability**: The functional approach is more concise but may be harder to understand for those unfamiliar with functional array methods.

2. **Performance**: The imperative approach **modifies state directly**, which can be slightly faster in certain scenarios, while the functional approach may **create additional arrays**, consuming more memory.

3. **Maintainability**: Functional programming **reduces side effects**, making the code easier to maintain and refactor.

Choosing the Right Approach

Factor	Imperative	Functional
Readability	Clear for beginners	More concise but abstract
Performance	Efficient for large datasets	May involve extra processing
Maintainability	Requires explicit management of variables	More modular and reusable

143

If **performance is a priority**, imperative programming might be preferable. However, if **maintainability and conciseness** are key concerns, functional programming is often the better choice.

Both functional and imperative programming styles have their strengths. The best approach depends on the project's **requirements, team familiarity, and codebase complexity**. In modern PHP, functional programming is increasingly favored for **data transformations**, while imperative programming remains essential for algorithms requiring **fine control over execution flow**.

Module 15:
Metaprogramming and Reflective Programming

Metaprogramming allows developers to write code that can modify or generate other code dynamically. This technique enables advanced functionality such as dynamic method invocation, automatic object construction, and runtime class manipulation. PHP provides powerful tools for metaprogramming, including **magic methods**, the **Reflection API**, and **runtime class manipulation**. This module explores these techniques and their practical applications, culminating in a case study where a dynamic plugin system is built.

Utilizing Magic Methods for Dynamic Function Execution

Magic methods in PHP allow objects to handle method calls, property access, and object instantiation dynamically. These special methods, prefixed with __ (double underscore), include __get(), __set(), __call(), and __invoke(), among others. They enable features like **lazy property initialization**, **method overloading**, and **dynamic proxies**.

For example, __call() and __callStatic() handle calls to undefined methods, allowing developers to implement **interceptors** or **delegators**. Similarly, __get() and __set() control access to inaccessible properties, making it possible to create **virtual properties**. These capabilities are widely used in PHP frameworks to provide clean and flexible APIs.

Leveraging PHP's Reflection API for Class Introspection

PHP's Reflection API allows developers to **inspect and manipulate classes, methods, properties, and functions** at runtime. It is particularly useful for **debugging, automated testing, and dependency injection frameworks**. With Reflection, it is possible to analyze class structures, extract metadata, and invoke methods dynamically.

For example, ReflectionClass can be used to examine the methods of an object, check its properties, or dynamically instantiate classes. This is useful when building **automatic form generators, API documentation tools, and dependency injection containers**. The Reflection API also allows modification of method visibility and invocation of private methods, making it a powerful tool for **framework and library development**.

Implementing Runtime Class Manipulation for Dynamic Features

Runtime class manipulation enables developers to **dynamically modify classes, add methods, or create new behaviors** without altering the original class definition. This technique is often

145

used in **ORMs (Object-Relational Mappers)**, **dependency injection containers**, and **plugin architectures**.

Using create_function() (deprecated) or Closure::bind(), developers can dynamically create and bind functions to objects at runtime. PHP 8 introduced **anonymous classes**, which allow defining new class instances on the fly. These techniques are useful for scenarios where class behavior needs to be extended dynamically, such as **middleware-based request handling or event-driven programming**.

Case Study: Creating a Dynamic Plugin System

A **plugin system** allows extending an application's functionality without modifying its core codebase. This case study demonstrates how PHP's metaprogramming capabilities can be used to create a dynamic plugin loader.

By utilizing **autoloading**, **magic methods**, and the **Reflection API**, the system dynamically loads and executes plugins based on configuration files or user input. Plugins can be registered, instantiated, and executed without hardcoding dependencies. This architecture is commonly used in **CMS platforms, e-commerce systems, and modular frameworks**, providing flexibility and scalability.

Metaprogramming in PHP enables **dynamic code execution, class introspection, and runtime manipulation**, making it an essential tool for building **flexible and scalable applications**. Magic methods allow dynamic behavior, the Reflection API provides introspection capabilities, and runtime class manipulation enables powerful design patterns. Mastering these techniques unlocks advanced PHP development capabilities, facilitating the creation of **dynamic and extensible software architectures**.

Utilizing Magic Methods for Dynamic Function Execution

Magic methods in PHP allow developers to implement dynamic behaviors by intercepting method calls, property access, object instantiation, and other operations. These special methods begin with a double underscore (__) and provide powerful ways to manipulate objects at runtime. Commonly used magic methods include __get(), __set(), __call(), and __invoke().

Handling Undefined Method Calls with __call() and __callStatic()

The __call() and __callStatic() methods are triggered when an inaccessible or undefined method is invoked on an object. This is useful for implementing **method overloading**, **delegation**, or **interceptors**.

```
class DynamicMethodHandler {
    public function __call($name, $arguments) {
        return "Method '$name' called with arguments: " . implode(', ',
            $arguments);
    }
```

```
    }
$obj = new DynamicMethodHandler();
echo $obj->someMethod('arg1', 'arg2');
// Output: Method 'someMethod' called with arguments: arg1, arg2
```

Similarly, __callStatic() works for static method calls:

```
class StaticMethodHandler {
    public static function __callStatic($name, $arguments) {
        return "Static method '$name' called.";
    }
}

echo StaticMethodHandler::undefinedMethod();
// Output: Static method 'undefinedMethod' called.
```

Using __get() and __set() for Dynamic Property Handling

The __get() and __set() magic methods allow handling the retrieval and assignment of inaccessible or undefined properties dynamically. This is useful for **lazy-loading properties** or **managing data storage**.

```
class DynamicProperties {
    private $data = [];

    public function __set($name, $value) {
        $this->data[$name] = $value;
    }

    public function __get($name) {
        return $this->data[$name] ?? "Property '$name' does not exist.";
    }
}

$obj = new DynamicProperties();
$obj->username = "JohnDoe";
echo $obj->username; // Output: JohnDoe
```

Using __invoke() to Treat an Object as a Function

The __invoke() method allows an object to be called like a function. This is useful for **creating callable objects**.

```
class CallableObject {
    public function __invoke($message) {
        return "Invoked with message: $message";
    }
}

$obj = new CallableObject();
echo $obj("Hello, PHP!");
// Output: Invoked with message: Hello, PHP!
```

Magic methods provide a **flexible mechanism for dynamic function execution** in PHP. They enable **dynamic method calls, property access, and function-like object invocation**, making them useful for **framework development, API wrappers, and**

147

dynamic data handling. Understanding these methods allows developers to write **cleaner, more adaptable code** for complex applications.

Leveraging PHP's Reflection API for Class Introspection

PHP's Reflection API allows developers to examine and manipulate classes, methods, properties, and functions at runtime. This capability is essential for metaprogramming, enabling **automated documentation, dependency injection, dynamic object creation, and debugging tools**. The Reflection API provides insights into **class structures, visibility, parameter details, and annotations**.

Examining Classes with ReflectionClass

ReflectionClass provides metadata about a class, including its **methods, properties, constants, and parent class**.

```php
class Example {
    private $privateVar;
    public function sampleMethod() {}
}

$reflection = new ReflectionClass('Example');
echo "Class: " . $reflection->getName() . PHP_EOL;
echo "Methods: " . implode(', ', array_map(fn($m) => $m->getName(), $reflection-
        >getMethods())) . PHP_EOL;
```

Output:

```
Class: Example
Methods: sampleMethod
```

This is useful for **inspecting third-party libraries, debugging, and automating object handling**.

Inspecting Methods with ReflectionMethod

ReflectionMethod helps **analyze method visibility, parameters, and return types**.

```php
class Test {
    public function sample($param1, int $param2): string {
        return "Hello";
    }
}

$method = new ReflectionMethod('Test', 'sample');
echo "Method: " . $method->getName() . PHP_EOL;
echo "Return Type: " . $method->getReturnType() . PHP_EOL;

$params = $method->getParameters();
foreach ($params as $param) {
    echo "Param: " . $param->getName() . " Type: " . ($param->getType() ?:
            'N/A') . PHP_EOL;
}
```

Output:

```
Method: sample
Return Type: string
Param: param1 Type: N/A
Param: param2 Type: int
```

Dynamically Invoking Methods with Reflection

Reflection enables calling **methods dynamically, even private ones**, by changing their visibility.

```php
class Hidden {
    private function secret() {
        return "Hidden message";
    }
}

$obj = new Hidden();
$method = new ReflectionMethod('Hidden', 'secret');
$method->setAccessible(true);
echo $method->invoke($obj); // Output: Hidden message
```

This technique is useful for **unit testing, debugging, and extending locked-down classes**.

Analyzing and Modifying Properties

ReflectionProperty provides access to **private, protected, and public properties**.

```php
class Example {
    private $hiddenValue = "Secret";
}

$property = new ReflectionProperty('Example', 'hiddenValue');
$property->setAccessible(true);

$obj = new Example();
echo $property->getValue($obj); // Output: Secret
```

The Reflection API is a **powerful tool for runtime class introspection**. It allows **dynamic analysis and manipulation of classes, methods, and properties**, making it essential for **framework development, dependency injection, and debugging utilities**. By leveraging reflection, PHP developers can create more **flexible, extensible, and automated systems**.

Implementing Runtime Class Manipulation for Dynamic Features

Runtime class manipulation in PHP enables developers to dynamically modify **classes, methods, and properties** at execution time. This approach is commonly used in **plugin systems, dependency injection, proxy objects, and testing frameworks**. PHP provides multiple techniques for runtime class manipulation, including **anonymous classes, dynamic method creation, and reflection-based property modification**.

Using Anonymous Classes for Runtime Object Manipulation

Anonymous classes allow on-the-fly class creation **without predefining a class in a separate file**. They are useful for **creating lightweight objects, implementing mock objects for testing, and modifying behaviors dynamically**.

```
interface Logger {
    public function log($message);
}

$logger = new class implements Logger {
    public function log($message) {
        echo "Logging: " . $message;
    }
};

$logger->log("This is a runtime class.");
```

Output:

```
Logging: This is a runtime class.
```

By using anonymous classes, developers can **extend classes and implement interfaces dynamically** without bloating the codebase.

Dynamically Adding Methods to Objects

PHP does not support adding methods to an instance dynamically, but it can be achieved using **closures and the __call() magic method**.

```
class DynamicObject {
    private $methods = [];

    public function addMethod($name, $callback) {
        $this->methods[$name] = $callback;
    }

    public function __call($name, $arguments) {
        if (isset($this->methods[$name])) {
            return call_user_func_array($this->methods[$name], $arguments);
        }
        throw new Exception("Method $name not found.");
    }
}

$obj = new DynamicObject();
$obj->addMethod("greet", function ($name) {
    return "Hello, $name!";
});

echo $obj->greet("John"); // Output: Hello, John!
```

This technique is useful for **extending objects at runtime, adding plugin-like features, or mocking objects in testing**.

Modifying Class Properties at Runtime

Reflection can be used to modify properties dynamically, even if they are **private**.

150

```
class Config {
    private $settings = "Default";
}

$config = new Config();
$reflection = new ReflectionProperty('Config', 'settings');
$reflection->setAccessible(true);
$reflection->setValue($config, "Modified at Runtime");

echo $reflection->getValue($config); // Output: Modified at Runtime
```

This method is useful for **testing, debugging, and modifying inaccessible properties in legacy code**.

Using eval() for Runtime Code Execution (With Caution!)

PHP's eval() function allows executing PHP code stored in a string, enabling **dynamic function creation**. However, **it should be used cautiously due to security risks**.

```
$code = 'function dynamicFunction() { return "Generated at runtime"; }';
eval($code);

echo dynamicFunction(); // Output: Generated at runtime
```

Instead of eval(), **anonymous functions, closures, and reflection** should be preferred for safer runtime manipulation.

Runtime class manipulation allows PHP developers to create **highly flexible and adaptive applications**. Techniques like **anonymous classes, dynamic method injection, and property modification** are useful in **plugin-based systems, dependency injection, and testing frameworks**. However, developers should balance **flexibility with security** to avoid vulnerabilities associated with runtime modifications.

Case Study: Creating a Dynamic Plugin System

A dynamic plugin system allows developers to **extend applications without modifying the core codebase**. By leveraging **autoloading, reflection, and runtime class manipulation**, PHP applications can **dynamically load and execute plugins**. This approach is widely used in **content management systems (CMS), e-commerce platforms, and frameworks** like WordPress, Magento, and Laravel.

Designing the Plugin Architecture

A well-structured plugin system requires:

1. **A defined interface** that plugins must implement.

2. **A plugin loader** to dynamically detect and load plugins.

3. **An event or hook system** to trigger plugin execution.

151

Step 1: Defining a Plugin Interface

Every plugin should follow a common interface to ensure **consistent behavior**.

```
interface PluginInterface {
    public function execute();
}
```

This interface enforces that all plugins implement the execute() method, ensuring compatibility with the plugin loader.

Step 2: Creating Sample Plugins

Each plugin **implements the interface** and defines its behavior.

```
class HelloPlugin implements PluginInterface {
    public function execute() {
        return "Hello from the plugin!";
    }
}

class DatePlugin implements PluginInterface {
    public function execute() {
        return "Today's date is: " . date('Y-m-d');
    }
}
```

These plugins provide different functionalities, such as **greeting messages** or **date display**.

Step 3: Implementing the Plugin Loader

The loader dynamically **detects and loads available plugins** from a directory.

```
class PluginLoader {
    private $plugins = [];

    public function loadPlugins($directory) {
        foreach (glob($directory . "/*.php") as $file) {
            require_once $file;
            $class = basename($file, ".php");
            if (class_exists($class) && in_array('PluginInterface',
        class_implements($class))) {
                $this->plugins[] = new $class();
            }
        }
    }

    public function executePlugins() {
        foreach ($this->plugins as $plugin) {
            echo $plugin->execute() . PHP_EOL;
        }
    }
}
```

- The loadPlugins() method scans a **plugin directory**, loads classes dynamically, and checks if they implement PluginInterface.

- The executePlugins() method **runs all loaded plugins**.

Step 4: Running the Plugin System

Now, let's initialize and execute the plugin system.

```
$loader = new PluginLoader();
$loader->loadPlugins("plugins"); // Assuming plugins are stored in a "plugins"
        directory
$loader->executePlugins();
```

If the plugins/ directory contains HelloPlugin.php and DatePlugin.php, the output might be:

```
Hello from the plugin!
Today's date is: 2025-03-17
```

Enhancing the Plugin System

To improve the system, additional features can be added:

- **Event-driven execution** – Plugins respond to specific application events.

- **Database-driven plugins** – Plugin configurations are stored in a database.

- **Security measures** – Restrict execution to **approved** plugins only.

A dynamic plugin system allows PHP applications to be **extensible and modular**. By using **interfaces, reflection, and autoloading**, developers can create **scalable and maintainable** plugin architectures. This approach is valuable for **CMS platforms, e-commerce systems, and SaaS applications**, enabling **third-party integrations without modifying the core system**.

Module 16:
Structured and Security-Oriented Programming

Modern PHP applications require a balance between **structured programming principles** and **robust security measures** to ensure code maintainability and prevent vulnerabilities. This module explores how structured programming improves code organization, discusses security best practices, and examines PHP security tools. The case study demonstrates a **secure user authentication system**, applying principles learned throughout the module.

Applying Structured Programming Principles in PHP

Structured programming is a **fundamental programming paradigm** that enhances readability, maintainability, and debugging efficiency. It encourages **modular code design**, avoiding **spaghetti code** by enforcing logical structures such as **sequences, selections, and loops**.

Key structured programming principles in PHP include:

- **Encapsulation** – Grouping related logic into functions or classes.

- **Modularity** – Breaking code into reusable components.

- **Code clarity** – Using meaningful variable and function names.

- **Avoiding deep nesting** – Simplifying logic to improve readability.

By adhering to structured programming practices, PHP developers can create **scalable, maintainable, and efficient** applications. This approach is essential for large-scale projects where multiple developers contribute to the same codebase.

Implementing Secure Coding Practices and Preventing Vulnerabilities

Security is a **critical aspect** of PHP programming. Common vulnerabilities include **SQL injection, cross-site scripting (XSS), and cross-site request forgery (CSRF)**. Secure coding practices help mitigate these threats and ensure application integrity.

Key secure coding practices include:

- **Input validation** – Sanitize and validate all user inputs before processing.

- **Parameterized queries** – Use prepared statements to prevent SQL injection.

154

- **Output escaping** – Sanitize output to prevent XSS attacks.

- **CSRF protection** – Use anti-CSRF tokens to secure user sessions.

- **Session security** – Implement secure session management to prevent session hijacking.

By integrating these security measures, PHP developers can significantly **reduce attack surfaces** and enhance the **reliability and trustworthiness** of their applications.

Using PHP Security Tools for Authentication and Encryption

Authentication and encryption are **essential security mechanisms** in modern PHP applications. Authentication ensures that only **authorized users** access the system, while encryption protects **sensitive data** from unauthorized access.

PHP offers several security tools and libraries:

- **password_hash() and password_verify()** – Secure password storage and verification.

- **OpenSSL** – Encrypts and decrypts sensitive data.

- **JWT (JSON Web Tokens)** – Provides secure authentication and API authorization.

- **PHP security frameworks** – Laravel and Symfony offer built-in authentication and encryption features.

By leveraging these tools, developers can **protect user credentials, encrypt sensitive information, and establish secure authentication mechanisms** for PHP applications.

Case Study: Developing a Secure User Authentication System

A secure authentication system is a **core component** of web applications. This case study walks through building a **user login and registration system** using **secure password hashing, token-based authentication, and session management**.

Key implementation steps include:

1. **User registration** – Securely storing passwords using password hashing.

2. **User login** – Verifying passwords using secure authentication mechanisms.

3. **Session management** – Protecting against session hijacking and fixation.

4. **Access control** – Restricting access to authenticated users.

This case study demonstrates how to **apply structured programming and security best practices** to develop a **robust and secure authentication system** in PHP.

Structured and security-oriented programming ensures that PHP applications are **efficient, maintainable, and protected against vulnerabilities**. By following structured programming principles and implementing **secure coding practices**, developers can create **reliable and scalable** applications. The **case study** reinforces these concepts by demonstrating **real-world authentication system development**, ensuring **secure user interactions and data protection**.

Applying Structured Programming Principles in PHP

Structured programming is a programming paradigm that enhances **code readability, maintainability, and debugging efficiency**. It focuses on breaking complex logic into smaller, well-organized modules. PHP, being a flexible language, allows both structured and unstructured code, but adhering to structured programming principles results in **more efficient and scalable applications**.

Core Principles of Structured Programming

1. **Sequence** – Code executes in a defined, logical order.

2. **Selection (Decision-Making)** – Using control structures like if, switch to guide execution.

3. **Iteration (Loops)** – Using for, while, and foreach loops for repetitive tasks.

4. **Modularity** – Breaking code into functions or classes for better organization.

Encapsulation and Modularity in PHP

Encapsulation and modularity help manage **complex applications** by organizing code into reusable functions and classes. Instead of writing redundant logic, developers can define **reusable functions** or **class methods** to improve code clarity.

```php
function calculateArea($length, $width) {
    return $length * $width;
}
echo "Area: " . calculateArea(5, 10);
```

This function follows **structured programming principles** by encapsulating logic in a reusable block, making the code **clear and maintainable**.

Avoiding Deep Nesting

Deeply nested code is difficult to read and maintain. Instead, **early returns** or **guard clauses** should be used.

156

Bad Practice (Deep Nesting):

```
function checkAge($age) {
    if ($age >= 18) {
        echo "You are eligible.";
    } else {
        echo "You are not eligible.";
    }
}
```

Better Approach (Guard Clause):

```
function checkAge($age) {
    if ($age < 18) {
        return "You are not eligible.";
    }
    return "You are eligible.";
}
```

This approach improves **readability and maintainability**, aligning with structured programming principles.

Using Meaningful Variable and Function Names

Readable code uses **descriptive names** rather than generic ones:

```
// Bad practice
$a = 10;
$b = 20;
$c = $a + $b;

// Good practice
$price = 10;
$tax = 20;
$totalCost = $price + $tax;
```

Well-named variables and functions make code **self-documenting**, reducing the need for excessive comments.

Structured programming in PHP improves **code quality, maintainability, and reusability**. By **organizing logic**, avoiding **deep nesting**, and using **meaningful identifiers**, PHP developers can create efficient and scalable applications. Applying these principles ensures that **large codebases remain manageable** while enhancing **readability and debugging efficiency**.

Implementing Secure Coding Practices and Preventing Vulnerabilities

Security is a crucial aspect of PHP development. Poor coding practices can introduce vulnerabilities such as **SQL injection, cross-site scripting (XSS), cross-site request forgery (CSRF), and remote code execution**. Implementing secure coding practices helps prevent attacks, ensuring that web applications are resilient against threats.

Input Validation and Data Sanitization

User inputs should never be trusted. Validation ensures that inputs meet expected formats, while sanitization removes potentially harmful data.

Example of Input Validation:

```php
function validateEmail($email) {
    return filter_var($email, FILTER_VALIDATE_EMAIL);
}

$email = "user@example.com";
if (validateEmail($email)) {
    echo "Valid email";
} else {
    echo "Invalid email";
}
```

This function ensures only valid emails are processed, reducing security risks.

Preventing SQL Injection

SQL injection occurs when user inputs manipulate database queries. Using **prepared statements with parameterized queries** prevents such attacks.

Vulnerable Code (SQL Injection Risk):

```php
$userInput = $_GET['username'];
$query = "SELECT * FROM users WHERE username = '$userInput'"; // Unsafe!
$result = mysqli_query($conn, $query);
```

Secure Approach with Prepared Statements:

```php
$stmt = $conn->prepare("SELECT * FROM users WHERE username = ?");
$stmt->bind_param("s", $userInput);
$stmt->execute();
```

This prevents attackers from injecting malicious SQL code.

Cross-Site Scripting (XSS) Prevention

XSS attacks occur when unescaped data is displayed in the browser, allowing execution of malicious scripts. Use htmlspecialchars() or strip_tags() to escape output.

```php
$userInput = "<script>alert('Hacked!');</script>";
echo htmlspecialchars($userInput, ENT_QUOTES, 'UTF-8'); // Safe output
```

This ensures that malicious scripts are not executed.

Cross-Site Request Forgery (CSRF) Protection

CSRF attacks trick authenticated users into performing unintended actions. Generating and validating CSRF tokens prevent such attacks.

```php
session_start();
```

```
$csrfToken = bin2hex(random_bytes(32));
$_SESSION['csrf_token'] = $csrfToken;
```

The token should be verified before processing sensitive requests.

Secure File Uploads

Uploading files without proper validation can lead to remote code execution. Always check file types and store uploads securely.

```
$allowedTypes = ['image/jpeg', 'image/png'];
if (in_array($_FILES['file']['type'], $allowedTypes)) {
    move_uploaded_file($_FILES['file']['tmp_name'], "uploads/" .
            $_FILES['file']['name']);
}
```

Secure coding in PHP prevents common vulnerabilities and strengthens application security. By implementing **input validation, prepared statements, XSS protection, CSRF tokens, and secure file handling**, developers can build robust, attack-resistant applications. Security should always be a top priority in PHP development.

Using PHP Security Tools for Authentication and Encryption

Authentication and encryption are fundamental to securing PHP applications. Authentication ensures that users are who they claim to be, while encryption protects sensitive data from unauthorized access. PHP offers various security tools and libraries for implementing **secure authentication, password hashing, and data encryption**.

Implementing Secure User Authentication

User authentication requires a robust **login and session management** system. Instead of storing plain-text passwords, PHP provides the password_hash() and password_verify() functions for secure password management.

Secure User Registration (Password Hashing):

```
$password = "securepassword";
$hashedPassword = password_hash($password, PASSWORD_BCRYPT);
echo $hashedPassword; // Securely hashed password
```

Verifying the Password During Login:

```
$inputPassword = "securepassword"; // User input
if (password_verify($inputPassword, $hashedPassword)) {
    echo "Password is correct";
} else {
    echo "Invalid credentials";
}
```

Using **bcrypt** ensures that passwords are stored securely, preventing **rainbow table attacks**.

Session Security Best Practices

PHP sessions store user authentication details, making them a critical attack target. **Session hijacking** occurs when an attacker steals a session ID. To mitigate this:

1. **Regenerate session IDs after login:**

```php
session_start();
session_regenerate_id(true); // Prevents session fixation attacks
```

2. **Restrict session cookies to HTTP-only and Secure mode:**

```php
session_set_cookie_params([
    'httponly' => true,
    'secure' => true,
    'samesite' => 'Strict'
]);
```

Encrypting Sensitive Data with OpenSSL

PHP's OpenSSL extension allows **data encryption and decryption** for protecting sensitive user information.

Example of Encrypting Data:

```php
$key = openssl_random_pseudo_bytes(32);
$iv = openssl_random_pseudo_bytes(16);
$data = "Sensitive Information";
$encrypted = openssl_encrypt($data, 'AES-256-CBC', $key, 0, $iv);
```

Decrypting Data:

```php
$decrypted = openssl_decrypt($encrypted, 'AES-256-CBC', $key, 0, $iv);
echo $decrypted; // Outputs: Sensitive Information
```

AES-256 encryption ensures that sensitive data remains secure even if intercepted.

Using JWT for Secure API Authentication

JSON Web Tokens (JWT) allow stateless authentication for APIs. Popular PHP libraries like **Firebase JWT** (firebase/php-jwt) help generate secure JWT tokens.

Generating a JWT Token:

```php
use Firebase\JWT\JWT;
$payload = ["user_id" => 1, "exp" => time() + 3600]; // Token expires in 1 hour
$jwt = JWT::encode($payload, "secretkey", "HS256");
```

Verifying JWT on API Requests:

```php
$decoded = JWT::decode($jwt, new Key("secretkey", "HS256"));
echo $decoded->user_id; // Extract user data
```

JWT-based authentication eliminates the need for sessions in API-based applications.

PHP provides robust tools for **authentication and encryption**, ensuring that applications remain secure against attacks. **Password hashing, secure session handling, OpenSSL encryption, and JWT-based authentication** protect user data and prevent security breaches. Developers should **regularly update security practices** to safeguard PHP applications against evolving threats.

Case Study: Developing a Secure User Authentication System

Building a **secure user authentication system** in PHP requires careful implementation of **secure password handling, session management, and protection against common vulnerabilities**. This case study demonstrates a **best-practice approach** for implementing **user registration, login, and session management**, ensuring data security and preventing common attacks.

1. Secure User Registration

When a user registers, their **password must be securely hashed** before storing it in the database. Using **bcrypt hashing** ensures that even if the database is compromised, passwords remain protected.

Steps for Secure User Registration:

1. **Validate user input** (avoid SQL injection and XSS).

2. **Hash the password** before storing it.

3. **Use prepared statements** to prevent SQL injection.

Example Code:

```
$conn = new PDO("mysql:host=localhost;dbname=secure_app", "user", "password");

if ($_SERVER["REQUEST_METHOD"] == "POST") {
    $email = filter_var($_POST["email"], FILTER_SANITIZE_EMAIL);
    $password = password_hash($_POST["password"], PASSWORD_BCRYPT);

    $stmt = $conn->prepare("INSERT INTO users (email, password) VALUES (:email,
        :password)");
    $stmt->bindParam(":email", $email);
    $stmt->bindParam(":password", $password);
    $stmt->execute();

    echo "User registered successfully!";
}
```

This approach ensures that user passwords are **never stored in plaintext** and that the database query is protected from **SQL injection**.

2. Secure User Login and Session Handling

After registration, users must log in securely. The system should **verify the hashed password**, and securely manage sessions to prevent session hijacking and fixation attacks.

Example Login Script:

```
session_start();
$conn = new PDO("mysql:host=localhost;dbname=secure_app", "user", "password");

if ($_SERVER["REQUEST_METHOD"] == "POST") {
    $email = filter_var($_POST["email"], FILTER_SANITIZE_EMAIL);
    $stmt = $conn->prepare("SELECT id, password FROM users WHERE email =
            :email");
    $stmt->bindParam(":email", $email);
    $stmt->execute();
    $user = $stmt->fetch(PDO::FETCH_ASSOC);

    if ($user && password_verify($_POST["password"], $user["password"])) {
        session_regenerate_id(true); // Prevent session fixation
        $_SESSION["user_id"] = $user["id"];
        echo "Login successful!";
    } else {
        echo "Invalid credentials.";
    }
}
```

This method ensures that **only hashed passwords are verified** and that **session security** is maintained.

3. Implementing Secure Session Management

Sessions should be **protected against hijacking and fixation attacks** using security best practices.

Steps to Secure Sessions:

- **Regenerate session IDs on login:** Prevents session fixation.

- **Restrict session cookies:** Prevents JavaScript access and enforces HTTPS.

- **Set a session timeout:** Logs out inactive users.

Secure Session Configuration:

```
session_set_cookie_params([
    "httponly" => true,
    "secure" => true,
    "samesite" => "Strict"
]);

session_start();
```

This configuration ensures that **session cookies** cannot be accessed via JavaScript (preventing **XSS attacks**) and that they are only sent over **secure HTTPS connections**.

4. Two-Factor Authentication (2FA) for Enhanced Security

To add an **extra layer of security**, developers can implement **Two-Factor Authentication (2FA)** using **Google Authenticator** or **email-based OTPs**.

Generating a 2FA Code:

```php
$code = rand(100000, 999999);
$_SESSION["2fa_code"] = $code;

// Send the code via email (use a mailer library like PHPMailer)
echo "Enter the code sent to your email.";
```

Verifying the 2FA Code:

```php
if ($_POST["code"] == $_SESSION["2fa_code"]) {
    echo "2FA verified! Access granted.";
} else {
    echo "Invalid 2FA code.";
}
```

This adds an additional security step, ensuring that even if a password is compromised, attackers cannot access the account without the **one-time code**.

This case study demonstrates how to build a **secure user authentication system** using **password hashing, session security, and Two-Factor Authentication**. By following these best practices, developers can **mitigate common security threats** such as **SQL injection, session hijacking, and password breaches**, ensuring a **secure PHP application**.

Module 17:
Imperative and Procedural Programming Best Practices

Imperative and procedural programming are foundational paradigms in PHP development. This module explores best practices for writing **clear control flow statements, organizing procedural code, and creating reusable functions**. These techniques ensure code maintainability, scalability, and efficiency, particularly in large-scale PHP projects. The module concludes with a **case study on developing a command-line PHP tool**, demonstrating these principles in action.

Writing Clear and Explicit Control Flow Statements

Control flow structures are essential for guiding the execution of PHP programs. Imperative programming relies on explicit control flow, making code easier to understand. **Best practices** include **avoiding deeply nested structures**, using **early returns**, and applying **switch-case statements** effectively.

Conditional statements (if, else, switch) should be structured to enhance readability. Using **guard clauses** to exit functions early prevents unnecessary indentation and improves maintainability. **Loops** (for, while, foreach) should be optimized by minimizing redundant calculations within iterations.

Maintaining **consistent formatting**, such as **proper indentation and clear naming conventions**, ensures that procedural code remains readable and manageable. Using **Boolean flags sparingly** prevents confusion in complex conditionals.

Organizing Procedural Code for Better Maintainability

Maintaining well-structured procedural code is crucial for **scalability** and **collaborative development**. A key practice is **separating concerns**—dividing code into logical sections such as **input handling, processing, and output generation**.

Using **include and require statements** to separate reusable logic into external files helps keep scripts organized. Grouping related functions into files based on functionality prevents monolithic, hard-to-maintain scripts. Establishing a **naming convention** for functions and variables enhances readability.

Error handling is another crucial aspect of maintainability. Implementing **consistent error reporting** using try-catch blocks and error_log() ensures that issues are logged properly for debugging. Writing **self-documenting code**—using meaningful function and variable names—reduces reliance on excessive inline comments.

Creating Modular and Reusable Functions for Large-Scale Projects

Large-scale projects benefit significantly from **modular function design**. Instead of repeating code, procedural functions should be **reusable, parameterized, and single-responsibility-oriented**. Each function should perform **one well-defined task**, adhering to the **Single Responsibility Principle (SRP)**.

Using **default parameter values** increases function flexibility, while **strict type declarations** ensure predictable behavior. Returning values instead of modifying global variables improves testability and reusability. **Passing dependencies as arguments** instead of relying on hardcoded values makes functions more adaptable.

Encapsulating commonly used logic, such as **database queries, file handling, or data validation**, into reusable functions streamlines development and reduces redundancy. Organizing functions into **utility files** (helpers.php) further enhances maintainability.

Case Study: Developing a Command-Line PHP Tool

The principles of procedural programming are particularly useful for building **command-line PHP applications**. This case study focuses on developing a **simple, modular command-line tool** that processes user input, executes predefined operations, and returns formatted output.

By applying **clear control flow, organized procedural structure, and reusable functions**, this tool demonstrates **imperative programming best practices**. The case study emphasizes **error handling, input validation, and output formatting**, ensuring that the tool remains **efficient, maintainable, and user-friendly**.

This module provides a structured approach to writing **maintainable procedural PHP code**. By focusing on **explicit control flow, modular design, and reusable functions**, developers can build **scalable, efficient applications**. The final case study reinforces these concepts by applying best practices to a **real-world command-line PHP tool**, highlighting the benefits of procedural programming in PHP.

Writing Clear and Explicit Control Flow Statements

Control flow statements dictate how PHP programs execute, making them essential for writing structured procedural code. **Best practices** in control flow improve readability, reduce complexity, and enhance maintainability. PHP provides several control structures, including **conditional statements (if-else, switch)** and **loops (for, while, foreach)**. Writing clean, explicit control flow ensures that code remains easy to debug and extend.

Using if-else for Readable Conditions

The if-else statement should be structured clearly to avoid excessive nesting. A **guard clause** helps eliminate unnecessary indentation by returning early when a condition is met:

```php
function checkUserAge($age) {
    if ($age < 18) {
        return "Access denied: You must be 18 or older.";
    }
    return "Access granted!";
}

echo checkUserAge(16); // Outputs: Access denied
```

Here, the **early return prevents deep nesting**, improving clarity.

Optimizing switch Statements

switch is useful for handling multiple conditions efficiently. Instead of multiple if-else blocks, a switch simplifies logic:

```php
function getUserRole($role) {
    switch ($role) {
        case 'admin':
            return "Admin access granted.";
        case 'editor':
            return "Editor access granted.";
        case 'subscriber':
            return "Subscriber access granted.";
        default:
            return "No valid role assigned.";
    }
}

echo getUserRole('editor'); // Outputs: Editor access granted.
```

Using a **default case ensures completeness**, preventing unexpected results.

Enhancing Loops for Efficiency

Loops control repetitive tasks, but inefficient use can lead to performance issues. **Avoid redundant calculations inside loops:**

```php
$numbers = [1, 2, 3, 4, 5];
$length = count($numbers); // Avoid calculating inside the loop

for ($i = 0; $i < $length; $i++) {
    echo $numbers[$i] . " ";
}
```

By **precomputing the array length before the loop**, performance improves, especially with large datasets.

Using foreach for Readable Iteration

foreach is the most readable way to loop through arrays:

```php
$users = ["Alice", "Bob", "Charlie"];
```

```php
foreach ($users as $user) {
    echo "Welcome, $user!\n";
}
```

This approach eliminates the need for manual index tracking, making code **cleaner and easier to maintain**.

Writing **clear and explicit control flow statements** in PHP prevents logical errors and enhances maintainability. Using **guard clauses, structured conditionals, and optimized loops** ensures that programs execute efficiently. Well-structured control flow improves **readability, performance, and debugging**, making it an essential practice in procedural PHP development.

Organizing Procedural Code for Better Maintainability

Maintaining procedural PHP code effectively requires **structured organization, modularization, and readability**. Without proper structure, procedural scripts can become **hard to debug, extend, or reuse**. By organizing code into logical sections, following consistent naming conventions, and separating concerns, developers can write scalable procedural applications.

Using a Modular Approach

A common pitfall in procedural programming is writing large, monolithic scripts. Instead, breaking code into **smaller, reusable functions** improves maintainability:

```php
function getUserData($userId) {
    // Simulate fetching user data
    return [
        "id" => $userId,
        "name" => "John Doe",
        "email" => "john@example.com"
    ];
}

function displayUser($userData) {
    echo "User: " . $userData['name'] . " - Email: " . $userData['email'];
}

// Calling the functions
$user = getUserData(1);
displayUser($user);
```

By **separating logic into functions**, we **improve reusability and readability**.

Grouping Code into Logical Sections

Using **separate files** for different functionalities enhances structure. Consider a directory layout:

```
/project
├── includes/
│   ├── database.php
```

```
│    ├── functions.php
├── public/
│    ├── index.php
└── config.php
```

By separating concerns, **index.php** focuses on output, while **functions.php** contains reusable logic.

Following a Consistent Naming Convention

Consistent naming ensures clarity. Functions should follow **verb-noun patterns**:

- ✓ getUserProfile(), sendEmailNotification()

- ✗ profileGet(), mailSend()

Descriptive function names make code self-explanatory.

Using Configuration Files

Instead of hardcoding values, store settings in a **config file**:

```
define("DB_HOST", "localhost");
define("DB_USER", "root");
define("DB_PASS", "password");
define("DB_NAME", "my_database");
```

This approach centralizes settings, making updates easier.

Organizing procedural PHP code **improves readability, reusability, and maintainability**. By structuring code into **modular functions, using clear naming conventions, and separating concerns**, developers can create **scalable** and **manageable** applications.

Creating Modular and Reusable Functions for Large-Scale Projects

In large-scale PHP projects, writing modular and reusable functions enhances **maintainability, scalability, and code reusability**. Modularization helps prevent code duplication and makes it easier to debug and extend functionalities. By following best practices, procedural PHP can remain **structured and efficient** while handling complex business logic.

Breaking Down Complex Logic into Smaller Functions

Instead of writing **one long script**, breaking down logic into **small, single-purpose functions** makes the code cleaner and easier to understand.

✓ **Example of Modular Functions:**

168

```php
function sanitizeInput($input) {
    return htmlspecialchars(trim($input), ENT_QUOTES, 'UTF-8');
}

function validateEmail($email) {
    return filter_var($email, FILTER_VALIDATE_EMAIL) !== false;
}

function getUserByEmail($email, $pdo) {
    $stmt = $pdo->prepare("SELECT * FROM users WHERE email = ?");
    $stmt->execute([$email]);
    return $stmt->fetch(PDO::FETCH_ASSOC);
}
```

Each function handles a **specific task**, making it reusable across different parts of the project.

Using Function Libraries for Better Organization

Instead of defining functions in a single script, store them in a **dedicated file** (e.g., functions.php). This allows multiple scripts to reuse them.

📁 Project Structure Example:

```
/project
   ├── includes/
   │     ├── functions.php
   │     ├── database.php
   ├── public/
   │     ├── index.php
   └── config.php
```

📌 Reusing Functions from functions.php

```php
require_once "../includes/functions.php";
require_once "../includes/database.php";

$email = sanitizeInput($_POST['email']);

if (validateEmail($email)) {
    $user = getUserByEmail($email, $pdo);
    echo $user ? "User found: " . $user['name'] : "User not found.";
} else {
    echo "Invalid email format.";
}
```

This approach makes functions **centralized and reusable**, reducing code repetition.

Ensuring Function Reusability Across Multiple Files

For large-scale applications, defining **utility functions** and making them **universally accessible** enhances efficiency.

✅ Example: Creating a Utility Function File (utils.php)

```php
function generateUniqueID($length = 10) {
```

```php
    return substr(str_shuffle("0123456789abcdefghijklmnopqrstuvwxyz"), 0,
        $length);
}
```

📌 Using it in multiple scripts:

```php
require_once "utils.php";

$orderID = generateUniqueID(12);
echo "Generated Order ID: " . $orderID;
```

This function can be reused in **any part of the application** without duplication.

By breaking down complex logic into **small, reusable functions**, structuring code into **separate libraries**, and making functions easily accessible, large-scale PHP projects become **easier to manage and extend**. Writing modular functions **reduces redundancy** and ensures **clean, maintainable code** in procedural PHP applications.

Case Study: Developing a Command-Line PHP Tool

Command-line PHP applications are useful for **automation, data processing, and administrative tasks**. Unlike web applications, command-line scripts operate without a web server and are executed via the terminal. In this case study, we will develop a **CLI-based user management tool** in PHP that allows adding, listing, and deleting users from a file-based storage system.

Project Overview and Setup

Our PHP CLI tool will:
✅ Accept **commands and arguments** from the terminal.
✅ Store user data in a **JSON file** for persistence.
✅ Support functions like **adding, listing, and deleting users**.

Project Structure:

```
/cli-user-manager
    ├── users.json
    ├── user_manager.php
```

✅ Basic Setup of the PHP CLI Tool (user_manager.php)

```php
#!/usr/bin/php
<?php

if (php_sapi_name() !== "cli") {
    exit("This script must be run from the command line.\n");
}

echo "PHP CLI User Manager\n";
```

170

This ensures the script runs only in a **CLI environment**, preventing execution via a browser.

Accepting Command-Line Arguments

Command-line arguments are accessed using $argv, where $argv[0] is the script name and $argv[1] is the first parameter.

✅ Parsing Arguments in PHP:

```php
if ($argc < 2) {
    exit("Usage: php user_manager.php [add|list|delete] [arguments]\n");
}

$command = $argv[1];
```

Now, running php user_manager.php add John john@example.com passes add as $argv[1], John as $argv[2], and john@example.com as $argv[3].

Storing and Managing Users in a JSON File

✅ Function to Load and Save Users (users.json)

```php
function loadUsers() {
    return file_exists("users.json") ?
            json_decode(file_get_contents("users.json"), true) : [];
}

function saveUsers($users) {
    file_put_contents("users.json", json_encode($users, JSON_PRETTY_PRINT));
}
```

Adding a User to the System

✅ Defining the addUser Function:

```php
function addUser($name, $email) {
    $users = loadUsers();

    foreach ($users as $user) {
        if ($user['email'] === $email) {
            exit("Error: User with email $email already exists.\n");
        }
    }

    $users[] = ['name' => $name, 'email' => $email];
    saveUsers($users);
    echo "User $name added successfully.\n";
}
```

📌 Running the Script:

```php
php user_manager.php add John john@example.com
```

Listing Users

171

✅ Function to Display All Users:

```php
function listUsers() {
    $users = loadUsers();

    if (empty($users)) {
        exit("No users found.\n");
    }

    foreach ($users as $user) {
        echo "Name: {$user['name']}, Email: {$user['email']}\n";
    }
}
```

📌 Run:

```
php user_manager.php list
```

Deleting a User by Email

✅ Function to Delete a User:

```php
function deleteUser($email) {
    $users = loadUsers();
    $filteredUsers = array_filter($users, fn($user) => $user['email'] !==
            $email);

    if (count($filteredUsers) === count($users)) {
        exit("Error: User with email $email not found.\n");
    }

    saveUsers($filteredUsers);
    echo "User with email $email deleted successfully.\n";
}
```

📌 Run:

```
php user_manager.php delete john@example.com
```

Executing the Commands in the Main Script

```php
switch ($command) {
    case 'add':
        if ($argc < 4) exit("Usage: php user_manager.php add <name> <email>\n");
        addUser($argv[2], $argv[3]);
        break;

    case 'list':
        listUsers();
        break;

    case 'delete':
        if ($argc < 3) exit("Usage: php user_manager.php delete <email>\n");
        deleteUser($argv[2]);
        break;

    default:
        echo "Invalid command.\n";
}
```

This case study demonstrates how **procedural PHP** can be used to build a **functional CLI tool**. By structuring functions effectively and utilizing JSON for storage, we created a **simple yet practical** user management system. This approach can be extended to **database interactions, automation scripts, and more complex command-line applications** in PHP.

Module 18:

Service-Oriented and Reflective API Development

APIs are the backbone of modern applications, enabling seamless communication between different software systems. PHP, being a versatile language, supports both RESTful and SOAP APIs, as well as microservices architecture. This module explores API design, microservices implementation, and the use of PHP's Reflection API for dynamic API routing. The case study demonstrates how to build a flexible API gateway system, integrating these concepts into a scalable and efficient solution.

Designing and Building RESTful and SOAP APIs in PHP

RESTful APIs follow a **stateless architecture** and use **HTTP methods** (GET, POST, PUT, DELETE) for data manipulation. PHP's built-in support for handling HTTP requests, along with frameworks like **Laravel, Slim, and Lumen**, makes it an excellent choice for RESTful API development. Developers can leverage JSON responses, middleware for authentication, and tools like Postman for testing.

SOAP (Simple Object Access Protocol) APIs, although less popular today, are still used in enterprise applications. PHP's **SoapServer** and **SoapClient** classes allow easy implementation of SOAP services, handling XML-based messaging efficiently. Understanding both RESTful and SOAP APIs equips developers with the ability to work in diverse system environments, catering to different integration needs.

Implementing Microservices Architecture with PHP

Microservices architecture breaks down applications into **independent services** that communicate via APIs. Unlike monolithic applications, where all components are tightly coupled, microservices allow for **scalability, flexibility, and independent deployment**.

PHP supports microservices through frameworks like **Symfony, Laravel, and API Platform**, along with tools like **Docker and Kubernetes** for containerization. Each microservice handles a **specific domain**, such as authentication, payment processing, or user management. PHP developers can use **gRPC, RabbitMQ, or RESTful communication** to connect these services efficiently.

Additionally, implementing an **API Gateway** helps manage routing, load balancing, and security, ensuring smooth interaction between microservices. By adopting microservices, PHP applications become **resilient, scalable, and easier to maintain**.

Using Reflection for Dynamic API Routing and Metadata Handling

PHP's Reflection API enables **introspection** of classes, methods, and properties at runtime. This capability is useful in API development for **dynamic routing, automatic documentation generation, and metadata processing**.

Frameworks like **Symfony and Laravel** leverage reflection to implement **dependency injection and middleware handling dynamically**. Developers can use reflection to **scan controllers and route methods automatically**, reducing manual configuration and improving API flexibility.

Additionally, PHP annotations, combined with reflection, allow **dynamic validation, serialization, and request handling**. This approach makes API development more efficient by automating repetitive tasks and enabling adaptive behaviors based on metadata.

Case Study: Building a Flexible API Gateway System

An API gateway acts as a **centralized entry point** for all API requests, handling authentication, rate limiting, caching, and request forwarding. In this case study, we develop a PHP-based API gateway that **routes requests dynamically, applies authentication layers, and integrates with microservices**.

By leveraging **Laravel or Symfony**, we implement request validation, JWT authentication, and role-based access control. Using **Reflection API**, the gateway dynamically maps incoming requests to the appropriate microservices, reducing the need for hardcoded routes.

This case study showcases **best practices in service-oriented architecture**, ensuring that the API gateway is scalable, secure, and easy to maintain.

Service-oriented and reflective API development in PHP allows for **scalable, flexible, and maintainable software solutions**. By understanding RESTful and SOAP API implementations, microservices architecture, and dynamic routing through reflection, developers can create efficient and adaptable systems. The case study reinforces these principles by demonstrating a real-world application of a flexible API gateway, highlighting the benefits of structured API management.

Designing and Building RESTful and SOAP APIs in PHP

APIs are essential for modern applications, enabling seamless communication between different systems. PHP supports both **RESTful and SOAP** APIs, allowing developers to create services that interact with various platforms. RESTful APIs use **HTTP methods (GET, POST, PUT, DELETE)** and exchange data in **JSON format**, making them widely adopted. SOAP APIs, on the other hand, use **XML-based messaging** and are still used in enterprise applications requiring strict contracts. This section explores building **RESTful APIs using PHP frameworks** and implementing **SOAP APIs using PHP's built-in classes**, ensuring a solid understanding of API development in PHP.

Creating a RESTful API in PHP

A RESTful API should follow proper design principles, using meaningful URLs and HTTP methods. In PHP, you can build a simple REST API using **native PHP**, but using a framework like **Laravel** simplifies the process.

Below is an example of a **basic REST API endpoint** using Laravel:

```
use Illuminate\Http\Request;
use Illuminate\Support\Facades\Route;
use App\Http\Controllers\UserController;

Route::get('/users', [UserController::class, 'index']);
Route::post('/users', [UserController::class, 'store']);
Route::get('/users/{id}', [UserController::class, 'show']);
Route::put('/users/{id}', [UserController::class, 'update']);
Route::delete('/users/{id}', [UserController::class, 'destroy']);
```

The **UserController** handles API logic, retrieving, creating, updating, and deleting user data:

```
namespace App\Http\Controllers;
use Illuminate\Http\Request;
use App\Models\User;

class UserController extends Controller {
    public function index() {
        return response()->json(User::all());
    }

    public function store(Request $request) {
        $user = User::create($request->all());
        return response()->json($user, 201);
    }

    public function show($id) {
        return response()->json(User::findOrFail($id));
    }

    public function update(Request $request, $id) {
        $user = User::findOrFail($id);
        $user->update($request->all());
        return response()->json($user);
    }

    public function destroy($id) {
        User::findOrFail($id)->delete();
        return response()->json(null, 204);
    }
}
```

This example demonstrates RESTful principles, **returning JSON responses** and using **HTTP status codes** for better API communication.

Building a SOAP API in PHP

SOAP APIs use **XML for data exchange** and require strict contracts. PHP provides **SoapServer** and **SoapClient** classes to implement SOAP services.

Here's how to create a simple SOAP server in PHP:

```php
class UserService {
    public function getUser($id) {
        return ["id" => $id, "name" => "John Doe", "email" =>
            "john@example.com"];
    }
}

$options = ['uri' => 'http://localhost/soap-server'];
$server = new SoapServer(null, $options);
$server->setClass('UserService');
$server->handle();
```

A SOAP client can consume this service using **SoapClient**:

```php
$client = new SoapClient(null, ['location' => 'http://localhost/soap-server',
        'uri' => 'http://localhost/soap-server']);
$response = $client->getUser(1);
print_r($response);
```

SOAP is useful when working with **legacy systems** and **enterprise-grade applications** that require strict XML contracts.

Building **RESTful and SOAP APIs in PHP** enables seamless system communication. RESTful APIs, being lightweight and widely used, are easily implemented with frameworks like **Laravel**. SOAP APIs, though less common, still serve critical enterprise functions. Understanding both approaches equips PHP developers to handle diverse API development scenarios effectively.

Implementing Microservices Architecture with PHP

Microservices architecture is a **modular approach to building applications** where different services handle specific tasks independently. Instead of a monolithic PHP application, microservices allow **scalability, fault isolation, and independent deployments**. In PHP, microservices can be built using **Slim, Lumen, Laravel, or Symfony**, combined with **Docker, API gateways, and messaging systems like RabbitMQ** for efficient communication. This section explores how to design, develop, and deploy **PHP-based microservices**, ensuring loose coupling and high availability.

Building a Simple PHP Microservice

A PHP microservice should be **lightweight and stateless**, handling a specific function such as user management, authentication, or payments. Below is an example of a **user management microservice** using **Slim Framework**:

Step 1: Install Slim Framework

Run the following command to install Slim via Composer:

```
composer require slim/slim slim/psr7
```

Step 2: Create a Microservice API

Create a **index.php** file and define RESTful routes:

```php
use Psr\Http\Message\ServerRequestInterface as Request;
use Psr\Http\Message\ResponseInterface as Response;
use Slim\Factory\AppFactory;

require __DIR__ . '/vendor/autoload.php';

$app = AppFactory::create();

// Get all users
$app->get('/users', function (Request $request, Response $response) {
    $users = [["id" => 1, "name" => "John Doe"], ["id" => 2, "name" => "Jane
        Doe"]];
    $response->getBody()->write(json_encode($users));
    return $response->withHeader('Content-Type', 'application/json');
});

// Run the application
$app->run();
```

This **lightweight PHP microservice** exposes a GET /users endpoint to fetch user data in **JSON format**.

Service Communication in Microservices

Since microservices are independent, they must communicate efficiently. PHP microservices can use **REST APIs**, **RabbitMQ**, or **Kafka** for messaging. Below is an example of **calling another microservice via cURL**:

```php
function fetchOrders() {
    $url = "http://orders-service.local/orders";
    $response = file_get_contents($url);
    return json_decode($response, true);
}

$orders = fetchOrders();
print_r($orders);
```

This approach ensures microservices **retrieve data dynamically** instead of maintaining **tight dependencies**.

Deploying PHP Microservices with Docker

Microservices benefit from containerization using **Docker**. Below is a basic Dockerfile for deploying a PHP microservice:

```
FROM php:8.2-cli
WORKDIR /app
COPY . .
RUN docker-php-ext-install pdo pdo_mysql
CMD ["php", "-S", "0.0.0.0:8000"]
```

To run the containerized microservice, execute:

178

```
docker build -t php-microservice .
docker run -p 8000:8000 php-microservice
```

This makes the PHP microservice **scalable, portable, and deployable across cloud environments**.

PHP microservices provide **flexibility, modularity, and scalability** for modern applications. Using frameworks like **Slim or Lumen**, integrating **RESTful communication**, and leveraging **Docker for deployment** ensures robust service-oriented architectures. Microservices improve **performance, fault tolerance, and maintainability**, making them an essential approach for PHP development.

Using Reflection for Dynamic API Routing and Metadata Handling

Reflection in PHP allows **introspection of classes, methods, and properties at runtime**, making it useful for **dynamic API routing and metadata handling**. When developing APIs, manually defining routes for each method can be cumbersome. Instead, PHP's **Reflection API** enables automatic route generation by scanning controller classes, reducing boilerplate code and increasing maintainability.

This section explores how to **use Reflection to dynamically route API endpoints**, retrieve metadata from **annotations**, and apply them to **middleware, validation, and API documentation**.

Dynamically Routing API Endpoints with Reflection

A common challenge in API development is mapping **URL routes to controller methods**. Instead of manually defining routes, **Reflection** can dynamically scan controllers and map endpoints based on method names.

Step 1: Create a Controller with Annotated Methods

```php
class UserController {
    /**
     * @Route("/users")
     */
    public function getUsers() {
        return json_encode([["id" => 1, "name" => "John Doe"]]);
    }

    /**
     * @Route("/users/{id}")
     */
    public function getUserById($id) {
        return json_encode(["id" => $id, "name" => "User $id"]);
    }
}
```

Each method has a @Route annotation, indicating the **API endpoint**.

Step 2: Implement Reflection for Route Discovery

179

The following function scans the **UserController** class and registers its methods dynamically:

```
function registerRoutes($controller) {
    $reflection = new ReflectionClass($controller);
    foreach ($reflection->getMethods() as $method) {
        $docComment = $method->getDocComment();
        if (preg_match('/@Route\("(.+)"\)/', $docComment, $matches)) {
            $route = $matches[1];
            echo "Registered route: $route -> {$method->getName()}\n";
        }
    }
}

registerRoutes(UserController::class);
```

This script extracts @Route annotations and **automatically registers routes**, eliminating manual mappings.

Using Reflection for Middleware and Validation

Reflection can also handle **custom middleware** and **parameter validation** dynamically.

Step 1: Define Method Metadata

```
class AuthController {
    /**
     * @Middleware("auth")
     */
    public function getProfile() {
        return json_encode(["user" => "Authenticated User"]);
    }
}
```

Step 2: Apply Middleware via Reflection

```
function applyMiddleware($controller) {
    $reflection = new ReflectionClass($controller);
    foreach ($reflection->getMethods() as $method) {
        if (preg_match('/@Middleware\("(.+)"\)/', $method->getDocComment(),
            $matches)) {
            $middleware = $matches[1];
            echo "Applying middleware: $middleware to {$method->getName()}\n";
        }
    }
}

applyMiddleware(AuthController::class);
```

This technique dynamically applies **middleware rules**, improving flexibility.

Generating API Documentation with Reflection

Reflection enables automatic **API documentation generation** by extracting metadata.

```
function generateDocs($controller) {
    $reflection = new ReflectionClass($controller);
    foreach ($reflection->getMethods() as $method) {
```

```
        $docComment = $method->getDocComment();
        echo "Endpoint: {$method->getName()}\nDescription: " . trim($docComment)
            . "\n\n";
    }
}

generateDocs(UserController::class);
```

This approach simplifies **API documentation maintenance**.

PHP's Reflection API enhances **API development** by automating **routing, middleware application, and documentation generation**. Using **annotations** within controller methods reduces **manual configuration**, making APIs more **scalable and maintainable**.

Case Study: Building a Flexible API Gateway System

An **API Gateway** is a crucial component in a **microservices architecture**, acting as a single entry point for **routing, authentication, and request transformation**. Instead of making direct calls to multiple services, clients interact with the gateway, which **delegates requests to the appropriate microservices**. In this case study, we explore how to build a **dynamic API Gateway in PHP** using **Reflection and middleware**.

This API Gateway will:

- **Route requests dynamically** based on service metadata.

- **Apply middleware** for security and logging.

- **Forward requests** to microservices and handle responses.

1. Defining Microservices and Endpoints

In a microservices-based system, we have multiple services handling specific functionalities:

- UserService (handles user management)

- OrderService (handles orders)

Each service exposes RESTful endpoints, which the **API Gateway** will route dynamically.

Example: UserService API

```
class UserService {
    /**
     * @Route("/users", method="GET")
     */
    public function getUsers() {
        return json_encode(["users" => [["id" => 1, "name" => "John Doe"]]]);
    }
}
```

181

2. Implementing the API Gateway

The API Gateway dynamically discovers services, extracts route definitions, and maps client requests.

Step 1: Dynamic Route Registration Using Reflection

```
class APIGateway {
    private array $routes = [];

    public function registerService($service) {
        $reflection = new ReflectionClass($service);
        foreach ($reflection->getMethods() as $method) {
            if (preg_match('/@Route\("(.+)", method="(.+)"\)/', $method-
            >getDocComment(), $matches)) {
                $route = $matches[1];
                $httpMethod = $matches[2];
                $this->routes[$route][$httpMethod] = [$service, $method-
                >getName()];
            }
        }
    }

    public function handleRequest($requestUri, $requestMethod) {
        foreach ($this->routes as $route => $methods) {
            if ($route === $requestUri && isset($methods[$requestMethod])) {
                [$service, $method] = $methods[$requestMethod];
                return (new $service())->$method();
            }
        }
        return json_encode(["error" => "Route not found"]);
    }
}
```

This gateway:

- **Uses Reflection** to discover service routes.

- **Registers endpoints dynamically** without hardcoding routes.

- **Handles requests** by invoking the appropriate service method.

3. Adding Middleware for Security and Logging

Middleware can be used for **authentication, logging, and request transformation**.

Middleware Example: Authentication Handler

```
class AuthMiddleware {
    public static function handle($next) {
        if (!isset($_SERVER['HTTP_AUTHORIZATION'])) {
            return json_encode(["error" => "Unauthorized"]);
        }
        return $next();
    }
}
```

Integrating Middleware with the API Gateway

```php
function applyMiddleware($middleware, $callback) {
    return call_user_func([$middleware, 'handle'], $callback);
}
```

Now, all API requests **must pass through authentication middleware** before being processed.

4. Forwarding Requests to Microservices

Once an API request is authenticated, the **API Gateway forwards it to the respective microservice**.

```php
function forwardRequest($url, $method) {
    $gateway = new APIGateway();
    $gateway->registerService(UserService::class);

    return applyMiddleware(AuthMiddleware::class, function() use ($gateway,
            $url, $method) {
        return $gateway->handleRequest($url, $method);
    });
}

echo forwardRequest("/users", "GET");
```

Here's what happens:

1. **API Gateway registers microservices dynamically.**

2. **Requests pass through authentication middleware.**

3. **If authorized, the API Gateway routes the request to the correct service.**

5. Extending the API Gateway for Microservices

This API Gateway **can scale** by registering multiple microservices dynamically:

```php
$gateway = new APIGateway();
$gateway->registerService(UserService::class);
$gateway->registerService(OrderService::class);
```

It now acts as a **central hub** for all services, ensuring **secure and structured** API interactions.

A **dynamic API Gateway** built with PHP **simplifies microservices communication** by handling routing, authentication, and request forwarding. By **leveraging Reflection for route discovery** and **middleware for security**, PHP applications can efficiently manage **service-oriented architectures**, ensuring flexibility and scalability.

Part 3:

PHP Practical Applications and Case Studies - Real-World Applications and Industry Use Cases

PHP is widely recognized as a powerful server-side language for building web applications, but its capabilities extend far beyond conventional web pages. This part explores PHP's role in API development, command-line scripting, content management systems, e-commerce, game development, IoT, cryptography, and performance optimization. By mastering these advanced PHP applications, developers can build robust, scalable, and secure solutions tailored to various industries. This section focuses on leveraging PHP's flexibility in backend development, system automation, gaming, IoT integrations, and security implementations to meet modern software demands effectively.

API Development with PHP

APIs have become the backbone of modern web services, enabling seamless communication between applications. PHP supports both RESTful and GraphQL API development, allowing developers to build efficient, scalable, and maintainable web services. Frameworks like Laravel and Symfony provide built-in tools for API routing, request handling, and response formatting, making development more streamlined. Security and performance are crucial in API design, necessitating authentication mechanisms like OAuth, JWT, and API keys. Rate limiting and caching strategies enhance API efficiency while preventing abuse. A case study on implementing a payment gateway integration highlights the importance of secure API development in financial applications.

Web Development – Frontend & Backend with PHP

PHP remains a dominant force in dynamic web development, seamlessly integrating frontend and backend components. Templating engines like Twig and Blade facilitate structured HTML generation, improving code maintainability. PHP's built-in session and cookie handling mechanisms provide robust user authentication. Proper validation and sanitization of form inputs ensure data integrity and security against injection attacks. By handling dynamic content generation and form-based interactions, PHP powers a wide range of web applications. The case study focuses on developing a content-driven website, demonstrating how PHP efficiently manages user interactions and data presentation.

Command-Line Scripting in PHP

PHP's capabilities extend beyond web servers, making it a valuable tool for command-line scripting. Running PHP scripts via the Command Line Interface (CLI) enables developers to automate system tasks such as file manipulation, batch processing, and scheduled data migrations. PHP is also effective for log parsing, system monitoring, and report generation. CLI scripts integrate seamlessly with cron jobs, enabling scheduled tasks like sending automated email reports. The case study showcases how PHP can automate email reporting systems, demonstrating its efficiency in handling background processes and administrative operations.

Content Management Systems (CMS) in PHP

PHP powers some of the most widely used CMS platforms, including WordPress, Joomla, and Drupal. Understanding CMS architecture enables developers to extend and customize these platforms through theme and plugin development. For those requiring bespoke solutions, PHP provides the foundation for building custom CMS applications using MySQL for content storage and management. The case study examines the development of a custom blogging platform, emphasizing the importance of structured data management and modular architecture in content-driven applications.

PHP for E-Commerce Platforms

PHP is a preferred choice for building e-commerce platforms due to its extensive framework support and seamless integration with payment gateways. Developing shopping carts, managing user sessions, and handling orders require efficient backend logic. Secure payment processing via PayPal, Stripe, and other gateways ensures transaction safety. Inventory and customer account management further enhance e-commerce functionality. The case study demonstrates how PHP and WooCommerce power a complete online store, highlighting best practices for managing transactions and user data.

Game Development and Browser-Based PHP Games

While PHP is not a traditional game development language, it plays a crucial role in browser-based gaming. Backend logic, player authentication, and leaderboard systems rely on PHP's ability to process and store game-related data. Multiplayer game servers use PHP for session management, while real-time interactions can be facilitated through WebSockets. The case study showcases a turn-based online game, illustrating how PHP effectively supports game state persistence, user authentication, and leaderboard tracking.

PHP in IoT and Smart Devices

IoT (Internet of Things) applications benefit from PHP's server-side processing capabilities. PHP facilitates IoT data processing, device communication, and API integrations for real-time monitoring. Protocols like MQTT enable PHP to interact with smart devices, allowing remote control and automation. PHP-powered dashboards provide an intuitive interface for IoT device management. The case study explores the development of a home automation system, demonstrating PHP's ability to integrate with IoT hardware for smart control solutions.

Security & Cryptography in PHP Applications

Security is a fundamental aspect of PHP development, requiring best practices in authentication, encryption, and vulnerability mitigation. PHP provides built-in cryptographic functions for secure password hashing, API encryption, and data protection. Secure coding practices, including input validation and SQL injection prevention, safeguard applications against cyber threats. The case study focuses on implementing a secure user authentication system using modern cryptographic techniques, reinforcing PHP's ability to protect sensitive user data.

Server-Side Scripting and Performance Optimization

PHP's server-side capabilities extend to optimizing performance for high-traffic applications. Efficient server-side scripting ensures minimal execution time and resource usage. Techniques like caching, asynchronous processing, and database indexing significantly improve response times. Scalability considerations, such as load balancing and content delivery networks (CDNs), enhance the reliability of large-scale applications. The case study explores how PHP can scale a web service to handle high traffic, showcasing effective performance optimization strategies.

This part provides developers with the knowledge to extend PHP beyond basic web development, enabling its use in APIs, automation, CMS platforms, e-commerce, gaming, IoT, security, and high-performance applications.

Module 19:
API Development with PHP

API development is a fundamental aspect of modern PHP applications, enabling seamless communication between different systems. This module covers the key aspects of **building, securing, and optimizing APIs in PHP**, including RESTful and GraphQL architectures. By exploring **Laravel and Symfony frameworks**, developers will learn to build scalable and secure APIs. Furthermore, authentication and rate limiting strategies will be addressed to ensure API security and efficiency. Finally, the case study will demonstrate the real-world application of these principles by implementing a **payment gateway integration**, a common requirement for e-commerce and financial applications.

Understanding RESTful and GraphQL APIs in PHP

RESTful APIs follow the **Representational State Transfer (REST) architecture**, where **resources** are accessed using **standard HTTP methods** like GET, POST, PUT, and DELETE. REST is widely used due to its simplicity and compatibility with web technologies. It is stateless, meaning each request from a client contains all the necessary information.

GraphQL, in contrast, is a **query language** that allows clients to request **precise data** rather than predefined endpoints. This **reduces over-fetching and under-fetching** of data, making it more efficient than REST for some use cases. In PHP, GraphQL can be implemented using libraries like **webonyx/graphql-php**. This section will compare **REST and GraphQL**, highlighting their advantages, disadvantages, and best use cases.

Building Secure and Scalable APIs with Laravel and Symfony

PHP frameworks like **Laravel** and **Symfony** offer robust solutions for developing APIs. Laravel provides **Eloquent ORM**, API resource controllers, and built-in authentication, making API development efficient. Symfony, on the other hand, focuses on **flexibility and modular components**, allowing developers to build scalable APIs tailored to specific needs.

Scalability in APIs involves strategies such as **database optimization, caching mechanisms, and load balancing**. Laravel's **API rate limiting middleware** and Symfony's **Messenger component** help improve API performance. Additionally, handling **CORS (Cross-Origin Resource Sharing)** is crucial when exposing APIs to third-party applications. This section will guide developers in building high-performance APIs using these frameworks.

Handling Authentication and Rate Limiting in PHP APIs

API security is paramount, and **authentication mechanisms** like **OAuth2, JWT (JSON Web Tokens), and API tokens** are essential to protect sensitive data. OAuth2 allows third-party applications to authenticate without exposing user credentials, while JWT ensures secure token-based authentication for stateless communication.

Rate limiting helps prevent **abuse and DDoS attacks** by restricting the number of requests a client can make within a time frame. Laravel's **throttle middleware** and Symfony's **RateLimiter component** provide built-in solutions for this. Implementing **API keys and IP whitelisting** further enhances security. This section will discuss best practices for **protecting APIs** against common security threats.

Case Study: Implementing a Payment Gateway Integration

Integrating a **payment gateway** is a critical feature for e-commerce applications. This involves connecting to payment providers like **Stripe, PayPal, or Authorize.Net** via their APIs. The implementation includes **handling payment requests, processing transactions securely, and managing webhooks for status updates**.

This case study will guide developers through the **end-to-end process** of integrating a payment gateway in PHP. Key considerations include **handling errors, securing payment data (PCI DSS compliance), and providing a smooth user experience**. By implementing these concepts, developers will gain hands-on experience in **real-world API integration**.

API development in PHP is essential for building **modern, connected applications**. This module has explored **RESTful and GraphQL APIs, security measures, and framework-based solutions** for scalable API development. Authentication and rate limiting ensure **robust security**, while the **payment gateway integration** case study demonstrates practical API usage. By mastering these concepts, developers can build **secure, efficient, and scalable PHP APIs** for various applications.

Understanding RESTful and GraphQL APIs in PHP

APIs (Application Programming Interfaces) facilitate communication between software applications, and PHP provides robust tools for building them. RESTful APIs follow the **Representational State Transfer (REST)** architecture, where resources are manipulated using standard HTTP methods:

- GET for retrieving data

- POST for creating data

- PUT/PATCH for updating data

- DELETE for removing data

RESTful APIs return responses in **JSON format**, making them easy to integrate with frontend applications.

GraphQL, on the other hand, is a **query language for APIs** that allows clients to request specific data fields, avoiding over-fetching or under-fetching data. Unlike REST, where each request targets a fixed endpoint, GraphQL allows clients to structure queries dynamically.

Building a Simple RESTful API in PHP

A basic RESTful API can be built using PHP and a lightweight framework like **Slim** or **Lumen (Laravel's micro-framework)**. Below is an example of a simple RESTful API using **pure PHP**:

```php
header("Content-Type: application/json");

$method = $_SERVER['REQUEST_METHOD'];

if ($method == "GET") {
    echo json_encode(["message" => "Fetching data..."]);
} elseif ($method == "POST") {
    echo json_encode(["message" => "Data created"]);
} else {
    http_response_code(405);
    echo json_encode(["error" => "Method Not Allowed"]);
}
```

This script handles GET and POST requests while returning an error for unsupported methods.

Implementing GraphQL in PHP

GraphQL APIs allow clients to request only the data they need, reducing redundant data transfers. The **webonyx/graphql-php** library provides a PHP implementation of GraphQL. Below is an example of setting up a simple GraphQL API in PHP:

```php
require 'vendor/autoload.php';

use GraphQL\GraphQL;
use GraphQL\Type\Schema;
use GraphQL\Type\Definition\ObjectType;
use GraphQL\Type\Definition\Type;

$QueryType = new ObjectType([
    'name' => 'Query',
    'fields' => [
        'message' => [
            'type' => Type::string(),
            'resolve' => fn() => 'Hello, GraphQL!'
        ],
    ],
]);

$schema = new Schema(['query' => $QueryType]);

$query = '{ message }';
```

188

```
$result = GraphQL::executeQuery($schema, $query)->toArray();

header('Content-Type: application/json');
echo json_encode($result);
```

In this example, a **GraphQL schema** is defined with a message query, allowing clients to retrieve only the requested fields.

Choosing Between REST and GraphQL

- **Use REST** when dealing with simple CRUD operations, public APIs, and scenarios where caching is crucial.

- **Use GraphQL** when working with complex data relationships, mobile applications, or cases where reducing network requests is critical.

Both RESTful and GraphQL APIs have their place in PHP development. Mastering both allows developers to **select the best approach based on project requirements**.

Building Secure and Scalable APIs with Laravel and Symfony

Developing APIs in PHP requires robust frameworks that ensure security, maintainability, and scalability. Laravel and Symfony are two powerful PHP frameworks that provide built-in tools for creating high-performance APIs.

Laravel's **Eloquent ORM**, **Resource Controllers**, and **Sanctum or Passport authentication** make API development streamlined. Symfony, with its **API Platform** and **event-driven architecture**, provides flexibility and scalability for enterprise-grade applications.

This section explores how to build secure and scalable APIs using Laravel and Symfony, focusing on **routing, controllers, authentication, and optimization strategies**.

Creating an API with Laravel

Laravel simplifies API development through its **API routes and controllers**. To create an API, first set up a **route in routes/api.php**:

```
use App\Http\Controllers\UserController;
use Illuminate\Support\Facades\Route;

Route::get('/users', [UserController::class, 'index']);
```

Next, define the **controller logic** in UserController.php:

```
namespace App\Http\Controllers;

use App\Models\User;
use Illuminate\Http\Request;

class UserController extends Controller {
```

189

```
    public function index() {
        return response()->json(User::all());
    }
}
```

Laravel's built-in JSON response handling ensures that the output is structured correctly.

Securing Laravel APIs with Sanctum

Laravel **Sanctum** provides API authentication using **token-based authentication**. To install it:

```
composer require laravel/sanctum
php artisan vendor:publish --provider="Laravel\Sanctum\SanctumServiceProvider"
php artisan migrate
```

Add middleware protection in app/Http/Kernel.php:

```
protected $middlewareGroups = [
    'api' => [

            \Laravel\Sanctum\Http\Middleware\EnsureFrontendRequestsAreStateful::c
            lass,
        'throttle:api',
        \Illuminate\Routing\Middleware\SubstituteBindings::class,
    ],
];
```

Now, a user can **request a token** for authentication:

```
$user = User::find(1);
$token = $user->createToken('API Token')->plainTextToken;
return response()->json(['token' => $token]);
```

All protected routes will require the token for access.

Building APIs with Symfony API Platform

Symfony's **API Platform** provides an efficient way to develop RESTful APIs with built-in serialization, validation, and authentication. Install API Platform:

```
composer require api
```

Define an API resource in src/Entity/User.php:

```
use ApiPlatform\Core\Annotation\ApiResource;
use Doctrine\ORM\Mapping as ORM;

#[ApiResource]
#[ORM\Entity]
class User {
    #[ORM\Id, ORM\GeneratedValue, ORM\Column(type: "integer")]
    private ?int $id = null;

    #[ORM\Column(length: 255)]
    private string $name;
}
```

After running migrations, Symfony automatically generates an API endpoint for the User entity.

Securing Symfony APIs with JWT

Install JWT authentication:

```
composer require lexik/jwt-authentication-bundle
```

Then, configure the firewall in config/packages/security.yaml:

```
security:
    firewalls:
        api:
            pattern: ^/api/
            stateless: true
            jwt: ~
```

Now, only authenticated users can access protected endpoints.

Scaling APIs in PHP

For performance, APIs in Laravel and Symfony should implement:

- **Rate limiting** (throttle:api in Laravel, API Platform's rate limiter in Symfony)

- **Database optimization** (indexing, caching with Redis)

- **Load balancing** (horizontal scaling with Docker and Kubernetes)

Both Laravel and Symfony offer robust tools for building **secure, scalable APIs**. The choice depends on the project's complexity and developer preference.

Handling Authentication and Rate Limiting in PHP APIs

APIs require secure authentication and rate limiting to **protect against unauthorized access, brute-force attacks, and abuse**. PHP frameworks like Laravel and Symfony provide built-in authentication mechanisms, while custom implementations using JWT (JSON Web Tokens) or OAuth can be used for API security.

Rate limiting helps prevent excessive API requests from overloading servers. Strategies include **IP-based throttling, token-based rate limiting, and caching mechanisms like Redis**. This section explores authentication strategies and rate limiting techniques in PHP API development.

API Authentication Methods in PHP

Authentication ensures that only **authorized users and services** can access an API. The most common authentication methods include:

1. **Token-Based Authentication (JWT, OAuth2, Laravel Sanctum/Passport)**

2. **Session-Based Authentication (for web apps using cookies)**

3. **Basic Authentication (username/password in headers, rarely used in production)**

Using Laravel Sanctum for Token-Based Authentication

Laravel Sanctum provides simple, lightweight authentication for APIs. To enable Sanctum, install the package:

```
composer require laravel/sanctum
php artisan vendor:publish --provider="Laravel\Sanctum\SanctumServiceProvider"
php artisan migrate
```

Add the Sanctum middleware in app/Http/Kernel.php:

```
protected $middlewareGroups = [
    'api' => [

            \Laravel\Sanctum\Http\Middleware\EnsureFrontendRequestsAreStateful::c
            lass,
        'throttle:api',
        \Illuminate\Routing\Middleware\SubstituteBindings::class,
    ],
];
```

Users can now authenticate and receive a token:

```
$user = User::find(1);
$token = $user->createToken('API Token')->plainTextToken;
return response()->json(['token' => $token]);
```

Clients must send this token in requests:

```
Authorization: Bearer {token}
```

JWT Authentication in Symfony

Symfony supports JWT authentication via lexik/jwt-authentication-bundle:

```
composer require lexik/jwt-authentication-bundle
```

Then, configure the security firewall in config/packages/security.yaml:

```
security:
    firewalls:
        api:
            pattern: ^/api/
            stateless: true
            jwt: ~
```

Once configured, clients must send a JWT token in API requests. Symfony validates the token and grants access accordingly.

Implementing API Rate Limiting in PHP

Rate limiting **prevents excessive requests from a single user/IP**, mitigating DoS attacks. PHP frameworks provide built-in rate limiting tools:

Laravel Rate Limiting

Laravel defines API rate limits using middleware. In routes/api.php:

```
Route::middleware('throttle:60,1')->group(function () {
    Route::get('/users', [UserController::class, 'index']);
});
```

This limits users to **60 requests per minute**. Custom limits can be defined in app/Providers/RouteServiceProvider.php:

```
RateLimiter::for('api', function (Request $request) {
    return Limit::perMinute(100)->by($request->user()?->id ?: $request->ip());
});
```

Symfony Rate Limiting

Symfony API Platform includes rate limiting features. Configure it in config/packages/api_platform.yaml:

```
api_platform:
    formats:
        json: ['application/json']
    defaults:
        pagination_items_per_page: 20
        maximum_items_per_page: 100
        cache_headers:
            max_age: 3600
            shared_max_age: 3600
```

For **per-user rate limiting**, Symfony's RateLimiter component can be used. Install it with:

```
composer require symfony/rate-limiter
```

Define limits in services.yaml:

```
services:
    Symfony\Component\RateLimiter\RateLimiterFactory:
        arguments:
            - 'api_limit'
            - '{"limit": 100, "interval": "1 minute"}'
```

Requests exceeding this limit return a **429 Too Many Requests** response.

Implementing **authentication and rate limiting** ensures PHP APIs remain **secure, efficient, and resilient**. Laravel and Symfony provide built-in tools for managing authentication via **JWT, OAuth2, and API tokens**. Rate limiting helps prevent abuse using **middleware, caching, and request throttling techniques**. Proper security and throttling improve API **performance and reliability**.

Case Study: Implementing a Payment Gateway Integration

Payment gateway integration is crucial for applications requiring **online transactions**, such as e-commerce platforms, SaaS products, and digital marketplaces. A payment gateway securely processes payments, ensuring that sensitive data like credit card details remain **protected**. Popular payment gateways for PHP applications include **Stripe, PayPal, and Razorpay**, each offering APIs for seamless transactions.

This case study demonstrates how to integrate a **secure payment system** in a PHP application using **Stripe API**, focusing on transaction processing, security best practices, and error handling.

Setting Up Stripe in a PHP Project

Before integrating Stripe into a PHP application, install the Stripe PHP SDK using Composer:

```
composer require stripe/stripe-php
```

Then, configure the Stripe API keys. Store them in **environment variables** instead of hardcoding them to enhance security:

```
require 'vendor/autoload.php';

\Stripe\Stripe::setApiKey(getenv('STRIPE_SECRET_KEY'));
```

Ensure you have the **Stripe public and secret keys**, which can be found in the Stripe dashboard.

Processing a Payment with Stripe

A basic payment flow in Stripe involves:

1. **Creating a Payment Intent**: This generates a client secret, allowing the front end to process the transaction securely.

2. **Confirming the Payment**: The user submits their card details, and Stripe verifies them.

3. **Handling Payment Success or Failure**: The backend checks if the transaction was successful.

Creating a Payment Intent

On the **backend (PHP server-side)**, create a payment intent for the user's transaction:

```
$paymentIntent = \Stripe\PaymentIntent::create([
    'amount' => 5000, // Amount in cents ($50.00)
    'currency' => 'usd',
```

```
    'payment_method_types' => ['card'],
]);

echo json_encode(['client_secret' => $paymentIntent->client_secret]);
```

The frontend uses the client_secret to confirm the payment via Stripe.js.

Confirming the Payment

Once the payment intent is created, the user provides their card details on the frontend. After submitting, Stripe sends a response to the backend, confirming whether the payment was **successful** or **failed**.

On the backend, check the payment status:

```
$paymentIntent = \Stripe\PaymentIntent::retrieve($_POST['payment_intent_id']);

if ($paymentIntent->status === 'succeeded') {
    echo json_encode(['message' => 'Payment successful']);
} else {
    echo json_encode(['error' => 'Payment failed']);
}
```

Handling Webhooks for Payment Events

Webhooks allow the application to listen for payment events, such as **successful transactions, refunds, or chargebacks**. Set up a webhook endpoint in PHP:

```
$payload = @file_get_contents('php://input');
$event = json_decode($payload);

if ($event->type == 'payment_intent.succeeded') {
    $paymentIntent = $event->data->object;
    file_put_contents('payments.log', "Payment received: " . $paymentIntent-
        >id);
}
```

To test webhooks locally, use **Stripe CLI**:

```
stripe listen --forward-to localhost/webhook.php
```

Security Best Practices for Payment Gateway Integration

1. **Use HTTPS**: Ensure all API requests are made over **SSL/TLS** to prevent data interception.

2. **Tokenize Card Details**: Avoid storing credit card data by using **Stripe's tokenization feature**.

3. **Implement Error Handling**: Catch API errors to handle transaction failures gracefully.

4. **Monitor Transactions**: Log all payment attempts to detect suspicious activities.

195

A **payment gateway integration** in PHP ensures **secure, seamless transactions**. Stripe offers a powerful API for handling payments, refunds, and webhooks. Following **best security practices**, such as **tokenization, HTTPS enforcement, and logging**, ensures that transactions remain **protected from fraud** while providing users with a smooth payment experience.

Module 20:
Web Development – Frontend & Backend with PHP

Web development with PHP enables developers to build dynamic, interactive, and data-driven applications. PHP serves as the **backend powerhouse**, handling logic, database interactions, and security, while frontend technologies like **HTML, CSS, JavaScript, and templating engines** enhance the user experience. This module explores key aspects of PHP web development, including **dynamic content generation, user authentication, input validation, and session management**. The case study at the end demonstrates how to apply these concepts by **building a content-driven website**, integrating **frontend and backend functionalities** to create a seamless, robust web application.

Generating Dynamic Content with PHP and Templating Engines

PHP dynamically generates web pages by embedding **server-side logic within HTML**. This approach allows content to be **retrieved from databases, processed in PHP, and displayed dynamically** to users. However, mixing PHP logic with HTML can lead to **code clutter**, making maintenance challenging.

To solve this, **templating engines** like **Twig, Blade (Laravel), and Smarty** separate **presentation from business logic**. These engines provide features such as **variable substitution, control structures, and layout inheritance**, making templates **reusable and modular**. Understanding how PHP dynamically renders pages and integrates with templating engines is crucial for building **scalable, maintainable** web applications.

User Authentication, Sessions, and Cookies in Web Applications

User authentication is a fundamental aspect of **securing web applications**, allowing users to log in and manage personalized sessions. PHP provides **session management** using the $_SESSION superglobal, enabling developers to store user-specific data across requests.

Additionally, **cookies** help in tracking user preferences and maintaining login states. Proper handling of authentication includes **hashing passwords (e.g., using password_hash()), managing session timeouts, and implementing secure cookie storage**. Modern PHP applications often use **OAuth, JWT (JSON Web Tokens), or Laravel Passport** for authentication. Understanding how **PHP handles authentication and state management** ensures a secure, smooth user experience.

Handling Forms, User Inputs, and Validations in PHP

Forms are the primary method for user interaction on web applications, whether for **login, registration, feedback, or data submission**. Handling user input in PHP involves **validating, sanitizing, and securely processing data** to prevent security threats like **SQL injection and XSS attacks**.

PHP provides functions like filter_var() and htmlspecialchars() to **sanitize inputs**, ensuring only expected data is processed. Validation frameworks such as **Laravel's Validator** or standalone libraries help enforce rules like **required fields, email formats, and numeric values**. Proper input handling ensures **data integrity, security, and a smooth user experience**, reducing risks associated with **malicious input manipulation**.

Case Study: Developing a Content-Driven Website with PHP

A content-driven website, such as a **blog, news portal, or knowledge base**, requires a well-structured backend for **content management, user authentication, and templating integration**. This case study demonstrates how to develop a **scalable PHP-based website**, utilizing **a database for content storage, a templating engine for rendering views, and authentication mechanisms** for user access control.

The project integrates **dynamic content retrieval, secure session management, and robust input validation**, ensuring a **functional, user-friendly web application**. By combining **frontend design with PHP backend capabilities**, developers can build **fully interactive and engaging** web platforms.

PHP remains a powerful tool for **web development**, enabling **dynamic content generation, secure authentication, and efficient form handling**. Integrating **templating engines, session management, and data validation** enhances security and maintainability. By applying these principles in the **content-driven website case study**, developers gain practical insights into **building robust, scalable web applications**, leveraging **PHP's full potential** in modern web development.

Generating Dynamic Content with PHP and Templating Engines

Dynamic content generation is one of PHP's core strengths, allowing developers to create **interactive and database-driven web applications**. Instead of serving static HTML files, PHP dynamically generates content by processing **user inputs, database queries, and session data** before rendering output. While PHP can mix logic with HTML, **templating engines** provide a cleaner, structured approach to maintaining code readability and reusability.

Embedding PHP in HTML

PHP allows developers to embed scripts within HTML files using <?php ?> tags. This approach enables **conditional content rendering**, loops, and variable output directly inside HTML structures.

```
<!DOCTYPE html>
<html>
<head>
    <title>Dynamic Page</title>
</head>
<body>
    <h1>Welcome, <?php echo htmlspecialchars($_GET['name'] ?? 'Guest'); ?>!</h1>
</body>
</html>
```

This simple example displays a dynamic greeting based on a **query parameter**, ensuring that content changes **based on user input**.

Challenges of Mixing PHP with HTML

While embedding PHP directly in HTML is convenient, it can lead to **code clutter and difficult maintenance**, especially in large projects. Separating **presentation (HTML) from logic (PHP)** improves maintainability and readability, which is where **templating engines** become essential.

Using Templating Engines for Cleaner Code

Templating engines such as **Twig, Blade (Laravel), and Smarty** provide a **structured way to separate presentation from business logic**. These engines allow the use of **placeholders, control structures, and layout inheritance**, reducing **code duplication**.

Example with Twig

Twig, a popular templating engine, simplifies rendering by **separating PHP logic from HTML**.

1. **Install Twig via Composer:**

   ```
   composer require twig/twig
   ```

2. **Create a Twig template (template.html.twig):**

   ```
   <h1>Welcome, {{ name|e }}!</h1>
   ```

3. **Render the template in PHP:**

   ```
   require_once 'vendor/autoload.php';

   $loader = new \Twig\Loader\FilesystemLoader('templates');
   $twig = new \Twig\Environment($loader);

   echo $twig->render('template.html.twig', ['name' => 'John']);
   ```

Twig ensures **better security** by escaping output automatically ({{ name|e }}), preventing XSS attacks.

Blade Templating in Laravel

Laravel's Blade engine enhances templating with **components, loops, and template inheritance**.

1. **Base Layout (layout.blade.php)**

```
<html>
<head><title>@yield('title')</title></head>
<body>@yield('content')</body>
</html>
```

2. **Page Template (home.blade.php)**

```
@extends('layout')
@section('title', 'Home Page')
@section('content')
    <h1>Welcome, {{ $name }}</h1>
@endsection
```

Blade enhances **reusability and maintainability** in Laravel projects.

Dynamic content generation is essential in PHP web applications. While embedding PHP directly in HTML works for **small-scale projects**, using templating engines **ensures cleaner, maintainable code**. Whether using **Twig, Blade, or Smarty**, separating logic from presentation enhances **code organization, security, and scalability**.

User Authentication, Sessions, and Cookies in Web Applications

User authentication is essential for web applications to **secure user data, manage access control, and maintain user sessions**. PHP provides robust mechanisms for handling **authentication, session management, and cookies**, enabling developers to build **secure login systems** and retain user states across multiple requests.

Handling User Authentication in PHP

Authentication involves verifying user credentials (username and password) before granting access to restricted resources. The process typically follows these steps:

1. **User submits login credentials.**

2. **Server verifies credentials against a database.**

3. **A session or token is created upon successful login.**

4. **User remains authenticated for subsequent requests.**

A **secure login system** ensures **passwords are hashed**, prevents **SQL injection**, and protects against **session hijacking**.

Example: Secure Login System

1. **Create a MySQL users table:**

```sql
CREATE TABLE users (
    id INT AUTO_INCREMENT PRIMARY KEY,
    username VARCHAR(50) UNIQUE NOT NULL,
    password_hash VARCHAR(255) NOT NULL
);
```

2. **Register Users with Hashed Passwords**

```php
require 'config.php';

if ($_SERVER['REQUEST_METHOD'] === 'POST') {
    $username = $_POST['username'];
    $password = password_hash($_POST['password'], PASSWORD_DEFAULT);

    $stmt = $pdo->prepare("INSERT INTO users (username, password_hash) VALUES
        (?, ?)");
    $stmt->execute([$username, $password]);

    echo "User registered successfully!";
}
```

3. **Authenticate Users with Password Verification**

```php
session_start();
require 'config.php';

if ($_SERVER['REQUEST_METHOD'] === 'POST') {
    $username = $_POST['username'];
    $password = $_POST['password'];

    $stmt = $pdo->prepare("SELECT * FROM users WHERE username = ?");
    $stmt->execute([$username]);
    $user = $stmt->fetch();

    if ($user && password_verify($password, $user['password_hash'])) {
        $_SESSION['user_id'] = $user['id'];
        echo "Login successful!";
    } else {
        echo "Invalid credentials.";
    }
}
```

Managing User Sessions in PHP

Sessions allow data persistence across multiple page requests **without exposing sensitive information** in URLs.

- A session is **initialized** using session_start().

- Session variables are stored on the server and can be **accessed across pages**.

- A session ends when a user logs out or after inactivity.

Example: Using PHP Sessions

```php
session_start();
```

```php
$_SESSION['username'] = "JohnDoe";
echo "Session created for " . $_SESSION['username'];
```

To destroy a session, use:

```php
session_start();
session_destroy();
echo "Logged out successfully!";
```

Using Cookies for Persistent Authentication

Cookies store **small pieces of data on the client's browser**, often used for **"Remember Me"** login functionality.

Example: Setting a Cookie

```php
setcookie("username", "JohnDoe", time() + 3600, "/");
echo "Cookie set!";
```

Reading a Cookie

```php
if (isset($_COOKIE['username'])) {
    echo "Welcome back, " . $_COOKIE['username'];
}
```

Deleting a Cookie

```php
setcookie("username", "", time() - 3600, "/");
```

User authentication in PHP relies on **secure password hashing, session management, and cookies for persistent authentication**. By implementing these techniques securely, developers ensure **user data protection, session integrity, and enhanced user experience** in web applications.

Handling Forms, User Inputs, and Validations in PHP

Handling user inputs securely is a fundamental part of web development. PHP provides powerful tools for **handling form submissions, validating user inputs, and preventing security vulnerabilities** such as **cross-site scripting (XSS) and SQL injection**. This section explores **best practices for processing forms and validating data** to build secure and efficient web applications.

Processing Form Data in PHP

A typical HTML form contains input fields for collecting user data and a submit button. The form's action attribute specifies the PHP script that will handle the submission.

Example: Basic HTML Form

```html
<form action="process.php" method="post">
    <label for="username">Username:</label>
    <input type="text" name="username" required>
```

```
<label for="email">Email:</label>
<input type="email" name="email" required>

    <button type="submit">Submit</button>
</form>
```

When the form is submitted, the PHP script **retrieves and processes the data**.

Processing Form Submission (process.php)

```
if ($_SERVER["REQUEST_METHOD"] == "POST") {
    $username = $_POST['username'];
    $email = $_POST['email'];

    echo "Username: " . htmlspecialchars($username) . "<br>";
    echo "Email: " . htmlspecialchars($email);
}
```

The **htmlspecialchars() function** prevents XSS by converting special characters (<, >, &, etc.) into their HTML entities.

Validating User Input in PHP

Validating input ensures that **users provide expected data formats**, reducing errors and enhancing security. PHP provides multiple ways to validate input, such as **regular expressions, built-in filters, and manual validation functions**.

Example: Validating a User's Email

```
$email = $_POST['email'];

if (!filter_var($email, FILTER_VALIDATE_EMAIL)) {
    echo "Invalid email format!";
} else {
    echo "Valid email!";
}
```

Sanitizing Input Data

Sanitization removes potentially malicious input.

```
$email = filter_var($_POST['email'], FILTER_SANITIZE_EMAIL);
$username = filter_var($_POST['username'], FILTER_SANITIZE_STRING);
```

Preventing Common Security Vulnerabilities

1. Preventing SQL Injection

Use **prepared statements** when interacting with a database.

```
require 'config.php';

$stmt = $pdo->prepare("INSERT INTO users (username, email) VALUES (?, ?)");
$stmt->execute([$username, $email]);
```

203

2. Preventing Cross-Site Scripting (XSS)

Use **htmlspecialchars()** when displaying user-generated content.

```php
echo htmlspecialchars($comment);
```

3. Preventing Cross-Site Request Forgery (CSRF)

Generate and validate CSRF tokens for form submissions.

```php
session_start();
$token = bin2hex(random_bytes(32));
$_SESSION['csrf_token'] = $token;

<input type="hidden" name="csrf_token" value="<?php echo $token; ?>">
```

Validate the CSRF token before processing the form:

```php
if ($_POST['csrf_token'] !== $_SESSION['csrf_token']) {
    die("CSRF validation failed!");
}
```

Properly handling form data and user inputs in PHP involves **validating and sanitizing data, preventing XSS and SQL injection, and implementing CSRF protection**. By following these best practices, developers can create **secure, reliable, and efficient PHP applications** that process user inputs safely.

Case Study: Developing a Content-Driven Website with PHP

Building a **content-driven website** using PHP involves integrating **dynamic content management, user authentication, form handling, and security measures**. This case study explores the **development of a simple blog system**, demonstrating how PHP can be used to **manage content dynamically**, interact with a database, and ensure security.

Project Overview

A **content-driven website** requires the ability to:

- **Store** and **retrieve** posts from a database.

- Allow **users to submit and edit content** securely.

- Use **templating** to display content dynamically.

- Implement **user authentication** for admin access.

For this project, we will use **PHP, MySQL, and Bootstrap** for styling.

Step 1: Setting Up the Database

First, we create a posts table to store blog posts.

```
CREATE TABLE posts (
    id INT AUTO_INCREMENT PRIMARY KEY,
    title VARCHAR(255) NOT NULL,
    content TEXT NOT NULL,
    created_at TIMESTAMP DEFAULT CURRENT_TIMESTAMP
);
```

Step 2: Connecting to the Database

We establish a secure database connection using PDO.

```
$dsn = "mysql:host=localhost;dbname=blog";
$username = "root";
$password = "";

try {
    $pdo = new PDO($dsn, $username, $password, [PDO::ATTR_ERRMODE =>
            PDO::ERRMODE_EXCEPTION]);
} catch (PDOException $e) {
    die("Connection failed: " . $e->getMessage());
}
```

Step 3: Displaying Blog Posts

We create an index.php page to fetch and display posts dynamically.

```
require 'db.php';

$stmt = $pdo->query("SELECT * FROM posts ORDER BY created_at DESC");
$posts = $stmt->fetchAll();
?>

<!DOCTYPE html>
<html>
<head><title>My Blog</title></head>
<body>
    <h1>Blog Posts</h1>
    <?php foreach ($posts as $post): ?>
        <h2><?= htmlspecialchars($post['title']) ?></h2>
        <p><?= nl2br(htmlspecialchars($post['content'])) ?></p>
        <hr>
    <?php endforeach; ?>
</body>
</html>
```

Step 4: Adding New Blog Posts

We create a form for adding new posts.

```
<form action="add_post.php" method="post">
    <input type="text" name="title" placeholder="Title" required>
    <textarea name="content" placeholder="Content" required></textarea>
    <button type="submit">Publish</button>
</form>
```

The add_post.php script processes form submissions and inserts posts into the database.

```
require 'db.php';
```

```php
if ($_SERVER["REQUEST_METHOD"] == "POST") {
    $title = htmlspecialchars($_POST['title']);
    $content = htmlspecialchars($_POST['content']);

    $stmt = $pdo->prepare("INSERT INTO posts (title, content) VALUES (?, ?)");
    $stmt->execute([$title, $content]);

    header("Location: index.php");
}
```

Step 5: Implementing User Authentication

To restrict access, we create a **simple login system** with sessions.

```php
session_start();

if ($_POST['password'] === "admin123") {
    $_SESSION['admin'] = true;
    header("Location: admin.php");
} else {
    echo "Incorrect password!";
}
```

An **authenticated admin** can access admin.php to manage posts.

```php
session_start();
if (!isset($_SESSION['admin'])) {
    die("Access denied!");
}
```

This case study demonstrates how PHP can power a **dynamic content-driven website**, integrating **database interactions, form handling, user authentication, and security measures**. By following best practices, developers can build **scalable and secure web applications** with PHP.

Command-Line Scripting in PHP

PHP is commonly associated with web development, but it also offers powerful capabilities for **command-line scripting (CLI)**. This module explores how to use PHP from the command line, enabling automation, file processing, data migration, and system administration. By leveraging PHP's CLI features, developers can create efficient scripts for **task automation, log parsing, and reporting**.

Running PHP Scripts from the Command Line Interface (CLI)

PHP scripts can be executed outside a web server using the **command-line interface (CLI)**. This approach is useful for **task automation, debugging, and administrative scripting**. CLI scripts differ from web-based scripts as they do not rely on HTTP requests, making them more efficient for background processes.

To run a PHP script from the command line, the PHP interpreter is used directly. PHP's CLI mode provides access to **standard input/output**, system commands, and environment variables, enabling powerful shell interactions. This section covers setting up the PHP CLI, executing scripts, handling command-line arguments, and using interactive mode for rapid testing and debugging.

Automating System Tasks, File Operations, and Batch Processing

PHP CLI is particularly useful for **automating system tasks** such as **scheduled jobs, file manipulation, and batch processing**. Common tasks include **renaming files in bulk, archiving logs, processing images, and database maintenance**.

By using PHP's file system functions (fopen, fwrite, file_get_contents), developers can efficiently read, modify, and create files. PHP CLI scripts can also interact with operating system commands via the exec() function, enabling the automation of repetitive system administration tasks.

Batch processing is another major advantage of PHP CLI, allowing developers to **process large datasets in chunks**. This reduces memory usage and execution time compared to processing everything in a single operation.

Working with PHP for Log Parsing, Data Migration, and Reporting

Many enterprise applications require **log analysis, data migration, and automated reporting**, which can be efficiently handled with PHP CLI scripts. **Log parsing** involves extracting meaningful information from server logs, error logs, and access logs, which can then be analyzed for system monitoring and security audits.

Data migration scripts help transfer data from **one format or database to another**, ensuring smooth transitions between different systems. PHP CLI can connect to databases via PDO or MySQLi and perform **bulk inserts, updates, or exports**. Additionally, PHP CLI can generate automated **reports in CSV, JSON, or PDF formats**, which can then be emailed or stored for future analysis.

Case Study: Automating Email Reports with PHP CLI

This case study demonstrates how PHP CLI can be used to **automate email reporting** by **retrieving data from a database, formatting it into a report, and sending it via email**. By scheduling the script with a **cron job**, reports can be automatically generated at set intervals. The case study covers **database querying, data formatting, file generation, and email sending using PHP's mail functions or third-party libraries**.

PHP's command-line capabilities extend its functionality beyond web development, enabling developers to **automate tasks, manage files, process logs, and generate reports** efficiently. Understanding how to leverage PHP CLI for scripting and automation provides a powerful toolset for backend and system-level programming, making PHP a versatile language for various development scenarios.

Running PHP Scripts from the Command Line Interface (CLI)

PHP can be executed beyond the web server environment through its **Command-Line Interface (CLI)**. This feature enables developers to build automation scripts, system utilities, and administrative tools. Unlike web-based PHP scripts, CLI scripts do not depend on a web server, HTTP requests, or browser interactions, making them ideal for **task automation, cron jobs, and system operations**.

Setting Up PHP CLI

Before running PHP from the command line, ensure the **PHP CLI executable** is installed and accessible. Verify the installation by running:

```
php -v
To check if PHP CLI is available, run:

php -m | grep cli
```

If PHP is installed correctly, it should output the installed version and available modules.

Executing PHP Scripts via CLI

A PHP script can be executed by navigating to its directory and running:

```
php script.php
```

208

Alternatively, specify the full path:

```
php /path/to/script.php
```

To make a script directly executable, include the PHP **shebang** (#!/usr/bin/env php) at the top:

```
#!/usr/bin/env php
<?php
echo "Hello from CLI!\n";
```

Then, grant execute permission and run it:

```
chmod +x script.php
./script.php
```

Handling Command-Line Arguments

PHP provides $argv (array of arguments) and $argc (argument count) for handling user inputs:

```
<?php
if ($argc > 1) {
    echo "Argument received: " . $argv[1] . "\n";
} else {
    echo "No argument passed.\n";
}
```

Run it with an argument:

```
php script.php example
```

Interactive Mode and Debugging

PHP CLI includes an **interactive mode**, useful for quick tests. Start it by running:

```
php -a
```

Then, execute PHP commands directly. For debugging, **error reporting** should be enabled in CLI scripts:

```
error_reporting(E_ALL);
ini_set('display_errors', 1);
```

Using Environment Variables

PHP CLI can access system environment variables using getenv():

```
<?php
echo "User: " . getenv('USER') . "\n";
```

This is useful for secure configurations, avoiding hardcoded values.

Understanding PHP CLI allows developers to leverage PHP for **automation, administrative tasks, and system scripting**. Running PHP scripts directly from the command line is efficient, enabling better debugging, automation, and integration with other command-line tools. In the next sections, we explore automation, file operations, and data processing using PHP CLI.

Automating System Tasks, File Operations, and Batch Processing

PHP's Command-Line Interface (CLI) is a powerful tool for **automating system tasks, managing files, and batch processing** large amounts of data. Unlike web-based PHP applications, CLI scripts operate without a server, making them ideal for **cron jobs, file manipulations, backups, and scheduled processes**.

Automating System Tasks with PHP CLI

Automation is crucial for **server management, log maintenance, and data synchronization**. PHP CLI enables developers to schedule tasks using **cron jobs** on Unix-based systems or **Task Scheduler** on Windows. A scheduled PHP script can handle tasks like clearing cache, generating reports, or sending scheduled emails.

Example of a cron job that runs a PHP script every midnight:

```
0 0 * * * /usr/bin/php /path/to/script.php
```

For Windows Task Scheduler, create a **.bat** file:

```
php C:\path\to\script.php
```

Then schedule it via Windows Task Scheduler to run at set intervals.

Handling File Operations in PHP CLI

PHP provides functions for **reading, writing, copying, and deleting files**. CLI scripts can manage backups, logs, and data processing efficiently.

Reading a File:

```php
<?php
$filename = "data.txt";
if (file_exists($filename)) {
    $content = file_get_contents($filename);
    echo "File Content:\n" . $content;
} else {
    echo "File not found.\n";
}
```

Writing to a File:

```php
<?php
$filename = "output.txt";
file_put_contents($filename, "This is a CLI-generated file.\n", FILE_APPEND);
```

```
echo "Data written to file.\n";
```

Processing Large Files in Batches

Handling large files in PHP requires **memory-efficient batch processing**. Using fgets()
ensures the script processes files **line-by-line** instead of loading the entire file into
memory.

```php
<?php
$handle = fopen("large_data.csv", "r");
if ($handle) {
    while (($line = fgets($handle)) !== false) {
        echo "Processing: " . trim($line) . "\n";
    }
    fclose($handle);
} else {
    echo "Failed to open file.\n";
}
```

For **database imports**, batch execution prevents memory overload:

```php
<?php
$db = new PDO("mysql:host=localhost;dbname=testdb", "user", "password");
$handle = fopen("large_dataset.csv", "r");

while (($data = fgetcsv($handle)) !== false) {
    $stmt = $db->prepare("INSERT INTO records (name, email) VALUES (?, ?)");
    $stmt->execute([$data[0], $data[1]]);
}
fclose($handle);
echo "Import completed.\n";
```

Executing System Commands from PHP CLI

PHP CLI can interact with system commands using exec(), shell_exec(), or system().

```php
<?php
$output = shell_exec("ls -l");
echo $output;
```

This can be useful for running shell scripts, backing up databases, or managing files
dynamically.

PHP CLI is an efficient solution for **automating system tasks, managing files, and batch
processing**. By integrating it with cron jobs, file handling, and system commands,
developers can build **automated workflows, scheduled reports, and background tasks**
without relying on a web server. The next section explores PHP CLI's role in **log parsing,
data migration, and reporting**.

Working with PHP for Log Parsing, Data Migration, and Reporting

PHP's Command-Line Interface (CLI) is highly effective for **log parsing, data migration,
and automated reporting**. These tasks are essential for **server monitoring, database
management, and business intelligence**. CLI scripts provide efficient ways to process

large files, migrate databases, and generate analytical reports without requiring a web interface.

Log Parsing with PHP

System logs contain valuable insights into **errors, access attempts, and system performance**. PHP CLI can efficiently parse logs to extract key information.

Consider an **Apache access log** entry:

```
192.168.1.1 - - [17/Mar/2025:10:15:30 +0000] "GET /index.php HTTP/1.1" 200 1024
```

A PHP script to **extract IP addresses and requested pages**:

```php
<?php
$logFile = "/var/log/apache2/access.log";

if (file_exists($logFile)) {
    $handle = fopen($logFile, "r");
    while (($line = fgets($handle)) !== false) {
        if (preg_match('/^([\d\.]+).+"(GET|POST) (.+?)"/', $line, $matches)) {
            echo "IP: {$matches[1]}, Page: {$matches[3]}\n";
        }
    }
    fclose($handle);
} else {
    echo "Log file not found.\n";
}
```

This script scans the log file **line-by-line**, extracting **IP addresses** and **requested pages**, which can be used for **security analysis or traffic monitoring**.

Data Migration Using PHP CLI

Data migration is essential when **moving data between databases**, especially during **system upgrades or platform transitions**. PHP can extract, transform, and load (ETL) data efficiently.

A script to **migrate user data from MySQL to PostgreSQL**:

```php
<?php
$mysql = new PDO("mysql:host=localhost;dbname=old_db", "root", "");
$pgsql = new PDO("pgsql:host=localhost;dbname=new_db", "postgres", "password");

$query = $mysql->query("SELECT id, name, email FROM users");

while ($row = $query->fetch(PDO::FETCH_ASSOC)) {
    $stmt = $pgsql->prepare("INSERT INTO users (id, name, email) VALUES (?, ?,
        ?)");
    $stmt->execute([$row['id'], $row['name'], $row['email']]);
}

echo "Data migration completed.\n";
```

This script **fetches user data** from MySQL and **inserts it** into a PostgreSQL database, making it useful for system migrations.

Generating Reports from Databases

Business intelligence often requires **automated reports**. PHP CLI can **query databases**, format results, and generate reports in **CSV, PDF, or JSON formats**.

Generating a **CSV sales report**:

```php
<?php
$db = new PDO("mysql:host=localhost;dbname=sales_db", "user", "password");
$file = fopen("sales_report.csv", "w");

fputcsv($file, ["Order ID", "Customer", "Total"]);

$query = $db->query("SELECT id, customer_name, total_amount FROM orders");
while ($row = $query->fetch(PDO::FETCH_ASSOC)) {
    fputcsv($file, [$row['id'], $row['customer_name'], $row['total_amount']]);
}

fclose($file);
echo "Sales report generated: sales_report.csv\n";
```

This script extracts **order details**, saves them in a CSV file, and makes it available for **business analysis**.

PHP CLI is a powerful tool for **log parsing, data migration, and reporting**. With its ability to process large files and automate database tasks, it is indispensable for **system monitoring, analytics, and administrative automation**. The next section explores **automating email reports using PHP CLI**.

Case Study: Automating Email Reports with PHP CLI

Automating email reports is a common requirement in **business intelligence, server monitoring, and financial reporting**. Using **PHP CLI**, administrators can generate reports, format data, and email results to stakeholders without manual intervention. This case study explores how PHP CLI can automate email reports by extracting data, formatting it, and sending scheduled emails.

Step 1: Extracting Data for the Report

Data extraction is the first step in generating reports. The script must query a **database**, retrieve relevant records, and format them for **email-friendly output**. Consider an **automated sales report** that fetches daily sales data:

```php
<?php
$db = new PDO("mysql:host=localhost;dbname=sales_db", "user", "password");

$query = $db->query("SELECT order_id, customer_name, total_amount FROM orders
        WHERE DATE(order_date) = CURDATE()");

$reportData = "Daily Sales Report\n--------------------\n";
```

213

```php
while ($row = $query->fetch(PDO::FETCH_ASSOC)) {
    $reportData .= "Order ID: {$row['order_id']}, Customer:
            {$row['customer_name']}, Total: \${$row['total_amount']}\n";
}

file_put_contents("sales_report.txt", $reportData);
echo "Sales report generated.\n";
```

This script queries sales data for the **current day** and saves it in a text file for email distribution.

Step 2: Formatting Data for Email Reports

Email reports should be **structured and readable**. They can be formatted as **plain text, HTML, or attachments**. To format the extracted data as an **HTML email report**:

```php
<?php
$report = file_get_contents("sales_report.txt");

$htmlReport = "
<html>
<head><title>Daily Sales Report</title></head>
<body>
    <h2>Daily Sales Report</h2>
    <pre>{$report}</pre>
</body>
</html>
";

file_put_contents("sales_report.html", $htmlReport);
echo "HTML report generated.\n";
```

This script converts the **text report into an HTML format**, ensuring readability in email clients.

Step 3: Sending Automated Email Reports

PHP's mail() function or external libraries like **PHPMailer** can be used to send automated emails. The following example sends the **HTML sales report as an email** using PHPMailer:

```php
<?php
use PHPMailer\PHPMailer\PHPMailer;
use PHPMailer\PHPMailer\Exception;

require 'vendor/autoload.php';

$mail = new PHPMailer(true);
try {
    $mail->setFrom('reports@company.com', 'Sales Reports');
    $mail->addAddress('manager@company.com');
    $mail->Subject = 'Daily Sales Report';
    $mail->isHTML(true);
    $mail->Body = file_get_contents("sales_report.html");

    $mail->send();
    echo "Report email sent.\n";
} catch (Exception $e) {
    echo "Error sending email: {$mail->ErrorInfo}\n";
```

```
}
```

This script **loads the report, formats it in HTML, and emails it to stakeholders**. Using **PHPMailer** ensures better email handling, including attachments and SMTP authentication.

Step 4: Automating with Cron Jobs

To fully automate email reports, schedule the script to run at specific intervals using a **cron job** (Linux) or **Task Scheduler** (Windows).

Example cron job (runs daily at 7 AM):

```
0 7 * * * /usr/bin/php /path/to/report_script.php
```

This ensures the **email report is generated and sent automatically every morning**.

Automating email reports with **PHP CLI** improves efficiency in business operations. By integrating **database queries, HTML formatting, and email delivery**, businesses can generate **real-time reports** without manual effort. This approach is invaluable for **financial tracking, sales monitoring, and system notifications**, making PHP CLI a powerful automation tool.

Content Management Systems (CMS) in PHP

Content Management Systems (CMS) play a crucial role in modern web development, enabling users to manage digital content with minimal technical expertise. PHP, as a server-side language, powers many popular CMS platforms, including **WordPress, Joomla, and Drupal**. This module explores **PHP's role in CMS architecture, customization of existing platforms, and building a custom CMS from scratch**. The case study focuses on developing a **blogging platform** with PHP. Understanding CMS development helps programmers create **scalable, secure, and user-friendly content-driven websites** while leveraging PHP's flexibility for customization and extensibility.

Understanding CMS Architecture and PHP's Role in Content Management

A CMS is a **software application that manages digital content** through a structured interface. It typically consists of a **database, backend administration panel, and a frontend display system**. PHP acts as the **backend engine**, processing user requests, retrieving content from the database, and rendering it dynamically on web pages.

CMS platforms follow the **Model-View-Controller (MVC) architecture**, separating **data handling (Model), business logic (Controller), and presentation (View)**. PHP interacts with **databases like MySQL** to store and retrieve content efficiently. Features such as **user authentication, media management, and role-based access control** are also handled using PHP. By understanding CMS architecture, developers can enhance performance, improve security, and integrate third-party extensions effectively.

Customizing WordPress, Joomla, and Drupal Themes & Plugins

Popular PHP-based CMS platforms like **WordPress, Joomla, and Drupal** allow extensive customization through **themes and plugins**. Themes control the website's **appearance and layout**, while plugins extend functionality without modifying core files.

- **WordPress**: Uses **PHP templates and hooks** to modify layouts and add features. Developers can create **custom themes** by editing template files and develop **plugins** to add custom functionalities.

- **Joomla**: Utilizes **modules, components, and templates** for customization. Developers can create **Joomla extensions** to enhance user experience.

- **Drupal**: Offers a **modular architecture** where developers build **custom modules** to extend site capabilities.

Customization involves **modifying PHP files, using CMS APIs, and integrating third-party tools**. Developers must follow **best practices** to ensure compatibility and security when extending these CMS platforms.

Building a Custom CMS with PHP and MySQL

For projects requiring **greater flexibility** than existing CMS platforms, developers can build a **custom CMS** using PHP and MySQL. A basic CMS consists of:

1. **User Authentication System**: Secure login and role-based access control.

2. **Database Structure**: Tables for users, posts, categories, and media files.

3. **Content Management Features**: CRUD (Create, Read, Update, Delete) operations for posts and pages.

4. **Template Engine**: Separating business logic from presentation using PHP templating.

5. **Media Upload System**: Handling file uploads securely.

Developing a **custom CMS** allows for **optimized performance, custom-tailored features, and enhanced security**. Developers must ensure proper **validation, sanitization, and scalability** while designing their CMS.

Case Study: Developing a Blogging Platform with PHP

A blogging platform is a **practical example of a CMS** that allows users to create, manage, and publish blog posts. This case study explores how PHP and MySQL can be used to build a **lightweight, scalable blogging system** with essential features such as **user authentication, post management, and commenting systems**.

Developing a custom blogging platform demonstrates how **PHP interacts with databases, handles user-generated content, and ensures security through validation and authentication mechanisms**. By leveraging **best practices in CMS development**, developers can create a robust and efficient system that meets modern web development standards.

PHP's dominance in CMS development is evident in platforms like **WordPress, Joomla, and Drupal**. Understanding CMS architecture, customizing themes and plugins, and building a **custom CMS** from scratch are essential skills for developers. The case study on **developing a blogging platform** highlights the core principles of **content management, user authentication, and database-driven design**. Mastering these concepts allows developers to create **scalable, secure, and feature-rich** web applications using PHP.

Understanding CMS Architecture and PHP's Role in Content Management

A **Content Management System (CMS)** is an application that enables users to create, manage, and modify content without needing extensive programming knowledge. PHP, being a server-side scripting language, is the backbone of many CMS platforms like **WordPress, Joomla, and Drupal**, handling **database interactions, content storage, and dynamic rendering**.

Core Components of a CMS

A typical CMS consists of:

1. **Database (MySQL, PostgreSQL, MariaDB)**: Stores content, user data, and system configurations.

2. **Backend Administration Panel**: Allows content management and user access control.

3. **Frontend Display System**: Dynamically renders content based on stored data.

4. **Template Engine**: Separates content from presentation using reusable templates.

Many PHP-based CMS platforms use the **Model-View-Controller (MVC) architecture**, where:

- **Model** represents database interactions.

- **View** manages UI rendering.

- **Controller** processes requests and business logic.

PHP's Role in CMS Development

PHP dynamically retrieves and displays content stored in a database. The following code snippet demonstrates how PHP fetches and displays articles from a MySQL database:

```php
<?php
$mysqli = new mysqli("localhost", "username", "password", "cms_database");

// Check connection
if ($mysqli->connect_error) {
    die("Connection failed: " . $mysqli->connect_error);
}

// Fetch articles
$result = $mysqli->query("SELECT title, content FROM articles ORDER BY
            created_at DESC");

while ($row = $result->fetch_assoc()) {
    echo "<h2>" . htmlspecialchars($row['title']) . "</h2>";
    echo "<p>" . nl2br(htmlspecialchars($row['content'])) . "</p>";
```

```
}
$mysqli->close();
?>
```

This script connects to a **MySQL database**, retrieves articles, and displays them using **HTML sanitization** to prevent XSS attacks.

CMS User Authentication with PHP

A secure CMS must include **user authentication**. The example below demonstrates **user login** with password verification:

```php
<?php
session_start();
require 'db_connection.php';

if ($_SERVER["REQUEST_METHOD"] == "POST") {
    $username = $_POST['username'];
    $password = $_POST['password'];

    $stmt = $conn->prepare("SELECT id, password FROM users WHERE username = ?");
    $stmt->bind_param("s", $username);
    $stmt->execute();
    $stmt->store_result();

    if ($stmt->num_rows > 0) {
        $stmt->bind_result($userId, $hashedPassword);
        $stmt->fetch();

        if (password_verify($password, $hashedPassword)) {
            $_SESSION['user_id'] = $userId;
            header("Location: dashboard.php");
        } else {
            echo "Invalid credentials.";
        }
    } else {
        echo "User not found.";
    }
    $stmt->close();
}
?>
```

This script:

- Retrieves the user's hashed password from the database.

- Uses **password_verify()** to check authentication.

- Starts a session and redirects authenticated users to the **dashboard**.

Security Considerations in PHP-Based CMS

Since CMS platforms handle user input, security is crucial. Best practices include:

- **Input Sanitization**: Prevent **SQL Injection** using prepared statements ($stmt->bind_param()).

219

- **Role-Based Access Control (RBAC)**: Restrict administrative access.

- **Data Encryption**: Hash passwords using password_hash() before storage.

PHP is an essential language for CMS development due to its flexibility, scalability, and extensive community support. With proper **database interactions, authentication, and security measures**, developers can build a **robust, user-friendly, and secure** CMS to manage digital content effectively.

Customizing WordPress, Joomla, and Drupal Themes & Plugins

WordPress, Joomla, and Drupal are three of the most widely used **PHP-based CMS platforms**. Each of these systems allows for extensive **customization** using themes and plugins, enabling developers to modify both **frontend appearance** and **backend functionality**.

Customizing WordPress

Creating a WordPress Plugin

WordPress plugins extend the functionality of the platform by integrating **custom PHP code**. Below is an example of a **basic WordPress plugin** that creates a custom shortcode:

```php
<?php
/**
 * Plugin Name: Custom Shortcode Plugin
 * Description: A simple plugin to add a shortcode for displaying a welcome
            message.
 * Version: 1.0
 * Author: Your Name
 */

function custom_welcome_message() {
    return "<p>Welcome to our WordPress site!</p>";
}
add_shortcode('welcome_message', 'custom_welcome_message');
?>
```

- This code registers a **shortcode** [welcome_message] that displays a welcome message wherever placed in a WordPress post.

- **Shortcodes** are commonly used for embedding dynamic content.

Modifying a WordPress Theme

To modify an existing **WordPress theme**, developers typically edit the functions.php file. The following code **adds a custom footer message** dynamically:

```php
function custom_footer_message() {
    echo "<p>&copy; " . date("Y") . " My Custom WordPress Theme.</p>";
}
add_action('wp_footer', 'custom_footer_message');
```

This **wp_footer** action hook ensures that the **custom message** appears at the bottom of every page in the theme.

Customizing Joomla

Joomla uses **modules, components, and plugins** for customization. Developers can create **custom modules** to extend Joomla's functionality.

Creating a Joomla Module

The following steps outline how to create a **Joomla module** that displays a custom greeting:

1. Create a new folder inside modules/ (e.g., mod_customgreeting).

2. Inside this folder, create a file mod_customgreeting.php:

```php
<?php
defined('_JEXEC') or die;
echo "<h3>Welcome to Our Joomla Website!</h3>";
?>
```

3. Register the module in mod_customgreeting.xml:

```xml
<extension type="module" version="3.9">
    <name>Custom Greeting Module</name>
    <files>
        <filename
            module="mod_customgreeting">mod_customgreeting.php</filename>
    </files>
</extension>
```

This module can now be **installed** via the Joomla backend.

Customizing Drupal

Drupal allows customization using **modules** and **themes**.

Creating a Drupal Module

To create a **Drupal module**, follow these steps:

1. Inside the modules/custom/ directory, create a folder named custom_message.

2. Inside this folder, create a custom_message.info.yml file:

```yaml
name: 'Custom Message Module'
type: module
core_version_requirement: ^9
description: 'Displays a custom message on pages.'
```

3. Then, create a custom_message.module file:

```php
<?php
function custom_message_block() {
    return [
        '#markup' => '<p>Welcome to our Drupal-powered site!</p>',
    ];
}
?>
```

After enabling the module, the **custom message** will appear on pages.

Customizing **WordPress, Joomla, and Drupal** allows developers to extend CMS functionality and improve user experience. Whether adding **custom plugins, modules, or themes**, PHP remains the core technology enabling developers to tailor CMS platforms to specific business needs.

Building a Custom CMS with PHP and MySQL

A **Content Management System (CMS)** allows users to create, manage, and modify content on a website without needing extensive technical skills. While platforms like **WordPress, Joomla, and Drupal** provide ready-made solutions, building a **custom CMS** in PHP and MySQL offers more flexibility and control over data, features, and security.

1. Setting Up the Database

A CMS typically requires a database to store **users, posts, and categories**. Below is an SQL script to create essential tables:

```sql
CREATE DATABASE custom_cms;
USE custom_cms;

CREATE TABLE users (
    id INT AUTO_INCREMENT PRIMARY KEY,
    username VARCHAR(50) NOT NULL UNIQUE,
    password VARCHAR(255) NOT NULL
);

CREATE TABLE posts (
    id INT AUTO_INCREMENT PRIMARY KEY,
    title VARCHAR(255) NOT NULL,
    content TEXT NOT NULL,
    created_at TIMESTAMP DEFAULT CURRENT_TIMESTAMP
);
```

- The **users** table stores login credentials.

- The **posts** table manages website content.

2. Connecting to the Database

To interact with MySQL, we establish a **database connection** using PDO:

```php
<?php
```

222

```php
$host = 'localhost';
$dbname = 'custom_cms';
$username = 'root';
$password = '';

try {
    $pdo = new PDO("mysql:host=$host;dbname=$dbname", $username, $password);
    $pdo->setAttribute(PDO::ATTR_ERRMODE, PDO::ERRMODE_EXCEPTION);
} catch (PDOException $e) {
    die("Database connection failed: " . $e->getMessage());
}
?>
```

- **PDO (PHP Data Objects)** ensures **secure database interactions** and prevents SQL injection.

3. User Authentication System

A CMS requires **secure login functionality**. Below is a **user registration script** that hashes passwords before storing them in the database:

```php
<?php
if ($_SERVER["REQUEST_METHOD"] == "POST") {
    require 'db.php';

    $username = $_POST['username'];
    $password = password_hash($_POST['password'], PASSWORD_DEFAULT);

    $stmt = $pdo->prepare("INSERT INTO users (username, password) VALUES (?,
        ?)");
    $stmt->execute([$username, $password]);

    echo "User registered successfully!";
}
?>
<form method="POST">
    <input type="text" name="username" placeholder="Username" required>
    <input type="password" name="password" placeholder="Password" required>
    <button type="submit">Register</button>
</form>
```

- **Passwords are hashed** using password_hash(), preventing plaintext storage.

4. Adding and Displaying Posts

Users should be able to **add and manage content**. Below is a simple script to insert and display blog posts:

Adding a Post

```php
<?php
if ($_SERVER["REQUEST_METHOD"] == "POST") {
    require 'db.php';

    $title = $_POST['title'];
    $content = $_POST['content'];

    $stmt = $pdo->prepare("INSERT INTO posts (title, content) VALUES (?, ?)");
    $stmt->execute([$title, $content]);
```

223

```php
        echo "Post added successfully!";
}
?>
<form method="POST">
    <input type="text" name="title" placeholder="Post Title" required>
    <textarea name="content" placeholder="Post Content" required></textarea>
    <button type="submit">Add Post</button>
</form>
```

Displaying Posts

```php
<?php
require 'db.php';

$stmt = $pdo->query("SELECT * FROM posts ORDER BY created_at DESC");
while ($row = $stmt->fetch(PDO::FETCH_ASSOC)) {
    echo "<h2>{$row['title']}</h2>";
    echo "<p>{$row['content']}</p>";
    echo "<hr>";
}
?>
```

Building a **custom CMS** in PHP and MySQL provides full control over features, user management, and security. By implementing **database-driven content storage, authentication, and CRUD operations**, developers can create tailored solutions beyond what traditional CMS platforms offer.

Case Study: Developing a Blogging Platform with PHP

A **blogging platform** is a practical example of a **custom CMS**, allowing users to create, manage, and publish articles dynamically. This case study demonstrates how to build a lightweight **blog system** in PHP and MySQL, covering **user authentication, content management, and comment handling**.

1. Setting Up the Database

The blogging platform requires tables for **users, posts, and comments**. Below is the SQL schema:

```sql
CREATE DATABASE blog_cms;
USE blog_cms;

CREATE TABLE users (
    id INT AUTO_INCREMENT PRIMARY KEY,
    username VARCHAR(50) NOT NULL UNIQUE,
    password VARCHAR(255) NOT NULL
);

CREATE TABLE posts (
    id INT AUTO_INCREMENT PRIMARY KEY,
    user_id INT NOT NULL,
    title VARCHAR(255) NOT NULL,
    content TEXT NOT NULL,
    created_at TIMESTAMP DEFAULT CURRENT_TIMESTAMP,
    FOREIGN KEY (user_id) REFERENCES users(id) ON DELETE CASCADE
);

CREATE TABLE comments (
```

224

```
    id INT AUTO_INCREMENT PRIMARY KEY,
    post_id INT NOT NULL,
    author VARCHAR(50) NOT NULL,
    comment TEXT NOT NULL,
    created_at TIMESTAMP DEFAULT CURRENT_TIMESTAMP,
    FOREIGN KEY (post_id) REFERENCES posts(id) ON DELETE CASCADE
);
```

2. User Authentication (Login & Registration)

A **secure login system** ensures that only registered users can manage blog posts. Below is the **registration form with password hashing**:

```php
<?php
require 'db.php';

if ($_SERVER["REQUEST_METHOD"] == "POST") {
    $username = $_POST['username'];
    $password = password_hash($_POST['password'], PASSWORD_DEFAULT);

    $stmt = $pdo->prepare("INSERT INTO users (username, password) VALUES (?,
          ?)");
    $stmt->execute([$username, $password]);

    echo "User registered successfully!";
}
?>

<form method="POST">
    <input type="text" name="username" placeholder="Username" required>
    <input type="password" name="password" placeholder="Password" required>
    <button type="submit">Register</button>
</form>
```

For login, **password verification** is used:

```php
<?php
session_start();
require 'db.php';

if ($_SERVER["REQUEST_METHOD"] == "POST") {
    $stmt = $pdo->prepare("SELECT * FROM users WHERE username = ?");
    $stmt->execute([$_POST['username']]);
    $user = $stmt->fetch(PDO::FETCH_ASSOC);

    if ($user && password_verify($_POST['password'], $user['password'])) {
        $_SESSION['user_id'] = $user['id'];
        echo "Login successful!";
    } else {
        echo "Invalid credentials!";
    }
}
?>
```

3. Creating and Managing Blog Posts

Authenticated users should be able to **add blog posts**:

```php
<?php
session_start();
require 'db.php';

if ($_SERVER["REQUEST_METHOD"] == "POST") {
```

```php
    $stmt = $pdo->prepare("INSERT INTO posts (user_id, title, content) VALUES
        (?, ?, ?)");
    $stmt->execute([$_SESSION['user_id'], $_POST['title'], $_POST['content']]);

    echo "Post created successfully!";
}
?>
<form method="POST">
    <input type="text" name="title" placeholder="Title" required>
    <textarea name="content" placeholder="Content" required></textarea>
    <button type="submit">Create Post</button>
</form>
```

To **display posts**, we retrieve and loop through them:

```php
<?php
require 'db.php';

$stmt = $pdo->query("SELECT posts.id, title, content, created_at, username FROM
        posts
                JOIN users ON posts.user_id = users.id
                ORDER BY created_at DESC");

while ($post = $stmt->fetch(PDO::FETCH_ASSOC)) {
    echo "<h2>{$post['title']} by {$post['username']}</h2>";
    echo "<p>{$post['content']}</p>";
    echo "<small>Posted on {$post['created_at']}</small>";
    echo "<a href='comments.php?post_id={$post['id']}'>View Comments</a>";
    echo "<hr>";
}
?>
```

4. Implementing Comments System

Users should be able to **leave comments** under blog posts. Below is a simple **comment form and display section**:

Adding Comments

```php
<?php
require 'db.php';

if ($_SERVER["REQUEST_METHOD"] == "POST") {
    $stmt = $pdo->prepare("INSERT INTO comments (post_id, author, comment)
        VALUES (?, ?, ?)");
    $stmt->execute([$_POST['post_id'], $_POST['author'], $_POST['comment']]);

    echo "Comment added!";
}
?>
<form method="POST">
    <input type="hidden" name="post_id" value="<?php echo $_GET['post_id']; ?>">
    <input type="text" name="author" placeholder="Your Name" required>
    <textarea name="comment" placeholder="Your Comment" required></textarea>
    <button type="submit">Submit Comment</button>
</form>
```

Displaying Comments

```php
<?php
require 'db.php';
```

```php
$post_id = $_GET['post_id'];
$stmt = $pdo->prepare("SELECT * FROM comments WHERE post_id = ? ORDER BY
            created_at DESC");
$stmt->execute([$post_id]);

while ($comment = $stmt->fetch(PDO::FETCH_ASSOC)) {
    echo "<p><strong>{$comment['author']}:</strong> {$comment['comment']}</p>";
}
?>
```

This case study showcases the **core components of a blogging platform**, including **user authentication, content management, and comments**. The system can be **extended** with additional features such as **categories, tags, media uploads, and user roles**, providing a **fully functional and scalable PHP-based CMS**.

PHP for E-Commerce Platforms

E-commerce platforms are a vital part of online business, and PHP provides a powerful and flexible foundation for building feature-rich web stores. This module explores the key components required to develop an e-commerce system, including shopping carts, payment gateway integration, inventory management, and customer account handling. Through structured sections, readers will learn how to create secure and scalable online stores using PHP. The case study focuses on building an online store with WooCommerce, demonstrating best practices in PHP-based e-commerce development. By the end of this module, learners will have the skills to develop a full-fledged e-commerce solution.

Developing Shopping Carts and Handling User Sessions in PHP

A shopping cart is the core of any e-commerce platform, allowing customers to add products before making a purchase. Implementing a shopping cart in PHP requires session management to retain cart data across different pages. This section explores how to create an efficient shopping cart system, handling **product selection, quantity updates, and item removal** using PHP's session handling mechanisms. Additionally, it covers how to ensure cart data integrity, optimize performance, and maintain a smooth user experience. Readers will understand how to design a cart that adapts dynamically to user actions while maintaining session security and state persistence.

Integrating Payment Gateways (PayPal, Stripe, etc.) with PHP

Seamless payment processing is critical for e-commerce platforms. PHP allows integration with major payment gateways such as **PayPal, Stripe, and Authorize.net**. This section discusses the steps required to connect a PHP application to different payment providers, covering **API authentication, transaction validation, and handling payment responses**. Security considerations such as **encryption, tokenization, and fraud detection** are also highlighted. Additionally, the importance of **PCI DSS compliance** is discussed, ensuring that payment transactions remain secure. By the end of this section, readers will know how to implement payment systems that provide customers with a safe and efficient checkout experience.

Managing Inventory, Orders, and Customer Accounts in PHP Applications

An efficient e-commerce platform must manage **inventory, orders, and customer accounts**. This section explores how to structure a database for product management, track stock levels, and handle order processing. It also covers how to implement **customer authentication, order history tracking, and profile management** using PHP and MySQL. The section emphasizes secure handling of **user credentials, encryption of sensitive data, and role-based access**

control. Additionally, techniques such as **automated stock updates and order notifications** are discussed. By following this approach, developers can create a well-structured e-commerce system that maintains accurate inventory and order data.

Case Study: Building an Online Store with PHP and WooCommerce

WooCommerce, a PHP-based plugin for WordPress, is one of the most widely used e-commerce solutions. This section presents a case study on building an online store using WooCommerce, highlighting its **installation, configuration, and customization**. It demonstrates how PHP can be leveraged to extend WooCommerce functionalities, including **custom payment methods, automated order processing, and dynamic product recommendations**. Additionally, it explores integrating third-party APIs for enhanced features like shipping tracking and customer support. By the end of this case study, readers will understand how to create a **scalable, feature-rich online store using PHP and WooCommerce**.

This module provides a comprehensive guide to **developing PHP-based e-commerce platforms**, covering essential aspects such as **shopping carts, payment gateway integration, inventory management, and customer handling**. By combining these components, developers can create secure, efficient, and scalable online stores. The case study on WooCommerce offers a practical demonstration of PHP's role in e-commerce.

Developing Shopping Carts and Handling User Sessions in PHP

A shopping cart is a fundamental component of any e-commerce platform, enabling users to select products before proceeding to checkout. In PHP, shopping carts are typically managed using **sessions**, allowing cart data to persist across multiple pages. This section explores how to create a dynamic shopping cart system using PHP sessions, including adding items, updating quantities, and removing products. It also covers best practices for handling user sessions securely, optimizing cart performance, and preventing session hijacking. By the end of this section, readers will understand how to implement a robust shopping cart system in PHP.

Setting Up the Shopping Cart with Sessions

PHP sessions store cart data while a user navigates the website. The first step is initializing a session and checking if the cart array exists:

```
session_start(); // Start the session

if (!isset($_SESSION['cart'])) {
    $_SESSION['cart'] = []; // Initialize an empty cart if not set
}
```

Products can be stored in an array with unique identifiers such as product IDs. Adding items to the cart involves updating this session array:

```
function addToCart($productId, $quantity) {
    if (isset($_SESSION['cart'][$productId])) {
```

```
            $_SESSION['cart'][$productId] += $quantity;
        } else {
            $_SESSION['cart'][$productId] = $quantity;
        }
    }
}
```

Updating and Removing Items from the Cart

Users should be able to modify the quantity of items in the cart or remove them entirely. Updating quantities involves modifying session values:

```
function updateCart($productId, $quantity) {
    if (isset($_SESSION['cart'][$productId])) {
        if ($quantity > 0) {
            $_SESSION['cart'][$productId] = $quantity;
        } else {
            unset($_SESSION['cart'][$productId]); // Remove item if quantity is
            zero
        }
    }
}
```

To clear the cart, simply reset the session array:

```
function clearCart() {
    $_SESSION['cart'] = [];
}
```

Displaying the Cart and Calculating Totals

A well-structured cart page should display item details, including product name, price, and total cost. Fetching cart data from the session and displaying it dynamically ensures a responsive shopping experience:

```
function displayCart() {
    foreach ($_SESSION['cart'] as $productId => $quantity) {
        echo "Product ID: $productId | Quantity: $quantity <br>";
    }
}
```

A function to calculate the total price can fetch prices from a database:

```
function calculateTotal($products) {
    $total = 0;
    foreach ($_SESSION['cart'] as $productId => $quantity) {
        $total += $products[$productId]['price'] * $quantity;
    }
    return $total;
}
```

Security Considerations and Best Practices

Session hijacking is a major risk in e-commerce applications. To mitigate this, always **regenerate session IDs** upon login and enforce **session timeouts**:

```
session_regenerate_id(true);
```

Using **HTTPS** and secure cookies enhances cart security:

```
session_set_cookie_params(0, '/', '', true, true);
```

A shopping cart system in PHP relies on **sessions for data persistence**, **functions for adding and updating products**, and **security measures to prevent vulnerabilities**. By implementing a well-structured session-based cart, developers can create a seamless shopping experience for users. The next section explores integrating payment gateways into PHP applications.

Integrating Payment Gateways (PayPal, Stripe, etc.) with PHP

Processing online payments securely and efficiently is a crucial aspect of e-commerce platforms. PHP supports multiple payment gateways, including **PayPal**, **Stripe**, and other third-party providers. This section explores integrating **PayPal and Stripe** into a PHP-based e-commerce platform, covering **API authentication, handling transactions, and processing payments securely**. It also emphasizes best practices such as validating payments, encrypting sensitive data, and handling webhook responses. By the end of this section, readers will understand how to implement payment processing in PHP.

Integrating PayPal with PHP

PayPal provides a **REST API** for processing transactions. To integrate PayPal into a PHP application:

1. **Create a PayPal Developer Account** at PayPal Developer.

2. **Obtain API credentials** (Client ID and Secret) from the PayPal Developer dashboard.

3. **Install PayPal SDK** via Composer:

```
composer require paypal/rest-api-sdk-php
```

4. **Configure PayPal API credentials** in PHP:

```php
use PayPal\Rest\ApiContext;
use PayPal\Auth\OAuthTokenCredential;

$apiContext = new ApiContext(
    new OAuthTokenCredential('YOUR_CLIENT_ID', 'YOUR_SECRET')
);
```

5. **Create a payment request** in PHP:

```php
use PayPal\Api\Amount;
use PayPal\Api\Transaction;
use PayPal\Api\Payment;
use PayPal\Api\PaymentExecution;
use PayPal\Api\Payer;
```

231

```php
use PayPal\Api\RedirectUrls;

$payer = new Payer();
$payer->setPaymentMethod("paypal");

$amount = new Amount();
$amount->setTotal("50.00")->setCurrency("USD");

$transaction = new Transaction();
$transaction->setAmount($amount)->setDescription("E-commerce purchase");

$redirectUrls = new RedirectUrls();
$redirectUrls->setReturnUrl("http://yourwebsite.com/success.php")
             ->setCancelUrl("http://yourwebsite.com/cancel.php");

$payment = new Payment();
$payment->setIntent("sale")
        ->setPayer($payer)
        ->setRedirectUrls($redirectUrls)
        ->setTransactions([$transaction]);

try {
    $payment->create($apiContext);
    header("Location: " . $payment->getApprovalLink()); // Redirect to PayPal
} catch (Exception $e) {
    die($e->getMessage());
}
```

6. **Handle the payment response** in success.php:

```php
$paymentId = $_GET['paymentId'];
$payerId = $_GET['PayerID'];

$payment = Payment::get($paymentId, $apiContext);
$execution = new PaymentExecution();
$execution->setPayerId($payerId);

try {
    $payment->execute($execution, $apiContext);
    echo "Payment successful!";
} catch (Exception $e) {
    echo "Payment failed: " . $e->getMessage();
}
```

Integrating Stripe with PHP

Stripe offers a **developer-friendly API** for payment processing. To integrate Stripe into a PHP application:

1. **Sign up at Stripe** and obtain API keys.

2. **Install Stripe's PHP SDK** via Composer:

```
composer require stripe/stripe-php
```

3. **Configure Stripe API keys** in PHP:

```php
require 'vendor/autoload.php';
\Stripe\Stripe::setApiKey("YOUR_SECRET_KEY");
```

232

4. **Create a payment form**:

```html
<form action="charge.php" method="POST">
    <script src="https://checkout.stripe.com/checkout.js" class="stripe-
            button"
        data-key="YOUR_PUBLISHABLE_KEY"
        data-amount="5000"
        data-name="E-commerce Store"
        data-description="Purchase"
        data-currency="usd">
    </script>
</form>
```

5. **Process the payment in charge.php**:

```php
require 'vendor/autoload.php';

\Stripe\Stripe::setApiKey("YOUR_SECRET_KEY");

$token = $_POST['stripeToken'];
$charge = \Stripe\Charge::create([
    "amount" => 5000,
    "currency" => "usd",
    "source" => $token,
    "description" => "E-commerce purchase"
]);

echo "Payment successful!";
```

Best Practices for Secure Payment Processing

- **Use HTTPS** for all transactions.

- **Validate payments on the server-side** to prevent unauthorized modifications.

- **Implement webhook listeners** for real-time updates on payment status.

- **Avoid storing card details**; rely on tokenized transactions via Stripe or PayPal.

Integrating PayPal and Stripe in PHP allows secure transaction handling. This section demonstrated setting up PayPal and Stripe, processing payments, and implementing security best practices. The next section explores managing inventory, orders, and customer accounts in PHP applications.

Managing Inventory, Orders, and Customer Accounts in PHP Applications

Managing **inventory, orders, and customer accounts** is crucial for any e-commerce platform. PHP provides robust tools for handling product stock levels, processing customer orders, and managing user profiles. This section covers **implementing an inventory system, tracking orders, and handling customer accounts**, with best practices for **data validation, security, and efficiency**. By the end of this section, readers will be able to create a **basic order management system** that integrates these functionalities.

Building an Inventory Management System

A **database-driven inventory system** helps track available stock, prevent overselling, and update stock levels dynamically. The inventory system typically includes:

- **Products table** storing item details.

- **Stock levels** updated after purchases.

- **Alerts** for low-stock items.

Creating the Products Table

```
CREATE TABLE products (
    id INT AUTO_INCREMENT PRIMARY KEY,
    name VARCHAR(255) NOT NULL,
    description TEXT,
    price DECIMAL(10,2) NOT NULL,
    stock INT NOT NULL DEFAULT 0
);
```

Fetching Available Products in PHP

```
$conn = new PDO("mysql:host=localhost;dbname=ecommerce", "root", "");

$query = $conn->prepare("SELECT * FROM products WHERE stock > 0");
$query->execute();
$products = $query->fetchAll(PDO::FETCH_ASSOC);

foreach ($products as $product) {
    echo "{$product['name']} - {$product['price']} USD - Stock:
        {$product['stock']}<br>";
}
```

Processing Customer Orders

When a customer places an order, the system should:

1. **Validate stock availability**.

2. **Deduct stock upon order confirmation**.

3. **Store order details in the database**.

Creating the Orders Table

```
CREATE TABLE orders (
    id INT AUTO_INCREMENT PRIMARY KEY,
    customer_id INT NOT NULL,
    product_id INT NOT NULL,
    quantity INT NOT NULL,
    total_price DECIMAL(10,2) NOT NULL,
    order_date TIMESTAMP DEFAULT CURRENT_TIMESTAMP
);
```

Placing an Order in PHP

```php
$product_id = 1;
$customer_id = 5;
$quantity = 2;

// Fetch product details
$query = $conn->prepare("SELECT price, stock FROM products WHERE id = ?");
$query->execute([$product_id]);
$product = $query->fetch(PDO::FETCH_ASSOC);

// Check stock availability
if ($product['stock'] >= $quantity) {
    $total_price = $product['price'] * $quantity;

    // Insert order into database
    $insert = $conn->prepare("INSERT INTO orders (customer_id, product_id,
            quantity, total_price) VALUES (?, ?, ?, ?)");
    $insert->execute([$customer_id, $product_id, $quantity, $total_price]);

    // Update stock
    $update = $conn->prepare("UPDATE products SET stock = stock - ? WHERE id =
            ?");
    $update->execute([$quantity, $product_id]);

    echo "Order placed successfully!";
} else {
    echo "Insufficient stock!";
}
```

Managing Customer Accounts

A user-friendly **customer account system** enhances user experience by allowing order tracking and profile management.

Creating the Customers Table

```sql
CREATE TABLE customers (
    id INT AUTO_INCREMENT PRIMARY KEY,
    name VARCHAR(255) NOT NULL,
    email VARCHAR(255) UNIQUE NOT NULL,
    password VARCHAR(255) NOT NULL
);
```

Registering a Customer

```php
$password = password_hash("securepassword", PASSWORD_BCRYPT);
$query = $conn->prepare("INSERT INTO customers (name, email, password) VALUES
        (?, ?, ?)");
$query->execute(["John Doe", "john@example.com", $password]);
```

Verifying Login Credentials

```php
$email = "john@example.com";
$password = "securepassword";

$query = $conn->prepare("SELECT * FROM customers WHERE email = ?");
$query->execute([$email]);
$user = $query->fetch(PDO::FETCH_ASSOC);

if ($user && password_verify($password, $user['password'])) {
```

```
      echo "Login successful!";
} else {
      echo "Invalid credentials!";
}
```

Best Practices for Managing Inventory and Orders

- **Use prepared statements** to prevent SQL injection.

- **Implement order status tracking** (pending, shipped, delivered).

- **Send email notifications** to customers upon order confirmation.

- **Monitor inventory levels** to prevent out-of-stock situations.

This section demonstrated how to **manage inventory, process orders, and handle customer accounts** using PHP and MySQL. Implementing these features enhances the efficiency of an e-commerce platform. The next section will focus on **building a full online store** by integrating all e-commerce components.

Case Study: Building an Online Store with PHP and WooCommerce

Building an online store requires integrating multiple components, including product management, user authentication, payment processing, and order handling. **WooCommerce**, a widely used e-commerce solution for WordPress, provides a flexible and scalable framework to create an online store. This case study explores **setting up WooCommerce, customizing product pages, integrating PHP scripts, and handling transactions efficiently** to build a functional e-commerce platform.

Setting Up WooCommerce for an Online Store

WooCommerce is a WordPress plugin that enables **product management, checkout processing, and order tracking**. To get started:

1. **Install WordPress** on a server.

2. **Install and activate WooCommerce** from the WordPress plugin directory.

3. **Configure store settings** (currency, payment methods, shipping).

4. **Add products and categories** for sale.

Adding a New Product in WooCommerce

WooCommerce provides an easy-to-use dashboard, but products can also be added programmatically using PHP.

```
function add_custom_product() {
    $product = new WC_Product_Simple();
    $product->set_name("New Product");
    $product->set_price(19.99);
    $product->set_regular_price(25.99);
    $product->set_description("This is a test product.");
    $product->set_sku("TEST123");
    $product->save();
}
add_action('init', 'add_custom_product');
```

This function **programmatically adds a product** to WooCommerce when executed.

Customizing WooCommerce with PHP Hooks

WooCommerce allows customization through **action hooks and filters**. Developers can modify product displays, checkout processes, and email notifications.

Changing the "Add to Cart" Button Text

```
function custom_add_to_cart_text() {
    return __('Buy Now', 'woocommerce');
}
add_filter('woocommerce_product_add_to_cart_text', 'custom_add_to_cart_text');
```

Adding Custom Fields to Product Pages

```
function add_custom_product_field() {
    echo '<div class="custom-field"><label>Custom Note:</label>';
    echo '<input type="text" name="custom_note" /></div>';
}
add_action('woocommerce_before_add_to_cart_button', 'add_custom_product_field');
```

Handling Transactions and Payment Processing

WooCommerce supports **multiple payment gateways** like PayPal and Stripe. Developers can integrate custom payment methods using PHP.

Creating a Custom Payment Gateway

```
class Custom_Gateway extends WC_Payment_Gateway {
    public function __construct() {
        $this->id = 'custom_gateway';
        $this->title = __('Custom Payment', 'woocommerce');
        $this->method_title = __('Custom Gateway', 'woocommerce');
        $this->init_form_fields();
        $this->init_settings();
    }

    public function process_payment($order_id) {
        $order = wc_get_order($order_id);
        $order->payment_complete();
        return ['result' => 'success', 'redirect' => $order-
            >get_checkout_order_received_url()];
    }
}
add_filter('woocommerce_payment_gateways', function($gateways) {
    $gateways[] = 'Custom_Gateway';
    return $gateways;
```

```
});
```

This code defines a **custom WooCommerce payment gateway**, allowing users to pay with a non-standard method.

Managing Orders and Customer Data

Once an order is placed, WooCommerce **tracks order status, customer details, and shipping information**. PHP functions help retrieve and process order data.

Fetching Recent Orders with PHP

```
$orders = wc_get_orders([
    'limit' => 5,
    'status' => 'completed'
]);

foreach ($orders as $order) {
    echo "Order #" . $order->get_id() . " - Total: $" . $order->get_total() .
        "<br>";
}
```

Automatically Sending Custom Email Notifications

```
function send_custom_email($order_id) {
    $order = wc_get_order($order_id);
    $to = $order->get_billing_email();
    $subject = "Your Order is Being Processed";
    $message = "Hello, your order #" . $order_id . " is being prepared!";
    wp_mail($to, $subject, $message);
}
add_action('woocommerce_thankyou', 'send_custom_email');
```

This function **automatically sends an email** when an order is placed.

Best Practices for WooCommerce PHP Development

- **WooCommerce hooks** to modify checkout and product pages efficiently.

- **Ensure security** by validating payment gateways and user input.

- **Optimize store performance** by caching queries and images.

- **Automate tasks** like order confirmation emails and stock updates.

This case study demonstrated **how to build and customize an online store** using PHP and WooCommerce. From product management to **payment processing and order handling**, WooCommerce provides powerful APIs and hooks for extending e-commerce functionality. The next module will explore **advanced PHP applications in web development**.

Game Development and Browser-Based PHP Games

PHP, traditionally used for web applications, can also serve as a powerful backend for browser-based games. This module explores **game logic implementation, backend processing, leaderboard management, multiplayer functionality, and real-time interaction** using PHP. By leveraging PHP's database capabilities, session management, and WebSocket support, developers can create engaging online games.

Understanding Game Logic and Backend Processing with PHP

Game development requires a structured approach to **handling logic, player interactions, and backend data processing**. While frontend technologies like JavaScript manage visuals and gameplay, PHP is crucial for **game state management, database interactions, and authentication**.

PHP can **store player progress, manage game sessions, and validate user actions** in real-time. For example, in a turn-based game, PHP can track player moves, ensure game rules are followed, and update the database accordingly. Additionally, PHP frameworks like Laravel or CodeIgniter can provide structured development approaches for handling complex game logic.

A well-structured **backend ensures fairness, prevents cheating, and maintains game integrity** by controlling interactions between players and the server.

Building Leaderboards and User Authentication for Online Games

Leaderboards are essential for **player engagement** in competitive games. PHP allows **secure tracking of scores**, ensuring fairness by preventing manual score tampering. By integrating a **MySQL database**, PHP can store and retrieve player rankings dynamically.

User authentication ensures that **each player has a unique profile, tracks progress, and prevents unauthorized access**. PHP's **session management and hashing functions** provide secure login mechanisms. Implementing **OAuth authentication** (Google, Facebook) can also enhance security and user convenience.

In addition, PHP scripts can **regularly update leaderboards** based on player achievements, rewarding top performers with badges or rewards.

Using PHP for Multiplayer Game Servers and Real-Time Interaction

Multiplayer games require **real-time communication** between players. PHP, when combined with **WebSockets (Ratchet PHP) and AJAX polling**, enables real-time updates without excessive server load.

PHP can handle **player matchmaking, game state synchronization, and in-game chat functionalities**. By using **Redis for in-memory storage**, PHP can efficiently manage fast-paced game data, such as player movements and score updates.

For turn-based multiplayer games, PHP can track **game turns, validate actions, and store results in a database**. Meanwhile, real-time games require efficient **WebSocket connections** to broadcast live updates to all connected players.

A well-optimized PHP-based multiplayer game ensures **low latency, smooth user experience, and synchronized gameplay** across different devices.

Case Study: Developing a Turn-Based Online Game with PHP

This case study explores **building a browser-based turn-based game** using PHP as the backend. The game includes **player authentication, turn validation, leaderboards, and multiplayer interaction**. PHP handles **matchmaking, turn processing, and data storage**, ensuring smooth game progression.

Key components include:

- **User Authentication** – Players log in to save progress.

- **Turn-Based Logic** – PHP validates and processes player turns.

- **Leaderboard System** – Scores are stored and ranked in a database.

- **Multiplayer Synchronization** – PHP updates the game state dynamically.

By following this structured approach, developers can build an engaging **browser-based game with PHP**.

Game development with PHP involves **backend logic, user authentication, leaderboard tracking, and real-time updates**. By leveraging PHP with **databases, WebSockets, and frameworks**, developers can create dynamic online games. This module lays the foundation for building browser-based PHP games, demonstrating how PHP extends beyond traditional web applications into the gaming industry.

Understanding Game Logic and Backend Processing with PHP
Game development requires structured backend processing to manage **game state, player interactions, and data storage**. While frontend technologies like JavaScript handle

rendering and animations, PHP plays a crucial role in **validating moves, tracking scores, managing user sessions, and enforcing game rules**.

A PHP-powered game backend processes player actions and updates the database accordingly. Consider a **turn-based game** where PHP must verify each player's move, enforce game rules, and update the game state before sending data back to the client. Here's an example of how PHP can **process game turns and store game state** in a database:

```php
<?php
session_start();
$conn = new mysqli("localhost", "root", "", "game_db");

function processMove($gameId, $playerId, $move) {
    global $conn;

    // Fetch current game state
    $query = $conn->prepare("SELECT current_turn FROM games WHERE id = ?");
    $query->bind_param("i", $gameId);
    $query->execute();
    $result = $query->get_result();
    $game = $result->fetch_assoc();

    if ($game['current_turn'] != $playerId) {
        return "Not your turn!";
    }

    // Update game state with the move
    $updateQuery = $conn->prepare("UPDATE games SET last_move = ?, current_turn
            = (current_turn % 2) + 1 WHERE id = ?");
    $updateQuery->bind_param("si", $move, $gameId);
    $updateQuery->execute();

    return "Move recorded successfully!";
}

// Example usage
echo processMove(1, $_SESSION['player_id'], "X at (2,3)");
?>
```

In this example:

- The system **checks if it is the player's turn** before accepting a move.

- The **game state updates dynamically**, ensuring fairness.

- The **next player's turn is set**, preventing unauthorized moves.

Game Session Management

A session in PHP allows tracking player activity **between game rounds**. PHP's session_start() initializes a session, and variables can be used to store player-specific data.

```php
<?php
session_start();
$_SESSION['player_id'] = 1;
```

```php
$_SESSION['username'] = "Gamer123";
?>
```

When designing game backends, PHP ensures **secure game logic, prevents cheating, and synchronizes game data with databases**.

PHP provides a powerful backend for browser-based games, ensuring **smooth game logic, database integration, and player session management**. By handling turn-based interactions, enforcing rules, and maintaining a structured database, PHP enables developers to create **fair, engaging, and interactive** online games.

Building Leaderboards and User Authentication for Online Games

Leaderboards and user authentication are essential for **competitive gaming experiences**. A leaderboard ranks players based on **scores, achievements, or win/loss ratios**, while authentication ensures **secure access** to player accounts. PHP facilitates both by managing **user sessions, storing game scores, and retrieving rankings** dynamically.

User Authentication with PHP

A secure authentication system prevents unauthorized access and **tracks player progress** across sessions. Here's how to implement **player login and registration** in PHP:

User Registration

```php
<?php
$conn = new mysqli("localhost", "root", "", "game_db");

if ($_SERVER["REQUEST_METHOD"] == "POST") {
    $username = $_POST['username'];
    $password = password_hash($_POST['password'], PASSWORD_BCRYPT); // Secure
        password hashing

    $stmt = $conn->prepare("INSERT INTO users (username, password) VALUES (?,
        ?)");
    $stmt->bind_param("ss", $username, $password);
    $stmt->execute();

    echo "Registration successful!";
}
?>
```

User Login

```php
<?php
session_start();
$conn = new mysqli("localhost", "root", "", "game_db");

if ($_SERVER["REQUEST_METHOD"] == "POST") {
    $username = $_POST['username'];
    $password = $_POST['password'];

    $stmt = $conn->prepare("SELECT id, password FROM users WHERE username = ?");
    $stmt->bind_param("s", $username);
    $stmt->execute();
    $result = $stmt->get_result();
```

```
        if ($user = $result->fetch_assoc()) {
            if (password_verify($password, $user['password'])) {
                $_SESSION['player_id'] = $user['id'];
                echo "Login successful!";
            } else {
                echo "Invalid password!";
            }
        } else {
            echo "User not found!";
        }
    }
?>
```

In this system:

- Passwords are **hashed** for security.

- PHP verifies credentials before logging in a player.

- Sessions maintain user authentication **across multiple game rounds**.

Building a Game Leaderboard

A leaderboard ranks players dynamically based on scores stored in a database. PHP retrieves and sorts the **top players** using SQL queries.

Leaderboard Database Structure

```
CREATE TABLE leaderboard (
    id INT AUTO_INCREMENT PRIMARY KEY,
    player_id INT,
    username VARCHAR(50),
    score INT,
    FOREIGN KEY (player_id) REFERENCES users(id)
);
```

Updating Player Scores

```
<?php
$conn = new mysqli("localhost", "root", "", "game_db");

function updateScore($playerId, $score) {
    global $conn;

    $stmt = $conn->prepare("UPDATE leaderboard SET score = score + ? WHERE
            player_id = ?");
    $stmt->bind_param("ii", $score, $playerId);
    $stmt->execute();
}
updateScore($_SESSION['player_id'], 10); // Example: Increase score by 10
?>
```

Displaying the Leaderboard

```
<?php
$conn = new mysqli("localhost", "root", "", "game_db");
```

```php
$result = $conn->query("SELECT username, score FROM leaderboard ORDER BY score
        DESC LIMIT 10");

echo "<h2>Leaderboard</h2><ol>";
while ($row = $result->fetch_assoc()) {
    echo "<li>{$row['username']} - {$row['score']} points</li>";
}
echo "</ol>";
?>
```

This script:

- Fetches the **top 10 players** sorted by **highest score**.

- Dynamically displays the leaderboard.

Leaderboards and authentication **enhance the competitive gaming experience**. PHP handles **secure logins, password hashing, and score tracking**, ensuring **fair rankings and smooth gameplay**. With a structured database, PHP efficiently manages **real-time player statistics and leaderboard updates**, making it an excellent choice for **browser-based multiplayer games**.

Using PHP for Multiplayer Game Servers and Real-Time Interaction

Multiplayer games require **real-time interaction** between players, which PHP can facilitate using **WebSockets, AJAX polling, or long polling**. PHP enables **handling game events, updating player states, and managing concurrent connections**. This section explores how PHP can power **multiplayer game servers** and facilitate **live communication** between players.

Setting Up a Multiplayer Game Server

A **multiplayer server** maintains **player states, synchronizes actions, and relays messages**. PHP, combined with **Ratchet (WebSockets)**, allows real-time data exchange.

Installing Ratchet WebSockets

Use **Composer** to install Ratchet:

```
composer require cboden/ratchet
```

Creating a WebSocket Server in PHP

```php
<?php
use Ratchet\MessageComponentInterface;
use Ratchet\ConnectionInterface;

require 'vendor/autoload.php';

class GameServer implements MessageComponentInterface {
    protected $clients;
```

```php
    public function __construct() {
        $this->clients = new \SplObjectStorage;
    }

    public function onOpen(ConnectionInterface $conn) {
        $this->clients->attach($conn);
        echo "New connection! ({$conn->resourceId})\n";
    }

    public function onMessage(ConnectionInterface $from, $msg) {
        foreach ($this->clients as $client) {
            if ($from !== $client) {
                $client->send($msg);
            }
        }
    }

    public function onClose(ConnectionInterface $conn) {
        $this->clients->detach($conn);
        echo "Connection {$conn->resourceId} closed.\n";
    }

    public function onError(ConnectionInterface $conn, \Exception $e) {
        echo "Error: {$e->getMessage()}\n";
        $conn->close();
    }
}

$server = \Ratchet\Server\IoServer::factory(
    new \Ratchet\WebSocket\WsServer(new GameServer()),
    8080
);

$server->run();
?>
```

- This server listens for **WebSocket connections** on **port 8080**.

- Clients can send messages, and the server **broadcasts** them to others.

- It ensures real-time **multiplayer communication**.

Connecting Clients to the Game Server

On the **frontend**, use JavaScript to **connect players**:

```javascript
const socket = new WebSocket("ws://localhost:8080");

socket.onopen = () => console.log("Connected to game server");
socket.onmessage = (event) => console.log("Game update: " + event.data);

function sendMove(move) {
    socket.send(JSON.stringify(move));
}
```

- Players **connect via WebSocket** to exchange game moves.

- The **server broadcasts actions**, ensuring **real-time synchronization**.

Tracking Player Positions in PHP

245

Store **player positions** in a database for persistent multiplayer states:

Database Table for Player States

```
CREATE TABLE player_positions (
    player_id INT PRIMARY KEY,
    x INT,
    y INT
);
```

Updating Player Positions in PHP

```php
<?php
$conn = new mysqli("localhost", "root", "", "game_db");

function updatePosition($playerId, $x, $y) {
    global $conn;
    $stmt = $conn->prepare("UPDATE player_positions SET x = ?, y = ? WHERE
            player_id = ?");
    $stmt->bind_param("iii", $x, $y, $playerId);
    $stmt->execute();
}
?>
```

When a **player moves**, their position is **updated**, ensuring the **server tracks real-time locations**.

PHP enables **real-time multiplayer interactions** using **WebSockets**. With **Ratchet**, PHP can handle **live game events, player movements, and messaging** efficiently. A **structured database** ensures smooth **state tracking**, while **WebSockets allow instant communication**, making PHP an excellent choice for **browser-based multiplayer games**.

Case Study: Developing a Turn-Based Online Game with PHP

Turn-based games involve **sequential player actions**, requiring **state management, turn tracking, and real-time updates**. PHP, combined with **WebSockets, AJAX, and databases**, provides an efficient backend for managing game logic. This case study explores building a **turn-based multiplayer game** using PHP.

Game Concept and Requirements

We will build a **simple turn-based strategy game** where **two players take turns to make moves**. The **core requirements** include:

- **User authentication** for identifying players.

- **Game state management** to track player actions.

- **Turn handling** to ensure correct sequencing.

- **Real-time updates** via **WebSockets** or **AJAX polling**.

246

Setting Up the Game Database

The database tracks **games, players, and turns**.

Game Sessions Table

```
CREATE TABLE games (
    game_id INT AUTO_INCREMENT PRIMARY KEY,
    player1_id INT,
    player2_id INT,
    current_turn INT DEFAULT 1,
    status ENUM('waiting', 'active', 'finished') DEFAULT 'waiting',
    created_at TIMESTAMP DEFAULT CURRENT_TIMESTAMP
);
```

- **player1_id** and **player2_id** store participants.

- **current_turn** tracks whose turn it is.

- **status** indicates if the game is **active** or **finished**.

Game Moves Table

```
CREATE TABLE moves (
    move_id INT AUTO_INCREMENT PRIMARY KEY,
    game_id INT,
    player_id INT,
    move_data TEXT,
    created_at TIMESTAMP DEFAULT CURRENT_TIMESTAMP
);
```

- Each move is recorded with **player ID** and **game ID**.

Handling Player Turns in PHP

Players take turns making moves. The backend must **validate turns** and **update the game state**.

Processing a Player's Move

```php
<?php
$conn = new mysqli("localhost", "root", "", "game_db");

function makeMove($gameId, $playerId, $moveData) {
    global $conn;

    // Get the current turn
    $stmt = $conn->prepare("SELECT current_turn, player1_id, player2_id FROM
            games WHERE game_id = ?");
    $stmt->bind_param("i", $gameId);
    $stmt->execute();
    $result = $stmt->get_result()->fetch_assoc();

    $currentTurn = $result['current_turn'];
    $expectedPlayer = ($currentTurn % 2 == 1) ? $result['player1_id'] :
            $result['player2_id'];
```

```php
    if ($playerId != $expectedPlayer) {
        return "Not your turn!";
    }

    // Record the move
    $stmt = $conn->prepare("INSERT INTO moves (game_id, player_id, move_data)
            VALUES (?, ?, ?)");
    $stmt->bind_param("iis", $gameId, $playerId, $moveData);
    $stmt->execute();

    // Update the turn
    $stmt = $conn->prepare("UPDATE games SET current_turn = current_turn + 1
            WHERE game_id = ?");
    $stmt->bind_param("i", $gameId);
    $stmt->execute();

    return "Move recorded!";
}
?>
```

- Checks if it's the **correct player's turn**.

- Saves the **move data**.

- Increments **turn counter** to allow the next player to move.

Displaying the Game Board

Players see the **game state** through an interface. The frontend **fetches moves** via AJAX.

Fetching Game Moves in PHP

```php
<?php
$conn = new mysqli("localhost", "root", "", "game_db");

function getMoves($gameId) {
    global $conn;
    $stmt = $conn->prepare("SELECT player_id, move_data FROM moves WHERE game_id
            = ?");
    $stmt->bind_param("i", $gameId);
    $stmt->execute();
    $result = $stmt->get_result();

    $moves = [];
    while ($row = $result->fetch_assoc()) {
        $moves[] = $row;
    }
    echo json_encode($moves);
}
?>
```

- Retrieves **all moves** for a given game session.

- Sends **JSON data** to the frontend for rendering.

Frontend JavaScript to Fetch Moves

```javascript
function fetchMoves(gameId) {
    fetch(`get_moves.php?game_id=${gameId}`)
```

```
        .then(response => response.json())
        .then(data => {
            console.log("Game Moves:", data);
        });
}
```

- Calls the PHP script to get **move history**.

- Updates the **game board dynamically**.

PHP facilitates **turn-based game development** by managing **game state, turns, and real-time updates**. By integrating **WebSockets or AJAX**, players receive **seamless feedback**. This structured approach allows for **scalable, multiplayer PHP games**, demonstrating PHP's versatility beyond traditional web applications.

PHP in IoT and Smart Devices

PHP, traditionally a server-side language, has found applications in **Internet of Things (IoT) ecosystems**. With its robust API handling, database connectivity, and ability to interact with **MQTT brokers**, PHP can process IoT data, manage smart devices, and provide web-based dashboards. This module explores how PHP can integrate with IoT devices, handle data streams, and build IoT-focused applications.

PHP for IoT Data Processing and API Integrations

IoT devices generate large amounts of **sensor data**, which must be processed, stored, and analyzed in real-time. PHP plays a crucial role in handling **data ingestion, storage, and retrieval**. With its extensive API capabilities, PHP can integrate with **RESTful APIs, WebSockets, and cloud platforms** to manage IoT ecosystems.

Using PHP's **cURL and HTTP request handling**, developers can retrieve data from IoT endpoints, process it, and store it in relational databases such as **MySQL or PostgreSQL**. Additionally, PHP-based APIs can serve as **middleware** for edge devices, allowing seamless communication between **hardware components and web-based dashboards**. This section explores best practices for **efficient data processing and API integration** in IoT applications.

Communicating with IoT Devices Using PHP and MQTT

Message Queuing Telemetry Transport (MQTT) is a lightweight protocol optimized for IoT communication. Unlike traditional HTTP-based communication, MQTT uses a **publish-subscribe model** that allows efficient, low-latency messaging between IoT devices and PHP-based applications.

PHP can interact with **MQTT brokers (like Mosquitto or HiveMQ)** to receive real-time updates from IoT sensors. By leveraging PHP's **MQTT libraries**, developers can subscribe to topics, process incoming messages, and trigger specific actions.

This section details how to establish **MQTT connections**, manage **data streams**, and integrate **PHP-based MQTT clients** into IoT infrastructures. The goal is to enable PHP applications to **control and monitor smart devices in real-time**, making it a viable backend for IoT automation systems.

Building IoT Dashboards and Smart Device Management Systems

IoT applications often require **real-time dashboards** to display device status, sensor readings, and system alerts. PHP, combined with **JavaScript frameworks (Vue.js, React, or Chart.js)**, can generate **interactive IoT dashboards** that visualize live data.

PHP-based management systems can also provide **remote control capabilities**, allowing users to **send commands** to IoT devices. Through **AJAX requests, WebSockets, and API endpoints**, PHP applications can facilitate **bi-directional communication** between users and smart devices.

Key components of an IoT dashboard include:

- **Device authentication and user access control**

- **Real-time sensor data visualization**

- **Control panels for adjusting device settings**

- **Logging and alerting for critical events**

This section explains how PHP can power **smart device management** systems, ensuring **secure and efficient** remote administration.

Case Study: Developing a PHP-Based Home Automation System

To illustrate PHP's role in IoT, this case study explores the development of a **home automation system** powered by PHP. The system integrates with **smart sensors, relays, and MQTT brokers** to control devices such as **lights, thermostats, and security systems**.

The case study details:

- **Setting up an MQTT-enabled PHP backend**

- **Building a web-based control panel for smart devices**

- **Automating home routines based on sensor data**

This example demonstrates how PHP can drive IoT innovations, offering a **cost-effective, flexible** approach to smart device management.

PHP's adaptability makes it a powerful tool for **IoT data processing, device communication, and real-time monitoring**. Through **API integrations, MQTT messaging, and interactive dashboards**, PHP can serve as a **backend for IoT ecosystems**, enabling efficient **automation and remote device control**. This module highlights **best practices** for developing **scalable, PHP-driven IoT applications**.

PHP for IoT Data Processing and API Integrations

The **Internet of Things (IoT)** relies on vast amounts of sensor data that need to be collected, processed, and acted upon efficiently. PHP, despite being a server-side language, can play a significant role in managing IoT data flows by acting as a middleware or backend system. It enables seamless **data processing, storage, and API integrations** with cloud platforms and third-party services. In this section, we will explore how PHP can handle **incoming IoT data**, process it in real-time, and communicate with **external APIs** to extend IoT applications.

Receiving and Processing IoT Data

IoT devices often send **HTTP requests** or push data via **RESTful APIs**. PHP can handle these requests, extract data, and store it in a **MySQL or NoSQL database**. The following example demonstrates a **PHP API endpoint** that receives sensor data from an IoT device:

```php
<?php
// Connect to MySQL database
$pdo = new PDO("mysql:host=localhost;dbname=iot_data", "user", "password");

// Get incoming JSON data
$data = json_decode(file_get_contents("php://input"), true);

// Insert sensor data into database
$query = "INSERT INTO sensors (device_id, temperature, humidity, timestamp)
          VALUES (:device_id, :temperature, :humidity, NOW())";
$stmt = $pdo->prepare($query);
$stmt->execute([
    'device_id' => $data['device_id'],
    'temperature' => $data['temperature'],
    'humidity' => $data['humidity']
]);

echo json_encode(["status" => "success"]);
?>
```

Here, PHP listens for incoming sensor data, extracts relevant values, and stores them in a **relational database**. This approach ensures that IoT data is **organized and accessible** for further processing.

Integrating PHP with Third-Party APIs

IoT applications often need to **send data to cloud platforms** or external APIs. PHP's **cURL library** allows seamless API interactions. The following example demonstrates how PHP can send sensor data to an external IoT analytics service:

```php
<?php
// Data to send
$postData = [
    'device_id' => 'sensor_123',
    'temperature' => 25.4,
    'humidity' => 60
];

// Initialize cURL
$ch = curl_init("https://api.iotanalytics.com/data");
curl_setopt($ch, CURLOPT_RETURNTRANSFER, true);
```

```php
curl_setopt($ch, CURLOPT_POST, true);
curl_setopt($ch, CURLOPT_POSTFIELDS, json_encode($postData));
curl_setopt($ch, CURLOPT_HTTPHEADER, ['Content-Type: application/json']);

// Execute and get response
$response = curl_exec($ch);
curl_close($ch);

echo "Response from API: " . $response;
?>
```

This script sends **sensor readings** to a remote IoT analytics platform, demonstrating how PHP can act as a **gateway between IoT devices and cloud services**.

Real-Time IoT Data Processing with PHP

While PHP is not a real-time language, it can be combined with **message queues** such as **Redis, RabbitMQ, or WebSockets** to process data efficiently. PHP scripts can **fetch queued data**, process it, and trigger necessary actions.

For example, using **Redis Pub/Sub**, PHP can listen for IoT updates:

```php
<?php
$redis = new Redis();
$redis->connect('127.0.0.1', 6379);

$redis->subscribe(['iot_channel'], function ($redis, $channel, $message) {
    echo "Received message: " . $message;
});
?>
```

This approach enables **event-driven IoT applications**, where PHP processes data only when necessary, improving efficiency.

PHP is well-suited for **handling IoT data streams, integrating with APIs, and processing information efficiently**. By leveraging **RESTful APIs, cURL, WebSockets, and message queues**, PHP can serve as a powerful **middleware** for IoT applications, ensuring **scalability and real-time responsiveness**. This section has demonstrated **best practices** for PHP-powered IoT data processing.

Communicating with IoT Devices Using PHP and MQTT

The **Message Queuing Telemetry Transport (MQTT)** protocol is widely used in **IoT applications** for lightweight and efficient communication between devices. Unlike traditional HTTP-based requests, MQTT enables **real-time, low-latency, and reliable messaging**, making it ideal for **sensor networks, smart home devices, and industrial IoT** systems. PHP can act as an MQTT **client**, allowing it to send and receive messages from **IoT brokers**. This section explores how PHP interacts with MQTT, sending commands to IoT devices and receiving sensor data.

Understanding MQTT for IoT Communication

MQTT follows a **publish-subscribe (Pub/Sub)** model, where devices (clients) **publish** messages to topics, and other devices **subscribe** to those topics to receive updates. A central **MQTT broker** (such as **Mosquitto or HiveMQ**) facilitates communication. PHP, although not designed for real-time messaging, can still interact with MQTT brokers to **send commands and process incoming data**.

Key components of MQTT include:

- **Broker:** Manages message distribution between clients.

- **Publishers:** Send messages to specific topics.

- **Subscribers:** Receive messages from subscribed topics.

- **Topics:** Channels through which messages are transmitted (e.g., "home/livingroom/temperature").

Setting Up an MQTT Broker for PHP Communication

Before using PHP with MQTT, ensure an MQTT broker is installed. For local testing, **Mosquitto** can be installed using:

```
sudo apt update
sudo apt install mosquitto mosquitto-clients
```

To test the broker, publish a message:

```
mosquitto_pub -h localhost -t "home/livingroom/temp" -m "25.4"
```

Then, subscribe to the topic:

```
mosquitto_sub -h localhost -t "home/livingroom/temp"
```

Now, PHP can interact with MQTT using a **PHP MQTT client library**, such as php-mqtt/client.

Publishing Messages to an IoT Device with PHP

To send data to an IoT device via MQTT, install the **php-mqtt/client** library using Composer:

```
composer require php-mqtt/client
```

Then, use the following PHP script to publish a temperature update to an MQTT topic:

```
<?php
require 'vendor/autoload.php';

use PhpMqtt\Client\MqttClient;
```

```php
$server   = 'mqtt.example.com';   // Replace with your broker address
$port     = 1883;
$clientId = 'php_mqtt_client';

$mqtt = new MqttClient($server, $port, $clientId);
$mqtt->connect();

$topic = "home/livingroom/temp";
$message = "25.4"; // Temperature value

$mqtt->publish($topic, $message, 0);
$mqtt->disconnect();

echo "Message published to $topic";
?>
```

This script connects to an **MQTT broker**, sends a **temperature reading**, and disconnects. IoT devices listening to "home/livingroom/temp" receive the message in **real time**.

Subscribing to IoT Sensor Data with PHP

PHP can also act as an **MQTT subscriber** to receive updates from IoT devices. The following script listens for messages on a topic:

```php
<?php
require 'vendor/autoload.php';

use PhpMqtt\Client\MqttClient;

$server   = 'mqtt.example.com';
$port     = 1883;
$clientId = 'php_mqtt_subscriber';

$mqtt = new MqttClient($server, $port, $clientId);
$mqtt->connect();

$mqtt->subscribe('home/livingroom/temp', function ($topic, $message) {
    echo "Received message on $topic: $message\n";
}, 0);

$mqtt->loop(true);
?>
```

This script continuously listens for **temperature updates**, making it ideal for **real-time monitoring applications**.

Integrating PHP-MQTT with IoT Dashboards

PHP can store incoming **sensor data** in a database and display it on a **web dashboard**. Using AJAX and WebSockets, PHP can provide **live updates** from IoT devices.

A simple example of retrieving stored sensor data using PHP:

```php
<?php
$pdo = new PDO("mysql:host=localhost;dbname=iot_data", "user", "password");

$query = $pdo->query("SELECT * FROM sensors ORDER BY timestamp DESC LIMIT 10");
$data = $query->fetchAll(PDO::FETCH_ASSOC);
```

```
echo json_encode($data);
?>
```

This allows a **web application** to retrieve and display recent sensor readings.

PHP can effectively interact with **MQTT brokers**, enabling real-time **IoT device communication**. By **publishing messages to IoT devices, subscribing to sensor data, and integrating with web dashboards**, PHP extends its role in **IoT ecosystems**. This section demonstrated how **PHP and MQTT** facilitate **seamless IoT communication** for smart applications.

Building IoT Dashboards and Smart Device Management Systems

A **smart device management system** enables users to **monitor, control, and interact with IoT devices** from a central web-based dashboard. PHP, when integrated with **databases, WebSockets, and APIs**, can create **real-time IoT dashboards** that display sensor data, trigger device actions, and log device interactions. This section explores building an IoT dashboard using PHP and modern web technologies.

Key Features of an IoT Dashboard

An effective **IoT dashboard** should provide:

1. **Live Data Visualization:** Real-time display of sensor readings (e.g., temperature, humidity, motion).

2. **Device Control Panel:** Interface for sending commands (e.g., turning devices ON/OFF).

3. **Historical Data Logs:** Storage and retrieval of past device readings for analysis.

4. **User Authentication:** Secure access to dashboard functionalities.

5. **Alerts and Notifications:** Triggered when sensor values exceed thresholds.

PHP serves as the **backend processor**, handling device communication, database interactions, and front-end data rendering.

Storing IoT Data in a Database

To track sensor readings over time, create a **MySQL table** for logging IoT data:

```
CREATE TABLE sensor_data (
    id INT AUTO_INCREMENT PRIMARY KEY,
    device_name VARCHAR(50),
    sensor_type VARCHAR(50),
    value FLOAT,
    timestamp TIMESTAMP DEFAULT CURRENT_TIMESTAMP
);
```

256

When IoT devices send data to the server, PHP stores it in the database:

```php
<?php
$pdo = new PDO("mysql:host=localhost;dbname=iot_dashboard", "user", "password");

$device = $_POST['device_name'];
$sensor = $_POST['sensor_type'];
$value  = $_POST['value'];

$query = $pdo->prepare("INSERT INTO sensor_data (device_name, sensor_type,
        value) VALUES (?, ?, ?)");
$query->execute([$device, $sensor, $value]);

echo "Data recorded successfully!";
?>
```

IoT devices send data via **HTTP POST requests** to this script, ensuring real-time database updates.

Fetching and Displaying Sensor Data on the Dashboard

To retrieve stored sensor readings, use the following **PHP API** endpoint:

```php
<?php
header("Content-Type: application/json");
$pdo = new PDO("mysql:host=localhost;dbname=iot_dashboard", "user", "password");

$query = $pdo->query("SELECT * FROM sensor_data ORDER BY timestamp DESC LIMIT
        10");
$data = $query->fetchAll(PDO::FETCH_ASSOC);

echo json_encode($data);
?>
```

A **JavaScript frontend** can periodically call this API to update the dashboard:

```javascript
setInterval(() => {
    fetch("fetch_sensor_data.php")
        .then(response => response.json())
        .then(data => console.log(data));
}, 5000);
```

This approach keeps the **dashboard refreshed** with real-time sensor readings.

Controlling IoT Devices from the Dashboard

To send commands to IoT devices, create a PHP script that updates the device state:

```php
<?php
$pdo = new PDO("mysql:host=localhost;dbname=iot_dashboard", "user", "password");

$device  = $_POST['device_name'];
$command = $_POST['command']; // Example: 'ON' or 'OFF'

$query = $pdo->prepare("UPDATE devices SET status = ? WHERE device_name = ?");
$query->execute([$command, $device]);

echo "Command sent to $device";
```

```
?>
```

A frontend **button click** can trigger this script using AJAX:

```
function sendCommand(device, command) {
    fetch("send_command.php", {
        method: "POST",
        body: new URLSearchParams({ device_name: device, command: command })
    }).then(response => response.text())
      .then(data => console.log(data));
}
```

This allows users to control **smart devices remotely** via the dashboard.

Using WebSockets for Real-Time Updates

Instead of relying on periodic API calls, **WebSockets** provide **instant updates** from IoT devices to the dashboard. A **PHP WebSocket server** listens for device messages and broadcasts updates to connected clients.

Setting Up a PHP WebSocket Server

```
<?php
$server = new WebSocketServer("0.0.0.0", 8080);
$server->on("message", function ($conn, $msg) {
    $conn->send("Received: $msg");
});
$server->run();
?>
```

IoT devices send messages to this WebSocket, which **immediately updates the dashboard**, eliminating the need for frequent AJAX requests.

By combining **PHP, MySQL, WebSockets, and AJAX**, an interactive **IoT dashboard** can be built for **smart device management**. PHP facilitates **real-time data visualization, device control, and secure communication**, making it a powerful tool for **monitoring and controlling IoT ecosystems**.

Case Study: Developing a PHP-Based Home Automation System

A **home automation system** allows users to remotely control devices such as **lights, thermostats, security cameras, and smart appliances**. Using **PHP as the backend**, MQTT for IoT messaging, and WebSockets for real-time communication, we can build a system that enables **smart home control** through a web-based dashboard.

System Architecture

A **PHP-based home automation system** consists of:

1. **IoT Devices**: Sensors and actuators (lights, motion detectors, smart plugs).

2. **PHP Backend**: Handles API requests, processes data, and manages device states.

3. **Database (MySQL)**: Stores device configurations and user preferences.

4. **MQTT Broker**: Facilitates communication between PHP and IoT devices.

5. **Web Dashboard**: Provides an interface for monitoring and controlling devices.

This architecture ensures **scalability, real-time updates, and secure device management**.

Setting Up Device Control with PHP and MQTT

IoT devices often use **MQTT (Message Queuing Telemetry Transport)** to communicate with the backend. The **PHP MQTT client (phpMQTT)** can be used to send commands.

Installing phpMQTT (via Composer)

```
composer require bluerhinos/phpmqtt
```

Sending MQTT Commands to a Smart Device

```php
<?php
require("phpMQTT.php");

$server = "mqtt.example.com";
$port = 1883;
$client_id = "php_mqtt_client";

$mqtt = new phpMQTT($server, $port, $client_id);
if ($mqtt->connect()) {
    $mqtt->publish("home/lights/livingroom", "ON", 0);
    $mqtt->close();
    echo "Command sent!";
}
?>
```

When this script runs, the **MQTT broker** relays the command to subscribed smart devices, switching the **living room light ON**.

Receiving Sensor Data from IoT Devices

IoT sensors publish **temperature, motion, or light levels** via MQTT topics. The PHP backend listens for these updates and stores them in a **MySQL database**.

```php
<?php
require("phpMQTT.php");

$server = "mqtt.example.com";
$port = 1883;
$client_id = "php_mqtt_subscriber";

$mqtt = new phpMQTT($server, $port, $client_id);
if ($mqtt->connect()) {
    $topics["home/sensors/temperature"] = ["qos" => 0, "function" => "logData"];
    $mqtt->subscribe($topics);
}
```

```php
function logData($topic, $message) {
    $pdo = new PDO("mysql:host=localhost;dbname=home_automation", "user",
        "password");
    $query = $pdo->prepare("INSERT INTO sensor_data (sensor, value) VALUES (?,
        ?)");
    $query->execute([$topic, $message]);
}

$mqtt->close();
?>
```

Now, each time a **temperature sensor** publishes a reading, PHP **records** it in the database.

Creating a Web Dashboard for Smart Home Control

A **PHP web dashboard** enables users to **view sensor data and control devices** via an intuitive interface.

Fetching Sensor Data for Display

```php
<?php
header("Content-Type: application/json");
$pdo = new PDO("mysql:host=localhost;dbname=home_automation", "user",
        "password");

$query = $pdo->query("SELECT * FROM sensor_data ORDER BY timestamp DESC LIMIT
        5");
echo json_encode($query->fetchAll(PDO::FETCH_ASSOC));
?>
```

A **JavaScript frontend** can call this API to update the dashboard dynamically:

```javascript
setInterval(() => {
    fetch("fetch_sensor_data.php")
        .then(response => response.json())
        .then(data => console.log(data));
}, 5000);
```

Sending Commands from the Web Dashboard

To **turn a device ON/OFF**, the frontend sends a **POST request** to PHP:

```php
<?php
$device = $_POST['device'];
$command = $_POST['command']; // ON or OFF

file_get_contents("http://mqtt.example.com/send?device=$device&command=$command"
        );
?>
```

The frontend **triggers this script** on button clicks:

```javascript
function controlDevice(device, command) {
    fetch("control_device.php", {
        method: "POST",
        body: new URLSearchParams({ device: device, command: command })
    });
}
```

This setup enables **real-time control** of smart home devices from the dashboard.

Implementing User Authentication for Secure Access

To **restrict access**, implement **PHP user authentication** with sessions.

```php
<?php
session_start();
if (!isset($_SESSION['user_id'])) {
    header("Location: login.php");
    exit();
}
?>
```

Now, only **authenticated users** can access the **home automation dashboard**.

A **PHP-based home automation system** integrates **IoT devices, MQTT messaging, and real-time dashboards** to provide seamless **smart home control**. With **secure authentication, live monitoring, and device management**, PHP proves to be a powerful backend for **IoT-driven automation**.

Module 26:
Security & Cryptography in PHP Applications

Security is a critical aspect of PHP development, ensuring that applications protect user data, prevent unauthorized access, and maintain integrity. This module explores various **security mechanisms** in PHP, including **secure password hashing, encryption, protection against vulnerabilities, and secure API communications**. A case study will illustrate how to build a **robust authentication system** using PHP's best security practices.

Implementing Secure Password Hashing and User Authentication

User authentication is the backbone of secure PHP applications. Secure password management involves **salting and hashing** to prevent attacks such as **rainbow table and brute-force attacks**. PHP provides the **password_hash()** function for hashing and **password_verify()** for checking password validity. Additionally, multi-factor authentication (MFA) can enhance security by requiring users to provide additional verification, such as a time-based one-time password (TOTP).

Session management is another crucial component. PHP sessions store user authentication states but must be handled securely to prevent **session fixation and hijacking**. Implementing **HTTP-only cookies and regenerating session IDs** can help mitigate these risks. Proper access control mechanisms should also be in place, enforcing **role-based authentication** to prevent unauthorized actions.

Using PHP for Data Encryption and Secure API Communications

Data encryption ensures sensitive information remains protected, whether **stored in databases or transmitted over networks**. PHP provides robust encryption mechanisms using **OpenSSL and Sodium libraries** for **symmetric and asymmetric encryption**. **AES encryption** (Advanced Encryption Standard) is commonly used for securing stored data, while **RSA encryption** is often used for securing API communications.

For secure API communications, PHP applications should implement **SSL/TLS encryption**, ensuring all data exchanged between clients and servers is encrypted. **OAuth 2.0 and JWT (JSON Web Token)** provide secure authentication for APIs, ensuring **only authorized clients can access protected resources**.

Another critical security measure is **HMAC (Hash-based Message Authentication Code)**, which ensures the integrity and authenticity of API requests. By using **HMAC with SHA-256**, PHP applications can verify that API messages have not been tampered with.

Protecting Against Common Web Vulnerabilities in PHP Applications

Web applications are prone to several vulnerabilities if not properly secured. The most common threats include **SQL injection, cross-site scripting (XSS), cross-site request forgery (CSRF), and remote code execution (RCE)**. PHP provides built-in functions and best practices to mitigate these risks.

- **SQL Injection Prevention**: Using **prepared statements and parameterized queries** in **PDO** prevents attackers from injecting malicious SQL code.

- **XSS Protection**: User inputs should be sanitized using **htmlspecialchars()** to prevent execution of malicious scripts in browsers.

- **CSRF Mitigation**: Implementing **CSRF tokens** in forms ensures that malicious actors cannot forge unauthorized requests on behalf of a user.

- **Input Validation**: All user inputs should be validated using **filter_var()** to prevent unexpected code execution or data manipulation.

By adopting secure coding practices, PHP applications can significantly reduce vulnerabilities and ensure a **safe user experience**.

Case Study: Building a Secure User Authentication System with PHP

To illustrate the concepts covered in this module, a **secure user authentication system** will be implemented. This system will use **password hashing, secure session management, multi-factor authentication, and role-based access control**. API security measures such as **JWT authentication and encrypted user data storage** will also be integrated to ensure a **comprehensive security framework**.

Security and cryptography are fundamental to building **reliable PHP applications**. By implementing **secure password storage, encryption, secure API communication, and protection against common vulnerabilities**, PHP developers can **ensure application security and user data integrity**. This module provides a **practical guide to securing PHP applications**, reinforced by a **real-world authentication system case study**.

Implementing Secure Password Hashing and User Authentication

In PHP applications, securing user authentication is essential for protecting sensitive user data. Passwords should never be stored in plaintext but rather hashed using secure algorithms. PHP provides the password_hash() function, which applies **bcrypt**, **Argon2**, or

263

other secure hashing methods to store passwords safely. Similarly, the password_verify() function is used to validate user passwords securely.

Hashing Passwords Securely

PHP's password_hash() function simplifies password security by automatically handling the generation of a cryptographic salt. Here's an example of how to **hash a password before storing it in a database**:

```php
$password = 'user_secure_password';
$hashedPassword = password_hash($password, PASSWORD_DEFAULT);
echo $hashedPassword;
```

This hashed password can then be stored in a database rather than storing the plaintext password.

Verifying a Password

When a user logs in, their inputted password must be compared against the stored hash:

```php
$inputPassword = 'user_secure_password';
if (password_verify($inputPassword, $hashedPassword)) {
    echo "Password is correct!";
} else {
    echo "Invalid password!";
}
```

Using this approach prevents attackers from gaining access to plaintext passwords, even if they obtain the database.

Session Management and Secure Authentication

Session hijacking and fixation attacks are common threats in web applications. PHP uses session variables to track user authentication, but these must be secured to prevent unauthorized access.

Starting a Secure Session

```php
session_start();
$_SESSION['user_id'] = $userID;
$_SESSION['authenticated'] = true;
```

To protect against **session fixation attacks**, regenerate the session ID after login:

```php
session_regenerate_id(true);
```

Using HTTP-Only and Secure Cookies

Setting session cookies as **HTTP-only** and **secure** ensures that they cannot be accessed by JavaScript (mitigating XSS attacks) and are only transmitted over HTTPS:

```
session_set_cookie_params([
    'lifetime' => 0,
    'path' => '/',
    'domain' => '',
    'secure' => true,
    'httponly' => true,
    'samesite' => 'Strict'
]);
```

Implementing Multi-Factor Authentication (MFA)

For additional security, **multi-factor authentication (MFA)** can be implemented. One common method is Time-Based One-Time Passwords (TOTP) using the **Google Authenticator** or similar services. PHP's random_bytes() can be used to generate secure **MFA secrets**.

```
$secret = bin2hex(random_bytes(10));
echo "Your MFA Secret: " . $secret;
```

The generated secret is then used to validate one-time passwords entered by the user.

Role-Based Access Control (RBAC)

Enforcing **Role-Based Access Control (RBAC)** ensures that users can only perform actions permitted by their assigned roles.

```
function checkUserRole($userRole) {
    $allowedRoles = ['admin', 'editor'];
    if (in_array($userRole, $allowedRoles)) {
        return true;
    }
    return false;
}
```

By integrating **password hashing, secure sessions, MFA, and role-based authentication**, PHP applications can **ensure robust user security and prevent unauthorized access**.

Using PHP for Data Encryption and Secure API Communications

In modern PHP applications, securing sensitive data and ensuring safe API communication is crucial. PHP provides robust encryption mechanisms using **OpenSSL** and **Sodium** libraries to protect data at rest and in transit. This section explores how to implement encryption and secure API communications using PHP.

Encrypting and Decrypting Data in PHP

To prevent unauthorized access to sensitive data, encryption is essential. PHP's **OpenSSL extension** allows for symmetric encryption using AES (Advanced Encryption Standard).

Encrypting Data with OpenSSL

```
function encryptData($data, $key) {
```

```php
    $cipher = "aes-256-cbc";
    $iv = openssl_random_pseudo_bytes(openssl_cipher_iv_length($cipher));
    $encrypted = openssl_encrypt($data, $cipher, $key, 0, $iv);
    return base64_encode($iv . $encrypted);
}

$secretKey = "my_secure_key_32_chars";
$plainText = "Sensitive Information";
$encryptedData = encryptData($plainText, $secretKey);
echo "Encrypted Data: " . $encryptedData;
```

Here, we use **AES-256-CBC**, a strong encryption algorithm. The **IV (Initialization Vector)** ensures that identical inputs produce different encrypted outputs, enhancing security.

Decrypting Data

```php
function decryptData($encryptedData, $key) {
    $cipher = "aes-256-cbc";
    $data = base64_decode($encryptedData);
    $ivLength = openssl_cipher_iv_length($cipher);
    $iv = substr($data, 0, $ivLength);
    $ciphertext = substr($data, $ivLength);
    return openssl_decrypt($ciphertext, $cipher, $key, 0, $iv);
}

$decryptedText = decryptData($encryptedData, $secretKey);
echo "Decrypted Data: " . $decryptedText;
```

This method ensures that encrypted data can only be decrypted using the correct **secret key**.

Securing API Communications with HTTPS and JWT

Forcing HTTPS in API Requests

All API requests should be served over **HTTPS** to prevent **Man-in-the-Middle (MITM) attacks**. A PHP script can enforce HTTPS:

```php
if (empty($_SERVER['HTTPS']) || $_SERVER['HTTPS'] !== 'on') {
    header("HTTP/1.1 403 Forbidden");
    exit("Secure HTTPS connection required.");
}
```

This ensures that clients cannot access the API over an insecure connection.

Implementing JSON Web Tokens (JWT) for API Authentication

JWT is widely used for **stateless authentication** in APIs. It consists of a **header**, **payload**, and **signature**, ensuring data integrity. The **Firebase JWT PHP library** can be used for generating and verifying tokens.

Generating a JWT Token in PHP

```php
use Firebase\JWT\JWT;
```

```php
$key = "my_secret_key";
$payload = [
    "user_id" => 123,
    "exp" => time() + 3600
];

$jwt = JWT::encode($payload, $key, 'HS256');
echo "JWT Token: " . $jwt;
```

Verifying a JWT Token

```php
use Firebase\JWT\JWT;
use Firebase\JWT\Key;

$decoded = JWT::decode($jwt, new Key($key, 'HS256'));
print_r($decoded);
```

This implementation ensures that only authenticated users can access API resources.

Using **encryption** and **secure API authentication** prevents data breaches and unauthorized access. By integrating **OpenSSL encryption**, **HTTPS enforcement**, and **JWT authentication**, PHP applications can ensure that sensitive data remains **confidential, secure, and tamper-proof** during storage and transmission.

Protecting Against Common Web Vulnerabilities in PHP Applications

Web applications face numerous security threats, including **SQL injection, cross-site scripting (XSS), cross-site request forgery (CSRF), and remote code execution (RCE)**. Protecting against these vulnerabilities is crucial for ensuring the safety of PHP applications. This section covers best practices and techniques to mitigate these security risks.

Preventing SQL Injection

SQL injection occurs when malicious SQL code is inserted into input fields, allowing attackers to manipulate database queries. The **PDO (PHP Data Objects) prepared statements** provide a secure way to handle database queries.

Unsafe SQL Query (Vulnerable to SQL Injection)

```php
$pdo = new PDO("mysql:host=localhost;dbname=test", "root", "password");
$userInput = $_GET['username'];
$query = "SELECT * FROM users WHERE username = '$userInput'"; // Vulnerable!
$stmt = $pdo->query($query);
```

Secure SQL Query Using Prepared Statements

```php
$stmt = $pdo->prepare("SELECT * FROM users WHERE username = :username");
$stmt->execute(['username' => $_GET['username']]);
$user = $stmt->fetch();
```

By using **bound parameters**, this approach prevents **malicious SQL injection attacks**.

Mitigating Cross-Site Scripting (XSS)

XSS attacks inject malicious scripts into webpages viewed by users. These scripts can steal cookies, session tokens, or redirect users to phishing websites.

Unsafe Code (Vulnerable to XSS)

```
echo "Welcome, " . $_GET['name']; // If input is:
        <script>alert('Hacked');</script>
```

Safe Code Using HTML Escaping

```
echo "Welcome, " . htmlspecialchars($_GET['name'], ENT_QUOTES, 'UTF-8');
```

Using **htmlspecialchars()** prevents scripts from executing by converting characters like < and > into safe HTML entities.

Defending Against Cross-Site Request Forgery (CSRF)

CSRF tricks users into executing unwanted actions on a trusted site by using their authenticated session. Implementing CSRF tokens helps protect against this attack.

Generating a CSRF Token

```
session_start();
if (empty($_SESSION['csrf_token'])) {
    $_SESSION['csrf_token'] = bin2hex(random_bytes(32));
}
```

Using CSRF Token in Forms

```
<form method="POST">
    <input type="hidden" name="csrf_token" value="<?= $_SESSION['csrf_token'];
        ?>">
    <input type="submit" value="Submit">
</form>
```

Validating the CSRF Token

```
if ($_POST['csrf_token'] !== $_SESSION['csrf_token']) {
    die("CSRF token validation failed.");
}
```

This ensures that only legitimate requests from authenticated users are processed.

Preventing Remote Code Execution (RCE)

RCE attacks occur when user input is executed as PHP code, leading to system compromise. Functions like eval(), exec(), and system() should be avoided.

Unsafe Code (Vulnerable to RCE)

```php
$command = $_GET['cmd'];
system($command); // If input is: rm -rf /
```

Safe Code Using Whitelisted Commands

```php
$allowedCommands = ['ls', 'whoami'];
$command = $_GET['cmd'];
if (in_array($command, $allowedCommands)) {
    echo shell_exec(escapeshellcmd($command));
} else {
    echo "Command not allowed!";
}
```

Securing PHP applications requires a proactive approach. Using **prepared statements**, **escaping user input**, **CSRF protection**, and **avoiding dangerous functions** can **significantly reduce** the risk of common vulnerabilities. Implementing these best practices ensures a **secure, resilient, and trusted** PHP application.

Case Study: Building a Secure User Authentication System with PHP

User authentication is a critical component of secure web applications. A well-implemented authentication system protects against attacks such as password breaches, session hijacking, and unauthorized access. This case study walks through the **design and implementation** of a secure authentication system in PHP, incorporating **password hashing, session management, and authentication controls**.

Step 1: Database Schema for User Authentication

The first step is designing a **users table** with secure password storage. Instead of storing plain-text passwords, **password hashing** using password_hash() should be used.

Users Table Schema (MySQL)

```sql
CREATE TABLE users (
    id INT AUTO_INCREMENT PRIMARY KEY,
    username VARCHAR(50) UNIQUE NOT NULL,
    email VARCHAR(100) UNIQUE NOT NULL,
    password_hash VARCHAR(255) NOT NULL,
    created_at TIMESTAMP DEFAULT CURRENT_TIMESTAMP
);
```

This table securely stores user credentials, ensuring that passwords are **hashed** before being saved.

Step 2: User Registration with Password Hashing

During user registration, the password should be hashed using PHP's password_hash() function before being stored in the database.

Registration Script (register.php)

```php
<?php
require 'db.php';

if ($_SERVER["REQUEST_METHOD"] == "POST") {
    $username = $_POST['username'];
    $email = $_POST['email'];
    $password = $_POST['password'];

    // Hash the password
    $passwordHash = password_hash($password, PASSWORD_DEFAULT);

    // Insert into database
    $stmt = $pdo->prepare("INSERT INTO users (username, email, password_hash)
            VALUES (?, ?, ?)");
    $stmt->execute([$username, $email, $passwordHash]);

    echo "Registration successful!";
}
?>
```

This ensures that even if the database is compromised, **plain-text passwords are not exposed**.

Step 3: Secure User Login with Password Verification

When a user logs in, the system verifies the hashed password using password_verify().

Login Script (login.php)

```php
<?php
session_start();
require 'db.php';

if ($_SERVER["REQUEST_METHOD"] == "POST") {
    $username = $_POST['username'];
    $password = $_POST['password'];

    $stmt = $pdo->prepare("SELECT id, password_hash FROM users WHERE username =
            ?");
    $stmt->execute([$username]);
    $user = $stmt->fetch();

    if ($user && password_verify($password, $user['password_hash'])) {
        $_SESSION['user_id'] = $user['id']; // Store user session
        echo "Login successful!";
    } else {
        echo "Invalid credentials!";
    }
}
?>
```

Using **password_verify()** prevents login attempts from working with precomputed hashes (rainbow table attacks).

Step 4: Implementing Secure Sessions

After successful authentication, **sessions** should be managed securely.

Best Practices for Secure Sessions

- Use session_regenerate_id(true) after login to **prevent session fixation**.

- Store **only minimal user information** in session variables.

- Set session cookies to **HttpOnly and Secure** in php.ini:

```
session.cookie_httponly = 1
session.cookie_secure = 1
```

Logout Script (logout.php)

```php
<?php
session_start();
session_unset();
session_destroy();
header("Location: login.php");
exit;
?>
```

This ensures that sessions are **properly destroyed** when users log out.

Step 5: Implementing Account Lockout and Rate Limiting

To prevent **brute-force attacks**, account lockout mechanisms can be implemented.

Brute-force Protection: Rate Limit Logins

```php
$ip = $_SERVER['REMOTE_ADDR'];
$stmt = $pdo->prepare("SELECT COUNT(*) FROM login_attempts WHERE ip_address = ?
          AND attempt_time > NOW() - INTERVAL 10 MINUTE");
$stmt->execute([$ip]);
$attempts = $stmt->fetchColumn();

if ($attempts > 5) {
    die("Too many failed attempts. Try again later.");
}
```

Tracking failed login attempts helps in detecting and blocking repeated unauthorized access attempts.

This case study demonstrates how to build a **secure user authentication system in PHP**, incorporating **password hashing, secure session management, and brute-force protection**. By following best security practices, developers can **safeguard user credentials and protect applications** from common authentication vulnerabilities.

Module 27:
Server-Side Scripting and Performance Optimization

PHP plays a vital role in server-side processing, enabling dynamic web applications to function efficiently. This module delves into PHP's responsibilities in server-side scripting, performance optimization techniques, and managing large-scale applications. It also explores caching strategies to enhance scalability. The module concludes with a case study on optimizing a high-traffic PHP web service.

Understanding the Role of PHP in Server-Side Processing

PHP is a **server-side scripting language** that processes requests and generates responses dynamically before delivering them to the client. Unlike frontend languages such as JavaScript, PHP executes on the server, handling **database interactions, user authentication, session management, and file processing**.

PHP operates in a request-response cycle. When a client requests a PHP script, the web server processes it via an interpreter (such as PHP-FPM) and returns the output as HTML. This enables **dynamic content generation**, allowing websites to customize responses based on user input or database queries.

Understanding how PHP interacts with the server, manages requests, and executes scripts efficiently is key to building optimized applications. By leveraging server-side capabilities, PHP enables **secure, efficient, and scalable** web applications.

Optimizing PHP Applications for High Performance and Scalability

Performance optimization is crucial for PHP applications, especially when handling large amounts of data or high user traffic. Optimization techniques include **code efficiency, database indexing, caching, and resource management**.

Efficient PHP applications reduce execution time by minimizing **loops, redundant function calls, and unnecessary computations**. Using **PHP's built-in functions** instead of writing custom logic improves performance. For instance, array_map() is often faster than using loops for modifying arrays.

Database performance is enhanced through **query optimization, proper indexing, and connection pooling**. Reducing database calls using **prepared statements and caching**

272

mechanisms minimizes load and improves response time. **Opcode caching with OPcache** can significantly reduce script execution time by storing precompiled script bytecode.

Leveraging **asynchronous processing** and background jobs allows PHP to handle intensive tasks without slowing down web pages. **Job queues like Redis and RabbitMQ** offload heavy operations such as image processing and email sending to background workers. These techniques improve both **scalability and user experience**.

Managing Large-Scale Web Applications with PHP and Caching Strategies

Scaling PHP applications involves **load balancing, caching, and database replication**. When traffic increases, using multiple servers with **horizontal scaling** ensures availability. Load balancers distribute requests among multiple PHP servers to prevent bottlenecks.

Caching plays a vital role in improving speed. **Server-side caching strategies** include:

- **Opcode caching** (OPcache) stores precompiled PHP scripts to reduce CPU load.

- **Object caching** with **Memcached or Redis** stores frequently accessed data in memory to avoid repeated database queries.

- **Full-page caching** with **Varnish** accelerates response times by serving pre-generated HTML.

- **CDN (Content Delivery Networks)** store static assets closer to users, reducing latency.

Database management is also key in large-scale applications. **Sharding, replication, and indexing** improve performance by distributing load efficiently. Using **connection pooling** and persistent connections ensures the database can handle multiple concurrent requests without degradation.

Case Study: Scaling a PHP-Based Web Service for High Traffic

A high-traffic web service faces performance bottlenecks due to increased users, database queries, and resource-intensive operations. This case study explores optimizing a PHP-based web service for scalability by implementing **load balancing, caching, and asynchronous processing**.

The first step is analyzing bottlenecks using **profiling tools like Xdebug and New Relic**. Identifying slow queries, excessive memory usage, and inefficient code paths helps determine optimization strategies.

Load balancing is introduced using **NGINX or Apache reverse proxy**, distributing traffic across multiple PHP servers. This prevents overloading a single server and enhances **high availability**.

Next, caching layers are implemented. **Redis** is used for object caching, reducing repeated database queries. **Varnish** serves cached pages instantly, improving response time for frequently accessed pages.

Database optimization involves **indexing, query caching, and replication**. Read-heavy operations are handled by **read replicas**, offloading queries from the primary database. **Write operations are optimized** by batching queries and using prepared statements.

By implementing these strategies, the web service achieves improved **performance, reduced latency, and seamless scalability**, ensuring it can handle high traffic efficiently.

This module highlights PHP's server-side role, performance optimization strategies, and techniques for managing large-scale applications. Effective **caching, load balancing, and asynchronous processing** ensure scalable and high-performing applications. The case study provides a practical approach to handling high traffic in PHP-based web services. By applying these techniques, developers can create robust, efficient, and scalable PHP applications.

Understanding the Role of PHP in Server-Side Processing

PHP is a powerful **server-side scripting language** designed to handle requests, process data, and dynamically generate web content. Unlike frontend languages such as JavaScript, which execute in the browser, PHP runs on the server, interacting with databases, managing user sessions, and executing business logic before sending responses to clients.

How PHP Works on the Server

PHP scripts are executed on a web server, typically using **Apache, NGINX, or PHP-FPM**. When a client makes an HTTP request, the web server passes it to the PHP interpreter, which processes the script and returns the output as HTML or JSON. The request-response cycle follows these steps:

1. A user requests a PHP page via a browser (index.php).

2. The web server processes the request and hands it to PHP.

3. PHP executes the script, fetching data from a database if necessary.

4. The generated HTML or JSON response is sent back to the browser.

Basic PHP Server-Side Processing

A simple example of PHP's server-side processing is generating dynamic content:

```php
<?php
// Display a greeting based on the time of day
$hour = date("H");

if ($hour < 12) {
```

```php
    echo "Good morning!";
} elseif ($hour < 18) {
    echo "Good afternoon!";
} else {
    echo "Good evening!";
}
?>
```

This script runs on the server and dynamically determines the greeting based on the server's time.

Handling Form Data in PHP

PHP processes form submissions by capturing user input from **GET** or **POST** requests.

```php
<?php
if ($_SERVER["REQUEST_METHOD"] == "POST") {
    $name = htmlspecialchars($_POST['name']);
    echo "Hello, $name!";
}
?>

<form method="POST">
    <input type="text" name="name">
    <button type="submit">Submit</button>
</form>
```

The script captures input, processes it on the server, and returns a response. The htmlspecialchars() function prevents **cross-site scripting (XSS)** attacks by escaping HTML characters.

Database Interactions in PHP

PHP efficiently interacts with databases like MySQL and PostgreSQL. The following script fetches data from a MySQL database using **PDO (PHP Data Objects)**:

```php
<?php
$pdo = new PDO("mysql:host=localhost;dbname=exampledb", "user", "password");

$query = $pdo->query("SELECT * FROM users");

while ($row = $query->fetch(PDO::FETCH_ASSOC)) {
    echo "User: " . $row['username'] . "<br>";
}
?>
```

PHP's role in server-side processing extends to **authentication, API development, background jobs, and session management**. Mastering its execution flow ensures the development of secure, efficient, and scalable applications.

Optimizing PHP Applications for High Performance and Scalability

Performance optimization is critical for PHP applications, especially as traffic and data complexity increase. Without proper optimizations, PHP scripts can become slow, inefficient, and resource-intensive. Optimizing performance involves improving code execution speed, database queries, caching mechanisms, and server configurations.

1. Efficient Code Execution

Writing clean, optimized PHP code reduces execution time. Best practices include:

- **Minimizing Loops and Function Calls**: Avoid unnecessary iterations and use array functions like array_map() instead of foreach.

- **Using Native PHP Functions**: PHP's built-in functions are optimized in C and run faster than custom implementations.

- **Avoiding Unnecessary Computation**: Reduce expensive operations by precomputing values and reusing them.

Example of optimized looping:

```php
<?php
// Inefficient
$sum = 0;
for ($i = 0; $i < count($numbers); $i++) {
    $sum += $numbers[$i];
}

// Efficient
$sum = array_sum($numbers);
?>
```

2. Optimizing Database Queries

Database interactions are often the biggest bottleneck in PHP applications. Optimization techniques include:

- **Using Indexed Queries**: Adding indexes speeds up searches in large datasets.

- **Reducing Query Execution Time**: Minimize the number of queries by using JOIN instead of multiple queries.

- **Using Prepared Statements**: Prevent SQL injection and improve query performance.

Example of an optimized query with **prepared statements**:

```php
<?php
$pdo = new PDO("mysql:host=localhost;dbname=mydb", "user", "password");

// Prepared Statement
$stmt = $pdo->prepare("SELECT * FROM users WHERE email = ?");
$stmt->execute(["user@example.com"]);

$user = $stmt->fetch(PDO::FETCH_ASSOC);
?>
```

3. Implementing Caching

Caching reduces redundant database queries and speeds up page loads. Common PHP caching strategies include:

- **Opcode Caching (OPcache)**: Stores compiled PHP scripts in memory.

- **Object and Data Caching**: Use Redis or Memcached to store frequently accessed data.

- **Full-Page Caching**: Cache rendered HTML pages using Varnish or NGINX.

Example of caching with Redis:

```php
<?php
$redis = new Redis();
$redis->connect('127.0.0.1', 6379);

// Store a value
$redis->set("username", "JohnDoe");

// Retrieve the value
echo $redis->get("username");
?>
```

4. Load Balancing and Asynchronous Processing

For high-traffic applications, distribute traffic using:

- **Load Balancers (NGINX, HAProxy)**: Distribute requests across multiple PHP servers.

- **Queue Processing (RabbitMQ, Redis, Laravel Queues)**: Offload background tasks like sending emails.

Example of background task processing using Laravel Queues:

```
php artisan queue:work
```

Optimizing PHP applications ensures **better performance, lower latency, and higher scalability**, making them robust for handling increased user demands.

Managing Large-Scale Web Applications with PHP and Caching Strategies

Managing large-scale PHP applications requires handling high traffic, optimizing database performance, and implementing caching strategies to ensure fast response times. Without proper architecture, PHP applications can suffer from bottlenecks, excessive memory usage, and slow performance. Caching, load balancing, and database optimization are critical to scaling PHP applications effectively.

1. Scaling PHP Applications

When scaling a PHP application, consider **vertical scaling** (adding more CPU/memory to a single server) and **horizontal scaling** (adding more servers). Horizontal scaling is achieved using **load balancers** such as NGINX or HAProxy to distribute traffic across multiple PHP servers.

Example of an NGINX configuration for load balancing:

```
upstream php_servers {
    server 192.168.1.100;
    server 192.168.1.101;
    server 192.168.1.102;
}

server {
    listen 80;
    server_name mywebsite.com;

    location / {
        proxy_pass http://php_servers;
    }
}
```

2. Optimizing Database Performance

A poorly optimized database can slow down even the most efficient PHP application. Strategies for handling large-scale databases include:

- **Indexing Frequently Queried Columns**: Increases retrieval speed.

- **Partitioning Large Tables**: Splits large datasets into smaller, manageable pieces.

- **Replication and Sharding**: Distribute data across multiple servers for load balancing.

Example of indexing for faster queries:

```
CREATE INDEX idx_email ON users(email);
```

3. Implementing Caching Strategies

Caching reduces server load and speeds up response times by storing frequently accessed data. Types of caching in PHP applications include:

- **Opcode Caching**: Using OPcache to store precompiled script code.

- **Object Caching**: Storing data in-memory using **Memcached** or **Redis**.

- **Full Page Caching**: Caching entire rendered HTML pages using **Varnish**.

Example of caching with **Memcached**:

```php
<?php
$memcached = new Memcached();
$memcached->addServer("127.0.0.1", 11211);

// Storing a value
$memcached->set("homepage", "Cached content", 600);

// Retrieving the cached value
echo $memcached->get("homepage");
?>
```

4. Asynchronous Processing and Job Queues

To prevent long-running tasks from slowing down a PHP application, use **asynchronous job queues**. These help with:

- **Email sending**

- **Data processing**

- **Scheduled background tasks**

Example of using Laravel Queues for asynchronous tasks:

```
php artisan queue:work
```

By implementing caching, load balancing, and database optimizations, PHP applications can efficiently handle large-scale traffic while maintaining performance and reliability.

Case Study: Scaling a PHP-Based Web Service for High Traffic

Scaling a PHP-based web service for high traffic requires strategic optimizations, including server load balancing, database performance tuning, caching mechanisms, and asynchronous job processing. In this case study, we explore how a high-traffic PHP web service was successfully scaled using these techniques to handle millions of daily requests efficiently.

1. The Challenge: Handling Increasing Traffic

A PHP-based web service running an e-commerce platform experienced a surge in user traffic, leading to:

- **Slow page load times** due to heavy database queries.

- **Server overload**, causing downtime during peak hours.

279

- **Inconsistent performance**, affecting user experience.

The goal was to scale the application efficiently while maintaining stability and performance.

2. Solution: Implementing Load Balancing and Auto-Scaling

The first step was **distributing traffic** across multiple servers using **NGINX as a load balancer**. This ensured even workload distribution and prevented a single server from being overwhelmed.

Example NGINX load balancing configuration:

```
upstream php_servers {
    server 192.168.1.101;
    server 192.168.1.102;
    server 192.168.1.103;
}

server {
    listen 80;
    server_name example.com;

    location / {
        proxy_pass http://php_servers;
    }
}
```

In addition, **auto-scaling** was configured in AWS to automatically spin up new PHP servers based on traffic spikes.

3. Database Optimization for Performance

The MySQL database was experiencing slow queries due to large datasets. Several optimizations were applied:

- **Read/Write Splitting:** Using **replication** to separate read and write queries.

- **Indexing Key Columns:** Improving query speed.

- **Partitioning Large Tables:** Distributing data across multiple physical tables.

Example of read/write splitting with MySQL replication:

```
$mysqli = new mysqli("replica-db", "user", "password", "database");

$result = $mysqli->query("SELECT * FROM orders WHERE status='pending'");
while ($row = $result->fetch_assoc()) {
    echo $row['order_id'];
}
```

4. Caching Strategies for Faster Responses

To reduce server load and improve response times, caching mechanisms were implemented:

- **OPcache** for PHP script caching.

- **Redis** for session and object caching.

- **Varnish** for full-page caching.

Example of using Redis for caching query results:

```
$redis = new Redis();
$redis->connect('127.0.0.1', 6379);

$cacheKey = "top_products";
if (!$products = $redis->get($cacheKey)) {
    $products = $db->query("SELECT * FROM products ORDER BY sales DESC LIMIT
            10")->fetchAll();
    $redis->set($cacheKey, serialize($products), 600);
} else {
    $products = unserialize($products);
}
```

5. Asynchronous Processing with Job Queues

Heavy tasks, such as order processing and email notifications, were offloaded using **RabbitMQ** for job queues, ensuring real-time processing without slowing down the user experience.

Example of dispatching a Laravel job:

```
dispatch(new SendOrderConfirmationEmail($orderId));
```

By implementing **load balancing, database optimization, caching, and job queues**, the PHP web service successfully handled millions of users while maintaining high availability and low latency. This case study demonstrates the importance of scalability strategies in high-traffic PHP applications.

Part 4:

PHP Frameworks and Design Patterns

PHP frameworks and design patterns play a crucial role in structuring modern applications by promoting reusability, maintainability, and efficiency. This part introduces developers to widely used PHP frameworks and their underlying architectural patterns. Frameworks provide predefined structures that simplify development, while design patterns offer reusable solutions to common programming challenges. Understanding both helps developers write scalable and organized code that adheres to industry best practices. By exploring various PHP frameworks and pattern-based programming, developers will be equipped with essential knowledge to build reliable, maintainable applications.

Introduction to PHP Frameworks and Design Patterns

PHP frameworks serve as the foundation for rapid application development by enforcing best practices and reducing redundant coding efforts. They provide built-in tools for routing, database management, and authentication, making it easier to build complex applications efficiently. Popular frameworks such as Laravel, Symfony, and CodeIgniter offer structured approaches to application development. At the core of many frameworks lies the Model-View-Controller (MVC) pattern, which separates logic, presentation, and data handling. Design patterns, on the other hand, provide structured solutions to common programming problems. Patterns like Singleton, Factory, and Observer improve maintainability by ensuring modular and reusable code. Understanding these patterns and frameworks allows developers to create applications that scale without unnecessary complexity.

Laravel - The Most Popular PHP Framework

Laravel has established itself as the most popular PHP framework due to its expressive syntax, robust features, and developer-friendly environment. Its built-in tools, such as Artisan CLI for task automation, Eloquent ORM for database interaction, and Blade templating engine for UI rendering, make development seamless. Laravel follows the MVC architecture, promoting clean separation between logic and presentation layers. The framework incorporates key design patterns like Singleton for centralized resource management, Factory for object creation, and Dependency Injection for reducing tight coupling. Laravel excels in building APIs, enterprise applications, and large-scale web platforms, making it a go-to choice for modern developers.

Symfony and CodeIgniter - Enterprise and Lightweight Frameworks

Symfony is an enterprise-grade framework known for its modular components, allowing developers to use only what they need. Its reusable bundles facilitate large-scale application development with efficient code management. CodeIgniter, in contrast, is a lightweight and high-speed framework that requires minimal configuration, making it ideal for small projects and rapid prototyping. Symfony extensively uses design patterns such as Strategy for flexible logic execution and Observer for event-driven programming. CodeIgniter embraces the MVC pattern while prioritizing performance and simplicity. While Symfony powers enterprise applications with high customization needs, CodeIgniter is well-suited for smaller, performance-sensitive web solutions.

CakePHP, Yii, and Phalcon - High-Performance Frameworks

CakePHP, Yii, and Phalcon are designed for developers seeking high performance and structured application development. CakePHP provides a rapid development environment with built-in validation, security, and CRUD operations. Yii is optimized for speed and security, making it ideal for large applications handling sensitive data. Phalcon, written in C, offers the fastest execution among PHP frameworks by leveraging low-level optimizations.

These frameworks implement patterns like Singleton for shared resource management, Builder for assembling complex objects, and Abstract Factory for modular component creation. Their emphasis on speed and reliability makes them suitable for data-intensive applications.

Slim, Lumen, and FuelPHP - Microframeworks

Microframeworks are lightweight alternatives to full-fledged frameworks, focusing on speed and simplicity. Slim is widely used for building RESTful APIs, offering essential middleware and routing capabilities. Lumen, developed by Laravel, is a microframework optimized for high-performance microservices. FuelPHP introduces a hybrid MVC-HMVC architecture, allowing developers to build flexible applications with modular components. These frameworks integrate patterns like Adapter for database abstraction, Proxy for controlled access to resources, and Facade for simplifying complex subsystems. They provide developers with the flexibility to build scalable and efficient applications without the overhead of larger frameworks.

Zend Framework / Laminas and Medoo - Specialized Frameworks

Zend Framework, now rebranded as Laminas, is an enterprise-oriented framework offering extensive modularity and scalability. It is designed for complex applications requiring high performance and maintainability. Medoo, on the other hand, is a minimalist database framework that simplifies SQL interactions with an intuitive API. Laminas incorporates design patterns like Chain of Responsibility for middleware processing, State for dynamic object behavior, and Composite for hierarchical structures. Medoo, while lightweight, benefits from abstraction layers that streamline database operations. These frameworks cater to specialized development needs, from enterprise applications to simplified database management.

Introduction to PHP Design Patterns

Design patterns provide reusable solutions to common programming challenges, improving code maintainability and flexibility. Creational patterns like Singleton and Factory simplify object instantiation. Structural patterns such as Adapter and Decorator facilitate modular architecture, while behavioral patterns like Observer and Strategy enable dynamic application behavior. PHP's support for these patterns allows developers to build applications that are scalable, flexible, and maintainable. Understanding when and how to use design patterns is crucial for writing efficient, reusable code that adheres to best practices.

Creational Patterns - Singleton, Factory, Abstract Factory, Builder

Creational design patterns simplify object creation and instantiation. The Singleton pattern ensures that only one instance of a class exists, preventing redundant resource allocation. The Factory pattern centralizes object creation, allowing flexible instantiation based on parameters. Abstract Factory extends this concept by creating families of related objects, ensuring consistency in application architecture. The Builder pattern structures object creation step-by-step, making it ideal for complex object construction. By mastering these patterns, developers gain control over how objects are instantiated and managed in PHP applications.

Structural and Behavioral Patterns

Structural patterns focus on organizing relationships between components for better maintainability. Adapter allows classes with incompatible interfaces to work together, while Decorator enhances objects dynamically without modifying their structure. Proxy controls access to resources efficiently, and Facade simplifies complex subsystems by providing a unified interface. Behavioral patterns govern object interactions: Observer enables event-driven programming, Strategy facilitates interchangeable algorithms, and Command decouples request execution. These patterns enhance PHP applications by promoting clean architecture, reducing redundancy, and improving flexibility.

This part equips developers with the knowledge of PHP frameworks and design patterns, enabling them to build scalable, maintainable, and high-performance applications with structured, reusable code.

Module 28:
Introduction to PHP Frameworks and Design Patterns

PHP frameworks and design patterns play a crucial role in modern PHP development by enhancing code structure, maintainability, and scalability. This module introduces the importance of frameworks, provides an overview of major PHP frameworks, explains the concept of design patterns, and highlights how frameworks and design patterns improve application development efficiency. Understanding these concepts is essential for building robust, secure, and high-performance PHP applications.

Role of Frameworks in PHP Development: Understanding Frameworks and Their Importance

Frameworks provide a structured foundation for PHP development by offering pre-built modules, libraries, and best practices that streamline coding and application management. They enforce design patterns, reduce development time, and improve code consistency across projects. PHP frameworks simplify repetitive tasks such as routing, authentication, and database management, enabling developers to focus on business logic rather than boilerplate code. Additionally, frameworks enhance security by implementing standard security mechanisms, such as input validation and CSRF protection. Adopting a PHP framework allows for rapid development, promotes modular programming, and ensures scalability for applications of any size, from small websites to enterprise-level software solutions.

Overview of Key PHP Frameworks: Brief Intro to 12 Major Frameworks

There are numerous PHP frameworks available, each catering to different development needs. Some of the most widely used PHP frameworks include:

1. **Laravel** – A powerful, elegant framework with built-in authentication, ORM (Eloquent), and Blade templating.

2. **Symfony** – A highly flexible framework used for complex enterprise applications.

3. **CodeIgniter** – A lightweight, fast framework ideal for beginners.

4. **Zend Framework (Laminas)** – An enterprise-grade framework with extensive features.

5. **Yii** – A high-performance framework for developing large-scale applications.

6. **Phalcon** – An ultra-fast framework written in C for PHP extensions.

7. **CakePHP** – A rapid development framework with built-in scaffolding.

8. **Slim** – A micro-framework designed for lightweight RESTful API development.

9. **FuelPHP** – A flexible, community-driven framework with MVC support.

10. **Lumen** – A minimalist framework built by Laravel for microservices and APIs.

11. **Fat-Free Framework (F3)** – A simple, lightweight, yet powerful PHP framework.

12. **PHPixie** – A modular framework focused on high performance and low overhead.

Each of these frameworks has its strengths and ideal use cases, making it essential to choose one based on the project's requirements.

What Are Design Patterns?: Introduction to Design Patterns in PHP

Design patterns are reusable solutions to common software design problems. They help standardize coding practices, making applications easier to manage and scale. In PHP development, design patterns provide a structured approach to writing maintainable and flexible code. Some common categories of design patterns include:

- **Creational Patterns** (e.g., Singleton, Factory, Builder) – Focus on object creation mechanisms.

- **Structural Patterns** (e.g., MVC, Adapter, Decorator) – Define object composition and relationships.

- **Behavioral Patterns** (e.g., Observer, Strategy, Command) – Manage object communication and behavior.

By implementing design patterns, developers can improve code reusability, enhance maintainability, and ensure adherence to best programming practices in PHP applications.

Benefits of Design Patterns and Frameworks: How They Improve Scalability, Maintainability, and Speed

Using PHP frameworks and design patterns significantly enhances scalability, maintainability, and application speed. Frameworks provide built-in tools that streamline development, reduce code redundancy, and improve security. Design patterns, on the other hand, promote modular programming, allowing developers to build applications that are easy to modify and expand. These approaches also facilitate team collaboration by enforcing consistent coding standards. Moreover, frameworks optimize database queries, caching, and request handling, leading to faster execution and performance improvements. By leveraging frameworks and design patterns, developers can build scalable, robust, and maintainable PHP applications that meet modern development demands.

PHP frameworks and design patterns form the backbone of efficient PHP development. Frameworks provide structured workflows, security features, and automation, while design patterns enhance code organization and reusability. Understanding and utilizing both frameworks and design patterns help developers create maintainable, scalable, and high-performance applications. Mastering these concepts is essential for any PHP developer aiming to build professional-grade software solutions.

Role of Frameworks in PHP Development: Understanding Frameworks and Their Importance

PHP frameworks simplify and streamline web development by providing structured code organization, pre-built functionalities, and standardized development practices. They enable developers to build applications faster, enforce security, and improve code maintainability. Frameworks follow the MVC (Model-View-Controller) pattern, promoting separation of concerns, making debugging easier, and allowing teams to collaborate efficiently.

Why Use a PHP Framework?

A PHP framework abstracts repetitive tasks such as request handling, routing, session management, and database interactions, allowing developers to focus on business logic. Some of the key benefits include:

1. **Code Reusability** – Frameworks provide reusable modules, reducing redundant coding.

2. **Security Enhancements** – Built-in protection against SQL injection, cross-site scripting (XSS), and CSRF attacks.

3. **Scalability** – Frameworks facilitate application scaling through modular structures.

4. **Rapid Development** – Features like ORM (Object-Relational Mapping), authentication, and templating speed up coding.

5. **Community Support** – Popular frameworks have strong developer communities that provide support, plugins, and updates.

Common Features of PHP Frameworks

Most PHP frameworks offer a set of features that help developers build robust applications:

- **Routing System** – Allows clean, readable URLs for accessing different parts of an application.

- **Database ORM** – Simplifies database operations by using models instead of direct SQL queries.

- **Middleware** – Enables request filtering and authentication before processing.

- **Session & Cookie Management** – Provides easy handling of user authentication and data storage.

- **Templating Engine** – Separates logic from presentation for better code organization.

Example: Creating a Basic Route in Laravel

Laravel provides a simple way to define routes in the routes/web.php file:

```
use Illuminate\Support\Facades\Route;

Route::get('/hello', function () {
    return "Hello, PHP Frameworks!";
});
```

This route listens for a GET request to /hello and returns a response. Such routing mechanisms simplify application structuring compared to traditional PHP scripts.

Frameworks provide an organized, scalable, and efficient way to develop PHP applications. They promote best practices, enhance security, and reduce development time. Whether building small applications or enterprise solutions, adopting a framework helps streamline workflow and improve maintainability. Understanding how frameworks function is essential for any PHP developer aiming for professional development.

Overview of Key PHP Frameworks: Brief Intro to 12 Major Frameworks

PHP frameworks provide developers with structured tools to build applications efficiently. They enforce best practices, improve code maintainability, and enhance security. Below is an overview of 12 major PHP frameworks, highlighting their key features and usage examples.

1. Laravel

Laravel is the most popular PHP framework, offering an elegant syntax, MVC architecture, and built-in features such as authentication, queues, and caching.

Example of routing in Laravel:

```
use Illuminate\Support\Facades\Route;
```

```
Route::get('/hello', function () {
    return response()->json(['message' => 'Hello from Laravel']);
});
```

2. Symfony

Symfony is a powerful framework focused on modularity and reusability, making it suitable for large-scale applications.

Example of a Symfony controller:

```
namespace App\Controller;

use Symfony\Component\HttpFoundation\Response;
use Symfony\Component\Routing\Annotation\Route;

class HelloController
{
    #[Route('/hello', name: 'hello')]
    public function hello(): Response
    {
        return new Response('Hello from Symfony');
    }
}
```

3. CodeIgniter

CodeIgniter is a lightweight framework known for its speed and minimal configuration.

Example of a simple CodeIgniter route:

```
class Welcome extends CI_Controller {
    public function index() {
        echo "Hello from CodeIgniter!";
    }
}
```

4. Yii

Yii is a high-performance framework that supports caching, security, and RESTful APIs.

Example of a Yii action:

```
class SiteController extends \yii\web\Controller {
    public function actionHello() {
        return "Hello from Yii!";
    }
}
```

5. Zend Framework (Laminas Project)

Zend, now Laminas, is an enterprise-level framework offering high security and flexibility.

Example of a Zend router:

```
use Zend\Expressive\Application;

$app->get('/hello', function ($request, $response) {
    $response->getBody()->write("Hello from Zend!");
    return $response;
});
```

6. Phalcon

Phalcon is an ultra-fast framework written in C, used as a PHP extension.

Example of a Phalcon controller:

```
use Phalcon\Mvc\Controller;

class IndexController extends Controller {
    public function indexAction() {
        echo "Hello from Phalcon!";
    }
}
```

7. Slim

Slim is a micro-framework used for APIs and lightweight applications.

Example of a Slim route:

```
use Slim\Factory\AppFactory;

$app = AppFactory::create();
$app->get('/hello', function ($request, $response) {
    $response->getBody()->write("Hello from Slim!");
    return $response;
});
$app->run();
```

8. FuelPHP

FuelPHP follows the HMVC pattern, improving code reusability.

Example of a FuelPHP controller:

```
class Controller_Hello extends Controller {
    public function action_index() {
        return "Hello from FuelPHP!";
    }
}
```

9. CakePHP

CakePHP uses a convention-over-configuration approach, simplifying development.

Example of a CakePHP controller:

```
namespace App\Controller;
```

```
use App\Controller\AppController;

class HelloController extends AppController {
    public function index() {
        return $this->response->withStringBody('Hello from CakePHP!');
    }
}
```

10. Laminas (Successor to Zend)

Laminas continues the legacy of Zend, offering enterprise-grade solutions.

Example of a Laminas router:

```
$app->get('/hello', function ($request, $response) {
    $response->getBody()->write("Hello from Laminas!");
    return $response;
});
```

11. Lumen

Lumen is a stripped-down version of Laravel, optimized for microservices.

Example of a Lumen route:

```
$app->get('/hello', function () {
    return response()->json(['message' => 'Hello from Lumen']);
});
```

12. Medoo

Medoo is a lightweight database framework, simplifying database interactions.

Example of a Medoo query:

```
$database = new Medoo\Medoo([
    'database_type' => 'mysql',
    'database_name' => 'test',
    'server' => 'localhost',
    'username' => 'root',
    'password' => ''
]);

$data = $database->select("users", ["name"], ["id" => 1]);
print_r($data);
```

Choosing the right PHP framework depends on project requirements. Laravel and Symfony are great for full-scale applications, while Slim and Lumen are ideal for APIs. CodeIgniter and Yii support rapid development, while Laminas and Phalcon cater to enterprise needs. Understanding these frameworks helps developers build robust and scalable PHP applications.

What Are Design Patterns?: Introduction to Design Patterns in PHP

291

Design patterns are reusable solutions to common programming problems, improving code maintainability, scalability, and readability. PHP supports various design patterns that help structure applications efficiently. This section explores essential design patterns, demonstrating their practical application in PHP development.

1. Singleton Pattern

The Singleton pattern ensures that a class has only one instance and provides a global access point.

Example of a Singleton in PHP:

```php
class Database {
    private static ?Database $instance = null;
    private function __construct() { }  // Private constructor prevents
            instantiation

    public static function getInstance(): Database {
        if (self::$instance === null) {
            self::$instance = new Database();
        }
        return self::$instance;
    }
}

$db1 = Database::getInstance();
$db2 = Database::getInstance();
var_dump($db1 === $db2); // true (same instance)
```

This pattern is useful for managing shared resources like database connections.

2. Factory Pattern

The Factory pattern provides a way to instantiate objects without specifying the exact class.

Example of a Factory in PHP:

```php
class Car {
    public function drive() {
        return "Driving a car!";
    }
}

class Bike {
    public function ride() {
        return "Riding a bike!";
    }
}

class VehicleFactory {
    public static function createVehicle($type) {
        return match($type) {
            'car' => new Car(),
            'bike' => new Bike(),
            default => throw new Exception("Invalid vehicle type")
        };
```

```
    }
}
$car = VehicleFactory::createVehicle('car');
echo $car->drive(); // Output: Driving a car!
```

This pattern helps encapsulate object creation logic, making code modular and easier to maintain.

3. Observer Pattern

The Observer pattern establishes a one-to-many dependency between objects, ensuring that when one object changes, all dependents are notified.

Example of an Observer in PHP:

```
class Subject {
    private array $observers = [];

    public function attach($observer) {
        $this->observers[] = $observer;
    }

    public function notify() {
        foreach ($this->observers as $observer) {
            $observer->update();
        }
    }
}
class Observer {
    public function update() {
        echo "Observer notified!\n";
    }
}

$subject = new Subject();
$observer1 = new Observer();
$observer2 = new Observer();

$subject->attach($observer1);
$subject->attach($observer2);
$subject->notify(); // Output: Observer notified! (twice)
```

This pattern is commonly used in event-driven programming and real-time notifications.

4. Strategy Pattern

The Strategy pattern allows selecting an algorithm at runtime, promoting flexibility.

Example of a Strategy in PHP:

```
interface PaymentStrategy {
    public function pay($amount);
}

class PayPalPayment implements PaymentStrategy {
    public function pay($amount) {
        echo "Paying $$amount using PayPal.";
```

```php
        }
}

class CreditCardPayment implements PaymentStrategy {
    public function pay($amount) {
        echo "Paying $$amount using Credit Card.";
    }
}

class PaymentContext {
    private PaymentStrategy $strategy;

    public function setStrategy(PaymentStrategy $strategy) {
        $this->strategy = $strategy;
    }

    public function executePayment($amount) {
        $this->strategy->pay($amount);
    }
}

$context = new PaymentContext();
$context->setStrategy(new PayPalPayment());
$context->executePayment(100); // Output: Paying $100 using PayPal.
```

This pattern is widely used in e-commerce platforms for payment processing.

Understanding design patterns enhances PHP development by making code more reusable, maintainable, and scalable. Patterns like Singleton, Factory, Observer, and Strategy solve real-world programming challenges, improving software architecture. Applying design patterns ensures a cleaner, more efficient, and structured approach to PHP programming.

Benefits of Design Patterns and Frameworks: How They Improve Scalability, Maintainability, and Speed

Design patterns and PHP frameworks significantly enhance software development by promoting structured, reusable, and scalable code. This section explores how they improve scalability, maintainability, and performance, making PHP applications more robust and efficient.

1. Scalability: Handling Growing Application Needs

Scalability ensures that an application can handle increased user loads without performance degradation. Design patterns like **Factory**, **Singleton**, and **Observer** improve the modularity of the application, making it easier to scale.

Example: Using Factory Pattern for Scalable Object Creation

```php
interface Logger {
    public function log(string $message);
}

class FileLogger implements Logger {
    public function log(string $message) {
        file_put_contents('log.txt', $message . PHP_EOL, FILE_APPEND);
    }
}
```

```php
class DatabaseLogger implements Logger {
    public function log(string $message) {
        echo "Saving log to database: $message";
    }
}

class LoggerFactory {
    public static function createLogger(string $type): Logger {
        return match($type) {
            'file' => new FileLogger(),
            'database' => new DatabaseLogger(),
            default => throw new Exception("Invalid logger type"),
        };
    }
}

$logger = LoggerFactory::createLogger('file');
$logger->log("Application started.");
```

By using the Factory pattern, different logging mechanisms can be introduced without modifying existing code, enhancing scalability.

2. Maintainability: Reducing Code Complexity

Maintainability ensures that applications remain easy to modify and extend over time. PHP frameworks like **Laravel**, **Symfony**, and **CodeIgniter** encourage structured development practices, making maintenance efficient.

Example: Using Laravel's MVC Structure for Maintainability

Laravel separates concerns into **Models**, **Views**, and **Controllers** (MVC), making the codebase cleaner.

```php
// routes/web.php
use App\Http\Controllers\UserController;
Route::get('/users', [UserController::class, 'index']);

// app/Http/Controllers/UserController.php
namespace App\Http\Controllers;
use App\Models\User;
use Illuminate\Http\Request;

class UserController extends Controller {
    public function index() {
        return view('users', ['users' => User::all()]);
    }
}

// resources/views/users.blade.php
@foreach($users as $user)
    <p>{{ $user->name }}</p>
@endforeach
```

This structure improves maintainability by separating logic, UI, and database operations.

3. Performance: Enhancing Speed and Efficiency

Frameworks and caching strategies optimize PHP applications for speed and efficiency. **Caching**, **lazy loading**, and **database indexing** improve performance.

Example: Using Caching in Laravel for Performance Optimization

```
use Illuminate\Support\Facades\Cache;

$users = Cache::remember('users', 600, function () {
    return User::all();
});
```

Here, Cache::remember() stores the result for 10 minutes, reducing redundant database queries.

Design patterns and frameworks streamline PHP development by improving **scalability, maintainability, and performance**. Patterns like **Factory**, **Observer**, and **Singleton** enhance modularity, while frameworks like **Laravel** and **Symfony** provide structured development approaches. Leveraging these tools ensures efficient, optimized, and easily manageable PHP applications.

Module 29:
Laravel - The Most Popular PHP Framework

Laravel has established itself as the most popular PHP framework due to its elegant syntax, built-in features, and robust ecosystem. It simplifies web application development by offering powerful tools like **Artisan CLI**, **Eloquent ORM**, and **Blade templating**. This module explores Laravel's core features, how to build applications using Laravel, key design patterns it employs, and its ideal use cases in large applications and APIs.

Overview of Laravel: Laravel's Features Like Artisan CLI, Eloquent ORM, and Blade

Laravel is a modern PHP framework that provides a structured way to develop web applications efficiently. One of its key strengths is **Artisan CLI**, a command-line interface that automates repetitive tasks like migrations, testing, and scaffolding. Another major feature is **Eloquent ORM**, which simplifies database interactions by using an expressive syntax for querying databases. Laravel also includes **Blade**, a lightweight and flexible templating engine that allows developers to create dynamic views efficiently. With built-in features like authentication, routing, and caching, Laravel reduces development time while ensuring best practices in modern PHP programming.

Building Applications with Laravel: A Quick Laravel Project Example

Laravel follows the **Model-View-Controller (MVC)** architecture, making application development more organized. A typical Laravel application consists of **routes**, **controllers**, **models**, and **views**. Developers can quickly scaffold a project using **Artisan commands**, reducing boilerplate code. Laravel's routing system is straightforward, allowing developers to define application logic easily. Database operations are efficiently managed using **Eloquent ORM**, while views are created using **Blade templates** for dynamic content rendering. With Laravel's built-in features, developers can rapidly build applications ranging from small projects to large-scale enterprise solutions.

Key Design Patterns in Laravel: MVC, Singleton, and Factory Patterns

Laravel implements several well-established **design patterns**, ensuring maintainability and scalability. The **Model-View-Controller (MVC)** pattern separates concerns, making code easier to manage. The **Singleton pattern** is used in services like database connections, ensuring a single instance is reused throughout the application, improving efficiency. Laravel also leverages the **Factory pattern** for creating objects dynamically, especially in database seeding and service container bindings. These patterns not only enhance code organization but also make Laravel applications scalable and easy to extend, allowing developers to build robust and modular web applications efficiently.

Use Cases for Laravel: Ideal Use Cases in Large Applications and APIs

Laravel is widely used in **large-scale applications** due to its scalability, security, and modularity. It is ideal for **enterprise applications**, **content management systems (CMS)**, and **e-commerce platforms**, thanks to its powerful authentication and authorization mechanisms. Laravel is also well-suited for **RESTful APIs**, as it provides built-in API authentication, request handling, and response formatting features. Additionally, Laravel's queue system and event broadcasting make it ideal for real-time applications such as chat applications and notification systems. With its extensive ecosystem, including packages like Laravel Passport and Laravel Horizon, Laravel is an excellent choice for modern web application development.

Laravel stands out as the most popular PHP framework due to its **elegant syntax, built-in tools, and powerful features**. It simplifies web development through **Artisan CLI, Eloquent ORM, and Blade templating**. Laravel's use of **MVC, Singleton, and Factory patterns** ensures code maintainability and scalability. Its robustness makes it the **framework of choice for large applications, APIs, and enterprise-level projects**.

Overview of Laravel: Laravel's Features Like Artisan CLI, Eloquent ORM, and Blade

Laravel is a powerful PHP framework that provides a structured approach to building web applications. It includes **Artisan CLI**, a command-line tool for automating tasks, **Eloquent ORM**, which simplifies database interactions, and **Blade**, a templating engine for dynamic views. These features enable developers to build robust applications with minimal effort.

Artisan CLI

Artisan is Laravel's command-line interface that automates repetitive tasks such as creating models, controllers, and database migrations. For instance, to generate a model and migration, you can use:

```
php artisan make:model Post -m
```

This command creates a Post model and a migration file, streamlining the development process.

Eloquent ORM

Eloquent simplifies database operations by allowing developers to interact with databases using object-oriented syntax. Instead of writing raw SQL, Eloquent enables querying like this:

```
$posts = Post::where('status', 'published')->get();
```

This retrieves all published posts, making database interactions more intuitive.

Blade Templating Engine

Blade is Laravel's lightweight templating engine, which allows developers to create dynamic views using simple syntax:

```
@if($user->isAdmin())
    <p>Welcome, Admin!</p>
@endif
```

Blade provides **layouts, sections, and template inheritance**, making front-end development in Laravel efficient.

Laravel's combination of **Artisan CLI, Eloquent ORM, and Blade** significantly enhances developer productivity, making it the **preferred PHP framework** for modern web development.

Building Applications with Laravel: A Quick Laravel Project Example

Laravel simplifies web application development by providing a well-structured environment with built-in features. This section demonstrates a basic Laravel project by building a simple **task management application** with routes, controllers, models, and views.

Step 1: Setting Up Laravel

First, install Laravel using Composer:

```
composer create-project --prefer-dist laravel/laravel TaskManager
cd TaskManager
php artisan serve
```

This starts the local development server. Access the application at **http://127.0.0.1:8000**.

Step 2: Creating the Model and Migration

Generate a model with a migration for managing tasks:

```
php artisan make:model Task -m
```

In the database/migrations/ folder, open the generated migration file and define the task schema:

```
public function up()
{
    Schema::create('tasks', function (Blueprint $table) {
        $table->id();
        $table->string('title');
        $table->boolean('completed')->default(false);
```

299

```
        $table->timestamps();
    });
}
```

Run the migration to create the table:

```
php artisan migrate
```

Step 3: Creating the Controller

Generate a controller to handle requests:

```
php artisan make:controller TaskController
```

Inside TaskController.php, add methods to retrieve and store tasks:

```
use App\Models\Task;
use Illuminate\Http\Request;

class TaskController extends Controller
{
    public function index()
    {
        return view('tasks.index', ['tasks' => Task::all()]);
    }

    public function store(Request $request)
    {
        Task::create($request->validate(['title' => 'required']));
        return redirect()->route('tasks.index');
    }
}
```

Step 4: Defining Routes

Modify routes/web.php to define application routes:

```
use App\Http\Controllers\TaskController;

Route::get('/tasks', [TaskController::class, 'index'])->name('tasks.index');
Route::post('/tasks', [TaskController::class, 'store'])->name('tasks.store');
```

Step 5: Creating the View

In resources/views/tasks/index.blade.php, define the HTML structure using Blade:

```
<!DOCTYPE html>
<html>
<head><title>Task Manager</title></head>
<body>
    <h1>Tasks</h1>
    <form action="{{ route('tasks.store') }}" method="POST">
        @csrf
        <input type="text" name="title" required>
        <button type="submit">Add Task</button>
    </form>
    <ul>
        @foreach($tasks as $task)
            <li>{{ $task->title }}</li>
        @endforeach
```

```
    </ul>
  </body>
</html>
```

This simple Laravel project demonstrates the **MVC structure**, allowing developers to build robust applications efficiently.

Key Design Patterns in Laravel: MVC, Singleton, and Factory Patterns

Laravel follows established design patterns to enhance **scalability, maintainability, and efficiency**. Three key patterns in Laravel are **Model-View-Controller (MVC)** for structuring applications, **Singleton** for managing single-instance objects, and **Factory** for dynamic object creation.

MVC Pattern in Laravel

The **Model-View-Controller (MVC)** pattern is the core architectural pattern of Laravel, separating application logic into three components:

- **Model:** Handles database interactions.

- **View:** Manages the presentation layer (Blade templates).

- **Controller:** Processes user requests and retrieves data for the views.

Example: Suppose we are building a **blog application**. The Post model represents a blog post, while the PostController handles business logic.

Defining the Model

```
namespace App\Models;

use Illuminate\Database\Eloquent\Factories\HasFactory;
use Illuminate\Database\Eloquent\Model;

class Post extends Model
{
    use HasFactory;
    protected $fillable = ['title', 'content'];
}
```

Creating the Controller

```
namespace App\Http\Controllers;

use App\Models\Post;
use Illuminate\Http\Request;

class PostController extends Controller
{
    public function index()
    {
        return view('posts.index', ['posts' => Post::all()]);
```

```
        }
}
```

Defining the Route

```
use App\Http\Controllers\PostController;
Route::get('/posts', [PostController::class, 'index']);
```

Creating the View (Blade Template)

```
@foreach($posts as $post)
    <h2>{{ $post->title }}</h2>
    <p>{{ $post->content }}</p>
@endforeach
```

This demonstrates the **MVC pattern** where the **Model interacts with the database, the Controller processes logic, and the View presents the data**.

Singleton Pattern in Laravel

The **Singleton Pattern** ensures that a class has only one instance and provides a global point of access. In Laravel, **services** such as database connections, caching, and logging use **Singletons**.

Example: Creating a singleton database service in Laravel using the **service container**.

Defining the Singleton in a Service Provider

In AppServiceProvider.php:

```
use App\Services\DatabaseConnection;
use Illuminate\Support\ServiceProvider;

class AppServiceProvider extends ServiceProvider
{
    public function register()
    {
        $this->app->singleton(DatabaseConnection::class, function () {
            return new DatabaseConnection();
        });
    }
}
```

Now, anywhere in the application, DatabaseConnection::class will return the same instance.

Factory Pattern in Laravel

The **Factory Pattern** is used in Laravel for dynamically creating instances, especially in **seeding databases**.

Example: Using Laravel **factories** to generate fake data for testing.

Creating a Factory for the Post Model

```
namespace Database\Factories;

use App\Models\Post;
use Illuminate\Database\Eloquent\Factories\Factory;

class PostFactory extends Factory
{
    protected $model = Post::class;

    public function definition()
    {
        return [
            'title' => $this->faker->sentence,
            'content' => $this->faker->paragraph,
        ];
    }
}
```

Seeding the Database with Factory

```
Post::factory()->count(10)->create();
```

This generates **10 fake blog posts**, useful for testing.

Laravel heavily relies on design patterns like **MVC for application structure, Singleton for single-instance services, and Factory for object creation**. Mastering these patterns ensures **better code organization, maintainability, and scalability** in Laravel projects.

Use Cases for Laravel: Ideal Use Cases in Large Applications and APIs

Laravel is one of the most widely used PHP frameworks, offering **robust tools, scalability, and security**. It is particularly well-suited for **large-scale applications** and **RESTful APIs**. Laravel's features like **Eloquent ORM, middleware, queue handling, and authentication** make it an excellent choice for enterprise projects.

1. Laravel for Large Web Applications

Laravel provides built-in tools that **simplify development for complex, high-traffic applications**. Some key features that support scalability include:

- **Queue Management:** Offloads time-consuming tasks, improving performance.

- **Caching:** Supports Redis, Memcached, and other caching systems.

- **Task Scheduling:** Automates routine background processes.

Example: Queue Management in a Large Web Application

Imagine an e-commerce platform sending **email notifications** after a purchase. Instead of delaying the checkout process, Laravel queues the email task.

```
namespace App\Jobs;

use Illuminate\Bus\Queueable;
use Illuminate\Contracts\Queue\ShouldBeUnique;
use Illuminate\Contracts\Queue\ShouldQueue;
use Illuminate\Foundation\Bus\Dispatchable;
use Illuminate\Queue\InteractsWithQueue;
use Illuminate\Queue\SerializesModels;
use App\Mail\OrderConfirmation;
use Illuminate\Support\Facades\Mail;

class SendOrderEmail implements ShouldQueue
{
    use Dispatchable, InteractsWithQueue, Queueable, SerializesModels;

    protected $order;

    public function __construct($order)
    {
        $this->order = $order;
    }

    public function handle()
    {
        Mail::to($this->order->user->email)->send(new OrderConfirmation($this->order));
    }
}
```

This job runs asynchronously, **improving response times and user experience**.

2. Laravel for RESTful APIs

Laravel is a **great choice for developing APIs** due to its:

- **Built-in API authentication (Laravel Passport, Sanctum).**

- **Resourceful controllers for structuring endpoints.**

- **Eloquent ORM for efficient database interactions.**

Example: Creating an API Endpoint in Laravel

Creating an API for retrieving **products**:

```
namespace App\Http\Controllers\API;

use App\Http\Controllers\Controller;
use App\Models\Product;
use Illuminate\Http\Request;

class ProductController extends Controller
{
    public function index()
    {
```

```
        return response()->json(Product::all());
    }
}
```

Defining API Routes

```
use App\Http\Controllers\API\ProductController;
Route::get('/products', [ProductController::class, 'index']);
```

This API returns all products in JSON format, making it easy to integrate with **mobile apps or frontend frameworks like React or Vue.js**.

3. Laravel for Multi-Tenant Applications

Laravel supports **multi-tenant applications**, meaning a single codebase can serve multiple businesses with **separate databases or shared tables**.

*   **Example:** A SaaS platform providing separate dashboards for different companies.

*   **Key Features Used:** Laravel Tenancy package, subdomain routing, and database separation.

Example: Defining a Multi-Tenant Middleware

```
namespace App\Http\Middleware;

use Closure;
use Illuminate\Http\Request;
use App\Models\Tenant;

class IdentifyTenant
{
    public function handle(Request $request, Closure $next)
    {
        $tenant = Tenant::where('domain', $request->getHost())->first();
        if (!$tenant) {
            abort(404, "Tenant not found");
        }

        app()->instance('tenant', $tenant);

        return $next($request);
    }
}
```

This middleware **identifies tenants based on subdomains** and ensures requests are processed in the right context.

4. Laravel for Enterprise-Grade Applications

Laravel's **modular structure, caching mechanisms, event broadcasting, and job handling** make it ideal for **enterprise applications** like:

*   **Customer Relationship Management (CRM) systems.**

- **Enterprise Resource Planning (ERP) software.**

- **Advanced content management systems (CMS).**

Laravel is best suited for **large-scale applications, APIs, multi-tenant platforms, and enterprise solutions**. Its ability to handle **complex business logic, background tasks, and security** makes it the preferred framework for modern **high-performance PHP applications**.

Module 30:
Symfony and CodeIgniter - Enterprise and Lightweight Frameworks

PHP offers a variety of frameworks, each catering to different project needs. **Symfony** is a robust, modular framework suited for enterprise-level applications, while **CodeIgniter** is a lightweight framework designed for simplicity and speed. This module explores the key features of both frameworks, their architectural patterns, and their ideal use cases in web development.

Symfony Overview: Modular Components, Reusable Bundles, and Flexibility

Symfony is a **high-performance, feature-rich PHP framework** designed for building large-scale applications. It follows a **modular architecture**, allowing developers to use only the components they need. Symfony's **flexibility** makes it a preferred choice for custom applications, API development, and enterprise solutions.

One of Symfony's standout features is its **component-based architecture**. Developers can use **independent Symfony components** in any PHP project, even outside the framework. These components include **Routing, Console, Dependency Injection, and Twig templating**. Additionally, Symfony's **bundles (pre-packaged modules)** allow developers to extend functionality without rewriting code, making it highly **maintainable and reusable**.

Symfony also includes **Symfony Flex**, a tool that simplifies package management, enabling rapid project setup and configuration. With built-in **security features, caching mechanisms, and debugging tools**, Symfony is well-suited for **enterprise applications requiring long-term stability and scalability**.

CodeIgniter Overview: Lightweight and Fast with Minimal Configuration

Unlike Symfony, **CodeIgniter** is a lightweight framework that emphasizes **simplicity, minimal configuration, and performance**. It is an excellent choice for **small-to-medium-sized projects** that require **rapid development and high efficiency**.

CodeIgniter follows the **Model-View-Controller (MVC) pattern**, but it allows for a more **flexible implementation**, making it **less restrictive** than other frameworks. The framework is **easy to install**, does not require a command-line interface (CLI), and has **low server resource requirements**, making it ideal for **shared hosting environments and budget-constrained projects**.

307

One of CodeIgniter's strengths is its **small footprint and fast execution**. Unlike Symfony, which uses an event-driven architecture, CodeIgniter is **optimized for speed**, making it ideal for applications where **quick responses and minimal overhead** are required. Additionally, its built-in **security features**, such as **XSS filtering, CSRF protection, and query binding**, ensure safe application development.

CodeIgniter is particularly useful for projects that **do not require heavy dependencies** or complex functionalities. It is commonly used for **basic CRUD applications, simple RESTful APIs, and small business websites**.

Design Patterns in Symfony and CodeIgniter: MVC, Strategy, and Observer

Both Symfony and CodeIgniter utilize **key software design patterns** to improve code organization and maintainability.

1. **MVC (Model-View-Controller) Pattern**

   o Both frameworks follow the **MVC pattern**, separating application logic (**Model**), presentation (**View**), and request handling (**Controller**) for better structure and maintainability.

2. **Strategy Pattern**

   o Symfony employs the **Strategy Pattern** in dependency injection, allowing multiple authentication methods or routing strategies to be swapped without modifying core logic.

   o CodeIgniter allows similar flexibility through **libraries and helper classes**, where different strategies can be applied based on specific use cases.

3. **Observer Pattern**

   o Symfony heavily uses the **Observer Pattern** in its event dispatcher, allowing applications to respond dynamically to various triggers.

   o CodeIgniter also supports **event-driven development**, though in a more lightweight manner compared to Symfony's extensive event handling system.

Understanding these patterns allows developers to make better design choices when working with either framework.

Use Cases: Symfony for Enterprise Apps vs. CodeIgniter for Small Projects

Symfony and CodeIgniter serve different purposes in the PHP ecosystem:

- **Symfony for Enterprise Applications**

  - Suitable for **large-scale web applications, enterprise software, and long-term projects** that require **high customization, modularity, and security**.

  - Ideal for **RESTful APIs, complex CMS platforms, and high-traffic applications**.

  - Used by companies like **Drupal, Magento, and Laravel (which incorporates Symfony components)**.

- **CodeIgniter for Small Projects**

  - Best for **simple web applications, small business websites, and MVP (Minimum Viable Product) development**.

  - Provides **fast execution, low resource consumption, and ease of deployment**.

  - Often used by startups and developers who **prioritize speed and simplicity over heavy configurations**.

Symfony and CodeIgniter are **two powerful PHP frameworks** with distinct strengths. Symfony is ideal for **enterprise-level applications**, offering **modularity, reusable components, and security**, while CodeIgniter is perfect for **lightweight projects requiring speed and minimal configuration**. Choosing the right framework depends on **project complexity, scalability needs, and resource constraints**.

Symfony Overview: Modular Components, Reusable Bundles, and Flexibility

Symfony is a **highly flexible PHP framework** designed for building **enterprise-grade applications**. It provides a **component-based architecture**, allowing developers to use Symfony components independently or as part of the full framework. Symfony supports **long-term maintainability, security, and scalability**, making it a popular choice for **large-scale applications and APIs**.

Installing Symfony

Symfony requires **Composer** for installation. The following command sets up a new Symfony project:

```
composer create-project symfony/skeleton my_project
cd my_project
php -S 127.0.0.1:8000 -t public
```

This installs the **Symfony skeleton** and starts a local development server.

Key Features of Symfony

1. **Routing Component**: Handles URL mapping to controllers.

2. **Dependency Injection**: Enhances modular development and maintainability.

3. **Twig Templating Engine**: Provides clean and efficient views.

4. **Doctrine ORM**: Manages database interactions with an object-relational mapper.

5. **Event Dispatcher**: Implements an observer-based architecture for extensibility.

Routing and Controllers in Symfony

Symfony's **routing system** maps URLs to controllers. Define routes in config/routes.yaml:

```
home:
  path: /
  controller: App\Controller\HomeController::index
```

The controller handling this route:

```
// src/Controller/HomeController.php
namespace App\Controller;

use Symfony\Component\HttpFoundation\Response;
use Symfony\Component\Routing\Annotation\Route;

class HomeController
{
    #[Route("/", name: "home")]
    public function index(): Response
    {
        return new Response("<h1>Welcome to Symfony</h1>");
    }
}
```

Symfony uses **annotations** (#[Route]) for clean routing configurations.

Using Bundles in Symfony

Symfony's **bundles** extend functionality without modifying core code. Popular bundles include:

- **SecurityBundle**: Handles authentication and authorization.

- **MonologBundle**: Manages logging.

- **DoctrineBundle**: Provides database ORM capabilities.

To install a bundle (e.g., Doctrine):

```
composer require symfony/orm-pack
```

Then configure it in .env:

```
DATABASE_URL="mysql://user:password@127.0.0.1:3306/mydb"
```

Run migrations:

```
php bin/console doctrine:migrations:migrate
```

Symfony is a **powerful framework** built for **scalability and maintainability**. Its **modular components, flexible routing, dependency injection, and ORM support** make it ideal for **enterprise applications**. By leveraging **bundles and reusable components**, developers can build **high-performance web applications** with Symfony.

CodeIgniter Overview: Lightweight and Fast with Minimal Configuration

CodeIgniter is a **lightweight PHP framework** designed for **speed and simplicity**. It is well-suited for **small to medium projects**, offering a minimal footprint while maintaining high performance. Unlike Symfony, which emphasizes modularity and enterprise features, **CodeIgniter prioritizes rapid development with minimal setup**.

Installing CodeIgniter

To set up a new CodeIgniter project, use Composer:

```
composer create-project codeigniter4/appstarter my_project
cd my_project
php spark serve
```

This installs **CodeIgniter 4** and starts a built-in development server.

Key Features of CodeIgniter

1. **Lightweight Framework**: Requires minimal configuration, making it faster than heavier frameworks.

2. **MVC Architecture**: Enforces a separation between logic and presentation.

3. **Built-in Security**: Provides protection against **CSRF, XSS, and SQL injection**.

4. **Database Management**: Supports multiple database connections using Query Builder.

5. **Routing System**: Simple routing mechanism for clean URL structures.

Routing and Controllers in CodeIgniter

CodeIgniter defines routes in app/Config/Routes.php:

```
$routes->get('/', 'Home::index');
```

A simple controller for handling requests:

```
// app/Controllers/Home.php
namespace App\Controllers;

use CodeIgniter\Controller;

class Home extends Controller
{
    public function index()
    {
        return "Welcome to CodeIgniter!";
    }
}
```

Using Models in CodeIgniter

CodeIgniter uses **models** to interact with the database. Example model:

```
// app/Models/UserModel.php
namespace App\Models;

use CodeIgniter\Model;

class UserModel extends Model
{
    protected $table = 'users';
    protected $primaryKey = 'id';
    protected $allowedFields = ['name', 'email', 'password'];
}
```

Querying the database in a controller:

```
$userModel = new \App\Models\UserModel();
$users = $userModel->findAll();
```

Building Views in CodeIgniter

CodeIgniter uses a **view system** for rendering templates:

```
// app/Views/welcome_message.php
<html>
<head><title>CodeIgniter</title></head>
<body>
    <h1>Welcome to CodeIgniter</h1>
</body>
</html>
```

To load this view from a controller:

```
return view('welcome_message');
```

CodeIgniter is a **fast and minimal PHP framework** ideal for **small projects and rapid development**. Its **lightweight architecture, simple routing, and built-in security features** make it a great choice for **developers seeking speed without complexity**.

Design Patterns in Symfony and CodeIgniter: MVC, Strategy, and Observer

Design patterns are essential in PHP frameworks to **structure applications efficiently, improve code maintainability, and ensure scalability**. Symfony and CodeIgniter use different design patterns to implement **modular, reusable, and flexible architectures**. The most common patterns in these frameworks include **MVC (Model-View-Controller), Strategy, and Observer patterns**.

MVC Pattern in Symfony and CodeIgniter

MVC (Model-View-Controller) is the foundational pattern in both frameworks. It separates concerns by handling **business logic (Model), user interface (View), and request handling (Controller).**

Symfony Example - MVC Implementation

Symfony uses a structured **controller-based** approach:

```php
// src/Controller/HomeController.php
namespace App\Controller;

use Symfony\Bundle\FrameworkBundle\Controller\AbstractController;
use Symfony\Component\HttpFoundation\Response;

class HomeController extends AbstractController
{
    public function index(): Response
    {
        return $this->render('home/index.html.twig', [
            'message' => 'Welcome to Symfony!',
        ]);
    }
}
```

Here, the **Controller** handles the request and returns a rendered **Twig template (View)**.

CodeIgniter MVC Example:

```php
// app/Controllers/Home.php
namespace App\Controllers;

use CodeIgniter\Controller;

class Home extends Controller
{
    public function index()
    {
        return view('home_view', ['message' => 'Welcome to CodeIgniter!']);
    }
}
```

Both frameworks rely on **Models** for database interaction and **Views** for rendering.

Strategy Pattern in Symfony and CodeIgniter

313

The **Strategy pattern** is used to **dynamically switch between algorithms** without modifying core logic. This is commonly seen in **authentication systems, logging, and payment gateways**.

Symfony Example - Using Strategy for Payment Processing

```
interface PaymentStrategy {
    public function pay(float $amount);
}

class PayPalPayment implements PaymentStrategy {
    public function pay(float $amount) {
        echo "Paid $amount via PayPal.";
    }
}

class CreditCardPayment implements PaymentStrategy {
    public function pay(float $amount) {
        echo "Paid $amount via Credit Card.";
    }
}
```

Using the **Strategy pattern**, Symfony allows **switching between payment methods dynamically**.

Observer Pattern in Symfony and CodeIgniter

The **Observer pattern** is used to implement **event-driven programming**. It is ideal for scenarios like **user registration (triggering email notifications) and logging changes**.

Symfony Example - Event Listener for User Registration

```
namespace App\EventSubscriber;

use Symfony\Component\EventDispatcher\EventSubscriberInterface;
use Symfony\Component\Security\Http\Event\InteractiveLoginEvent;

class LoginSubscriber implements EventSubscriberInterface
{
    public static function getSubscribedEvents()
    {
        return [
            InteractiveLoginEvent::class => 'onLogin',
        ];
    }

    public function onLogin(InteractiveLoginEvent $event)
    {
        // Log user login
        file_put_contents('login.log', "User logged in at " . date('Y-m-d
            H:i:s'));
    }
}
```

In Symfony, the **Event Dispatcher Component** enables handling multiple observers.

CodeIgniter Example - Observer for Database Events

```
// app/Observers/UserObserver.php
namespace App\Observers;

use App\Models\UserModel;

class UserObserver
{
    public function created(UserModel $user)
    {
        log_message('info', "User {$user->id} created at " . date('Y-m-d
            H:i:s'));
    }
}
```

CodeIgniter allows attaching observers to **models for event-driven behavior**.

Symfony and CodeIgniter utilize **design patterns** to ensure **scalability, maintainability, and flexibility**. **MVC** provides a structured approach, **Strategy** enables dynamic behavior changes, and **Observer** allows event-driven programming. Understanding these patterns enhances **PHP framework expertise** and improves **enterprise-level application development**.

Use Cases: Symfony for Enterprise Apps vs. CodeIgniter for Small Projects

Symfony and CodeIgniter serve different purposes in PHP development. **Symfony** is ideal for **enterprise applications**, offering a **robust architecture, modular components, and built-in security features. CodeIgniter**, on the other hand, is a **lightweight framework** best suited for **small to medium-scale applications** where speed and simplicity are priorities. Understanding the right use cases for each framework helps developers **choose the best tool** for their projects.

Symfony for Enterprise Applications

Symfony is a **highly configurable** framework designed for **large-scale applications** with **complex business logic**. It is widely used in industries such as **finance, healthcare, and e-commerce** where security, performance, and modularity are critical.

Key Features for Enterprise Applications

1. **Modular Bundles** – Symfony allows **reusing components** across projects.

2. **Doctrine ORM** – A powerful **database abstraction layer**.

3. **Security Component** – Advanced **authentication and authorization mechanisms**.

4. **Twig Template Engine** – Optimized for **performance and flexibility**.

5. **Event Dispatcher** – Enables event-driven programming.

Example: Enterprise-Level API with Symfony

Symfony is excellent for building **RESTful APIs** in large applications.

```php
// src/Controller/ApiController.php
namespace App\Controller;

use Symfony\Bundle\FrameworkBundle\Controller\AbstractController;
use Symfony\Component\HttpFoundation\JsonResponse;
use Symfony\Component\Routing\Annotation\Route;

class ApiController extends AbstractController
{
    #[Route('/api/products', methods: ['GET'])]
    public function getProducts(): JsonResponse
    {
        $products = [
            ['id' => 1, 'name' => 'Laptop', 'price' => 1500],
            ['id' => 2, 'name' => 'Smartphone', 'price' => 800]
        ];

        return new JsonResponse($products);
    }
}
```

This **API endpoint** is **scalable, maintainable, and secure**, making it ideal for enterprise applications.

CodeIgniter for Small to Medium Projects

CodeIgniter is designed for **speed and simplicity**, making it **ideal for startups, personal projects, and small business applications**. It does not require extensive configurations and offers **fast performance** with **minimal overhead**.

Key Features for Small Applications

1. **Lightweight and Fast** – Minimal configuration, making it easy to set up.

2. **Built-in Helpers and Libraries** – Simplifies common tasks like form handling and security.

3. **MVC Architecture** – Ensures separation of concerns without excessive complexity.

4. **Easy Database Management** – Uses a simple **Active Record implementation**.

Example: Quick CRUD App with CodeIgniter

```php
// app/Controllers/ProductController.php
namespace App\Controllers;

use App\Models\ProductModel;
use CodeIgniter\Controller;

class ProductController extends Controller
{
```

```
public function index()
{
    $model = new ProductModel();
    $data['products'] = $model->findAll();
    return view('products/index', $data);
}
}
```

This simple controller retrieves products from the database and passes them to a **view**, perfect for small business applications.

Choosing Between Symfony and CodeIgniter

Feature	Symfony (Enterprise)	CodeIgniter (Small Projects)
Performance	Optimized for large apps	Fast for small projects
Scalability	High, with modular bundles	Moderate, lightweight
Security	Advanced security tools	Basic security features
Learning Curve	Steep	Easy to learn
Ideal Use Cases	APIs, e-commerce, large platforms	Blogs, startups, simple apps

Symfony and CodeIgniter **excel in different areas** of PHP development. Symfony is best suited for **complex, enterprise-grade applications** with strict security and modularity requirements, while CodeIgniter is an **efficient choice for smaller applications** requiring **speed and simplicity**. Choosing the right framework depends on **project scope, complexity, and long-term scalability**.

Module 31:

CakePHP, Yii, and Phalcon - High-Performance Frameworks

PHP development has evolved with the introduction of high-performance frameworks like **CakePHP, Yii, and Phalcon**, each offering unique advantages in terms of **speed, security, and scalability**. CakePHP emphasizes **rapid development** with built-in features, Yii focuses on **performance and security**, while Phalcon, being **C-based**, offers **unparalleled execution speed**. Understanding these frameworks helps developers **select the best tool** based on project requirements and performance needs.

CakePHP Overview: Rapid Development with Built-In Features

CakePHP is a **rapid development framework** that follows **convention over configuration**, minimizing the need for developers to make complex decisions about project structure. It includes a powerful **ORM (Object-Relational Mapping)** system, built-in **security features**, and an easy-to-use **scaffolding system** that speeds up development.

One of CakePHP's greatest strengths is its **built-in tools** for authentication, validation, and security. It enforces the **MVC (Model-View-Controller) architecture**, keeping business logic separate from the presentation layer. Additionally, CakePHP includes features like **CSRF protection, SQL injection prevention, and secure authentication mechanisms**. This makes it an excellent choice for **enterprise applications and large-scale projects** that require both **security and scalability** without sacrificing rapid development speed.

Yii Overview: High Performance and Security for Large Applications

Yii is a **high-performance PHP framework** designed for **large-scale applications** that demand **speed, security, and flexibility**. It uses **lazy loading**, meaning components are only loaded when needed, which significantly improves performance. Yii comes with a **powerful caching system**, supporting **memcached, Redis, and file-based caching** to optimize application speed.

Security is a core focus in Yii. The framework includes **input validation, output filtering, SQL injection prevention, and Cross-Site Scripting (XSS) protection**. It also has a built-in **RBAC (Role-Based Access Control)** system, which is crucial for applications that require **fine-grained permission management**. Yii's **modular structure** and support for **third-party extensions** make it a strong choice for complex applications such as **financial platforms, SaaS products, and e-commerce solutions**.

Phalcon Overview: Ultra-Fast Performance Due to Being C-Based

Phalcon is a **high-performance PHP framework** that stands out because it is **written in C** and compiled as a **PHP extension**. Unlike traditional PHP frameworks that rely on interpreted code, Phalcon executes natively at the **C level**, making it one of the **fastest PHP frameworks available**.

Because Phalcon runs as a C extension, it has **lower resource consumption** and **improved execution speed**, making it an excellent choice for **real-time applications, high-traffic APIs, and microservices**. It includes **Volt (a template engine)**, **Zephir (a PHP extension language)**, and a **low-level ORM** that provides database interaction at high speeds. Phalcon's speed and low overhead make it suitable for **applications requiring extreme efficiency, such as financial systems and large-scale web services**.

Key Design Patterns in These Frameworks: Singleton, Builder, and Abstract Factory Patterns

Each of these frameworks implements **design patterns** that promote scalability, maintainability, and performance.

1. **Singleton Pattern** – Ensures a class has only **one instance** and provides a global access point to it. Used in **CakePHP's configuration management** and **Yii's application components**.

2. **Builder Pattern** – Separates object construction from representation, used in **Yii's Query Builder** and **Phalcon's ORM** for efficient data management.

3. **Abstract Factory Pattern** – Creates families of related objects without specifying their concrete classes, used in **Phalcon's dependency injection container** for managing object creation efficiently.

CakePHP, Yii, and Phalcon are three **powerful PHP frameworks** that cater to different needs. CakePHP is **ideal for rapid development**, Yii is **optimized for high-performance and secure applications**, and Phalcon delivers **exceptional speed** due to its **C-based implementation**. Understanding these frameworks and their **design patterns** enables developers to **select the best framework** for their specific project requirements.

CakePHP Overview: Rapid Development with Built-In Features

CakePHP is a **modern PHP framework** designed to **accelerate development** while ensuring **maintainability** and **scalability**. It follows the **MVC (Model-View-Controller) pattern**, which promotes **code separation** and **reusability**. Developers can quickly build applications using CakePHP's **built-in ORM, validation mechanisms, security tools, and scaffolding system**.

One of CakePHP's standout features is its **convention over configuration** approach, meaning developers can **write less code** and still achieve well-structured applications. This results in **faster development cycles** without sacrificing functionality. Additionally, CakePHP includes built-in **CSRF protection, form tampering protection, and SQL injection prevention**, making it a **secure framework** suitable for enterprise applications.

Installing CakePHP

To install CakePHP, use **Composer**, the PHP dependency manager:

composer create-project --prefer-dist cakephp/app my_cakephp_app

Once installed, navigate to the project directory and start the built-in development server:

```
cd my_cakephp_app
bin/cake server
Now, open http://localhost:8765/ in a browser to see the CakePHP welcome screen.
```

MVC Architecture in CakePHP

CakePHP follows the **MVC pattern**, where:

- **Model** handles database interactions

- **View** manages UI presentation

- **Controller** processes requests and manages logic

Defining a Model

CakePHP's ORM allows defining database tables as models. Here's an example of a UsersTable.php model:

```
namespace App\Model\Table;

use Cake\ORM\Table;

class UsersTable extends Table {
    public function initialize(array $config): void {
        $this->setTable('users');
        $this->setPrimaryKey('id');
    }
}
```

Creating a Controller

Controllers handle user interactions and application logic. Here's a basic UsersController.php:

```
namespace App\Controller;

use App\Controller\AppController;

class UsersController extends AppController {
```

```
    public function index() {
        $users = $this->Users->find()->all();
        $this->set(compact('users'));
    }
}
```

Building a View

Views display data from controllers. Example index.php in templates/Users/:

```
<h1>Users List</h1>
<ul>
    <?php foreach ($users as $user): ?>
        <li><?= h($user->name) ?> - <?= h($user->email) ?></li>
    <?php endforeach; ?>
</ul>
```

Scaffolding in CakePHP

CakePHP provides a **scaffolding feature** that generates basic CRUD (Create, Read, Update, Delete) interfaces automatically. To scaffold a new model, run:

```
bin/cake bake all Users
```

This command **generates models, controllers, and views** for Users, allowing you to manage users via a web interface instantly.

Security Features

CakePHP includes **built-in security features** to protect against common vulnerabilities:

- **CSRF Protection**: Enabled by default

- **Input Validation**: Ensures data integrity

- **SQL Injection Prevention**: Uses prepared statements

- **Authentication**: Provides built-in authentication and authorization

Example of using **CakePHP's built-in password hashing**:

```
use Cake\Auth\DefaultPasswordHasher;

$hashedPassword = (new DefaultPasswordHasher())->hash('my_secure_password');
```

CakePHP is a **powerful framework** that enables **rapid PHP development** with **minimal configuration**. It enforces **security best practices**, integrates a **robust ORM**, and follows **the MVC pattern**, making it an **excellent choice for enterprise applications**. With **built-in scaffolding, authentication, and security mechanisms**, CakePHP remains a **top choice** for developers seeking **speed and reliability** in PHP development.

Yii Overview: High Performance and Security for Large Applications

Yii is a **high-performance, component-based PHP framework** designed for **fast and secure web applications**. It follows the **MVC (Model-View-Controller) pattern** and provides a **rich set of features**, including an **Active Record ORM, caching mechanisms, built-in authentication, and security features**. Yii is known for its **high speed**, making it a great choice for **large-scale applications**.

Yii offers two versions: **Yii 2**, which is the current stable release, and **Yii 3**, which is under development. With its **lazy loading technique**, Yii loads only the necessary components, reducing memory consumption and **optimizing performance**. It also includes **code generation tools like Gii**, allowing developers to quickly scaffold applications.

Installing Yii

To install Yii, use Composer:

```
composer create-project --prefer-dist yiisoft/yii2-app-basic my_yii_app
```

Navigate to the project directory and start the built-in PHP server:

```
cd my_yii_app
php yii serve
```

Visit http://localhost:8080/ in a browser to view the Yii application.

Yii MVC Architecture

Yii follows the **MVC pattern**, ensuring clean and organized code:

- **Model**: Handles database operations using **Active Record ORM**

- **View**: Manages UI representation

- **Controller**: Processes user requests and business logic

Defining a Model

Yii's **Active Record ORM** makes it easy to interact with the database. Example User.php model:

```
namespace app\models;

use yii\db\ActiveRecord;

class User extends ActiveRecord {
    public static function tableName() {
        return 'users';
    }
```

322

```
    }
```

Creating a Controller

Controllers handle HTTP requests and interact with models. Example UserController.php:

```
namespace app\controllers;

use yii\web\Controller;
use app\models\User;

class UserController extends Controller {
    public function actionIndex() {
        $users = User::find()->all();
        return $this->render('index', ['users' => $users]);
    }
}
```

Building a View

The view file index.php (inside views/user/) renders user data:

```
<h1>User List</h1>
<ul>
    <?php foreach ($users as $user): ?>
        <li><?= \yii\helpers\Html::encode($user->name) ?> - <?=
            \yii\helpers\Html::encode($user->email) ?></li>
    <?php endforeach; ?>
</ul>
```

Yii's Security Features

Security is a key focus in Yii, and it includes:

- **CSRF Protection**: Enabled by default

- **Input Validation**: Prevents invalid data entry

- **SQL Injection Prevention**: Uses parameterized queries

- **Password Hashing**: Uses Yii's built-in Security component

Example of **password hashing** in Yii:

```
use Yii;

$hashedPassword = Yii::$app->security-
        >generatePasswordHash('my_secure_password');
```

Yii also supports **RBAC (Role-Based Access Control)** for user authorization.

Yii Caching Mechanisms

Yii provides **multiple caching mechanisms** to optimize performance:

- **File Cache**

- **Database Cache**

- **Memcached and Redis**

Example of enabling **file caching**:

```
Yii::$app->cache->set('key', 'cached_data', 3600);
$data = Yii::$app->cache->get('key');
```

Gii - Yii's Code Generator

Yii includes **Gii**, a powerful code generator that helps create models, controllers, and forms:

```
php yii gii/model --tableName=users
```

This generates a **User model** based on the users table.

Yii is a **high-performance PHP framework** with **robust security and caching mechanisms**. Its **Active Record ORM**, **built-in authentication**, and **MVC architecture** make it an excellent choice for **large-scale applications**. With **lazy loading, Gii code generation, and flexible caching**, Yii is ideal for **secure and high-performance web development**.

Phalcon Overview: Ultra-Fast Performance Due to Being C-Based

Phalcon is a **high-performance PHP framework** written in **C**, designed to deliver **extremely fast execution times** while maintaining a rich set of features. Unlike traditional PHP frameworks, Phalcon is installed as a **PHP extension**, meaning it is compiled directly into the server's runtime environment. This significantly reduces the overhead associated with file parsing and execution, making Phalcon one of the **fastest PHP frameworks available**.

Phalcon follows the **MVC (Model-View-Controller) architecture**, supporting **ORM (Object-Relational Mapping)**, **caching**, **security features**, and **dependency injection** for modular application development. It is an excellent choice for **high-performance applications**, APIs, and real-time web services.

Installing Phalcon

Since Phalcon is a **C-based PHP extension**, installing it requires using a package manager or compiling it manually.

Installing Phalcon on Linux/macOS

Using Homebrew on macOS:

```
brew tap phalcon/extension
brew install phalcon
```

For Ubuntu/Linux:

```
sudo apt-add-repository ppa:phalcon/stable
sudo apt update
sudo apt install php-phalcon
```

After installation, enable the extension in your php.ini file:

```
extension=phalcon.so
```

Restart your web server for the changes to take effect.

Creating a Simple Phalcon Application

Phalcon uses its own **Micro** and **Full-Stack** modes. The **Micro mode** is useful for APIs and lightweight applications.

Basic Phalcon Micro Application

Create an index.php file with the following content:

```
use Phalcon\Mvc\Micro;

$app = new Micro();

$app->get('/', function () {
    return "Welcome to Phalcon!";
});

$app->handle($_SERVER["REQUEST_URI"]);
```

Run this script using a PHP development server:

```
php -S localhost:8000
```

Visiting http://localhost:8000/ will display:

```
Welcome to Phalcon!
```

Phalcon MVC Architecture

Phalcon provides a full-fledged **MVC framework** for large applications. Below is a breakdown of its components:

- **Model**: Manages database interactions using Phalcon ORM

- **View**: Handles HTML rendering

- **Controller**: Processes user requests and business logic

Defining a Model in Phalcon

Phalcon uses **its own ORM** to simplify database interactions. Example Users.php model:

```
use Phalcon\Mvc\Model;

class Users extends Model {
    public $id;
    public $name;
    public $email;
}
```

Creating a Controller in Phalcon

```
use Phalcon\Mvc\Controller;

class UserController extends Controller {
    public function indexAction() {
        $users = Users::find();
        foreach ($users as $user) {
            echo $user->name . " - " . $user->email . "<br>";
        }
    }
}
```

Setting Up a View in Phalcon

Phalcon views are stored in app/views/. Example index.volt template file:

```
<h1>User List</h1>
<ul>
    {% for user in users %}
        <li>{{ user.name }} - {{ user.email }}</li>
    {% endfor %}
</ul>
```

Phalcon's Performance Features

Phalcon's **C-based implementation** allows it to outperform traditional PHP frameworks. Some key features include:

- **Memory Resident Framework**: Avoids loading framework files on every request

- **Optimized Query Performance**: Uses Phalcon ORM for efficient database interactions

- **Built-in Caching**: Supports file, memory, and database caching

- **Dependency Injection**: Reduces unnecessary object instantiations

Example of using **Phalcon caching** with Redis:

```
use Phalcon\Cache\Adapter\Redis;
use Phalcon\Storage\SerializerFactory;
```

```
$serializer = new SerializerFactory();
$cache = new Redis($serializer, ['host' => '127.0.0.1', 'port' => 6379]);

$cache->set('key', 'Phalcon Cache Example');
echo $cache->get('key');
```

Security Features in Phalcon

Phalcon provides **built-in security mechanisms** to protect against **SQL injection, CSRF, and XSS attacks**.

Example of **password hashing** in Phalcon:

```
use Phalcon\Security;

$security = new Security();
$hashedPassword = $security->hash("secure_password");
```

To verify passwords:

```
if ($security->checkHash($userInput, $hashedPassword)) {
    echo "Password is valid!";
}
```

Phalcon is an **ultra-fast PHP framework** designed for **high-performance applications**. Its **C-based nature**, **memory-resident architecture**, and **built-in caching** make it an ideal choice for **large-scale web applications**. With support for **MVC architecture, ORM, security, and dependency injection**, Phalcon enables **efficient and scalable PHP development**.

Key Design Patterns in These Frameworks: Singleton, Builder, and Abstract Factory Patterns

PHP frameworks like **CakePHP, Yii, and Phalcon** implement **design patterns** to ensure **code reusability, maintainability, and scalability**. Some of the most widely used design patterns in these frameworks include **Singleton**, **Builder**, and **Abstract Factory**, each serving a specific role in structuring applications efficiently.

These design patterns help **standardize** application development and **enhance performance** by providing predefined best practices that minimize redundant code. In this section, we will explore **how each pattern works and how it is applied** in CakePHP, Yii, and Phalcon, along with practical implementations.

Singleton Pattern in CakePHP, Yii, and Phalcon

The **Singleton Pattern** ensures that a **class has only one instance** and provides a global access point to it. This pattern is commonly used for managing **database connections, caching, and application configurations**.

Example: Singleton Database Connection in CakePHP

327

In CakePHP, the database connection is usually handled via its ORM, but we can implement a **manual Singleton pattern** for a database connection:

```php
class Database {
    private static $instance = null;
    private $connection;

    private function __construct() {
        $this->connection = new PDO("mysql:host=localhost;dbname=test", "root",
            "");
    }

    public static function getInstance() {
        if (self::$instance == null) {
            self::$instance = new Database();
        }
        return self::$instance;
    }

    public function getConnection() {
        return $this->connection;
    }
}

// Usage
$db = Database::getInstance()->getConnection();
```

This ensures that only **one instance of the database connection** exists throughout the application.

Builder Pattern in Yii

The **Builder Pattern** is used to **construct complex objects step by step**, making it useful for creating **dynamic queries, form objects, and report generators** in Yii applications.

Example: Building a Query Object in Yii

Yii provides a built-in **query builder** that follows the Builder pattern:

```php
use yii\db\Query;

$query = (new Query())
    ->select(['id', 'name', 'email'])
    ->from('users')
    ->where(['status' => 'active'])
    ->orderBy(['name' => SORT_ASC]);

$users = $query->all();
```

This approach allows **flexible query construction** while maintaining **readability and maintainability**.

Abstract Factory Pattern in Phalcon

The **Abstract Factory Pattern** is used to create **families of related objects** without specifying their concrete classes. This is useful when dealing with **multiple database drivers, form elements, or dependency injection**.

Example: Abstract Factory in Phalcon Dependency Injection

Phalcon uses **dependency injection containers** to manage object creation dynamically:

```
use Phalcon\Di;
use Phalcon\Di\FactoryDefault;
use Phalcon\Db\Adapter\Pdo\Mysql;
use Phalcon\Db\Adapter\Pdo\Postgresql;

// Abstract Factory via Dependency Injection
$di = new FactoryDefault();

$di->setShared('db', function () {
    return new Mysql([
        "host"     => "localhost",
        "dbname"   => "test",
        "username" => "root",
        "password" => "",
    ]);
});

// Retrieve the database instance
$db = $di->get('db');
```

By using **dependency injection**, we can easily swap out database drivers **without modifying application logic**.

CakePHP, Yii, and Phalcon integrate **design patterns** like **Singleton, Builder, and Abstract Factory** to **enhance reusability, flexibility, and maintainability**. These patterns **streamline application architecture**, making it **easier to manage complex systems**. Understanding and applying these patterns effectively will significantly **improve the scalability and structure** of PHP applications.

Module 32:
Slim, Lumen, and FuelPHP - Microframeworks

Microframeworks are lightweight PHP frameworks designed for **small applications, APIs, and services** where a full-fledged framework like Laravel or Symfony would be overkill. They provide **minimalist architectures**, focusing on performance and flexibility. This module explores **Slim, Lumen, and FuelPHP**, highlighting their features, use cases, and integration with design patterns like **Adapter, Proxy, and Facade** to enhance modularity and scalability.

Slim Overview: Lightweight API Framework for Small Applications

Slim is a **minimalist PHP microframework** used primarily for building **RESTful APIs and microservices**. Unlike monolithic frameworks, Slim provides only the essentials: **routing, middleware support, dependency injection, and request handling**, making it highly efficient for lightweight applications.

Developers prefer Slim for **building APIs, single-page applications (SPA) backends, and lightweight web services**. It offers **flexibility**, allowing developers to integrate custom components or third-party libraries for additional features like database connections and authentication. Slim follows **PSR-7 and PSR-15 standards**, ensuring compatibility with modern PHP applications. Its middleware-based architecture allows developers to **handle authentication, logging, and request modification** efficiently without modifying core logic.

Lumen Overview: High-Performance Microframework from Laravel

Lumen is a **microframework developed by Laravel**, offering a stripped-down version of Laravel's ecosystem for high-performance API development. Built specifically for **speed and minimal resource usage**, Lumen is ideal for **stateless microservices, API gateways, and background processing services**.

Unlike Laravel, Lumen **removes unnecessary components**, focusing on essential functionalities like **routing, middleware, authentication, caching, and database interactions via Eloquent ORM**. It is designed to **scale efficiently**, leveraging Laravel's syntax while maintaining a **small memory footprint**. Lumen is often used for **developing large-scale distributed applications**, where individual microservices handle specific functionalities independently but communicate with a central application.

One of Lumen's biggest advantages is **easy migration to Laravel**. If a project outgrows Lumen's capabilities, it can be seamlessly upgraded to Laravel without major modifications.

FuelPHP Overview: Flexible and Secure Framework Supporting Both MVC and HMVC

FuelPHP is a **secure, modular, and flexible microframework** that supports both **MVC (Model-View-Controller)** and **HMVC (Hierarchical Model-View-Controller)** architectures. While other microframeworks primarily focus on routing and API development, FuelPHP is built for **robust full-stack application development** with microframework efficiency.

FuelPHP's **HMVC support** allows for better modularity, where applications can be structured into **independent sub-applications**, improving scalability and maintainability. It also includes **built-in security features** like **input filtering, output encoding, and CSRF protection**, making it a preferred choice for applications requiring **secure data handling**.

The framework's flexibility allows developers to choose their preferred architecture, whether a **traditional MVC or a more advanced HMVC structure**, providing greater control over application workflows.

Design Patterns in Microframeworks: Adapter, Proxy, and Facade Patterns

Microframeworks utilize design patterns to enhance their **modularity, scalability, and flexibility**. Three key patterns used in **Slim, Lumen, and FuelPHP** are **Adapter, Proxy, and Facade**.

- **Adapter Pattern**: This pattern helps bridge different interfaces, making it useful when integrating **third-party services, APIs, or database connections**.

- **Proxy Pattern**: Used in caching and middleware implementations, it allows **request modification before passing to the actual resource**, improving performance and security.

- **Facade Pattern**: Simplifies complex interactions by **providing a unified interface** to a set of classes, making the framework easier to work with.

Slim, Lumen, and FuelPHP are powerful **microframeworks** designed for lightweight and high-performance PHP applications. They provide **efficient routing, dependency injection, and middleware support** while maintaining flexibility. Understanding how **design patterns like Adapter, Proxy, and Facade** are implemented in these frameworks enhances **scalability and maintainability**, making them excellent choices for **modern API and microservice development**.

Slim Overview: Lightweight API Framework for Small Applications

Slim is a **minimalist PHP microframework** designed primarily for building **RESTful APIs, microservices, and small-scale web applications**. It is lightweight and fast, offering **core functionalities like routing, middleware support, request/response**

handling, and dependency injection while avoiding the complexity of full-stack frameworks like Laravel or Symfony.

One of Slim's most valuable features is its **middleware-based architecture**, which allows developers to **intercept and modify requests and responses** before reaching the core application logic. This makes it ideal for **implementing authentication, logging, caching, and security layers** without altering the core application code. Slim also follows **PSR-7 and PSR-15 standards**, ensuring compatibility with modern PHP libraries and third-party tools.

Installing and Setting Up Slim

To start using Slim, install it via **Composer**, the dependency manager for PHP:

```
composer require slim/slim:"^4.0"
composer require slim/psr7
```

Once installed, create a **basic Slim application**:

```php
<?php

require __DIR__ . '/vendor/autoload.php';

use Slim\Factory\AppFactory;

$app = AppFactory::create();

// Define a basic route
$app->get('/hello/{name}', function ($request, $response, $args) {
    $response->getBody()->write("Hello, " . $args['name']);
    return $response;
});

// Run the application
$app->run();
```

This script creates a **basic web application** that responds with "Hello, {name}" when accessed via GET /hello/{name}.

Routing in Slim

Slim provides a **flexible routing system** that allows developers to define application endpoints easily. Routes can handle different HTTP methods such as **GET, POST, PUT, DELETE**, making it an excellent choice for API development.

Example of multiple routes:

```php
$app->post('/user', function ($request, $response, $args) {
    $data = $request->getParsedBody();
    $response->getBody()->write("User Created: " . json_encode($data));
    return $response;
});

$app->put('/user/{id}', function ($request, $response, $args) {
```

332

```
    $response->getBody()->write("User ID {$args['id']} Updated");
    return $response;
});

$app->delete('/user/{id}', function ($request, $response, $args) {
    $response->getBody()->write("User ID {$args['id']} Deleted");
    return $response;
});
```

These routes allow creating, updating, and deleting a user via **API endpoints**.

Middleware in Slim

Middleware in Slim enables **pre-processing and post-processing of requests**. It is often used for **logging, authentication, CORS handling, and error management**.

Example of authentication middleware:

```
$authMiddleware = function ($request, $handler) {
    $apiKey = $request->getHeaderLine('Authorization');
    if ($apiKey !== 'valid_api_key') {
        $response = new \Slim\Psr7\Response();
        return $response->withStatus(401)-
            >withBody(\Slim\Psr7\Stream::create('Unauthorized'));
    }
    return $handler->handle($request);
};

$app->get('/secure-data', function ($request, $response, $args) {
    $response->getBody()->write("This is secure data!");
    return $response;
})->add($authMiddleware);
```

This middleware ensures that only requests with a valid API key can access the **secure-data** route.

Slim is an excellent **microframework** for **lightweight web services and APIs**. Its **flexible routing, middleware support, and compliance with modern PHP standards** make it a powerful choice for **rapid development**. Whether building **RESTful APIs, microservices, or small-scale applications**, Slim offers a simple yet robust solution with minimal overhead.

Lumen Overview: High-Performance Microframework from Laravel

Lumen is a **high-performance PHP microframework** developed by the creators of Laravel. It is specifically designed for **building lightning-fast microservices and RESTful APIs** while maintaining a similar structure to Laravel. Lumen is ideal for developers who require the power of Laravel but need an optimized framework for **speed and efficiency** in API development.

Lumen sacrifices some of Laravel's heavier features, such as **blade templating, session management, and HTTP middleware**, to achieve **better performance**. However, it retains essential features like **Eloquent ORM, routing, authentication, caching, and database migrations**, making it a **lightweight but powerful choice** for API-driven applications.

Installing and Setting Up Lumen

To install Lumen, use Composer:

```
composer create-project --prefer-dist laravel/lumen lumen-app
```

After installation, navigate to the project directory and start the built-in development server:

```
cd lumen-app
php -S localhost:8000 -t public
```

To verify the installation, modify the routes/web.php file:

```
$router->get('/', function () {
    return "Lumen is up and running!";
});
```

Visiting http://localhost:8000/ should display "Lumen is up and running!".

Routing and Controllers in Lumen

Lumen uses a simple and fast routing system similar to Laravel. Routes are defined in routes/web.php or routes/api.php.

Example of defining API routes in routes/api.php:

```
$router->get('/users', 'UserController@index');
$router->get('/users/{id}', 'UserController@show');
$router->post('/users', 'UserController@store');
$router->put('/users/{id}', 'UserController@update');
$router->delete('/users/{id}', 'UserController@destroy');
```

A sample UserController.php for handling these routes:

```
namespace App\Http\Controllers;
use Illuminate\Http\Request;
use App\Models\User;

class UserController extends Controller {
    public function index() {
        return response()->json(User::all());
    }

    public function show($id) {
        return response()->json(User::find($id));
    }

    public function store(Request $request) {
        $user = User::create($request->all());
        return response()->json($user, 201);
    }
```

```
    public function update(Request $request, $id) {
        $user = User::findOrFail($id);
        $user->update($request->all());
        return response()->json($user, 200);
    }

    public function destroy($id) {
        User::destroy($id);
        return response()->json(null, 204);
    }
}
```

This example demonstrates how to create, retrieve, update, and delete users using Lumen's **Eloquent ORM**.

Middleware and Authentication in Lumen

Lumen supports **middleware** to filter HTTP requests. You can register middleware inside bootstrap/app.php:

```
$app->middleware([
    App\Http\Middleware\ExampleMiddleware::class,
]);
```

A sample authentication middleware (ExampleMiddleware.php):

```
namespace App\Http\Middleware;
use Closure;

class ExampleMiddleware {
    public function handle($request, Closure $next) {
        if (!$request->header('Authorization')) {
            return response('Unauthorized', 401);
        }
        return $next($request);
    }
}
```

This middleware ensures that only authenticated users can access certain routes.

Lumen is an excellent choice for **microservices and high-performance APIs**, combining the simplicity of Laravel with optimized performance. Its **fast routing, built-in Eloquent ORM, and middleware support** make it a perfect solution for scalable web services. If you need **Laravel's power but with better performance**, Lumen is a great choice.

FuelPHP Overview: Flexible and Secure Framework Supporting Both MVC and HMVC

FuelPHP is a **highly flexible and secure PHP framework** designed for developers who need a modern, efficient, and extensible solution for web application development. Unlike traditional PHP frameworks that strictly adhere to the **Model-View-Controller (MVC) architecture**, FuelPHP also supports **Hierarchical Model-View-Controller (HMVC)**, making it an ideal choice for large-scale and modular applications.

FuelPHP emphasizes **security, flexibility, and performance**, providing built-in features like **input filtering, encoding, and CSRF protection** to prevent common vulnerabilities. Its HMVC structure enables **code reusability, improved performance, and better separation of concerns**, making it an excellent framework for complex projects.

Installing and Setting Up FuelPHP

To install FuelPHP, use Composer:

```
composer create-project fuel/fuel --prefer-dist fuel-app
```

Navigate to the project directory and start the built-in PHP server:

```
cd fuel-app
php -S localhost:8000 -t public
```

The default FuelPHP directory structure contains key folders such as:

- app/ (application logic)

- core/ (FuelPHP framework core)

- public/ (public-facing assets)

- packages/ (reusable packages)

FuelPHP HMVC Architecture and Routing

FuelPHP uses **HMVC (Hierarchical Model-View-Controller)**, allowing controllers to **call other controllers as sub-requests**, improving modularity and performance. Routes are defined in app/config/routes.php:

```
return [
    '_root_'   => 'welcome/index',  // Default route
    'about'    => 'page/about',      // Custom route
    'contact'  => 'page/contact',
];
```

A sample controller (app/classes/controller/page.php):

```
namespace App\Controller;
use Fuel\Core\Controller;
use Fuel\Core\View;

class Controller_Page extends Controller {
    public function action_about() {
        return View::forge('about');
    }

    public function action_contact() {
        return View::forge('contact');
    }
}
```

The views (app/views/about.php and app/views/contact.php) will contain HTML content rendered by the controller.

FuelPHP Security Features

FuelPHP provides built-in security mechanisms to protect against **XSS, CSRF, and SQL injection attacks**:

1. **Cross-Site Scripting (XSS) Protection**

   o Auto-encoding of output using Security::htmlentities().

2. **Cross-Site Request Forgery (CSRF) Protection**

   o Using CSRF tokens in forms:

```
echo Form::open();
echo Form::hidden(Config::get('security.csrf_token_key'),
        Security::fetch_token());
echo Form::close();
```

3. **SQL Injection Prevention**

   o FuelPHP's **Query Builder** prevents SQL injection automatically.

```
$users = DB::select()->from('users')->where('email', '=', 'test@example.com')-
        >execute();
```

Modules and Extensibility

FuelPHP allows applications to be **modular**, enabling better scalability and code separation. Modules are stored in the app/modules/ directory and can be loaded dynamically.

To enable a module in app/config/config.php:

```
'module_paths' => [
    APPPATH . 'modules' . DS,
],
```

Creating a module structure:

```
app/modules/
    blog/
        classes/controller/blog.php
        views/blog/index.php
```

Modules can be accessed like standard controllers using:

```
return [
    'blog' => 'blog/index',
];
```

FuelPHP is a **lightweight yet powerful** framework offering **security, modularity, and high performance** through **MVC and HMVC support**. Its flexibility, built-in security features, and extensibility make it an excellent choice for developers looking for a **modern and scalable PHP framework**.

Design Patterns in Microframeworks: Adapter, Proxy, and Facade Patterns

Microframeworks like **Slim, Lumen, and FuelPHP** are lightweight and designed for building APIs, small applications, and modular systems. Despite their simplicity, they can benefit from well-established **design patterns** to enhance maintainability, scalability, and flexibility. Three key design patterns—**Adapter, Proxy, and Facade**—are commonly used in microframeworks to improve structure and code efficiency.

These patterns help manage **external dependencies, optimize performance, and simplify complex functionalities**. The **Adapter pattern** allows seamless integration with third-party services, the **Proxy pattern** manages performance and security aspects, and the **Facade pattern** simplifies API interactions by providing a unified interface.

Adapter Pattern: Integrating Third-Party Libraries

The **Adapter pattern** allows an application to work with third-party libraries or APIs by converting their interfaces into a format compatible with the microframework. This pattern is particularly useful for integrating **external APIs, databases, or authentication systems**.

Example: Adapter for Logging System

Suppose a Slim application needs to support both **Monolog** and a custom logging system. The **Adapter pattern** can help unify their interfaces:

```
interface LoggerInterface {
    public function log($message);
}

class MonologAdapter implements LoggerInterface {
    private $monolog;

    public function __construct($monolog) {
        $this->monolog = $monolog;
    }

    public function log($message) {
        $this->monolog->info($message);
    }
}
```

This allows seamless integration of Monolog into a Slim application without modifying its core structure.

Proxy Pattern: Enhancing Security and Performance

The **Proxy pattern** controls access to objects by acting as an intermediary. It can be used for **caching responses, implementing authentication, or managing request limits**.

Example: Proxy for Rate Limiting API Requests

A Lumen microservice may require rate-limiting to prevent excessive API calls:

```php
class RateLimiterProxy {
    private $apiService;
    private $requests = [];

    public function __construct($apiService) {
        $this->apiService = $apiService;
    }

    public function request($user) {
        if ($this->isRateLimited($user)) {
            return "Too many requests. Try again later.";
        }
        return $this->apiService->fetchData();
    }

    private function isRateLimited($user) {
        $this->requests[$user] = $this->requests[$user] ?? 0;
        return $this->requests[$user]++ > 10;
    }
}
```

This proxy **throttles API requests**, improving security and performance.

Facade Pattern: Simplifying Complex Functionality

The **Facade pattern** provides a unified interface to a complex system, hiding implementation details. It's often used to simplify interactions with **framework components like database connections, authentication, or caching**.

Example: Facade for Database Queries in FuelPHP

Instead of writing complex queries repeatedly, a **Facade** can abstract the logic:

```php
class DBFacade {
    public static function getUsers() {
        return DB::select()->from('users')->execute();
    }

    public static function getUserById($id) {
        return DB::select()->from('users')->where('id', '=', $id)->execute();
    }
}
```

This simplifies database operations:

```php
$users = DBFacade::getUsers();
$user = DBFacade::getUserById(1);
```

Design patterns significantly **enhance microframework-based applications** by making code **more scalable, maintainable, and efficient**. The **Adapter pattern** integrates external services, the **Proxy pattern** optimizes performance and security, and the **Facade pattern** simplifies complex operations. Using these patterns in **Slim, Lumen, and FuelPHP** helps developers build **structured and robust PHP applications**.

Module 33:
Zend Framework / Laminas and Medoo - Specialized Frameworks

Zend Framework (now Laminas) and Medoo are specialized PHP frameworks that cater to different use cases. **Zend Framework/Laminas** is known for its **enterprise-level scalability and modularity**, making it suitable for large applications. **Medoo**, on the other hand, is a lightweight **database framework** designed for simplicity and efficiency. This module explores **Zend Framework's enterprise capabilities, Laminas' transition from Zend, Medoo's minimalist approach to database interactions**, and **design patterns like Composite, Chain of Responsibility, and State** that are applicable to these frameworks. Understanding these frameworks allows developers to make informed choices when handling complex or lightweight PHP projects.

Zend Framework Overview: Scalable Enterprise Applications

Zend Framework, now **Laminas**, is a **powerful object-oriented PHP framework** designed for **enterprise-level applications**. It provides a **modular MVC structure**, allowing developers to integrate only the components they need. Zend is **highly extensible** and supports various **database backends**, making it suitable for complex business applications.

A key advantage of Zend is its **service-oriented architecture (SOA)**, enabling smooth **API integrations, security features, and scalability**. Companies often use it for **banking, healthcare, and financial applications** that require **high performance, robust security, and maintainability**. Its **middleware support** makes it a great choice for **RESTful API development**, ensuring seamless service-oriented solutions.

Laminas Overview: Transitioning from Zend to Laminas for Modern PHP Development

Laminas is the **modernized evolution of Zend Framework**, backed by the **Laminas Project** under the **Linux Foundation**. The transition from Zend to Laminas introduces improvements in **modularity, performance, and security** while maintaining backward compatibility. Laminas continues to support **enterprise PHP applications** while enhancing **API-first development** through tools like **Laminas API Tools**.

Laminas is structured into **three major components: Laminas MVC (for large-scale applications), Mezzio (middleware-based framework for APIs), and Laminas Components (for reusable libraries)**. Developers migrating from Zend Framework to Laminas benefit from **active community support, long-term development roadmap, and enhanced security patches**, ensuring a sustainable framework for enterprise needs.

341

Medoo Overview: A Minimalist Database Framework

Medoo is a **lightweight PHP database framework** designed to simplify **SQL interactions** without the complexity of full ORM frameworks like **Doctrine or Eloquent**. It offers **a simple API** for handling database operations, making it ideal for **small to medium-sized projects** that require an efficient, low-overhead database solution.

Medoo supports **multiple database types** like **MySQL, SQLite, PostgreSQL, and MSSQL** while maintaining a **low footprint** of only **one file (~100KB)**. It provides built-in **data sanitization, prepared statements, and an intuitive query builder**, ensuring security and ease of use. Medoo is best suited for **rapid development, lightweight applications, and performance-sensitive environments**.

Design Patterns in Zend / Laminas and Medoo: Composite, Chain of Responsibility, and State Patterns

Composite Pattern is useful in Zend/Laminas applications where hierarchical structures need to be represented, such as **UI components and form elements**. It allows developers to manage **nested objects in a unified manner**, enhancing modularity.

The **Chain of Responsibility Pattern** is commonly used in **middleware-based architectures** in **Laminas Mezzio**. It enables the **sequential processing of requests**, improving code maintainability and scalability in **API development and request handling**.

State Pattern is applicable in Medoo when handling **workflow-based database interactions**. It allows objects to transition between different states efficiently, ensuring **scalability and maintainability** in complex database applications.

Zend Framework, Laminas, and Medoo each serve distinct purposes in PHP development. **Zend and Laminas are enterprise-oriented frameworks** designed for **scalable, modular, and API-driven applications**, while **Medoo is a minimalist database framework** that simplifies SQL interactions. Understanding these frameworks and the **Composite, Chain of Responsibility, and State Patterns** enables developers to build **structured, efficient, and maintainable PHP applications** across different project scales.

Zend Framework Overview: Scalable Enterprise Applications

Zend Framework, now Laminas, is a **high-performance, enterprise-level PHP framework** designed to build **scalable and modular applications**. With a **component-based architecture**, it allows developers to integrate only the necessary components, reducing unnecessary dependencies and enhancing performance. It follows **strict coding standards**, making it a preferred choice for **banking, healthcare, and financial applications** that demand high security, performance, and maintainability.

One of Zend's strongest features is its **Middleware and MVC (Model-View-Controller) support**, allowing developers to build structured, testable applications. Additionally, **Zend Service Manager** facilitates dependency injection, helping developers create **loosely coupled and maintainable applications**.

Installing Zend Framework

To install Zend Framework, use Composer, the dependency manager for PHP:

```
composer require zendframework/zend-mvc
```

After installation, create a **basic Zend MVC application** by defining a simple controller.

Creating a Simple Zend Controller

A **controller** in Zend follows a structured approach. Below is an example of a UserController that returns a JSON response:

```
namespace Application\Controller;

use Laminas\Mvc\Controller\AbstractActionController;
use Laminas\View\Model\JsonModel;

class UserController extends AbstractActionController {
    public function indexAction() {
        return new JsonModel([
            'status' => 'success',
            'message' => 'Welcome to Zend Framework!'
        ]);
    }
}
```

In this example:

- The JsonModel returns a **JSON response** instead of an HTML view.

- The controller extends AbstractActionController, a core **MVC component** in Zend.

Routing in Zend Framework

To define application routes, update the **module.config.php** file:

```
return [
    'router' => [
        'routes' => [
            'user' => [
                'type'    => 'Literal',
                'options' => [
                    'route'    => '/user',
                    'defaults' => [
                        'controller' =>
        Application\Controller\UserController::class,
                        'action'      => 'index',
                    ],
                ],
            ],
```

```
            ],
        ],
      ],
    ],
  ];
```

- This configuration maps the /user endpoint to the indexAction method in UserController.

- Zend Framework's **modular routing** allows developers to create highly structured applications.

Why Use Zend Framework for Enterprise Applications?

1. **Scalability** – The **modular approach** ensures large-scale applications remain manageable.

2. **Security** – Built-in **input filtering, CSRF protection, and authentication tools**.

3. **Performance** – Optimized for **high-traffic enterprise applications**.

4. **API Development** – Supports **RESTful API creation** with structured middleware.

5. **Extendability** – Offers **pre-built components** like Zend Form, Zend DB, and Zend Cache.

Zend Framework (Laminas) remains a **top choice for enterprise PHP applications** due to its **modularity, security, and performance capabilities**. It provides a **robust MVC architecture**, **RESTful API capabilities**, and **high scalability**, making it ideal for **large-scale business applications**. Developers can leverage **Zend's component-based architecture** to build **secure, maintainable, and scalable enterprise solutions**.

Laminas Overview: Transitioning from Zend to Laminas for Modern PHP Development

Laminas is the successor to Zend Framework, providing a **modern, flexible, and enterprise-ready** PHP framework. After Zend's transition, Laminas has continued to offer the same powerful **MVC architecture, middleware support, and component-based structure**, making it ideal for **enterprise and high-performance applications**. Laminas focuses on **modularity, security, and maintainability**, ensuring that businesses can build scalable solutions efficiently.

This transition brings **improved documentation, long-term support, and backward compatibility**, making it easy for developers to migrate from Zend. Additionally, Laminas is part of the **Linux Foundation's open-source projects**, ensuring its longevity and adoption across enterprise applications.

Installing Laminas

To install Laminas, use Composer:

```
composer require laminas/laminas-mvc
```

Once installed, developers can start building **modular and reusable** PHP applications with Laminas components.

Creating a Laminas Controller

Laminas retains the **MVC architecture** from Zend. Below is an example of a ProductController in Laminas:

```
namespace Application\Controller;

use Laminas\Mvc\Controller\AbstractActionController;
use Laminas\View\Model\JsonModel;

class ProductController extends AbstractActionController {
    public function listAction() {
        return new JsonModel([
            'products' => [
                ['id' => 1, 'name' => 'Laptop', 'price' => 1200],
                ['id' => 2, 'name' => 'Phone', 'price' => 800]
            ]
        ]);
    }
}
```

- This controller returns a **JSON response** containing product details.

- The Laminas **View Model** enables flexible data representation for APIs.

Routing in Laminas

Routes in Laminas are configured in module.config.php:

```
return [
    'router' => [
        'routes' => [
            'products' => [
                'type'    => 'Literal',
                'options' => [
                    'route'    => '/products',
                    'defaults' => [
                        'controller' =>
        Application\Controller\ProductController::class,
                        'action'     => 'list',
                    ],
                ],
            ],
        ],
    ],
];
```

This setup defines a /products route that maps to the listAction method in ProductController.

Key Improvements in Laminas Over Zend Framework

1. **Modernization** – Laminas follows **PSR-7, PSR-15, and PSR-17 standards**, making it **more compatible** with modern PHP applications.

2. **Middleware Support** – Improved middleware support through **Laminas Stratigility**, making API development more flexible.

3. **Security** – **Enhanced cryptographic support** for password hashing and encryption.

4. **Performance** – **Optimized for high-performance applications** with caching and memory improvements.

5. **Community Support** – Laminas is **backed by the Linux Foundation**, ensuring long-term support and active development.

Why Migrate to Laminas?

For existing Zend applications, transitioning to Laminas is **seamless**. The core architecture remains the same, and developers can gradually migrate their applications without breaking functionality. Laminas ensures that **enterprise-grade applications remain scalable, secure, and future-proof**.

Laminas builds upon Zend's legacy by offering **modern PHP development standards, middleware architecture, and enterprise scalability**. With continued **long-term support and security enhancements**, Laminas is a **powerful framework for business-critical applications**. Developers familiar with Zend can transition smoothly, ensuring that their applications remain **future-proof and optimized for modern PHP environments**.

Medoo Overview: A Minimalist Database Framework

Medoo is a **lightweight PHP database framework** designed for developers who need **simplicity and efficiency**. Unlike full-fledged ORMs, Medoo provides a **minimalist approach to database interactions** while still supporting powerful features like **SQL abstraction, security, and chainable query building**. It is ideal for developers who want a lightweight solution without the overhead of larger frameworks like Eloquent or Doctrine.

Medoo supports **multiple database engines** such as MySQL, PostgreSQL, SQLite, and SQL Server, making it a versatile choice for PHP applications. With **a single-file implementation**, Medoo is easy to integrate into existing projects, ensuring a seamless database interaction experience.

Installing Medoo

Medoo can be installed via Composer:

```
composer require catfan/medoo
```

This command pulls the latest Medoo package, allowing you to integrate it into your PHP project effortlessly.

Connecting to a Database with Medoo

Setting up Medoo to connect to a MySQL database is straightforward:

```
require 'vendor/autoload.php';
use Medoo\Medoo;

$database = new Medoo([
    'type' => 'mysql',
    'host' => '127.0.0.1',
    'database' => 'test_db',
    'username' => 'root',
    'password' => '',
]);
```

- The **configuration array** specifies the database type, host, name, username, and password.

- Medoo provides **out-of-the-box support** for various databases, making it flexible for different applications.

Performing CRUD Operations in Medoo

Inserting Data

```
$database->insert("users", [
    "name" => "John Doe",
    "email" => "john@example.com",
    "age" => 30
]);
```

Retrieving Data

```
$user = $database->select("users", "*", [
    "name" => "John Doe"
]);

print_r($user);
```

Updating Data

```
$database->update("users", [
    "age" => 31
], [
    "name" => "John Doe"
]);
```

Deleting Data

```
$database->delete("users", [
    "name" => "John Doe"
```

```
]);
```

Medoo's syntax is **concise and easy to understand**, reducing the complexity of direct SQL queries while maintaining flexibility.

Medoo's Security Features

1. **SQL Injection Prevention** – Medoo uses **prepared statements** internally to prevent SQL injection attacks.

2. **Data Sanitization** – Input validation mechanisms help ensure **data integrity and security**.

3. **Secure Query Building** – Chainable methods ensure that developers write safe and structured SQL queries.

Comparison: Medoo vs. Full ORMs

Feature	Medoo	Full ORMs (Eloquent, Doctrine)
Complexity	Low	High
Performance	Fast	Slower due to ORM overhead
Setup	Minimal	Requires configurations
Query Control	High	Abstracted query handling
Use Case	Small to medium apps	Enterprise applications

Medoo provides a **balance between raw SQL and full ORM solutions**, making it **ideal for lightweight applications** or cases where developers need direct control over queries.

When to Use Medoo?

Medoo is best suited for:

- **Small and Medium Projects** – Where full ORM overhead is unnecessary.

- **Microservices** – Where efficient database operations are required.

- **API Backends** – Due to its **fast execution** and **simple syntax**.

- **Prototyping** – Quick database interactions without heavy setup.

Medoo is a **powerful yet lightweight** PHP database framework designed for developers who need a simple, secure, and efficient way to interact with databases. Its **minimalist approach, security features, and ease of use** make it an excellent alternative to traditional

ORMs. With Medoo, PHP developers can build **fast, scalable, and secure applications** without unnecessary complexity.

Design Patterns in Zend / Laminas and Medoo: Composite, Chain of Responsibility, and State Patterns

Design patterns provide **structured solutions** to common software design challenges, making applications **more maintainable, scalable, and efficient**. Zend Framework (now Laminas) and Medoo both leverage **design patterns** to enhance functionality and ensure modular, reusable code. This section explores three key patterns used in these frameworks: **Composite, Chain of Responsibility, and State Patterns**.

Composite Pattern in Zend / Laminas

The **Composite Pattern** is used in Laminas to create **hierarchical structures** where individual objects and groups of objects are treated **uniformly**. This is particularly useful in **form handling, UI components, and complex data structures**.

Example: Composite Pattern in Laminas Form Elements

```
use Laminas\Form\Form;
use Laminas\Form\Element;

$form = new Form('user_form');

$name = new Element\Text('name');
$name->setLabel('Name');

$email = new Element\Email('email');
$email->setLabel('Email');

$form->add($name);
$form->add($email);

// Render the form with multiple elements in a composite structure
foreach ($form->getElements() as $element) {
    echo $element->getLabel() . ": <input type='" . $element-
            >getAttribute('type') . "' name='" . $element->getName() . "'><br>";
}
```

- The **form acts as a composite** that contains multiple elements (text, email, etc.).

- This **hierarchical composition** allows the form to handle **multiple elements in a unified way**.

Chain of Responsibility Pattern in Laminas Middleware

The **Chain of Responsibility Pattern** is widely used in Laminas middleware to **process HTTP requests through a chain of handlers**. This allows for **modular, flexible request handling** where each middleware component can **either handle the request or pass it along the chain**.

349

Example: Middleware Chain in Laminas

```
use Laminas\Stratigility\MiddlewarePipe;
use Laminas\Diactoros\ServerRequestFactory;
use Laminas\Diactoros\Response;

$pipeline = new MiddlewarePipe();

$pipeline->pipe(function ($request, $handler) {
    if ($request->getMethod() !== 'POST') {
        return new Response('php://memory', 405);
    }
    return $handler->handle($request);
});

$pipeline->pipe(function ($request, $handler) {
    $response = new Response();
    $response->getBody()->write("Request handled successfully.");
    return $response;
});

$request = ServerRequestFactory::fromGlobals();
$response = $pipeline->handle($request);

echo $response->getBody();
```

- **Middleware components** are executed in sequence.

- If a request is **not a POST request**, the first middleware stops further execution.

- Otherwise, the second middleware processes it successfully.

- This ensures **flexibility, modularity, and scalability** in handling HTTP requests.

State Pattern in Medoo Query Handling

The **State Pattern** is useful in **Medoo for dynamic query execution** based on different conditions. Instead of using **complex conditionals**, objects change their behavior **depending on their internal state**.

Example: State Pattern in Medoo Query Building

```
require 'vendor/autoload.php';
use Medoo\Medoo;

class QueryState {
    private $db;
    private $state;

    public function __construct(Medoo $db) {
        $this->db = $db;
        $this->state = "select";
    }

    public function setState($state) {
        $this->state = $state;
    }

    public function execute($table, $data) {
```

350

```php
        if ($this->state === "insert") {
            return $this->db->insert($table, $data);
        } elseif ($this->state === "update") {
            return $this->db->update($table, $data['values'],
            $data['conditions']);
        } else {
            return $this->db->select($table, "*");
        }
    }
}

$db = new Medoo([
    'type' => 'mysql',
    'host' => '127.0.0.1',
    'database' => 'test_db',
    'username' => 'root',
    'password' => '',
]);

$queryHandler = new QueryState($db);

// Select State
$queryHandler->setState("select");
print_r($queryHandler->execute("users", []));

// Insert State
$queryHandler->setState("insert");
$queryHandler->execute("users", ["name" => "Alice", "email" =>
        "alice@example.com"]);

// Update State
$queryHandler->setState("update");
$queryHandler->execute("users", [
    "values" => ["email" => "alice_new@example.com"],
    "conditions" => ["name" => "Alice"]
]);
```

- The **State Pattern** enables **dynamic query execution** based on the current state.

- Developers can **switch query types dynamically** without complex conditionals.

- Medoo's **concise syntax** makes this pattern highly efficient for query management.

Zend (Laminas) and Medoo leverage **design patterns** to **enhance modularity, maintainability, and scalability**. Laminas uses the **Composite Pattern** for form and UI structures, the **Chain of Responsibility** for middleware processing, and Medoo applies the **State Pattern** for flexible query execution. These patterns **streamline development** and **improve application architecture**, making PHP applications more efficient and scalable.

Module 34:
Introduction to PHP Design Patterns

Design patterns are **proven solutions** to common software development problems. They **streamline code organization, improve maintainability, and enhance scalability** in PHP applications. This module introduces **design patterns in PHP**, explaining how they **solve recurring challenges**. The focus will be on **creational, structural, and behavioral patterns**, each serving distinct purposes in software architecture.

What Are Design Patterns?

Design patterns are **blueprints for solving specific coding problems** that developers frequently encounter. They **standardize solutions**, making software **more modular, reusable, and easier to maintain**. Patterns are **not rigid code templates** but rather **conceptual approaches** that help developers structure their applications effectively.

There are **three major categories** of design patterns:

1. **Creational Patterns** - Deal with **object creation mechanisms** to ensure flexibility and reuse.

2. **Structural Patterns** - Focus on **object composition** and **relationship management** to improve code organization.

3. **Behavioral Patterns** - Define **communication** between objects, making interactions **more efficient and scalable**.

By understanding and applying these patterns, developers can write **more maintainable and scalable** PHP applications.

Creational Patterns: Singleton, Factory, Abstract Factory, and Builder

Creational patterns **manage object creation efficiently**, reducing complexity and dependencies.

- **Singleton Pattern** ensures only **one instance** of a class exists. Useful for **database connections, caching, and configuration management**.

- **Factory Pattern** provides a centralized way to **create objects** without specifying exact classes.

- **Abstract Factory** extends the Factory Pattern by creating **related objects** without specifying concrete implementations.

- **Builder Pattern** constructs **complex objects step by step**, useful for creating **large, structured objects like reports, forms, and configurations**.

These patterns **decouple object instantiation**, enhancing **code flexibility and maintainability**.

Structural Patterns: Adapter, Decorator, Proxy, and Facade

Structural patterns **define relationships between objects** to improve flexibility and extensibility.

- **Adapter Pattern** allows incompatible interfaces to work together by **translating method calls**.

- **Decorator Pattern** dynamically **adds new behaviors** to an object without modifying its structure.

- **Proxy Pattern** provides a **placeholder for another object**, useful for **lazy loading, security, and access control**.

- **Facade Pattern** simplifies complex systems by **providing a unified interface** to a set of related components.

These patterns **improve modularity, separation of concerns, and code maintainability**.

Behavioral Patterns: Observer, Strategy, Command, and State

Behavioral patterns **manage object interaction** by defining efficient **communication mechanisms**.

- **Observer Pattern** enables **one-to-many dependencies**, ensuring updates are automatically propagated (e.g., event listeners).

- **Strategy Pattern** defines a **family of algorithms**, allowing objects to choose a behavior dynamically.

- **Command Pattern** encapsulates requests as objects, supporting **undo/redo mechanisms and queuing**.

- **State Pattern** allows an object to **change behavior based on its state**, making it ideal for **workflow-based applications**.

These patterns **enhance flexibility, scalability, and maintainability in software design**.

PHP **design patterns** offer **proven strategies** for structuring applications **efficiently and flexibly**. Creational patterns focus on **object instantiation**, structural patterns define **relationships between objects**, and behavioral patterns enhance **object communication**.

Understanding these patterns helps **streamline development, improve maintainability, and optimize scalability** in PHP applications.

What Are Design Patterns?: A Deeper Dive into PHP Design Patterns

Design patterns are **well-established solutions** to common programming problems, offering a structured approach to software development. They help developers **write reusable, maintainable, and scalable** applications by following **predefined best practices**. Instead of reinventing the wheel, developers apply these patterns to **optimize code organization** and **enhance efficiency**.

PHP, being an **object-oriented programming (OOP) language**, supports various **design patterns** that make applications **modular and flexible**. These patterns solve recurring challenges like **object creation, structural organization, and behavior control**. The three major categories of design patterns—**Creational, Structural, and Behavioral**—each address different aspects of software design.

The Three Categories of Design Patterns

1. Creational Patterns

Creational patterns focus on **how objects are created and instantiated efficiently**. They help developers manage object creation **without tightly coupling code**. Some widely used creational patterns in PHP include:

- **Singleton Pattern** - Ensures that only **one instance of a class** exists throughout the application.

- **Factory Pattern** - Centralizes object creation, allowing easy instantiation **without specifying exact class names**.

- **Builder Pattern** - Constructs **complex objects step by step**, making object creation **more flexible**.

2. Structural Patterns

Structural patterns deal with **the organization and relationship between objects** to create **efficient and scalable** code. Common structural patterns include:

- **Adapter Pattern** - Allows incompatible interfaces to **communicate** by creating an **intermediary**.

- **Decorator Pattern** - Dynamically **adds functionality** to an object without modifying its structure.

- **Facade Pattern** - Provides a **simplified interface** for complex subsystems.

3. Behavioral Patterns

Behavioral patterns define **communication between objects**, making interactions **efficient and maintainable**. Key behavioral patterns include:

- **Observer Pattern** - Implements a **publish-subscribe model** to notify objects of changes.

- **Strategy Pattern** - Enables switching between **different algorithms dynamically**.

- **Command Pattern** - Encapsulates requests as objects, useful for **queueing, logging, and undo mechanisms**.

Example: Implementing the Singleton Pattern in PHP

The Singleton pattern ensures that only **one instance** of a class exists. Below is an implementation in PHP:

```php
class DatabaseConnection {
    private static $instance = null;
    private function __construct() {
        echo "Database connection established.\n";
    }
    public static function getInstance() {
        if (self::$instance == null) {
            self::$instance = new DatabaseConnection();
        }
        return self::$instance;
    }
}
$db1 = DatabaseConnection::getInstance();
$db2 = DatabaseConnection::getInstance();
```

Explanation:

- **Private constructor** prevents direct instantiation.

- **Static method getInstance()** ensures that only **one instance** of the class is created.

- When calling DatabaseConnection::getInstance() multiple times, it **returns the same instance** instead of creating a new one.

Design patterns in PHP **improve software design, scalability, and maintainability**. They provide **structured solutions** for object creation, system organization, and behavior management. By applying these patterns, developers can write **more efficient and optimized** PHP applications. The next sections will explore specific design patterns in greater detail with **practical examples**.

Creational Patterns: Singleton, Factory, Abstract Factory, and Builder

Creational patterns focus on **efficient object creation** while **reducing complexity** and **enhancing reusability**. They **decouple the instantiation process** from the client code, making applications more **flexible and maintainable**. The four key creational patterns in PHP are **Singleton, Factory, Abstract Factory, and Builder**.

1. Singleton Pattern

The **Singleton pattern** ensures that only **one instance of a class** exists throughout the application. This is useful for managing **shared resources**, such as database connections, loggers, or configuration settings.

Example: Singleton in PHP

```php
class Logger {
    private static $instance = null;
    private function __construct() {} // Prevent direct instantiation
    public static function getInstance() {
        if (self::$instance == null) {
            self::$instance = new Logger();
        }
        return self::$instance;
    }
    public function log($message) {
        echo "[LOG]: $message\n";
    }
}
$log1 = Logger::getInstance();
$log2 = Logger::getInstance();
$log1->log("This is a log message.");
```

Key Takeaways:

- The constructor is **private**, preventing direct instantiation.

- The getInstance() method ensures **only one instance** of the class exists.

- Useful for **global access** to shared resources.

2. Factory Pattern

The **Factory pattern** provides a centralized way to create objects **without exposing the class names**. It is useful when multiple subclasses share a **common interface** but require **different instantiations**.

Example: Factory Pattern in PHP

```php
interface Notification {
    public function send($message);
}
class EmailNotification implements Notification {
```

```php
    public function send($message) {
        echo "Sending Email: $message\n";
    }
}
class SMSNotification implements Notification {
    public function send($message) {
        echo "Sending SMS: $message\n";
    }
}
class NotificationFactory {
    public static function create($type) {
        return ($type === 'email') ? new EmailNotification() : new
            SMSNotification();
    }
}
$notification = NotificationFactory::create('sms');
$notification->send("Hello, this is a test.");
```

Key Takeaways:

- Centralizes **object creation logic**, making it **easier to extend**.

- The client **doesn't need to know** the class names.

- Reduces **tight coupling** between classes.

3. Abstract Factory Pattern

The **Abstract Factory pattern** is an extension of the **Factory pattern**, where a factory **creates related objects without specifying concrete classes**. It is useful for **complex object families**, such as UI elements, databases, or APIs.

Example: Abstract Factory Pattern in PHP

```php
interface Button {
    public function render();
}
class WindowsButton implements Button {
    public function render() {
        return "Rendering Windows Button\n";
    }
}
class MacOSButton implements Button {
    public function render() {
        return "Rendering MacOS Button\n";
    }
}
interface GUIFactory {
    public function createButton();
}
class WindowsFactory implements GUIFactory {
    public function createButton() {
        return new WindowsButton();
    }
}
class MacOSFactory implements GUIFactory {
    public function createButton() {
        return new MacOSButton();
    }
```

```
}
$factory = new MacOSFactory();
$button = $factory->createButton();
echo $button->render();
```

Key Takeaways:

- Creates **families of objects** without exposing **concrete classes**.

- Ensures **consistency** across object groups.

- Useful in **cross-platform development**.

4. Builder Pattern

The **Builder pattern** is used to **construct complex objects step by step**, separating the object **creation process** from its **representation**. It is useful for objects with **many optional parameters**.

Example: Builder Pattern in PHP

```
class Car {
    public $engine;
    public $wheels;
    public function showSpecs() {
        echo "Car with $this->engine engine and $this->wheels wheels.\n";
    }
}
class CarBuilder {
    private $car;
    public function __construct() {
        $this->car = new Car();
    }
    public function setEngine($engine) {
        $this->car->engine = $engine;
        return $this;
    }
    public function setWheels($wheels) {
        $this->car->wheels = $wheels;
        return $this;
    }
    public function build() {
        return $this->car;
    }
}
$car = (new CarBuilder())->setEngine("V8")->setWheels(4)->build();
$car->showSpecs();
```

Key Takeaways:

- Separates **object creation** from its **representation**.

- Supports **step-by-step configuration** of complex objects.

- Improves **code readability and flexibility**.

Creational patterns **optimize object creation** by ensuring **efficiency, flexibility, and maintainability**. The **Singleton pattern** manages global instances, the **Factory pattern** simplifies object instantiation, the **Abstract Factory pattern** handles object families, and the **Builder pattern** constructs complex objects step by step. Understanding these patterns is crucial for building **scalable and well-structured** PHP applications.

Structural Patterns: Adapter, Decorator, Proxy, and Façade

Structural design patterns focus on **organizing classes and objects** to ensure efficient and flexible software architecture. These patterns simplify relationships between objects, **promoting reusability and reducing complexity**. Four key structural patterns in PHP are **Adapter, Decorator, Proxy, and Facade**.

1. Adapter Pattern

The **Adapter pattern** allows two incompatible interfaces to work together by creating a **bridge** between them. It is useful when integrating **third-party libraries** or **legacy code** with modern systems.

Example: Adapter Pattern in PHP

```php
// Old system interface
class LegacyPrinter {
    public function printText($text) {
        echo "Printing: $text\n";
    }
}

// New system interface
interface Printer {
    public function printDocument($content);
}

// Adapter class
class PrinterAdapter implements Printer {
    private $legacyPrinter;

    public function __construct(LegacyPrinter $legacyPrinter) {
        $this->legacyPrinter = $legacyPrinter;
    }

    public function printDocument($content) {
        $this->legacyPrinter->printText($content);
    }
}

// Usage
$adapter = new PrinterAdapter(new LegacyPrinter());
$adapter->printDocument("Hello, world!");
```

Key Takeaways:

- Bridges **incompatible interfaces** without modifying existing code.

- Useful for **integrating old and new systems**.

- Improves **code maintainability and flexibility**.

2. Decorator Pattern

The **Decorator pattern** dynamically **adds new functionalities** to objects **without modifying** their structure. It is useful for **extending classes** without creating **multiple subclasses**.

Example: Decorator Pattern in PHP

```php
// Base interface
interface Coffee {
    public function cost();
}

// Basic coffee
class SimpleCoffee implements Coffee {
    public function cost() {
        return 5;
    }
}

// Decorator
class MilkDecorator implements Coffee {
    private $coffee;

    public function __construct(Coffee $coffee) {
        $this->coffee = $coffee;
    }

    public function cost() {
        return $this->coffee->cost() + 2;
    }
}

// Usage
$coffee = new MilkDecorator(new SimpleCoffee());
echo "Total Cost: $" . $coffee->cost();
```

Key Takeaways:

- Enhances **object functionality at runtime**.

- Avoids **class explosion** caused by multiple subclasses.

- Maintains **flexibility and scalability**.

3. Proxy Pattern

The **Proxy pattern** provides a **placeholder object** that controls access to another object. It is useful for **lazy initialization, security, and access control**.

Example: Proxy Pattern in PHP

```php
// Subject Interface
```

360

```php
interface Image {
    public function display();
}

// Real Object
class RealImage implements Image {
    private $filename;

    public function __construct($filename) {
        $this->filename = $filename;
        $this->loadFromDisk();
    }

    private function loadFromDisk() {
        echo "Loading image: $this->filename\n";
    }

    public function display() {
        echo "Displaying: $this->filename\n";
    }
}

// Proxy Object
class ImageProxy implements Image {
    private $filename;
    private $realImage;

    public function __construct($filename) {
        $this->filename = $filename;
    }

    public function display() {
        if ($this->realImage == null) {
            $this->realImage = new RealImage($this->filename);
        }
        $this->realImage->display();
    }
}

// Usage
$image = new ImageProxy("photo.jpg");
$image->display();  // Loads and displays
$image->display();  // Only displays (no loading)
```

Key Takeaways:

- Improves **performance** with **lazy initialization**.

- Controls **access** to expensive or sensitive resources.

- Useful in **security and remote object management**.

4. Facade Pattern

The **Facade pattern** provides a **simplified interface** to a complex subsystem, making it easier to use. It is helpful for **hiding complexity** in large applications.

Example: Facade Pattern in PHP

```php
// Subsystem components
```

361

```php
class CPU {
    public function start() {
        echo "CPU started\n";
    }
}
class Memory {
    public function load() {
        echo "Memory loaded\n";
    }
}
class HardDrive {
    public function read() {
        echo "Hard Drive reading data\n";
    }
}

// Facade class
class ComputerFacade {
    private $cpu;
    private $memory;
    private $hardDrive;

    public function __construct() {
        $this->cpu = new CPU();
        $this->memory = new Memory();
        $this->hardDrive = new HardDrive();
    }

    public function startComputer() {
        $this->cpu->start();
        $this->memory->load();
        $this->hardDrive->read();
        echo "Computer started successfully\n";
    }
}

// Usage
$computer = new ComputerFacade();
$computer->startComputer();
```

Key Takeaways:

- Hides **subsystem complexity** behind a **simple interface**.

- Improves **code readability and usability**.

- Useful in **large applications** to manage **modular components**.

Structural patterns **enhance code organization** and **reduce complexity** by managing object relationships. The **Adapter pattern** bridges incompatible interfaces, the **Decorator pattern** extends functionality dynamically, the **Proxy pattern** optimizes access control, and the **Facade pattern** simplifies complex subsystems. Mastering these patterns improves **code maintainability, flexibility, and efficiency** in PHP applications.

Behavioral Patterns: Observer, Strategy, Command, and State

Behavioral design patterns **define communication and interaction** between objects, making systems more **flexible and extensible**. These patterns focus on how objects **cooperate and delegate responsibilities**. The **Observer, Strategy, Command, and State**

patterns are widely used in PHP to improve **code modularity, maintainability, and reusability**.

1. Observer Pattern

The **Observer pattern** defines a **one-to-many dependency** between objects, ensuring that when one object changes state, all its dependents are notified automatically. It is useful for **event-driven programming** and is commonly used in **user interfaces, logging, and notifications**.

Example: Observer Pattern in PHP

```php
// Subject Interface
interface Subject {
    public function attach(Observer $observer);
    public function detach(Observer $observer);
    public function notify();
}

// Concrete Subject
class NewsPublisher implements Subject {
    private $observers = [];
    private $latestNews;

    public function attach(Observer $observer) {
        $this->observers[] = $observer;
    }

    public function detach(Observer $observer) {
        $this->observers = array_filter($this->observers, fn($obs) => $obs !==
            $observer);
    }

    public function setNews($news) {
        $this->latestNews = $news;
        $this->notify();
    }

    public function notify() {
        foreach ($this->observers as $observer) {
            $observer->update($this->latestNews);
        }
    }
}

// Observer Interface
interface Observer {
    public function update($news);
}

// Concrete Observer
class Subscriber implements Observer {
    private $name;

    public function __construct($name) {
        $this->name = $name;
    }

    public function update($news) {
        echo "$this->name received news update: $news\n";
    }
```

```
}

// Usage
$publisher = new NewsPublisher();
$alice = new Subscriber("Alice");
$bob = new Subscriber("Bob");

$publisher->attach($alice);
$publisher->attach($bob);

$publisher->setNews("Breaking: PHP 9 Released!");
```

Key Takeaways:

- Implements a **publisher-subscriber** relationship.

- Supports **event-driven systems**.

- Improves **modularity and decoupling**.

2. Strategy Pattern

The **Strategy pattern** defines a **family of algorithms** and encapsulates each one in a separate class, allowing the **behavior to be selected dynamically**. It is useful when an application needs to **switch between different algorithms** at runtime.

Example: Strategy Pattern in PHP

```php
// Strategy Interface
interface PaymentStrategy {
    public function pay($amount);
}

// Concrete Strategy 1
class PayPalPayment implements PaymentStrategy {
    public function pay($amount) {
        echo "Paid $amount using PayPal.\n";
    }
}

// Concrete Strategy 2
class CreditCardPayment implements PaymentStrategy {
    public function pay($amount) {
        echo "Paid $amount using Credit Card.\n";
    }
}

// Context Class
class ShoppingCart {
    private $paymentMethod;

    public function setPaymentMethod(PaymentStrategy $method) {
        $this->paymentMethod = $method;
    }

    public function checkout($amount) {
        $this->paymentMethod->pay($amount);
    }
}
```

```php
// Usage
$cart = new ShoppingCart();
$cart->setPaymentMethod(new PayPalPayment());
$cart->checkout(100);
```

Key Takeaways:

- Enables **switching algorithms dynamically**.

- Promotes **flexibility and maintainability**.

- Eliminates **conditional logic in methods**.

3. Command Pattern

The **Command pattern** encapsulates a **request as an object**, allowing requests to be **queued, logged, or executed at different times**. It is useful for **undo/redo operations, task scheduling, and event handling**.

Example: Command Pattern in PHP

```php
// Command Interface
interface Command {
    public function execute();
}

// Receiver Class
class Light {
    public function turnOn() {
        echo "Light is ON\n";
    }

    public function turnOff() {
        echo "Light is OFF\n";
    }
}

// Concrete Command 1
class TurnOnCommand implements Command {
    private $light;

    public function __construct(Light $light) {
        $this->light = $light;
    }

    public function execute() {
        $this->light->turnOn();
    }
}

// Concrete Command 2
class TurnOffCommand implements Command {
    private $light;

    public function __construct(Light $light) {
        $this->light = $light;
    }
```

```
    public function execute() {
        $this->light->turnOff();
    }
}

// Invoker
class RemoteControl {
    private $command;

    public function setCommand(Command $command) {
        $this->command = $command;
    }

    public function pressButton() {
        $this->command->execute();
    }
}

// Usage
$light = new Light();
$remote = new RemoteControl();

$remote->setCommand(new TurnOnCommand($light));
$remote->pressButton();

$remote->setCommand(new TurnOffCommand($light));
$remote->pressButton();
```

Key Takeaways:

- Encapsulates **requests as objects**.

- Supports **undo, redo, and logging**.

- Used in **task scheduling and event handling**.

4. State Pattern

The **State pattern** allows an object to **change its behavior** when its **internal state changes**. It is useful in scenarios where an object can **transition between different states dynamically**.

Example: State Pattern in PHP

```
// State Interface
interface State {
    public function handle();
}

// Concrete State 1
class HappyState implements State {
    public function handle() {
        echo "User is happy! ☺\n";
    }
}

// Concrete State 2
class SadState implements State {
    public function handle() {
```

366

```php
        echo "User is sad. ☹\n";
    }
}

// Context Class
class User {
    private $state;

    public function setState(State $state) {
        $this->state = $state;
    }

    public function express() {
        $this->state->handle();
    }
}

// Usage
$user = new User();

$user->setState(new HappyState());
$user->express();

$user->setState(new SadState());
$user->express();
```

Key Takeaways:

- Changes **behavior dynamically based on state**.

- Reduces **conditional statements**.

- Improves **code readability and structure**.

Behavioral patterns enhance **object interaction and communication**. The **Observer pattern** supports **event-driven** programming, the **Strategy pattern** enables **dynamic algorithm selection**, the **Command pattern** encapsulates **requests as objects**, and the **State pattern** allows **dynamic behavior changes**. These patterns **promote modular, flexible, and scalable** PHP applications.

Module 35:

Creational Patterns - Singleton, Factory, Abstract Factory, Builder

Creational design patterns focus on **efficient object creation** to improve maintainability, scalability, and flexibility in PHP applications. These patterns **encapsulate object instantiation logic**, reducing **tight coupling** and increasing **code reusability**. This module covers four essential creational patterns: **Singleton**, **Factory**, **Abstract Factory**, and **Builder**, each solving distinct instantiation challenges. Understanding these patterns helps PHP developers write **structured, scalable, and reusable code**.

Singleton Pattern: Ensuring a Single Instance Throughout the Application

The **Singleton pattern** ensures that a class **has only one instance** and provides a **global access point** to it. This is useful in scenarios where **a single shared resource** should be managed, such as **database connections, caching mechanisms, and logging services**. Instead of allowing multiple instances, the Singleton pattern **restricts instantiation** and provides a consistent interface.

In PHP, achieving a Singleton involves **private constructors**, **static properties**, and **a controlled instance retrieval method**. This pattern prevents **unnecessary memory consumption and resource duplication** by ensuring that multiple parts of an application rely on the same instance. However, developers should **use it with caution**, as excessive reliance on Singleton can lead to **hidden dependencies** and **reduced testability**.

Factory Pattern: Creating Objects Dynamically Based on Parameters

The **Factory pattern** provides an interface for **creating objects** without specifying their **exact class types**. It promotes **loose coupling** by delegating object instantiation to a dedicated method, making it easier to **introduce new object types** without modifying existing code.

This pattern is useful when an application needs to **create multiple object variants dynamically** based on **runtime conditions**. For example, in a **payment processing system**, different classes might handle **PayPal, Stripe, or credit card payments**, but the calling code should remain **agnostic** to specific implementations.

By implementing the Factory pattern in PHP, developers achieve **cleaner, more maintainable** code by **centralizing object creation logic**. Additionally, it enhances **extensibility**, allowing new classes to be integrated with minimal changes.

Abstract Factory Pattern: Family of Related Objects Creation

The **Abstract Factory pattern** builds on the **Factory pattern** by creating a set of **related objects** without specifying their **concrete classes**. Instead of a single Factory class, **multiple factories** handle **different but related object families**.

This pattern is particularly useful in **large-scale applications** that require **consistent object groups**, such as **UI components, database connections, or API clients**. By abstracting creation logic, the Abstract Factory ensures that objects **work seamlessly together**, preventing **incompatible combinations**.

A common use case is in **cross-platform applications**, where different factories generate **UI elements** for **desktop, web, and mobile** interfaces. By using an Abstract Factory, developers **maintain consistency** while allowing future modifications **without altering client code**.

Builder Pattern: Step-by-Step Construction of Complex Objects

The **Builder pattern** simplifies the construction of **complex objects** by **breaking down creation into manageable steps**. Instead of passing a large set of **constructor arguments**, the Builder pattern allows incremental object setup through **method chaining**.

This pattern is ideal for **configurable entities**, such as **reports, query builders, or structured API requests**, where objects require **optional parameters** or **differing configurations**. By using a Builder, developers create **readable and maintainable** code while **avoiding constructor overloads**.

An effective use case is in **database query builders**, where different components—**SELECT clauses, WHERE conditions, ORDER BY statements**—are constructed dynamically. The Builder pattern **enhances flexibility**, allowing developers to create objects with **varying levels of complexity** without **modifying class constructors**.

Creational patterns improve **object instantiation and management**, ensuring **scalability, maintainability, and flexibility** in PHP applications. The **Singleton pattern** enforces **single-instance usage**, while the **Factory and Abstract Factory** patterns provide **dynamic object creation**. The **Builder pattern** constructs **complex objects efficiently**. Mastering these patterns allows PHP developers to design **robust, well-structured, and reusable applications**.

Singleton Pattern: Ensuring a Single Instance throughout the Application

The **Singleton pattern** ensures that a class **has only one instance** throughout the application, providing **a single access point**. This is beneficial for managing **shared resources** such as **database connections, configuration settings, and logging systems**. By restricting instantiation, Singleton prevents **unnecessary memory usage** and **duplicate object creation**, ensuring consistency.

A **Singleton class in PHP** typically involves:

1. **A private static property** to store the single instance.

2. **A private constructor** to prevent direct instantiation.

3. **A public static method** to retrieve the single instance.

Implementing the Singleton Pattern in PHP

```php
class DatabaseConnection {
    private static ?DatabaseConnection $instance = null;
    private PDO $connection;

    private function __construct() {
        $this->connection = new PDO("mysql:host=localhost;dbname=mydb", "user",
            "password");
        $this->connection->setAttribute(PDO::ATTR_ERRMODE,
            PDO::ERRMODE_EXCEPTION);
    }

    public static function getInstance(): DatabaseConnection {
        if (self::$instance === null) {
            self::$instance = new self();
        }
        return self::$instance;
    }

    public function getConnection(): PDO {
        return $this->connection;
    }
}

// Usage
$db1 = DatabaseConnection::getInstance();
$db2 = DatabaseConnection::getInstance();

var_dump($db1 === $db2); // true, both variables reference the same instance
```

Key Features of the Singleton Pattern

1. **Private Constructor**: Prevents object instantiation using new.

2. **Static Property**: Holds the single instance.

3. **Static Method (getInstance)**: Ensures only one instance is created.

Benefits of the Singleton Pattern

- **Resource Management**: Ideal for **database connections** and **logging systems**.

- **Performance Optimization**: Prevents repeated **instantiations** and saves memory.

- **Global Access**: Ensures **a single point of access** across different parts of an application.

Potential Drawbacks of the Singleton Pattern

- **Hidden Dependencies**: Can lead to tight coupling.

- **Limited Testability**: Hard to mock singletons in unit tests.

- **Global State Issues**: If misused, it can introduce **unexpected behaviors**.

When to Use the Singleton Pattern

1. **Database Connections**: To prevent redundant connections.

2. **Logging Services**: A centralized logger across the application.

3. **Configuration Management**: To maintain application settings in a single instance.

The **Singleton pattern** is a powerful design pattern when used appropriately. It ensures that only one instance of a class exists, making it ideal for managing **shared resources**. However, overusing Singletons can introduce **tight coupling and testing difficulties**. Proper implementation ensures efficiency, performance, and maintainability in PHP applications.

Factory Pattern: Creating Objects Dynamically Based on Parameters

The **Factory Pattern** is a **creational design pattern** that provides an interface for creating objects **without specifying their exact class**. This pattern **centralizes object creation**, improving **code maintainability** and **flexibility** by allowing dynamic instantiation based on **runtime conditions**.

In PHP, the Factory Pattern is commonly used for:

- **Managing different database connections** (MySQL, PostgreSQL, SQLite).

- **Creating objects of different types based on user input or configuration**.

- **Decoupling object creation from client code**, making it easier to extend and modify.

Implementing the Factory Pattern in PHP

Let's create a **Factory class** that generates different types of Notification objects.

Step 1: Define an Interface

We start by defining a common interface for all notification types:

```
interface Notification {
```

```
        public function send(string $message): void;
    }
```

Step 2: Create Concrete Implementations

Now, we implement different notification types:

```
class EmailNotification implements Notification {
    public function send(string $message): void {
        echo "Sending Email: $message\n";
    }
}

class SMSNotification implements Notification {
    public function send(string $message): void {
        echo "Sending SMS: $message\n";
    }
}

class PushNotification implements Notification {
    public function send(string $message): void {
        echo "Sending Push Notification: $message\n";
    }
}
```

Step 3: Create the Factory Class

The factory class is responsible for **instantiating the correct notification type** based on input:

```
class NotificationFactory {
    public static function createNotification(string $type): Notification {
        return match ($type) {
            "email" => new EmailNotification(),
            "sms" => new SMSNotification(),
            "push" => new PushNotification(),
            default => throw new InvalidArgumentException("Invalid notification
        type"),
        };
    }
}
```

Step 4: Using the Factory to Create Objects

Now, let's use the Factory Pattern to dynamically create and send notifications:

```
$notificationType = "sms"; // This could come from user input or a config file
$notification = NotificationFactory::createNotification($notificationType);
$notification->send("Hello, this is a test notification!");
```

Benefits of the Factory Pattern

1. **Encapsulation**: Object creation logic is contained in one place.

2. **Flexibility**: Easily extendable—new types can be added without modifying existing code.

3. **Decoupling**: Client code does not need to know class names or dependencies.

When to Use the Factory Pattern

- When object creation logic is **complex or repetitive**.

- When a **class needs to delegate** its instantiation to a separate component.

- When **multiple subclasses** share a common interface, and selection depends on **runtime conditions**.

The **Factory Pattern** is a powerful tool for **dynamic object creation** in PHP applications. It enhances **maintainability, scalability, and code organization** while ensuring a **clean separation of concerns**. By using this pattern, developers can simplify object instantiation and improve **code flexibility** across various application layers.

Abstract Factory Pattern: Family of Related Objects Creation

The **Abstract Factory Pattern** is a **creational design pattern** used for creating **families of related objects without specifying their concrete classes**. Unlike the **Factory Pattern**, which focuses on creating a **single type of object**, the **Abstract Factory** pattern provides an **interface for creating multiple related objects** that belong to a common theme.

In PHP, the Abstract Factory Pattern is useful when:

- An application needs to **support multiple database engines** (MySQL, PostgreSQL, SQLite).

- There are **multiple UI themes**, and each theme has different components.

- The application needs **cross-platform compatibility**, such as web, mobile, and desktop views.

Implementing the Abstract Factory Pattern in PHP

Let's build an **Abstract Factory** to create **different UI components** (Buttons and Checkboxes) for **Windows and MacOS interfaces**.

Step 1: Define Abstract Interfaces

We define the **common interfaces** for buttons and checkboxes:

```
interface Button {
    public function render(): void;
}

interface Checkbox {
    public function toggle(): void;
```

```
}
```

Step 2: Create Concrete Implementations

Each **operating system (Windows, MacOS)** will have its own implementation of **Button** and **Checkbox**.

```
class WindowsButton implements Button {
    public function render(): void {
        echo "Rendering Windows-style Button\n";
    }
}

class MacOSButton implements Button {
    public function render(): void {
        echo "Rendering MacOS-style Button\n";
    }
}

class WindowsCheckbox implements Checkbox {
    public function toggle(): void {
        echo "Toggling Windows-style Checkbox\n";
    }
}

class MacOSCheckbox implements Checkbox {
    public function toggle(): void {
        echo "Toggling MacOS-style Checkbox\n";
    }
}
```

Step 3: Define the Abstract Factory Interface

Now, we define an **Abstract Factory** to create families of objects:

```
interface GUIFactory {
    public function createButton(): Button;
    public function createCheckbox(): Checkbox;
}
```

Step 4: Implement Concrete Factories

Each OS-specific factory **creates its corresponding UI components**:

```
class WindowsFactory implements GUIFactory {
    public function createButton(): Button {
        return new WindowsButton();
    }

    public function createCheckbox(): Checkbox {
        return new WindowsCheckbox();
    }
}

class MacOSFactory implements GUIFactory {
    public function createButton(): Button {
        return new MacOSButton();
    }

    public function createCheckbox(): Checkbox {
        return new MacOSCheckbox();
```

```
        }
    }
```

Step 5: Using the Abstract Factory

Now, let's create **a client that uses the factory** to instantiate components dynamically:

```
function renderUI(GUIFactory $factory): void {
    $button = $factory->createButton();
    $checkbox = $factory->createCheckbox();

    $button->render();
    $checkbox->toggle();
}

// Selecting factory based on OS
$os = "MacOS"; // This could come from system settings

$factory = ($os === "Windows") ? new WindowsFactory() : new MacOSFactory();
renderUI($factory);
```

Benefits of the Abstract Factory Pattern

1. **Ensures Consistency**: All objects in a product family match, preventing incompatible components.

2. **Decouples Object Creation**: The client doesn't need to know concrete classes, making the system easier to extend.

3. **Improves Maintainability**: New themes, OS variations, or configurations can be introduced without modifying existing code.

When to Use the Abstract Factory Pattern

• When the system **needs to create families of related objects dynamically**.

• When ensuring **consistent object behavior** across different environments.

• When using **multiple configurations**, such as **light and dark themes**, different UI libraries, or **cross-platform components**.

The **Abstract Factory Pattern** is a **powerful approach to creating related objects dynamically** in PHP applications. It enhances **code organization, flexibility, and maintainability**, making it an excellent choice for **modular UI systems, database layers, and scalable architecture designs**.

Builder Pattern: Step-by-Step Construction of Complex Objects

The **Builder Pattern** is a **creational design pattern** that allows constructing **complex objects step by step** without exposing their **internal representations**. Instead of using a

large constructor with multiple parameters, the Builder pattern **separates object construction from representation**, making it easier to **create variations of an object**.

This pattern is useful in PHP when:

- An object has **many optional attributes**.

- The same **construction process** must create **different representations** (e.g., JSON, XML, HTML).

- The object **requires validation before creation**.

Implementing the Builder Pattern in PHP

Let's build a **Builder Pattern** to construct a **complex "User" object** with optional attributes like **name, email, age, and address**.

Step 1: Define the Complex Object (Product)

```php
class User {
    public string $name;
    public string $email;
    public ?int $age;
    public ?string $address;

    public function __construct(string $name, string $email, ?int $age = null,
            ?string $address = null) {
        $this->name = $name;
        $this->email = $email;
        $this->age = $age;
        $this->address = $address;
    }

    public function display(): void {
        echo "User: {$this->name}, Email: {$this->email}, Age: " . ($this->age
            ?? 'N/A') . ", Address: " . ($this->address ?? 'N/A') . "\n";
    }
}
```

Step 2: Create the Builder Interface

A **Builder Interface** defines the methods for **incremental object construction**.

```php
interface UserBuilder {
    public function setName(string $name): self;
    public function setEmail(string $email): self;
    public function setAge(int $age): self;
    public function setAddress(string $address): self;
    public function build(): User;
}
```

Step 3: Implement the Concrete Builder

The **Concrete Builder** follows the **Builder Interface** and **stores intermediate values** while constructing the object.

```php
class ConcreteUserBuilder implements UserBuilder {
    private string $name;
    private string $email;
    private ?int $age = null;
    private ?string $address = null;

    public function setName(string $name): self {
        $this->name = $name;
        return $this;
    }

    public function setEmail(string $email): self {
        $this->email = $email;
        return $this;
    }

    public function setAge(int $age): self {
        $this->age = $age;
        return $this;
    }

    public function setAddress(string $address): self {
        $this->address = $address;
        return $this;
    }

    public function build(): User {
        return new User($this->name, $this->email, $this->age, $this->address);
    }
}
```

Step 4: Using the Builder to Construct Objects

Now, let's **use the builder** to construct a **User** with optional attributes.

```php
$builder = new ConcreteUserBuilder();

$user1 = $builder->setName("John Doe")
                 ->setEmail("john@example.com")
                 ->setAge(30)
                 ->setAddress("123 Main St")
                 ->build();

$user2 = $builder->setName("Alice Smith")
                 ->setEmail("alice@example.com")
                 ->build();

$user1->display();  // Output: User: John Doe, Email: john@example.com, Age: 30,
          Address: 123 Main St
$user2->display();  // Output: User: Alice Smith, Email: alice@example.com, Age:
          N/A, Address: N/A
```

Benefits of the Builder Pattern

1. **Simplifies Object Creation**: Avoids **complex constructors** with **many parameters**.

2. **Encapsulates Construction Logic**: Users don't need to **know the order of parameters**.

377

3. **Provides Step-by-Step Customization**: Users can **construct an object incrementally**.

4. **Ensures Immutability**: Once an object is built, it **remains unchanged**.

When to Use the Builder Pattern

- When an object has **a large number of optional parameters**.

- When objects need **different representations**, such as **JSON, XML, or UI components**.

- When you **want to separate object construction** from its **actual representation**.

The **Builder Pattern** is a powerful **object creation strategy** in PHP applications, allowing for **clean, flexible, and scalable object construction**.

Module 36:
Structural and Behavioral Patterns

Design patterns provide reusable solutions to common problems in software development. This module covers **structural and behavioral patterns**, focusing on how they improve code organization and maintainability in PHP applications. **Structural patterns** simplify object relationships, while **behavioral patterns** define interaction and communication among objects. Additionally, the **Composite Pattern** is introduced for handling hierarchical structures. By understanding when and where to apply these patterns, PHP developers can create flexible and scalable applications. This module offers **practical advice on applying these patterns effectively** in PHP projects to enhance modularity, extensibility, and efficiency in real-world applications.

Structural Patterns: Adapter, Decorator, Proxy, and Facade

Structural design patterns **simplify object composition** and help create larger structures by defining relationships between components. The **Adapter Pattern** allows incompatible interfaces to work together, enabling integration between different classes. The **Decorator Pattern** enhances object functionality **dynamically without modifying existing code**, promoting extensibility. The **Proxy Pattern** acts as an intermediary, managing access control, caching, or security, improving efficiency. Lastly, the **Facade Pattern** simplifies complex system interactions by **providing a unified interface**, making it easier to interact with multiple subsystems. These patterns **increase modularity and reusability** while maintaining flexibility in PHP application design.

Behavioral Patterns: Observer, Strategy, Command, and State

Behavioral patterns **define object interactions**, focusing on communication, responsibility delegation, and action execution. The **Observer Pattern** enables event-driven programming by notifying multiple objects when a state changes, making it useful for logging, notifications, and data synchronization. The **Strategy Pattern** allows algorithms to be swapped dynamically, promoting flexible logic execution without modifying existing code. The **Command Pattern** encapsulates actions as objects, supporting undo operations and queuing requests, ideal for task execution and UI commands. Lastly, the **State Pattern** enables objects to change behavior dynamically based on internal states, reducing complexity in workflow management and state-dependent operations.

Composite Pattern: Treating Individual Objects and Compositions Uniformly

The **Composite Pattern** provides a way to work with **individual objects and groups of objects in the same way**, simplifying tree structures such as menus, file systems, and UI components.

This pattern **treats hierarchical structures uniformly**, allowing clients to interact with both simple and complex elements without distinguishing them. In PHP applications, it enables recursive operations on nested objects, ensuring scalability and ease of modification. By structuring data in this manner, applications maintain **flexibility and cohesion**, reducing redundancy while allowing efficient manipulation of grouped elements like product catalogs, organizational hierarchies, and multi-level UI components.

When to Use These Patterns in PHP Applications

Applying **structural and behavioral patterns** requires understanding the **problem domain** and choosing the right pattern for the situation. Structural patterns should be used when there's a **need for simplified object relationships** or **integration with different components**. Behavioral patterns are most useful when **communication between objects needs flexibility**, such as event-driven systems or workflow management. The Composite Pattern works well for **nested or hierarchical data structures**, where **treating individual and grouped elements uniformly** simplifies development. By incorporating these patterns into PHP applications, developers can create **scalable, maintainable, and well-structured codebases** suitable for diverse project needs.

Structural Patterns: Adapter, Decorator, Proxy, and Facade Explained with PHP Examples

Structural design patterns focus on **organizing classes and objects efficiently** to enhance reusability, maintainability, and scalability. This section covers **Adapter, Decorator, Proxy, and Facade** patterns, demonstrating their implementation in PHP.

Adapter Pattern

The **Adapter Pattern** allows objects with **incompatible interfaces** to communicate by acting as a bridge. This is useful when integrating third-party libraries or working with legacy code.

Example: Converting Data Format

```
interface XMLData {
    public function getXML();
}

class XMLProvider implements XMLData {
    public function getXML() {
        return "<data><item>PHP</item></data>";
    }
}

// Adapter to convert XML to JSON
class XMLToJSONAdapter {
    private $xmlProvider;

    public function __construct(XMLData $xmlProvider) {
        $this->xmlProvider = $xmlProvider;
    }
```

```php
    public function getJSON() {
        $xml = simplexml_load_string($this->xmlProvider->getXML());
        return json_encode($xml);
    }
}

// Usage
$adapter = new XMLToJSONAdapter(new XMLProvider());
echo $adapter->getJSON(); // Converts XML to JSON
```

Decorator Pattern

The **Decorator Pattern** dynamically adds functionality to an object **without modifying its class**. It's useful for extending features like logging, authentication, or formatting.

Example: Adding Formatting to a Text Output

```php
interface Text {
    public function render();
}

class PlainText implements Text {
    private $text;
    public function __construct($text) {
        $this->text = $text;
    }
    public function render() {
        return $this->text;
    }
}

class BoldDecorator implements Text {
    private $text;

    public function __construct(Text $text) {
        $this->text = $text;
    }

    public function render() {
        return "<b>" . $this->text->render() . "</b>";
    }
}

// Usage
$plainText = new PlainText("Hello, PHP!");
$boldText = new BoldDecorator($plainText);
echo $boldText->render(); // Outputs: <b>Hello, PHP!</b>
```

Proxy Pattern

The **Proxy Pattern** controls access to an object by acting as a substitute. It's useful for **caching, lazy loading, and security validation**.

Example: Lazy Loading a Database Connection

```php
class Database {
    public function connect() {
        return "Database Connection Established";
    }
```

```php
}
class DatabaseProxy {
    private $database;
    private $connected = false;

    public function connect() {
        if (!$this->connected) {
            $this->database = new Database();
            $this->connected = true;
        }
        return "Using Cached Database Connection";
    }
}

// Usage
$db = new DatabaseProxy();
echo $db->connect(); // First call initializes connection
echo $db->connect(); // Subsequent calls reuse connection
```

Facade Pattern

The **Facade Pattern** provides a **simplified interface** to a complex system, making it easier to interact with multiple subsystems.

Example: Simplifying Email Sending

```php
class SMTP {
    public function connect() { return "Connected to SMTP server."; }
}

class Mailer {
    public function send($message) { return "Email Sent: " . $message; }
}

// Facade Class
class EmailFacade {
    private $smtp;
    private $mailer;

    public function __construct() {
        $this->smtp = new SMTP();
        $this->mailer = new Mailer();
    }

    public function sendEmail($message) {
        $this->smtp->connect();
        return $this->mailer->send($message);
    }
}

// Usage
$email = new EmailFacade();
echo $email->sendEmail("Hello World!");
```

Structural design patterns like **Adapter, Decorator, Proxy, and Facade** improve **code flexibility and reusability**. The Adapter Pattern **bridges incompatible interfaces**, the Decorator Pattern **enhances objects dynamically**, the Proxy Pattern **optimizes resource management**, and the Facade Pattern **simplifies system interactions**. These patterns help developers build **modular, efficient, and scalable** PHP applications.

Behavioral Patterns: Observer, Strategy, Command, and State Patterns in Action

Behavioral design patterns focus on how objects **communicate and interact** within a system. These patterns help manage complex workflows, improve code organization, and increase flexibility. This section covers four key behavioral patterns: **Observer, Strategy, Command, and State**, with practical PHP implementations.

Observer Pattern

The **Observer Pattern** allows an object (subject) to notify multiple dependent objects (observers) of state changes **automatically**. It's commonly used in event-driven programming and **implementing event listeners**.

Example: User Registration with Email Notifications

```php
// Subject (Observable)
class User {
    private $observers = [];

    public function addObserver($observer) {
        $this->observers[] = $observer;
    }

    public function register($username) {
        echo "User $username registered.\n";
        foreach ($this->observers as $observer) {
            $observer->notify($username);
        }
    }
}

// Observer Interface
interface Observer {
    public function notify($username);
}

// Concrete Observer (Email Notification)
class EmailNotifier implements Observer {
    public function notify($username) {
        echo "Sending email to $username\n";
    }
}

// Usage
$user = new User();
$user->addObserver(new EmailNotifier());
$user->register("JohnDoe");
```

Strategy Pattern

The **Strategy Pattern** defines a family of interchangeable algorithms and allows them to be selected dynamically at runtime. It is useful for **implementing different sorting, authentication, or payment methods**.

Example: Different Payment Methods

```php
// Strategy Interface
interface PaymentStrategy {
    public function pay($amount);
}

// Concrete Strategies
class PayPalPayment implements PaymentStrategy {
    public function pay($amount) {
        echo "Paid $amount via PayPal\n";
    }
}

class CreditCardPayment implements PaymentStrategy {
    public function pay($amount) {
        echo "Paid $amount via Credit Card\n";
    }
}

// Context Class
class PaymentProcessor {
    private $strategy;

    public function __construct(PaymentStrategy $strategy) {
        $this->strategy = $strategy;
    }

    public function executePayment($amount) {
        $this->strategy->pay($amount);
    }
}

// Usage
$payment = new PaymentProcessor(new PayPalPayment());
$payment->executePayment(100);
```

Command Pattern

The **Command Pattern** encapsulates a request as an object, allowing users to **queue, log, or execute commands at different times**. This is useful for **undo/redo functionality, task scheduling, and remote controls**.

Example: Light Switch Commands

```php
// Command Interface
interface Command {
    public function execute();
}

// Receiver (Light)
class Light {
    public function turnOn() {
        echo "Light turned ON\n";
    }

    public function turnOff() {
        echo "Light turned OFF\n";
    }
}

// Concrete Commands
class TurnOnCommand implements Command {
    private $light;
```

```php
    public function __construct(Light $light) {
        $this->light = $light;
    }

    public function execute() {
        $this->light->turnOn();
    }
}

class TurnOffCommand implements Command {
    private $light;

    public function __construct(Light $light) {
        $this->light = $light;
    }

    public function execute() {
        $this->light->turnOff();
    }
}

// Invoker (Switch)
class RemoteControl {
    private $command;

    public function setCommand(Command $command) {
        $this->command = $command;
    }

    public function pressButton() {
        $this->command->execute();
    }
}

// Usage
$light = new Light();
$remote = new RemoteControl();
$remote->setCommand(new TurnOnCommand($light));
$remote->pressButton();
```

State Pattern

The **State Pattern** allows an object to **alter its behavior based on its internal state**, avoiding complex conditional statements. It is useful for **workflow management, state machines, and game development**.

Example: Order Processing System

```php
// State Interface
interface OrderState {
    public function process();
}

// Concrete States
class PendingState implements OrderState {
    public function process() {
        echo "Order is pending.\n";
    }
}

class ShippedState implements OrderState {
    public function process() {
        echo "Order has been shipped.\n";
```

```php
        }
    }
// Context Class
class Order {
    private $state;

    public function setState(OrderState $state) {
        $this->state = $state;
    }

    public function processOrder() {
        $this->state->process();
    }
}
// Usage
$order = new Order();
$order->setState(new PendingState());
$order->processOrder();

$order->setState(new ShippedState());
$order->processOrder();
```

Behavioral patterns like **Observer, Strategy, Command, and State** optimize **workflow management, communication, and runtime behavior** in PHP applications. Observer handles event-based interactions, Strategy enables flexible algorithm choices, Command structures actions as objects, and State manages transitions **efficiently**. These patterns **enhance code maintainability, scalability, and flexibility** in real-world projects.

Composite Pattern: Treating Individual Objects and Compositions Uniformly

The **Composite Pattern** is a structural design pattern that allows **individual objects** and **composite groups of objects** to be treated **uniformly**. This is particularly useful when building hierarchical structures like **file systems, graphical user interfaces (GUIs), or menus**, where individual and grouped elements need to be handled in the same way.

Understanding the Composite Pattern

The core idea of the **Composite Pattern** is to have an interface that represents both **single objects (leaf nodes)** and **groups of objects (composite nodes)**. This enables operations to be applied **consistently** across both.

The pattern consists of the following components:

- **Component (Interface/Abstract Class)** – Defines a common interface for both individual objects and composite objects.

- **Leaf (Individual Object)** – Represents individual elements that do not contain children.

- **Composite (Group of Objects)** – A container that holds **multiple leaf nodes or other composite nodes**, allowing hierarchical structures.

Example: Implementing a File System Structure in PHP

Consider a **file system**, where both individual files and folders need to be treated the same way. A folder may contain **multiple files** or **other subfolders**, and operations like **displaying contents** should work on both files and directories uniformly.

Step 1: Define the Component Interface

```php
// Component Interface
interface FileSystemComponent {
    public function display();
}
```

Step 2: Create the Leaf Class (File)

```php
// Leaf Node (File)
class File implements FileSystemComponent {
    private $name;

    public function __construct($name) {
        $this->name = $name;
    }

    public function display() {
        echo "File: " . $this->name . "\n";
    }
}
```

Step 3: Create the Composite Class (Folder)

```php
// Composite Node (Folder)
class Folder implements FileSystemComponent {
    private $name;
    private $items = [];

    public function __construct($name) {
        $this->name = $name;
    }

    public function addItem(FileSystemComponent $item) {
        $this->items[] = $item;
    }

    public function display() {
        echo "Folder: " . $this->name . "\n";
        foreach ($this->items as $item) {
            echo "  - ";
            $item->display();
        }
    }
}
```

Step 4: Demonstrate Usage

```php
// Creating Files
$file1 = new File("Document.txt");
```

```
$file2 = new File("Image.png");

// Creating Folders and Adding Files
$folder1 = new Folder("Projects");
$folder1->addItem($file1);
$folder1->addItem($file2);

$folder2 = new Folder("Work");
$folder2->addItem($folder1);
$folder2->addItem(new File("Report.pdf"));

// Display Folder Structure
$folder2->display();
```

Output:

```
Folder: Work
  - Folder: Projects
    - File: Document.txt
    - File: Image.png
  - File: Report.pdf
```

Advantages of the Composite Pattern

1. **Uniform Treatment** – Both single objects and composite objects are treated uniformly, reducing complexity in hierarchical structures.

2. **Flexibility** – Easily extendable; additional elements (e.g., more file types) can be added without modifying existing structures.

3. **Recursive Processing** – Since composite objects contain other objects, recursive operations (like rendering elements or traversing directories) can be implemented **seamlessly**.

4. **Simplifies Client Code** – The client does not need to check whether an object is a leaf or composite; operations like display() work **consistently** across all elements.

Real-World Applications

- **GUI Elements:** Components like **buttons, panels, and containers** can use the Composite Pattern to manage hierarchical UI elements.

- **File System Management:** Operating systems **treat files and directories** as the same entity for operations like renaming, copying, or deleting.

- **Menu Structures:** Website navigation menus, where **menus contain submenus**, use the **Composite Pattern** for managing nested options efficiently.

- **Document Structures:** Word processors **treat paragraphs, tables, and images** as composable document elements.

The **Composite Pattern** is a powerful **structural pattern** that simplifies hierarchical object management in PHP applications. It ensures uniformity in handling **both individual elements and complex compositions**, making it essential for applications involving **trees, menus, GUIs, and document structures**. By leveraging this pattern, developers can create **scalable and maintainable** architectures that elegantly handle nested elements.

When to Use These Patterns: Practical Advice on Applying These Patterns in PHP Applications

Design patterns provide **structured solutions** to common programming challenges. Structural and behavioral patterns, such as **Adapter, Decorator, Proxy, Facade, Observer, Strategy, Command, and State**, enhance PHP applications by **improving maintainability, flexibility, and scalability**. Understanding **when** to apply these patterns is key to designing efficient systems.

When to Use Structural Patterns

Structural patterns focus on organizing code efficiently by defining **relationships between components**. Here's when you should use them:

1. Adapter Pattern: When You Need Compatibility Between Incompatible Interfaces

- Use the Adapter pattern when integrating **third-party libraries, legacy systems, or different APIs** that do not naturally work together.

- Example: If your application uses a **new logging system**, but an older module relies on a different logging format, an **Adapter** can bridge the gap.

2. Decorator Pattern: When You Need Dynamic Behavior Without Modifying a Class

- Use Decorator when extending an object's functionality **without altering the original class**.

- Example: Enhancing a User object with **roles, permissions, or access control layers** dynamically, instead of modifying the base class.

3. Proxy Pattern: When You Need Controlled Access to an Object

- Useful for **lazy loading, caching, and security control** before granting access to an object.

- Example: Implementing an **authentication proxy** for restricting access to sensitive data.

4. Facade Pattern: When You Need a Simplified Interface for a Complex System

- Use Facade to provide a **single access point** to a set of functionalities.

- Example: Wrapping multiple database operations in a **DatabaseManager** class that abstracts complex query handling.

When to Use Behavioral Patterns

Behavioral patterns focus on **managing object interactions** and improving system flexibility.

1. Observer Pattern: When You Need Automatic Event Notification

- Use the Observer pattern when an object's state change needs to trigger updates in dependent objects.

- Example: Implementing **event-driven systems** like a user registration system that triggers email notifications.

2. Strategy Pattern: When You Need to Dynamically Switch Between Different Algorithms

- Use Strategy when an operation has **multiple possible implementations** that should be interchangeable.

- Example: **Payment processing**, where the same checkout system can dynamically switch between PayPal, Stripe, or credit card payments.

3. Command Pattern: When You Need to Encapsulate Requests as Objects

- Use Command for **queuing, undoing, or executing delayed operations**.

- Example: Implementing **task scheduling** in PHP applications, where jobs are encapsulated and processed asynchronously.

4. State Pattern: When an Object's Behavior Changes Based on Its State

- Use State when an object needs to change behavior **without modifying its class**.

- Example: **Order processing systems**, where an order transitions from **Pending** → **Shipped** → **Delivered** with different rules.

Final Considerations

Choosing the **right** design pattern depends on:

✓ **Project Requirements** – What problem are you solving?
✓ **Code Maintainability** – Will this pattern make future changes easier?
✓ **Performance Trade-offs** – Will the pattern introduce unnecessary complexity?

By **strategically** applying design patterns, PHP developers create **scalable, maintainable, and flexible** applications that adapt to evolving needs.

Review Request

Thank you for reading "PHP Programming: Versatile, Server-Side, Multi-Purpose Programming Language"

I truly hope you found this book valuable and insightful. Your feedback is incredibly important in helping other readers discover the CompreQuest series. If you enjoyed this book, here are a few ways you can support its success:

1. **Leave a Review:** Sharing your thoughts in a review on Amazon is a great way to help others learn about this book. Your honest opinion can guide fellow readers in making informed decisions.

2. **Share with Friends:** If you think this book could benefit your friends or colleagues, consider recommending it to them. Word of mouth is a powerful tool in helping books reach a wider audience.

3. **Stay Connected:** If you'd like to stay updated with future releases and special CompreQuest series offers, please visit my author ptofile on Amazon at https://www.amazon.com/stores/Theophilus-Edet/author/B0859K3294 or follow me on social media facebook.com/theoedet, twitter.com/TheophilusEdet, or Instagram.com/edettheophilus. Besides, you can mail me at theo.edet@comprequestseries.com, or visit us at https://www.comprequestseries.com/.

Thank you for your support and for being a part of our community. Your enthusiasm for learning and growing in the field of PHP Programming is greatly appreciated.

Wishing you continued success on your programming journey!

Theophilus Edet

Embark on a Journey of ICT Mastery with CompreQuest Series

Discover a realm where learning becomes specialization, and let CompreQuest Series guide you toward ICT mastery and expertise

- **CompreQuest's Commitment**: We're dedicated to breaking barriers in ICT education, empowering individuals and communities with quality courses.

- **Tailored Pathways**: Each series offers personalized journeys with tailored courses to ignite your passion for ICT knowledge.

- **Comprehensive Resources**: Seamlessly blending online and offline materials, CompreQuest Series provide a holistic approach to learning. Dive into a world of knowledge spanning various formats.

- **Goal-Oriented Quests**: Clear pathways help you confidently pursue your career goals. Our curated reading guides unlock your potential in the ICT field.

- **Expertise Unveiled**: CompreQuest Series isn't just content; it's a transformative experience. Elevate your understanding and stand out as an ICT expert.

- **Low Word Collateral**: Our unique approach ensures concise, focused learning. Say goodbye to lengthy texts and dive straight into mastering ICT concepts.

- **Our Vision**: We aspire to reach learners worldwide, fostering social progress and enabling glamorous career opportunities through education.

Join our community of ICT excellence and embark on your journey with CompreQuest Series.

www.ingramcontent.com/pod-product-compliance
Lightning Source LLC
LaVergne TN
LVHW081512050326
832903LV00025B/1465